Pacific CRYSTAL Centre for Science, Mathematics, and Technology Literacy: Lessons Learned

Pacific CRYSTAL Centre for Science, Mathematics, and Technology Literacy: Lessons Learned

Edited by

Larry D. Yore
Eileen Van der Flier-Keller
David W. Blades
Timothy W. Pelton
University of Victoria
Victoria, British Columbia, Canada

David B. Zandvliet
Simon Fraser University
Burnaby, British Columbia, Canada

SENSE PUBLISHERS
ROTTERDAM/BOSTON/TAIPEI

A C.I.P. record for this book is available from the Library of Congress.

ISBN: 978-94-6091-504-8 (paperback)
ISBN: 978-94-6091-505-5 (hardback)
ISBN: 978-94-6091-506-2 (e-book)

Published by: Sense Publishers,
P.O. Box 21858,
3001 AW Rotterdam,
The Netherlands
www.sensepublishers.com

Printed on acid-free paper

TABLE OF CONTENTS

LIST OF PACIFIC CRYSTAL PROJECT LEADERS
(2005–2011)

John O. Anderson, Department of Educational Psychology and Leadership Studies, University of Victoria

Robert J. Anthony, Department of Curriculum and Instruction, University of Victoria

David W. Blades, Department of Curriculum and Instruction, University of Victoria

Cathy Carolsfeld, WestWind SeaLab Supplies, Victoria, BC

Yvonne Coady, Department of Computer Science, University of Victoria

Rachel Cooper, Department of Psychology, Vancouver Island University

Steven Earle, Department of Earth Science, Vancouver Island University

Leslee Francis Pelton, Department of Curriculum and Instruction, University of Victoria

E. Anne Marshall, Department of Educational Psychology and Leadership Studies, University of Victoria

Asit Mazumder, Department of Biology, University of Victoria

Timothy W. Pelton, Department of Curriculum and Instruction, University of Victoria

Wolff-Michael Roth, Department of Curriculum and Instruction, University of Victoria

Ulrike Stege, Department of Computer Science, University of Victoria

Eileen Van der Flier-Keller, School of Earth and Ocean Sciences, University of Victoria

Andrew Weaver, School of Earth and Ocean Sciences, University of Victoria

Nikki Wright, SeaChange Marine Conservation Society, Brentwood Bay, BC

Larry D. Yore, Department of Curriculum and Instruction, University of Victoria

David B. Zandvliet, Faculty of Education, Simon Fraser University

ACKNOWLEDGEMENTS

The Co-editors acknowledge the contributions of the Natural Sciences and Engineering Research Council of Canada, the University of Victoria, Simon Fraser University, and other funding agencies for their financial support for the Pacific CRYSTAL Project from which the research and development projects and the chapters in this book arose. We especially thank the First Nations, schools, teachers, students, volunteers, professional associations, nongovernmental agencies, and other participants who contributed so freely to the success of these projects. The potential cognitive symbiosis within science, mathematics, and technology literacies—specifically between language and understanding of science, mathematics, and technology—is fundamental to address pressing science, technology, society, and environment issues. We are pleased to share our research and development results about these literacies, high-quality professional learning experiences, instructional resources, classroom practices, and student achievements.

We thank Pat Bright and Joanne Westby, Department of Curriculum and Instruction, University of Victoria, for their financial management and accounting services over the duration of the Pacific CRYSTAL Project (2005–2011). Special thanks are given to Shari Yore, SAY Professional Services, Saanichton, BC, for her efforts in managing this book project and for her thorough editorial work; authors explicitly mentioned her professional and helpful comments on format, style, references, and internal consistency.

Larry D. Yore
Eileen Van der Flier-Keller
David W. Blades
Timothy W. Pelton
David B. Zandvliet
Co-editors

I. OVERVIEW, COMMON THEMES, AND THEORETICAL FRAMEWORKS

LARRY D. YORE AND EILEEN VAN DER FLIER-KELLER

1. PACIFIC CRYSTAL CENTRE FOR SCIENCE, MATHEMATICS, AND TECHNOLOGY LITERACY: LESSONS LEARNED

Overview

The Centres for Research in Youth, Science Teaching and Learning (CRYSTAL; Natural Sciences and Engineering Research Council of Canada [NSERC], 2009) were funded by NSERC as a 5-year pilot project (2005–2010) to foster science and mathematics education research and development (R&D). These five Canadian centres (see Notes) focused on science, mathematics, and technology (SMT), including engineering and computer science, in response to the widespread and growing recognition that the SMT literacies are vital skills in the 21st century economy. CRYSTAL has provided a forum for the many partners who share an interest in developing and enhancing the skills of and resources available to teachers, nongovernmental agencies, and public awareness educators and in enriching the SMT preparation of young Canadians. The CRYSTAL projects have attempted to:
– improve understanding of the skills and resources needed to enhance the quality of science, mathematics, and technology education (K–12), and
– improve understanding of the best ways to enrich the preparation of youth in these foundation subjects.
The five interuniversity and interdisciplinary centres are composed of one or more universities and colleges, faculties of education, science and engineering, local community partners, and nongovernmental agencies. Partners and agencies were recruited from user groups that focused on the public awareness of SMT, First Nations, informal learning environments, public and private schools, and ministries of education.

CONCEPTUAL FOCUS AND ORGANIZATION OF PACIFIC CRYSTAL

Pacific CRYSTAL consisted of a partnership of universities (University of Victoria, Simon Fraser University, and Vancouver Island University [formerly Malaspina University College]), faculties within the universities (Education, Science, and Engineering), British Columbia school districts on Vancouver Island and the Lower Mainland, First Nations (Saanich First Nations including Tsartlip and Tsawout), and nongovernmental agencies (Canadian Geological Foundation, Centre for Excellence in Teaching and Learning Science, Constructivist Education Resources Network,

L. D. Yore et al (Eds.), Pacific CRYSTAL Centre for Science, Mathematics, and Technology Literacy: Lessons Learned, 3–22.

EdGEO, Victoria Foundation, SeaChange, and WestWind SeaLabs). Pacific CRYSTAL examined ways to improve SMT teaching and learning in elementary, middle, and secondary schools by building on Canada's successful foundation, as demonstrated by recent (2003, 2006, 2009) general mathematics and scientific literacy performances on the Programme of International Student Assessment (PISA; Organisation for Economic Co-operation and Development [OECD], n.d.). General SMT literacies are focused on citizenship and active participation in society. Improving SMT literacies among youth as a whole helps address access and equity issues and increases the supply of students qualified for and interested in science, mathematics, engineering, and technology programs at postsecondary levels, thereby addressing the higher-level elite literacies related to SMT careers and the needs of the provincial, national, and international economies.

Pacific CRYSTAL and its projects emphasized research inquiries that develop and evaluate knowledge about SMT literacies, underserved and underrepresented peoples, and science and technology fields including biology (ocean ecosystems, botany), environmental science, earth science (weather, climate, geologic history, plate tectonics, natural hazards, resources), chemistry (water quality, qualitative and quantitative analyses), computer science (problem solving, graph theory, foundation concepts, programming, robotics), and mathematics (data displays, probability, geometry) in Years 1–3 (2005–2008). Greater emphasis was placed on education, professional development, and leadership for teachers, wider implementation, dissemination and outreach activities to influence public policies, education and curricular decisions, classroom practices, and instructional resources in Years 4–5 (2008–2010). A no-cost extension request was approved to complete ongoing projects, finalize resources, disseminate outcomes, and influence policy makers (Year 6, 2010–2011). Over the duration of the project, the participants changed (~30%) as projects were completed and graduate students finished their research programs. As well, the focus of the Centre and projects morphed to meet changing emphases and interpretations of the CRYSTAL program and to reflect the Centre's successes, progress, and opportunities.

Pacific CRYSTAL established a mission statement through a deliberative process involving faculty members, partners, and research associates as a centre *to promote scientific, mathematical, and technological literacy for responsible citizenship through research partnerships with university and educational communities.* A strategic Build–Expand–Lead plan was developed in which ideas, resources, and research inquiries would *evolve from small-scale authentic learning opportunities viewed as extra-curricular and outside the prescribed curriculum and school program (Build), to controlled applications of evidence-based classroom practices and resources (Expand), and to scaled dissemination and implementation, leadership experiences, and policy actions (Lead).* The emphasis changed from small-scale authentic opportunities in the early years to classroom-scale trials in the middle years and finally to systemic-scale implementation, leadership, and knowledge transfer efforts in the final years. The partners identified project foci and intentions within the mission statement and formed three functional nodes under a central leadership and administration node at the University of Victoria, which was guided by (a) an

International Advisory Board of scientists, community members, science educators, and cognitive scientists, (b) an Executive Committee of principal investigators from the University of Victoria and community partners, and (c) Co-directors (see Appendix for complete listing of these groups).

The functional organization involved a hub-and-spoke model for administrative purposes, with the central management node radiating out to the three R&D nodes. However, as the projects developed, much more integration and collaboration occurred among the researchers and participants in the separate nodes. A central, internodal goal was to increase the leadership capacity for SMT education through production of highly qualified personnel (HQP) for schools, partner agencies, and universities. Therefore, wherever possible, internships, graduate fellowships, and research apprenticeships were utilized to provide authentic experiences in SMT areas. While only some projects are featured in the following chapters, a listing of HQP, graduate projects, theses and dissertations, articles, conference presentations, chapters, reports, and instructional products is provided in the book's Appendix.

Node 1 (*Build*) involved developing authentic experiences designed to provide real SMT opportunities to students and then documentation and evaluation of what happened in these experiences to assess their effectiveness in improving SMT literacies, fostering interest in the disciplines, and establishing disciplinary identity. Innovative experiences and approaches to SMT literacy included self-exploration of identity, career awareness, attitudes toward the disciplines; internships in university science laboratories, community education groups, and traditional and western knowledge about nature; field-based ecology programs; intertidal systems and aquaria in classrooms; hands-on earth science field trips and activities; and problem-solving workshops with computer science concepts. These experiences, applications, and resources were informed by constructivist pedagogies and self-efficacy as well as inquiry, design, and problem-solving based learning in both formal and informal learning environments.

Node 2 (*Expand*) involved implementing classroom experiences that provide a variety of instructional approaches regarding thinking, language, mathematics, and engineering design with unique resources and information communication technologies (ICT) to enhance SMT literacies. Research conducted on these approaches focused on establishing interdisciplinary relationships amongst science, mathematics, and language arts; integrating instructional resources and strategies developed in Node 1 into classroom experiences; examining science literacy through reading, writing, and oral discourse; and developing weather units and online assessment tools. Projects included explicit literacy instruction in middle schools; community mapping in environmental studies, socioscientific issues, earth science activities and strategies in teacher education and professional development; and use of automated weather stations, a weather unit, and an inventory of weather concepts. Teachers collaborating with researchers benefited and contributed professionally through involvement in the research projects, professional development workshops associated with the projects, and individual graduate research projects integrated with the node's objectives.

Node 3 (*Lead*) involved researchers seeking to engage and build partnerships with teachers and to better understand and support the teacher's role in improving students' SMT literacies and instruction. This node focused on hierarchical linear modeling (HLM) analyses of the PISA datasets for science, mathematics, and reading literacies to better understand the relationships between student performance and student, home, and community characteristics; implementing change, establishing a foundation for educational policy involving SMT education, developing model programs, and producing a legacy of SMT advocates and lead teachers. This node emphasized leadership through professional development, cascading leadership in which participants assumed responsibility for professional development activities as projects evolved, demonstration or lighthouse schools, teacher workshops, teacher involvement, and programs for preservice teachers. Lighthouse schools investigated the development of excellence in classroom instruction with school-wide professional development, resulting in K–5 science units, a water quality exploration, and environmental literacy, awareness, and activities. Teacher education in earth science was fostered through a specialized laboratory section for pre-Education students in a first year Earth and Ocean Science course. Leadership and knowledge transfer (also termed *knowledge mobilization* and *knowledge utilization*) were central to all projects in this node.

INTEGRATIVE THEMES AND IDEAS

Early efforts were devoted to shaping the mission statement and strategic evolution plan and to ensuring shared understanding of the goals and working frameworks amongst a diverse group of scientists, educators, and partners. These efforts identified a set of interconnected themes and ideas that crossed and integrated many of the independent projects within Pacific CRYSTAL, for example, constructivist learning and teaching approaches, SMT literacies, learner resources, informal and formal environments, professionalism, teacher education, professional learning and leadership, evidence-based practices, knowledge transfer, and policy advocacy.

Constructivist Learning and Teaching Approaches

Education—a horizontal knowledge structure—has conflicting or alternative views of learning that coexist without the normal evolution, integration, or replacement of competing views found in the vertical knowledge structure in the sciences and mathematics (Lerman, 2010). This allows views of learning, curricula, instruction, and assessment practices based on outdated or questionable foundations to exist (United States National Research Council [NRC], 2000, 2007). Science education and mathematics education are no exceptions since some views of learning and instruction are based on behaviouralism (drill and practice, objective test items), while others are based on cognitive development (developmental appropriate tasks, performance assessments), and still others are based on cognitive psychology (sociocultural, sociocognitive perspectives, authentic assessments). Some of these views do not recognize the importance of learners' prior knowledge (including misconceptions, informal experiences, metacognition, language, and intuition), and they stress rote content learning and emphasize learner deficits (NRC, 2005a, 2005b, 2007).

"Students often have limited opportunities to understand or make sense of topics because many curricula have emphasized memory rather than understanding" (NRC, 2000, pp. 8–9).

The diverse participants in Pacific CRYSTAL embraced constructivism and recognized that this view of learning includes a spectrum of views from information processing, interactive-constructivism, social constructivism, and radical constructivism (Henriques, 1997; Yore, 2003). Constructivist approaches consider learning as sense making; the nature of SMT; the constructive, persuasive, and communicative roles of language in doing and learning these disciplines; the importance of prior knowledge, values, and beliefs; cultural perspectives about these disciplines; intuitive reasoning, critical or creative thinking, reflection, and metacognition; and the utilization of these resources to construct understanding.

Most project leaders implicitly or explicitly endorsed centralist views of constructivism with a sociocognitive interpretation that considered sociocultural influences, group dynamics and negotiations, and individual reflection and sense making while emphasizing a balance of self-directed and teacher-guided approaches. Many of the pragmatic teaching approaches utilized some form of a modified learning cycle (5Es [engage, explore, explain, elaborate, evaluate], EECA [engage, explore, consolidate, assess], or EDU [explore, discuss, understand]) and inquiry-oriented, problem-solving, and design-based approaches (teacher-structured, teacher-guided, open) involving hands-on experiences, multiple information sources, small-group negotiations, teacher-scaffolded discussions, and assessment for and of learning. These approaches assume that learners construct understanding based on their ontological assumptions, epistemological beliefs, prior knowledge, concurrent sensory experiences, available information sources, and interpersonal interactions within a sociocultural context. Teacher-directed instruction and modelling focused on requisite concepts or abilities are provided as *just-in-time* teaching on an *as-needed* basis, and the instruction considers the metacognitive awareness (declarative, procedural, and conditional knowledge) and executive control (planning, monitoring, regulating) necessary to facilitate students' explorations and learning. Assessment *for* learning involved ongoing formative techniques that empowered learning and informed instruction, while assessment *of* learning involved summative techniques that provided cumulative information for evaluation and accountability purposes.

Science, Mathematics, and Technology Literacies

Participants were generally in agreement that science, mathematics, and technology are disciplines with unique but interconnected and related attributes. They were supportive of the idea that SMT literacies ultimately resulted in *fuller participation in the public debate about science, technology, society, and environment (STSE) issues leading to informed decisions and sustainable solutions and actions.* Science is generally characterized as inquiry, mathematics as problem solving, and technology as design but all involve argumentation (AAAS, 1990; International Technology Education Association, 2007; United States National Academy of Engineering, 2010; United States National Council of Teachers of Mathematics, 2000; NRC, 1996, 2007).

Analyses of the USA reform documents in SMT indicated common goals, pedagogy and assessment focused on all students, disciplinary literacy, constructivist teaching approaches, and authentic assessments (Ford, Yore, & Anthony, 1997). However, even with international support of SMT literacies, there are no commonly shared definitions that provide a working framework and details. The lack of clear working frameworks for each of the SMT literacies, the central goal of the project, was identified as a requirement to improve Pacific CRYSTAL and to encourage integration across projects.

Collaboration among CRYSTAL Alberta, Pacific CRYSTAL, and the National Science Council of Taiwan resulted in mathematical and scientific literacy frameworks that provided fine structure to these literacies building on earlier analyses of the USA reform documents (Ford et al., 1997). The resulting frameworks for mathematics and scientific literacies and the development of a parallel framework for technological literacy are reported in Chapter 2 (Yore, this book). Special issues of the *International Journal of Science and Mathematics Education* (Anderson, Chiu, & Yore, 2010; Yore, Pimm, & Tuan, 2007) sought mathematics and science education research involving forms of these literacies. These IJSME special issues synthesized the current international and Canadian reforms to produce (a) parallel frameworks of mathematical and scientific literacy and (b) a secondary analyses of the 2000, 2003, and 2006 PISA results on literacies in reading, mathematics, and science. PISA, unlike other international assessments, used noncurricular definitions of these literacies, which morphed somewhat over the 2000–2006 period but retained focus on adult needs, real-world applications, and informational text (OECD, n.d.). The very high correlations (0.78–0.88) at student-level performances amongst reading, mathematics, and science literacies illustrate shared variances (61–77%) and potential associations amongst these literacies, which do not necessarily indicate causal relationships but are too large to ignore (Anderson et al., 2010). These results were used to support the interactive nature of fundamental literacy in a discipline and the derived understanding of that discipline found in the proposed frameworks.

Learner Resources: Prior Knowledge, Experiences, Beliefs, and Perceptions of Self

Learning theories and models prior to constructivism put much emphasis on learner qualities (IQ, logico-mathematical operations, socioeconomic background, etc.) as fixed traits unreceptive to change and growth. Therefore, many teaching approaches using these interpretations incorporated a *deficit model* in which instruction (e.g., learning assistance, special education, etc.) had to first address the deficit before the actual teaching and learning could occur. Applicants of constructivism incorporated the positive and negative lessons learned from these special approaches and re-engineered instruction to view all learner attributes as resources from and on which to facilitate learning. The basic principles are to ascertain what learners know and can do and then teach them accordingly (Ausubel, 1968) and to realize that teaching is in service of learning—without learning, teaching did not occur (Hand, 2007). Prior experiences and knowledge, including misconceptions, become springboards or foundations for further inquiries, designs, and problem solving.

Many students have misconceptions about the nature of SMT that influence learning (AAAS, 1993). Minority cultural beliefs and views of the SMT disciplines can be used to anchor instruction that respects sociocultural perspectives, enables honourable engagement, and guides the learning and teaching progressions.

Language is an important cognitive, persuasive, and communicative tool or technology in learning (NRC, 2000, 2007). It is documented that, like English language learners (ELL), most students in SMT courses face the 3-language problem involving transitions between home, school, and disciplinary languages (Yore & Treagust, 2006). Therefore, SMT students are science language learners (SLL), mathematics language learners (MLL), and technology language learners (TLL). The border crossings for some ELL, SLL, MLL, and TLL involve more than memorizing scientific, mathematical, and technological terminology; it involves being initiated into the culture, discourse, and metalanguage of these disciplines and into how language is used to construct, shape, justify, and report knowledge.

A major resource of interest for the underrepresented and underserved target populations of Pacific CRYSTAL were students' identities in and with the SMT disciplines. The NRC (2007) stated, "Students' motivation, their beliefs about science [and likely mathematics and technology], and their identities as learners affect their participation in the ... [SMT] classroom[s] and have consequences for the quality of their learning." (p. 195). These identity attributes (i.e., cognitive—belief about self; emotional or affective—values, interest, motivation, and attitudes; and behavioural—persistence, effort, and attention) are captured under the general headings of "[s]elf-concept[, which] refers to global ideas about one's identity and one's role relations to others. ... [and s]elf-esteem[, which] refers to the value one places on himself or herself." (Koballa & Glynn, 2007, p. 92). Both self-concept and self-esteem appear to be discipline- and context-specific where young people may have strong to weak interpretations of self in, for example, music, athletics, gangs, and academics.

The NRC (2007) suggested that students who have stronger beliefs and sense of competence in SMT tend to use deep learning strategies and exert more academic effort. Furthermore, there appear to be gender and cultural differences in these beliefs about role-stereotyped domains of SMT that may provide insights into the current and future participation, success, and career choices of underrepresented and underserved populations. The SMT cultures are "foreign to many students, both mainstream and nonmainstream, and the challenges of ... [SMT] learning may be greater for students whose cultural traditions are discontinuous with the way of knowing characteristic of [these disciplines and school programs in these disciplines]" (NRC, 2007, p. 201). de Abreu (2002) stated, that in mathematics education:

> The need for a better account of the interplay between the cultural, social, and person systems is needed. ... There were issues related to the uniqueness of the individual and patterns of development in the reconstruction of the cultural tools at the person level and also issues related to the social valorization of knowledge, changes in social structures, and the person's and the group's sense of identity. (p. 341)

The NRC (2007) stated, "some students in a group may disidentify with a particular domain, like school or ... [SMT], due to widely held stereotypes about their lack of ability in it. To protect their own sense of self, some students disidentify with the domain and stop trying to achieve in it." (p. 197).

Self-efficacy is a more specific interpretation of self and identity involving "beliefs in one's capabilities to organize and execute the courses of action required to produce given attainments" (Bandura, 1997, p. 3). Self-efficacy has two dimensions: beliefs about abilities and the expectation that these competencies can be successfully applied. Koballa and Glynn (2007) pointed out that self-efficacy within science and specific domains or topics were reasonable predictors of achievement and test performance; however, questionnaires that address specific areas may be more useful than those that address science generally. Such instruments have been developed for science and mathematics but not for technology (Enochs & Riggs, 1990; Enochs, Smith, & Huinker, 2000).

Goal orientations, such as performance and mastery, provide insights into students' intellectual resources and inform teaching. Performance orientation focuses on favourable evaluation while mastery orientation focuses on skill development, conceptual understanding, and learning. Performance orientation is well suited to test-driven learning environments while mastery orientation is well suited to interactive-constructivist learning environments where students and teachers collaborate to set the learning agenda.

Informal and Formal Environments

One goal of Pacific CRYSTAL was to use informal environments as an incubator for developing and evaluating authentic SMT learning activities that could then be implemented and disseminated to classroom and school environments and for the public awareness and engagement of SMT. (See comprehensive literature review at http://education2.uvic.ca/pacificcrystal/literature/index.html.) The NRC (2009) provided a comprehensive overview and value-added insights of informal environments beyond classrooms and schools. The "narrow focus on traditional academic activities and learning outcomes is fundamentally at odds with the ways in which individuals learn across various social settings: ... in potentially all the places they experience and pursuits they take on" (p. 27). The report recognizes life-long, life-wide, and life-deep learning and the significant contribution that lived experiences make to formal learning within constructivist, people-centred, place-centred, and culture-centred learning. The "[s]tandardized, multiple-choice test, [which] has become monoculture species for demonstrating outcomes in the K–12 education system, is at odds with the types of activities, learning and reasons for participation that characterize informal experiences" (p. 56). Formal assessments *of* learning are antithetical to assessment *for* self-directed learning, and these techniques may threaten learners' self-esteem and self-concept of the SMT activities. "In sum, although the nature and extent of ... [SMT]-related learning may vary considerably from one life stage to another, most people develop relevant abilities and intuitive knowledge from the days immediately after birth and expand on these in later stages of their life." (p. 99).

Informal environments include people-built designed settings, programs for various age groups, and media. Designed settings (including exhibits, demonstrations, and programs at institutions such as museums, science centres, aquaria, and environmental centres) are fluid spaces to be engaged with episodically and navigated freely, with limited or no directions, guidance, and facilitation by external scaffolding or staff to explore the target ideas emphasized by the design features. Programs—including after-school and out-of-school learning programs for children and youth, adult programs such as citizen science programs and teacher professional development programs, as well as programs for older adults—reflect societal changes in childcare, career changes, and leisure time. After-school, weekend, and summer programs (e.g., robotics contests, girls in science, and Science Venture) can cause tensions with in-school programs. However, Pacific CRYSTAL research and learning initiatives clearly supported the belief that "The potential of programs for ... [SMT] learning is great, given the broader population patterns" and require careful consideration, research, documentation, and evaluation (NRC, 2009, p. 199). Informal environments can address diversity, culture, and equity issues faced by underrepresented and underserved populations since many of these issues have their roots in other educational systems and lack of opportunities. "Environments should be developed in ways that expressly draw upon participants' cultural practices, including everyday language, linguistic practices and common cultural experiences" (pp. 236–237). Mass and interactive media (e.g., print, education broadcast, popular entertainment, and other immersive media—IMAX, planetaria, laser-projection systems) have significant roles in the public awareness and engagement. "[SMT]-related media are likely to continue to play a major role in the ways that people learn about ... [SMT] informally. The public often cites broadcast, print and digital media as their major sources of scientific[, mathematical, and technological] information." (p. 277).

Professionalism, Teacher Education, Professional Learning, and Leadership

Professions—communities of practice regulated by defined associations, authorities, or judicial panels—control entrance, acceptable practices, ethical conduct, and discipline. Teaching professions are not as tightly controlled as the accounting, engineering, legal, medical, or other recognized professions. Colleges of teachers or provincial governments control licensure requirements for initial entry into teaching and teacher education programs directly or indirectly in Canada. Some school districts require or encourage continued professional learning or advanced degrees to maintain effectiveness and to progress to higher lanes of salary structures. Universities, professional associations, and school districts can formally offer these experiences as credit or noncredit courses. There is reasonable evidence that high-quality professional development and high-quality instructional resources will change classroom practices, but there is very limited evidence that this triad leads to improved student achievement (Shymansky, Yore, Annetta, & Everett, 2008).

There is a growing realization that initial teacher education programs cannot provide the content (CK), pedagogical (PK), and pedagogical-content (PCK) knowledge for career-long, effective performance in rapidly changing classrooms and curricular contexts. Many teachers desire personalized approaches that value self-directed or community-based professional learning to maintain or enhance effectiveness and to address the ever-changing curriculum and instructional demands. The US National Board for Professional Teaching Standards (NBPTS) certificate is one such post-entry program designed to improve high-quality professionalism, classroom practice, and school leadership (http://www.nbpts.org/). Central requirements of NBPTS certificates are evaluation, reflection, regulation, and justification of curricular, instructional, and assessment decisions about preparing for and establishing favourable contexts, and advancing and supporting student learning by professional teachers. This places prime importance on rational, evidence-based decisions about what to teach, how to teach, and what data justify learning and teaching effectiveness.

Many of the Pacific CRYSTAL projects focused on teacher enhancement, curriculum development, and instructional resources that attempted to utilize authentic learning activities and leadership opportunities from informal environments to develop leaders, evidence-based practices, and tested resources for classroom and school environments. Therefore, internships, professional development experiences, fellowships, and apprenticeships were utilized to provide authentic learning, teaching, research, and leadership experiences for the SMT education areas. These experiences used community-based designs to (a) identify needs and set agendas, (b) deliver professional learning experiences focused on CK, PK, and PCK, and (c) provide mentoring and peer tutoring between and amongst university, school, First Nations, and nongovernmental participants within the realities of SMT research, development, and teaching.

Evidence-based Practices

Millar and Osborne (2009) considered practices that might have sufficient evidential-basis and suggested that wait time (Rowe, 1974a, 1974b), formative assessment (Black & Wiliam, 1998a, 1998b), and cognitive acceleration (Adey & Shayer, 1990) had enough research support for such acceptance and teacher uptake. Interestingly, learning styles and inquiry teaching, although popular with teachers or widely promoted in education literature, do not appear to enjoy the same degree of evidence or actual teacher uptake. These and other instructional practices appear to be popularized by promotional efforts but not empirical research findings.

The evidence-based practice model requires that (a) practitioners (here, teachers of SMT literacy) read the research on curricular and instructional practices, (b) this research addresses teachers as the target audience and end users, and (c) professional codes and recommendations are based on quality research results in sufficient quantity and consistency to define best practices (Hayward & Phillips, 2009). The US Institute for Educational Sciences provided standards for quality of evidence considered to be strong, possible, or weak for specific instructional programs, resources, and practices based on research design, rigorous methods, valid and reliable measurements, comprehensive data sources, appropriate data analysis, and compelling arguments involving legitimate claims, strong theoretical backings, and sound warrants of the data as evidence for or against specific claims or counterclaims (Shelley, 2009).

Recent analyses of science teacher journal articles dealing with scientific literacy from Australia, the United Kingdom, and the United States revealed that most recommended literacy strategies and activities were poorly justified (Hand, Yore, Jagger, & Prain, 2010). A more in-depth analysis of the 1998–2009 National Science Teachers Association journals for elementary, middle, and secondary school teachers on the same topic revealed that 61% of the recommendations were based on no or weak evidence (Jagger & Yore, 2010). Several North American agencies provided synthesis of evidence and have identified best practices:

– Best Evidence Encyclopedia (http://www.bestevidence.org/)
– The Campbell Collaboration (http://www.campbellcollaboration.org/)
– Comprehensive School Reform Quality Center (http://www.csrq.org/)
– What Works Clearinghouse (http://ies.ed.gov/ncee/wwc/)

Pacific CRYSTAL has attempted to provide similar insights by means of its publications, presentations, and resources.

Knowledge Transfer and Policy Advocacy

A central concern of the CRYSTAL project was for wider dissemination of its R&D results and the influence of public policy. It is widely recognized that writing research reports for highly regarded, peer-reviewed academic journals and assuming that end users (i.e., teachers, administrators, parents, bureaucrats, elected politicians) will access and use these results has not worked; few education policies are influenced by SMT education research. Successful knowledge transfer and policy influence involves much more; specifically, considering the end users from the outset and understanding the political structures and policy process, end users' preferred access and sources of information, and normative values of the political context. Reporting to these audiences as intended targets and speaking truth to powerful people is a complex, poorly understood, and time-consuming process. Shelley (2009) stated, "In highly abbreviated form, the essential point is how to reach across the gulf that is created by an unequal distribution of power (researchers having rather little and decision makers having very much more) to transmit understanding to those who are able to compel binding decisions." (p. 444). Unfortunately, "[a]mong policy makers and many scholars, educational research has a reputation of being amateurish, unscientific, and generally beside the point" (Henig, 2008, p. 357).

Research results are not the prime influence on public policy since research evidence or findings are more often used to confirm or justify a position rather than to inform or change positions (Rees, 2008). The structure, information flow, and decision process of most political organizations involve the ultimate decision makers—politicians, high-ranking appointees, etc. (first community), academics (second community), and policy advisers, consultants, research officers, support staff, lobbyists, special interest groups, advocates (third community) in the policy system (Cohn, 2006). Academics infrequently have direct access to the first community but may have direct or indirect access to the third community. The actors in the third community use knowledge and information to produce useful position papers or briefs in the language of decision makers and then disseminate them to influence or advise decision makers.

Effective communication with and persuasion of these end users mean using appropriate sources, format, language, and style; stressing cooperation and collaboration rather than conflict; and recognizing possible claims, counterclaims, and rebuttals. Members of the K–12 education and policy communities are more likely to rely on ICT and generalist journals rather than high-level, peer-reviewed research journals (Henig, 2008). Knowledge mobilization and lobby efforts need to provide information that recognizes the central function (persuasion) and the window of opportunity. The Society for Research in Child Development (n.d.), for example, prepares 2-page, research-based briefs on social policy topics concerning children, families, and other issues in print and electronic form that are concise and informative.

Canada, unlike many nations, does not have a national ministry or office of education. Education is a provincial or territorial mandate that is vigorously guarded; therefore, provincial and territorial ministries of education are the focal point for any lobby actions and policy influence. However, there have been nonbinding cooperatives of governmental education agencies focused on policy, curricula, and assessments. The Council of Ministers of Education, Canada (CMEC) is one of the few national entities—it is a collective of the ministers of education from the provinces and territories that comprise the nation.

The *Victoria Declaration* was developed by the ministers of education in September 1993 and provided a directive to harmonize education by promoting curriculum compatibility and assessment. The first initiative related to the Declaration was the development of the *School Achievement Indicators Program*, which assessed reading, writing, mathematics, and science performance of 13- and 16-year-old students until it was replaced by the *Pan-Canadian Assessment Program*. The CMEC next adopted the *Pan-Canadian Protocol for Collaboration on School Curriculum*, which recognized provincial jurisdiction for education and that, by sharing human and financial resources, the quality and efficiency of education could be increased. The first curriculum effort led to the *Common Framework of Science Learning Outcomes, K to 12* (CMEC, 1997), a nationally (albeit that Quebec did not officially participate) developed curriculum document that harmonized learning goals and science instruction in Canadian schools to provide the highest quality of education.

The Western and Northern Protocol for Canada (WNPC; http://www.wncp.ca/) is a regional interprovincial and interterritorial collaboration (composed of British Columbia, Alberta, Saskatchewan, Manitoba, the Yukon, Northwest Territories, and Nunavut) formed to develop coordinated perspectives on some common curricular areas. The WNCP *Common Curriculum Framework for K–9 Mathematics* (2006) is a guide with learning outcomes that reflects general trends in international mathematics education reforms. No similar national or regional effort has addressed K–12 computer science, engineering, environmental, and technology education.

Royal task forces and commissions are used to build consensus and lay the foundation for policies in Canada and other countries. The deliberative mechanisms appear to be democratic processes, but they are not without political difficulties. Membership in these groups may be based on expertise, representation, or other criteria but, once formed, they all involve negotiation, persuasion, controversy, and compromise. Participants involved in science and mathematics education deliberations and reforms have attested to the internal and external struggles in producing a document based on diverse input and lengthy deliberations.

Three international reports have potential for influencing science literacy around the world and to illustrate potential pathways for mathematics and technology literacies (Fensham, 2008; Osborne & Dillon, 2008; Rocard et al., 2007). These 'plain talk' reports identify problems, provide recommendations, and supportive justification that could be used by policy and decision makers to craft policy briefs and procedures that would improve the articulation and coordination of science education goals, resources, and efforts regarding formal schooling and public awareness of science. They serve as reasonable models for what could be done for mathematics and technology education.

Knowledge transfer and policy influence require synthesis of qualitative and quantitative research using metasynthesis, meta-analysis, and systematic review techniques or secondary analysis of data sets and multiple results. The Pacific CRYSTAL HLM project that analyzed the PISA 2003 and 2006 results (Anderson et al., 2010; Milford, Anderson, & Luo, Chapter 11 this book) illustrates attempts to repackage international survey data into meaningful evidence for policy makers and decision makers. Milford, Jagger, Yore, and Anderson (2010) used document analyses and informant interviews to document the influence of the Pan-Canadian Science Framework (CMEC, 1997) on provincial and territorial K–12 science curricula. They found that the Framework was pervasive in both general directions and design elements and in the specific direct use of the document in curriculum development initiatives in the ministries of education throughout the nation. However, the influences of reform-oriented actions take significant time to influence educational policy and depend on curriculum development and implementation itself, which functions in a 7- to 12-year cycle.

Another issue identified was the need for specific operational definitions for implementing and evaluating the reform. For example, the centrality of scientific literacy is not matched by a specific definition of its meaning in terms of curriculum and instruction. Furthermore, given that the Pan-Canadian Science Framework is now in its second decade, there is a need for attention to currency and relevancy to science and science education. These findings also likely apply to mathematics and technology education reforms.

OVERVIEW OF BOOK, SECTIONS, AND CHAPTERS

This book addresses lessons learned during 5 years of R&D. These lessons provide insights for funding agencies regarding SMT literacies and instruction and into collaborative partnerships involving multiple agencies, scaling implementation from single teachers and classrooms to wider dissemination to schools and district-wide settings, building leadership capacity amongst SMT teachers, knowledge transfer, and influencing SMT educational policy and decisions.

Section I provides readers insights into CRYSTAL and especially Pacific CRYSTAL. **Chapter 1** provides an overview of the contextual and organizational goals, conceptual foundations, theoretical constructs, and integrative themes across the projects as they evolved from concept to testing and dissemination. The integrative themes of many of the projects are constructivist learning, SMT literacies, community-based R&D models, partnerships, learner attributes, informal environments, professional learning or development, teacher education, leadership capacity, systemic change, evidence-based practices, knowledge transfer or mobilization, and policy advocacy. **Chapter 2**, *Foundations of Scientific, Mathematical, and Technological Literacies—Common Themes and Theoretical Frameworks*, provides the working definitions and theoretical backings and research support for the central focus of Pacific CRYSTAL. These discipline-specific literacies have been discussed for many years and serve as the focus of international education reforms, but they lack well-accepted definitions that incorporate conceptual understanding, literacy, and contextual applications.

Section II, Authentic Learning—Informal Environments and Extracurricular Science, Mathematics, and Technology Opportunities: Anchoring and Bridging Real-world, Cultural, and School Experiences, describes projects from Node 1 that focused on building conceptual ideas and transforming them into instructional practices. **Chapter 3**, *Adolescents' Science Career Aspirations Explored through Identity and Possible Selves*, addresses making career decisions in secondary school—a challenging and often stressful experience for adolescents involving self-concept related to identity and self-efficacy. The Possible Selves Mapping Process is an experiential activity that is future-oriented and a personalized form of self-concept; it has direct relevance to how students' views of themselves guide their work and educational behaviours. **Chapter 4**, *Giving Voice to Science from Two Perspectives: A Case Study*, reports on an ethnobotanical program involving six First Nations members over 6 years in which opportunities to explore traditional and western knowledge about nature and naturally occurring events were made available at the University of Victoria and SNIT□E□ (pronounced *sneakwith*, SENĆOŦEN language for The Place of the Blue Grouse)—part of traditional territory utilized for hunting, fishing, shellfish gathering, and sacred ceremonies. **Chapter 5**, *Seaquaria in Schools: Participatory Approaches in the Evaluation of an Exemplary Environmental Education Program*, reports on the successful partnerships amongst nongovernmental agencies, schools, universities, and their communities that helped enliven a community of practice for public school educators in which all partners actively participated in setting agendas and developing programs. The successes and challenges provide insights into how to achieve long-term sustainability through active community partnerships and how this approach can be applied elsewhere. **Chapter 6**, *Teaching Problem Solving and Computer Science in the Schools: Concepts and Assessment*, explores expanding the age range of students exposed to computer science and computer science concepts (i.e., recursion, concurrency, graph theory) through the development and deployment of interesting and engaging hands-on computer science activities. It discusses encouraging findings from three studies as well as the strengths and weaknesses of assessment techniques in various classroom settings. **Chapter 7**, *Outreach Workshops, Applications, and Resources: Helping Teachers to Climb over the Science, Mathematics, and Technology Threshold by Engaging Their Classes*, illustrates how elementary and middle school teachers who lacked confidence and competence to teach SMT topics effectively adopted constructivist approaches. The outreach workshops made SMT topics more accessible to teachers by modelling the successful use of effective pedagogies, appropriate technologies, and authentic learning activities.

Section III, Moving Tested ideas into Classrooms, illustrates how conceptual ideas and practices were expanded and moved into larger settings. **Chapter 8,** *Explicit Literacy Instruction Embedded in Middle School Science Classrooms: A Community-based Professional Development Project to Enhance Scientific Literacy*, reports on the community-based project that identified, developed, and embedded explicit literacy instruction in science programs to achieve fundamental literacy in science and science understanding. **Chapter 9**, *Enhancing Science Education through an Online Repository of Controversial, Socioscientific News Stories*, reports an interactive teaching technique that employed controversial, socioscientific news stories as a means of developing scientific literacy and follows the development of the Science Times resource, its effectiveness and potential uses in similar learning opportunities and the larger learning community via Internet delivery. **Chapter 10,** *Promoting Earth Science Teaching and Learning: Inquiry-based Activities and Resources Anchoring Teacher Professional Development and Education*, focuses on developing teachers' interest in and positive attitudes toward Earth Science and to increase PCK and experience with scientific reasoning and practice. A series of inquiry-based activities and accompanying resources were developed for teacher professional development workshops, an Education Laboratory in a first year Earth and Ocean Sciences course that demonstrates relevance, constructivist approach, curriculum linkages, opportunities for interdisciplinary associations (including language arts, mathematics, and other sciences) and accompanying resources are key attributes of these successful activities, which are classroom tested and informed by teacher feedback.

Section IV, Knowledge Transfer, Systemic Implementation, and Building Leadership Capacity, addresses the lead phase of the evolutionary strategy. **Chapter 11**, *Modelling of Large-scale PISA Assessment Data: Science and Mathematics Literacy*, investigates relationships and patterns associated with student performance in the literacies of mathematics, science, and reading and student, school, home, and community characteristics. The PISA data sets were the central foci of the investigations using HLM. The findings reported go well beyond simple ranking of participating nations in terms of average performance scores. **Chapter 12**, *Time and Teacher Control in Curriculum Adoption: Lessons from the Lighthouse Schools Project*, reports on case studies involving an elementary and a middle school where teachers were provided with funding that enabled them to have the time to implement a new science education curriculum and total control over the change process. Initially conceived as a lighthouse project of peer interschool development, the teachers involved reconceptualized the lighthouse to serve their particular, local interests. Teacher control translated into unit planning and changes in the direction of funding support toward the middle school receiving students from the elementary school. While teachers were enthusiastic about this change in process and the availability of time to plan, analysis of the science education units developed at both schools revealed that curriculum change is complex and difficult, not easily addressed by providing time for planning, or by locating teachers as the sole agents of the change process. **Chapter 13**, *The Development of a Place-based Learning Environment at the Bowen Island Community School*, describes and documents one elementary lighthouse school's experiences in achieving its environmental literacy goals through the development of a place-based learning environment. The Ecological Education Project studied the complex ecology of the intersection between scientific knowledge, pedagogy, student learning, and curriculum. They identified and developed innovative approaches for the teaching of scientific and interdisciplinary topics around environmental education framed within the context of ecoliteracy.

Section V: Closing Remarks and Implications for the Future, provides a post hoc perspective to highlight themes that evolved from individual projects. **Chapter 14**, *Epilogue of Pacific CRYSTAL—Lessons Learned about Science, Mathematics, and Technology Literacy, Teaching and Learning*, provides a cross-case analysis and discussion of the themes emerging from the studies reported in this book. The common themes across these studies were community commitment and action planning, disciplinary literacy (science, mathematics, technology), evidence-based resources and practices, professional learning (teacher education and professional development), student performance (conceptual understanding, fundamental literacy, self-efficacy, identity), and educational leadership and advocacy.

The Appendix offers a listing of highly qualified personnel—postdoctoral and graduate students, undergraduate research assistants, and community interns—involved with Pacific CRYSTAL. It summarizes their contributions, including theses and dissertations, articles, conference presentations, and instructional resources. This Appendix documents the legacy of the Pacific CRYSTAL Project more so than any other document.

CLOSING REMARKS

Pacific CRYSTAL suggested a number of independent R&D projects in the original proposal to address the changed research and policy expectations of NSERC. As the project unfolded, both NSERC and the principal investigators in Pacific CRYSTAL became more realistic about the complexity of the central problems and the project design. Early R&D efforts involved a loose collection of diverse projects without the internal glue of a shared mission statement and strategic plan. Experiences during Year 1 led to national and project-wide deliberations and considerations of the central goals, organizational structure, operational procedures, and outcomes by the NSERC staff, project directors from the five CRYSTAL projects, and the Pacific CRYSTAL International Advisory Board, Executive Committee, and all participants. The traditional definitions of educational research (i.e., publication of peer-reviewed articles and presentation at international conferences) was revised to focus on teachers, policy makers, instructional resources, and a variety of local, provincial, and national professional conferences. The insights into processes and procedures are equally and likely more important than the number of peer-reviewed research articles, books, and chapters that flow from Pacific CRYSTAL. The following chapters provide theoretical, empirical, and practical documentation for several claims about SMT literacy and programs that promote fuller engagement of SMT learning and problems.

NOTES

CRYSTAL Alberta at the University of Alberta, Edmonton, AB, provided national coordination for all Centres (http://www.edpolicystudies.ualberta.ca/en/Centres InstitutesAndNetworks/CRYSTALAlberta.aspx): CRYSTAL Atlantique at the University of New Brunswick, St. John, NB (http://www.crystalatlantique.ca/); Centre de Recherché sur l'Enseignemeent et l'Apprentissage des Sciences at the University of Sherbrooke, Quebec (http://creas.educ.usherbrooke.ca/); CRYSTAL Manitoba at the University of Manitoba, Winnipeg, MB (http://umanitoba.ca/outreach/crystal/); and Pacific CRYSTAL at the University of Victoria, BC (http://www.educ.uvic.ca/ pacificcrystal/main.html).

REFERENCES

Adey, P. S., & Shayer, M. (1990). Accelerating the development of formal thinking in middle and high school students. *Journal of Research in Science Teaching, 27*(3), 267–285.

American Association for the Advancement of Science. (1990). *Science for all Americans: Project 2061.* New York: Oxford University Press.

American Association for the Advancement of Science. (1993). *Benchmarks for science literacy: Project 2061.* New York: Oxford University Press.

Anderson, J. O., Chiu, M.-H., & Yore, L. D. (2010). First cycle of PISA (2000–2006)—International perspectives on successes and challenges: Research and policy directions [Special issue]. *International Journal of Science and Mathematics Education, 8*(3), 373–388.

Ausubel, D. P. (1968). *Educational psychology: A cognitive view.* New York: Holt, Rinehart & Winston.

Bandura, A. (1997). *Self-efficacy: The exercise of control.* New York: W.H. Freeman.

Black, P. J., & Wiliam, D. (1998a). Assessment and classroom learning. *Assessment in Education: Principles, Policy & Practice, 5*(1), 7–74.

Black, P. J., & Wiliam, D. (1998b). *Inside the black box: Raising standards through classroom assessment.* London, England: King's College.

Cohn, D. (2006). Jumping into the political fray: Academics and policy-making. *Institute for Research on Public Policy (IRPP) Matters, 7*(3), 8–36. Retrieved from http://www.irpp.org/pm/archive/pmvol7no3.pdf

Council of Ministers of Education, Canada. (1997). *Common framework of science learning outcomes, K to 12.* Pan-Canadian protocol for collaboration on school curriculum. Retrieved from http:// publications.cmec.ca/science/framework/

de Abreu, G. (2002). Mathematics learning in out-of-school contexts: A cultural psychology perspective. In L. D. English (Ed.), *Handbook of international research in mathematics education* (pp. 323–353). Mahwah, NJ: Lawrence Erlbaum.

Enochs, L. G., & Riggs, I. M. (1990). Further development of an elementary science teaching efficacy belief instrument: A preservice elementary scale. *School Science and Mathematics, 90*(8), 694–706.

Enochs, L. G., Smith, P. L., & Huinker, D. (2000). Establishing factorial validity of the mathematics teaching efficacy beliefs instrument. *School Science and Mathematics, 100*(4), 194–202.

Fensham, P. J. (2008). *Science education policy-making: Eleven emerging issues.* Paris, France: UNESCO.

Ford, C. L., Yore, L. D., & Anthony, R. J. (1997, March). *Reforms, visions, and standards: A cross-curricular view from an elementary school perspective.* Paper presented at the annual meeting of the National Association for Research in Science Teaching, Oak Brook, IL, USA. Retrieved from ERIC database. (ED406168)

Hand, B. (Ed.). (2007). *Science inquiry, argument and language: A case for the science writing heuristic.* Rotterdam, The Netherlands: Sense.

Hand, B., Yore, L. D., Jagger, S., & Prain, V. (2010). Connecting research in science literacy and classroom practice: A review of science teaching journals in Australia, the UK, and the United States, 1998–2008. *Studies in Science Education, 46*(1), 45–68.

Hayward, D. V., & Phillips, L. M. (2009). Considering research quality and applicability through the eyes of stakeholders. In M. C. Shelley II, L. D. Yore, & B. Hand (Eds.), *Quality research in literacy and science education: International perspectives and gold standards* (pp. 139–148). Dordrecht, The Netherlands: Springer.

Henig, J. R. (2008). The evolving relationship between researchers and public policy. *Phi Delta Kappan, 89*(5), 357–360.

Henriques, L. (1997). *A study to define and verify a model of interactive-constructive elementary school science teaching.* Unpublished doctoral dissertation, University of Iowa, Iowa City, IA, USA.

International Technology Education Association. (2007). *Standards for technological literacy: Content for the study of technology* (3rd ed.). Reston, VA: Author.

Jagger, S., & Yore, L. D. (2010). *Evidence-based practice in science literacy for all: A case study of 1998–2009 NSTA articles as self-directed professional development* [Manuscript submitted for publication].

Koballa, T. R., Jr., & Glynn, S. M. (2007). Attitudinal and motivational constructs in science learning. In S. K. Abell & N. G. Lederman (Eds.), *Handbook of research on science education* (pp. 75–102). Mahwah, NJ: Lawrence Erlbaum.

Lerman, S. (2010, January 26). *Looking through theories in mathematics education research.* [Svend Pederson Award Lecture]. University of Stockholm, Sweden.

Milford, T. M., Jagger, S., Yore, L. D., & Anderson, J. O. (2010). National influences on science education reform in Canada. *Canadian Journal of Science, Mathematics and Technology Education, 10*(4), 370–381.

Millar, R., & Osborne, J. (2009). Research and practice: A complex relationship? In M. C. Shelley II, L. D. Yore, & B. Hand (Eds.), *Quality research in literacy and science education: International perspectives and gold standards* (pp. 41–61). Dordrecht, The Netherlands: Springer.

Natural Sciences and Engineering Research Council of Canada. (2009). *Centres for research in youth, science teaching and learning pilot program.* Retrieved from http://www.nserc-crsng.gc.ca/Promoter-Promotion/CRYSTAL-CREAS_eng.asp

Organisation for Economic Co-operation and Development. (n.d.). *Homepage.* Retrieved from http://www.pisa.oecd.org

Osborne, J., & Dillon, J. (2008). *Science education in Europe: Critical reflections.* London, England: Nuffield Foundation.

Rees, W. E. (2008, April-May). Science, cognition and public policy. *Academic Matters*, 9–12.

Rocard, M., Csermely, P., Jorde, D., Lenzen, D., Walberg-Henriksson, H., & Hemmo, V. (2007). *Science education now: A renewed pedagogy for the future of Europe.* Luxembourg, Belgium: European Commission.

Rowe, M. B. (1974a). Relation of wait-time and rewards to the development of language, logic, and fate control: Part II - Rewards. *Journal of Research in Science Teaching, 11*(4), 291–308.

Rowe, M. B. (1974b). Wait-time and rewards as instructional variables, their influence on language, logic, and fate control: Part I - Wait-time. *Journal of Research in Science Teaching, 11*(2), 81–94.

Shelley, M. C., II. (2009). Speaking truth to power with powerful results: Impacting public awareness and public policy. In M. C. Shelley II, L. D. Yore, & B. Hand (Eds.), *Quality research in literacy and science education: International perspectives and gold standards* (pp. 443–466). Dordrecht, The Netherlands: Springer.

Shymansky, J. A., Yore, L. D., Annetta, L. A., & Everett, S. A. (2008). Missouri-Iowa science cooperative (Science Co-op): Rural schools-urban universities collaborative project. *The Rural Educator, 29*(2), 1–3.

Society for Research in Child Development. (n.d.). *Homepage.* Retrieved from http://www.srcd.org/

United States National Academy of Engineering. (2010). *Standards for K–12 engineering education?* Committee on Standards for K–12 Engineering Education. Washington, DC: The National Academies Press.

United States National Council of Teachers of Mathematics. (2000). *Principles and standards for school mathematics*. Reston, VA: Author.

United States National Research Council. (1996). *The national science education standards*. Washington, DC: The National Academies Press.

United States National Research Council. (2000). *How people learn: Brain, mind, experience, and school— Expanded edition* (J. D. Bransford, A. L. Brown, & R. R. Cocking, Eds.). Committee on Developments in the Science of Learning. Commission on Behavioral and Social Sciences and Education. Washington, DC: The National Academies Press.

United States National Research Council. (2005a). *How students learn: Mathematics in the classroom*. Committee on *How people learn* (M. S. Donovan & J. D. Bransford, Eds.). A Targeted Report for Teachers. Division of Behavioral and Social Sciences and Education. Washington, DC: The National Academies Press.

United States National Research Council. (2005b). *How students learn: Science in the classroom* (M. S. Donovan & J. D. Bransford, Eds.). Committee on *How people learn*. A Targeted Report for Teachers. Division of Behavioral and Social Sciences and Education. Washington, DC: The National Academies Press.

United States National Research Council. (2007). *Taking science to school: Learning and teaching science in grades K–8* (R. A. Duschl, H. A. Schweingruber, & A. W. Shouse, Eds.). Committee on Science Learning, Kindergarten through Eighth Grade. Board on Science Education, Center for Education, Division of Behavioral and Social Sciences and Education. Washington, DC: The National Academies Press.

United States National Research Council. (2009). *Learning science in informal environments: People, places, and pursuits* (P. Bell, B. Lewenstein, A. W. Shouse, & M. A. Feder, Eds.). Committee on Learning Science in Informal Environments. Board on Science Education, Center for Education, Division of Behavioral and Social Sciences and Education. Washington, DC: The National Academies Press.

Western and Northern Canadian Protocol for Collaboration in Education. (2006). *The common curriculum framework for K–9 mathematics*. Retrieved from http://www.wncp.ca/english/subjectarea/mathematics/ccf.aspx

Yore, L. D. (2003). Quality science and mathematics education research: Considerations of argument, evidence and generalizability [Guest editorial]. *School Science and Mathematics, 103*(1), 1–7.

Yore, L. D., Pimm, D., & Tuan, H.-L. (Eds.). (2007). Language—An end and a means to mathematical literacy and scientific literacy [Special issue]. *International Journal of Science and Mathematics Education, 5*(4), 557–769.

Yore, L. D., & Treagust, D. F. (2006). Current realities and future possibilities: Language and science literacy—empowering research and informing instruction. *International Journal of Science Education, 28*(2/3), 291–314.

Larry D. Yore
Department of Curriculum and Instruction

Eileen Van der Flier-Keller
School of Earth and Ocean Sciences
University of Victoria
Victoria, British Columbia, Canada

APPENDIX

Pacific CRYSTAL Advisory Board and Executive Committee Members,
Co-directors as on June 30, 2010

Advisory Board

Dr. Chris Barnes, Director, Neptune Project, University of Victoria
Dr. Phillip Bell, Co-director, LASER Project, University of Washington, Seattle, WA
Dr. Jacques De'sautels, Laval University, Montreal, PQ
Dr. Reg Mitchell, Department of Chemistry, University of Victoria
Dr. Stephen Norris, National Coordinator, CRYSTAL, University of Alberta, Edmonton, AB
Mr. Lionel Sander, President, Edvantage Press, Victoria, BC
Dr. Rachel Scarth, Director of Research Services, University of Victoria

Executive Committee

Dr. David W. Blades, Department of Curriculum and Instruction, University of Victoria
Ms. Cathy Carolsfeld, WestWind SeaLab Supplies, Victoria, BC
Dr. Yvonne Coady, Department of Computer Science, University of Victoria
Mr. Calvin Parsons, Strawberry Vale Elementary School, Victoria, BC
Dr. Leslee Francis Pelton, Department of Curriculum and Instruction, University of Victoria
Dr. Ulrike Stege, Department of Computer Science, University of Victoria
Ms. Nikki Wright, SeaChange Marine Conservation Society, Brentwood Bay, BC

Co-directors

Dr. Larry D. Yore, Department of Curriculum and Instruction, University of Victoria
Dr. Eileen Van der Flier-Keller, School of Earth and Ocean Sciences, University of Victoria

LARRY D. YORE

2. FOUNDATIONS OF SCIENTIFIC, MATHEMATICAL, AND TECHNOLOGICAL LITERACIES—COMMON THEMES AND THEORETICAL FRAMEWORKS

The Pacific CRYSTAL Centre for Scientific and Technological Literacy was proposed knowing that many people in the academic and educational communities did not have or share common definitions of scientific literacy and mathematical literacy (also known as numeracy) and that the efforts to define and share technological, computer science, and engineering literacies were much more limited. However, Pacific CRYSTAL was designed on an interdisciplinary foundation involving (a) formal and informal environments for learning about science, mathematics, and technology; (b) scientists and engineers from these academic disciplines; and (c) educational researchers from counselling psychology, environmental education, indigenous studies, language and literacy, mathematics education, science education, and technology education. This broad involvement allowed Pacific CRYSTAL to adopt cognitive sciences (i.e., linguistic, pedagogical, ontological, epistemological, psychological, sociocultural) and constructivist perspectives for science, mathematics, and technology (SMT) literacies because these views were demonstrated to be part of contemporary educational reforms and practices (Ford, Yore, & Anthony, 1997). Surprisingly, there was very little collaboration amongst SMT educators in developing current reforms.

Technological literacy (International Technology Education Association [ITEA], 1996, 2003, 2006, 2007) and engineering literacy (United States National Academy of Engineering [NAE], 2010) standards have much shorter histories than the 50+ year history of scientific literacy and 20+ year history of mathematics literacy. In fact, "[the] 'E' in STEM [Science, Technology, Engineering, and Mathematics] has been silent" (NAE, p. vii) in USA education and totally missing in most of Canadian education; while the 'T' was associated with industrial or manual arts in both countries. There are some indications that the fragmented technology and engineering education is becoming consolidated in the USA with the recent (November 2010) name change of the major technology education association from the International Technology Education Association to the International Technology and Engineering Education Association (ITEEA); however, computer science education has not made a major impact in K–12 education.

Prior to the outset of Pacific CRYSTAL, much consideration had been given to scientific literacy (Ford et al., 1997; Hand, Prain, & Yore, 2001; Norris & Phillips,

L. D. Yore et al (Eds.), Pacific CRYSTAL Centre for Science, Mathematics, and Technology Literacy: Lessons Learned, 23–44.

2003; Yore, Bisanz, & Hand, 2003) that proposed a framework for literacy in the discipline and understanding the big ideas of the discipline, which promote fuller engagement with socioscientific issues. Early efforts in CRYSTAL projects addressed the need to articulate a similar definition of mathematics literacy. However, similar efforts were not apparent for technology literacy, which in part may be due to the definitions of technology being reasonably narrow or confused with computational tools, engineering being confused as simply applied science, and computer science being strongly attached to computer hardware.

Current definitions of technology and engineering are defined as design under constraints—with nature being the fundamental constraint—and "time, money, available materials, ergonomics, environmental regulations, manufacturability, reparability and political considerations" being others (NAE, 2010, p. 6). Computer science has been a new arrival in many engineering and technology departments, sometimes transferring from faculties of mathematics and sciences where its defining characteristics were not fully embraced. Computer science, technology, and engineering involve iterative design or problem-solving processes that begin "with the identification of a problem and [end] with a solution that takes into account the identified constraints and [meets] specifications for desired performance ... [and] do not have single, correct solutions[; technology, computer science, and engineering], by necessity, [are] creative [endeavours]" (NAE, pp. 6–7).

Therefore in this chapter, the development of a technological literacy framework, which includes engineering and computer science and parallels scientific and mathematics literacy, will be stressed. Technology is taken as a broad discipline spanning a continuum of inventors, technicians, technologists, professional engineers, and researchers. It is important to note that scientific, mathematical, and technological practices and literacies are distinct (scientific literacy—nature of the world; mathematical literacy—patterns and relationships of quantity, order, and shape; technological literacy—needs, problems, designs). However, many common features have been identified, such as "the use of mathematics, the interplay of creativity and logic, eagerness to be original," in both science and technology (American Association for the Advancement of Science [AAAS], 1990, ch. 3, p. 2). "It is the union of science, mathematics, and technology that forms the [techno-scientific] endeavor and that makes it so successful. Although each of these human enterprises has a character and history of its own, each is dependent on and reinforces the others" (AAAS, 1990, ch. 1, p. 1). Furthermore, engineering and computer sciences are frequently viewed as partially overlapping with technology or as part of the technological continuum and that the crowded school program and curriculum mitigate against the development of another stand-alone curricular entry (NAE, 2010).

SCIENCE, MATHEMATICS, AND TECHNOLOGY LITERACIES

Participants in Pacific CRYSTAL generally agreed that science, mathematics, and technology (including engineering and computer science) are disciplines with unique but interconnected and related attributes and supported the idea that general (mainstream) SMT literacies ultimately resulted in fuller participation in the public debate about science, technology, society, and environment (STSE) issues leading to informed decisions and sustainable solutions and actions. Although general literacy focuses on mainstream citizenship, it also serves as a platform or springboard for elite (pipeline) literacy, leading to further academic studies and SMT-oriented careers and professions. It was the sincere belief of most participating investigators in Pacific CRYSTAL that greater attention to the fundamental literacy, disciplinary understanding, and socioscientific applications of the mainstream focus would alleviate much of the pipeline problems for underserved and underrepresented peoples entering higher studies and careers in these disciplines.

Science is generally characterized as inquiry, mathematics as problem solving, and technology as design—but all involve argumentation consisting of logical reasoning about knowledge claims, problem solutions and innovations based on empirical evidence, established procedures, or theoretical assumptions and foundations. Collaboration among CRYSTAL Alberta, Pacific CRYSTAL, and the National Science Council of Taiwan focused on constructing theoretical and empirical foundations for scientific and mathematical literacies. These efforts resulted in frameworks that provided fine structure and research basis for scientific and mathematical literacies building on earlier analyses of the US mathematics (United States National Council of Teachers of Mathematics [NCTM], 2000) and science (AAAS, 1990, 1993; United States National Research Council [NRC], 1996) reform documents that demonstrated focus on disciplinary literacies involving conceptual understanding of big ideas, critical thinking, and communications (Yore, Pimm, & Tuan, 2007) and support for associations (0.78–0.88) and shared variances (61–77%) amongst student Programme for International Student Assessment (PISA) performance in reading, mathematics, and science literacies not reported elsewhere (Anderson, Chiu, & Yore, 2010). PISA used noncurricular definitions of these literacies, which have morphed somewhat over the 2000–2006 period; but they have retained focus on adult needs, real-world applications, and informational text (Table 1).

The following sections summarize key attributes of SMT literacies that use a common framework to promote public engagement with STSE issues. Each literacy will be defined and illustrated using common interacting senses of fundamental literacy in the discipline and derived understanding of the discipline—science, mathematics, or technology. A cautionary note must be considered here in that many standards are presented as learning progressions for primary, middle, and secondary schools; they are based on experts' hypotheses and not empirical research results.

Scientific Literacy

Science Literacy for All is a long promoted, but ill-defined general expectation (Hurd, 1958) with international cache (McEneaney, 2003), which runs the risk of being cast off as an outdated slogan, logo, or rally flag rather than an essential framework to guide science education (Yore, 2009). Science Literacy for All does not

Table 1. PISA definitions of mathematics, science, and reading literacy
(OECD 2000, 2003, & 2006 from Anderson et al., 2010, pp. 376–377)

Year	Mathematics	Science	Reading
2000	The capacity to identify, to understand, and to engage in mathematics and make well-founded judgments about the role that mathematics plays, as needed for an individual's current and future private life, occupational life, social life with peers and relatives, and life as a constructive, concerned, and reflective citizen.	The capacity to use scientific knowledge, to identify questions, and to draw evidence-based conclusions in order to understand and help make decisions about the natural world and the changes made to it through human activity.	Understanding, using, and reflecting on written texts in order to achieve one's goals, to develop one's knowledge and potential, and to participate in society.
2003	An individual's capacity to identify and understand the role that mathematics plays in the world, to make well-founded judgments, and to use and engage with mathematics in ways that meet the needs of that individual's life as a constructive, concerned, and reflective citizen.	The capacity to use scientific knowledge, to identify questions, and to draw evidence-based conclusions in order to understand and help make decisions about the natural world and the changes made to it through human activity.	An individual's capacity to understand, use, and reflect on written texts in order to achieve one's goals, to develop one's knowledge and potential, and to participate in society.
2006	An individual's capacity to identify and understand the role that mathematics plays in the world, to make well-founded judgments, and to use and engage with mathematics in ways that meet the needs of that individual's life as a constructive, concerned, and reflective citizen.	An individual's scientific knowledge and use of that knowledge to identify questions, to acquire new knowledge, to explain scientific phenomena, and to draw evidence-based conclusions about science-related issues, understanding of the characteristic features of science as a form of human knowledge and enquiry, awareness of how science and technology shape our material, intellectual, and cultural environments, and willingness to engage in science-related issues, and with the ideas of science, as a reflective citizen.	An individual's capacity to understand, use, and reflect on written texts in order to achieve one's goals, to develop one's knowledge and potential, and to participate in society.

assume or preclude elite-level studies and science-related careers (pipeline interpretation); rather, it embraces practical, civic, and cultural aspects (mainstream interpretation; Shen, 1975). Roberts (2007) classified definitions of science literacy as
emphasizing science understanding (Vision I) or contextual applications (Vision II).
Analyses of science education reforms (Ford et al., 1997; Hand et al., 2001) and the
theoretical construct (Norris & Phillips, 2003) identified interacting fundamental and
derived senses of science literacy. The fundamental sense subsumes abilities,
emotional dispositions, and information communication technologies (ICT) as well as
language (speaking–listening, writing–reading, representing–interpreting) and mathematics. The derived sense subsumes the content goals regarding understanding the
big ideas of science (nature of science, scientific inquiry, technological design, and
the relationships amongst STSE). These fundamental and derived senses of science
literacy lead to fuller and informed participation in the public debate about STSE
issues (Vision III). Table 2 illustrates the two interacting senses, components, and
cognitive symbiosis between the senses and amongst the components within both
senses. For example, peoples' views of science will influence their use of scientific
metalanguage (theory, proof, certainty, etc.), and their prior conceptual knowledge
about the domain and topic will influence their reading comprehension of texts
focused on the domain or topic. People's understanding of science will influence
their inquiries and explanations of the resulting data and their critical thinking will
influence their choice and interpretation of information accessed from the Internet.

Table 2. Interacting senses of scientific literacy—Cognitive symbiosis
(Yore et al., 2007, p. 568)

Fundamental sense	Derived sense
Cognitive and Metacognitive Abilities	Understanding the Big Ideas and Unifying Concepts of Science
Critical Thinking/Plausible Reasoning	Nature of Science
Habits of Mind	Scientific Inquiry
Scientific Language (including mathematical language)	Technological Design
Information Communication Technologies (ICT)	Relationships among Science, Technology, Society, and Environment (STSE)

Fundamental sense of scientific literacy. The fundamental sense of being literate
in a discipline is somewhat more contested and less well documented (Moje, 2008;
Shanahan & Shanahan, 2008), but it involves more than the ability to talk and read
science. The contents of this sense encompass the cognitive, affective, psychomotor,
and linguistic requirements of constructivist models of learning as making meaning
rather than taking meaning. The *cognitive and metacognitive* (awareness—declarative, procedural, and conditional knowledge; and executive control of cognition—
planning, monitoring, and regulating) abilities and strategies include a variety
of knowledge building and science processes, argumentation, and planning and
evaluating procedures. *Critical thinking/plausible reasoning* is about deciding what
to believe or do about a challenge and the abductive, inductive, deductive, and

hypothetico-deductive logics used in scientific reasoning. *Habits of mind* involve emotional dispositions (beliefs, values, attitudes, and critical-response skills) toward science and scientific inquiry (AAAS, 1993). *Scientific language* involves the use of metalanguage, words, symbols, numbers, and representations to develop procedures, build arguments, construct knowledge claims, and communicate these processes, arguments, and claims to others. Language, both natural and mathematical, shapes what is known as well as reports what is known and persuades others about these ideas. Most interpretations of the roles of language in science overemphasize the importance of mathematical language and the communicative role of language—while overlooking the constructive (language as cognitive technology/tool) and persuasive (argument) aspects in constructing understandings. Talking–listening about science with peers and with the teacher provides students with opportunities to make sense of their thinking, hear others' ideas, become aware of multiple perspectives, rethink ideas, evaluate others' ideas, and frame their ideas.

Unfortunately, K–12 teachers dominate classroom discussions and do the majority of talking. Therefore, students do not spend sufficient time producing language and interacting with others in exploratory talk, which allows them to process both language and content more deeply and to negotiate meaning and adjust their language to make it comprehensible to their audience. Writing–reading about ideas within an inquiry science context creates opportunities to propose claims, reinforce arguments, and revise conceptual knowledge and models for different modes of text, thereby building structures necessary for reading informational texts. Representing–interpreting various modes of text (print, numerical, graphic, etc.) influences depth of processing and understanding in science (Yore & Hand, 2010). Scientific-literate people construct and use multiple representations (including sketches, diagrams, models, tables, charts, maps, pictures, graphs); use visual and textual displays to reveal relationships; locate and evaluate information from various textual and digital sources; and choose and use appropriate vocabulary, spatial displays, numerical operations, and statistics. Scientists do science with and are limited by available technologies and use *ICT* to cooperate; coauthor; share databases; display, analyze, and model data; and construct new knowledge. Scientific-literate students use similar ICT to troubleshoot, solve problems; access, process, manage, interpret and communicate information; and create representations (Partnership for 21st Century Skills, 2004a).

Derived sense of scientific literacy. The derived sense of scientific literacy is reasonably well understood and accepted in the science education community and international science education reform documents (Yore, 2009). There is some disagreement on the specifics, but when taken at the general level, there is a reasonable consensus. The *big ideas and unifying concepts* consider the major content for biological, earth and space, and physical sciences that apply across domains and topics or provide a foundation for work in a specific domain. The *Pan-Canadian Framework of Science Learning Outcomes* (Council of Ministers of Education, Canada [CMEC], 1997) identified the following unifying concepts: constancy and change, energy, similarity and diversity, and system and interactions. The *nature of science* is frequently promoted as inquiry, but it could equally well be defined as argument. The specifics about the nature of science are contested; but there is reasonable agreement about science as people's attempt to systematically search out, describe, and explain generalized patterns of events in the natural world through observing, thinking, experimenting, and validating—also that the explanations stress natural physical causalities and cause-effect mechanisms, not supernatural, mystical, magical, or spiritual causes (Good, Shymansky, & Yore, 1999). However, traditional, modern, and postmodern interpretations vary significantly (Yore, Hand, & Florence, 2004) and cultural views differ from Western views (Yore, 2008). Attempts to engage diverse groups must be cautious of these differences to avoid misleading students about the nature of Western science. Respectfully, "Explanations about the natural world based on myths, personal beliefs, religious values, mystical inspiration, superstition, or authority may be personally useful and socially relevant, but they are not science" (NRC, 1996, p. 201). *Scientific inquiry* is a curiosity-driven, creative, dynamic, and recursive process while *technological design* is a mission-driven process seeking to adapt the environment to people's needs and to alleviate problems (ITEA, 2007). *STSE issues* (climate change; oil spills; fish farms; air, water, and land pollution; resource depletion; natural hazards, etc.) are major concerns currently facing people. These known and unknown issues are ultimate foci of and relevant contexts for scientific literacy.

Mathematical Literacy

Success in the 21st century society, world of work, and life involves mathematical understanding, quantitative reasoning, problem solving, modeling, visualizing, and making well-founded judgments and decisions (Organisation for Economic Co-operation and Development [OECD], 2003). Mathematical literacy is specifically used here to avoid numeracy, which is a contentious and contested term frequently focused on number sense and skills. Mathematical literacy is more than recalling basic facts, using memorized algorithms, and performing simple calculations; it involves understanding the mathematical enterprise and mathematics and the abilities, reasoning, emotional dispositions, language, and ICT to make sense of and solve quantitative problems.

Analyses of the Western and Northern Canadian Protocol (WNCP) for mathematics (WNCP for Collaboration in Education, 2006) and the USA's Principles and Standards for School Mathematics (NCTM, 2000) built on earlier analyses (Ford et al., 1997). The process and content standards were organized and supplemented to produce a framework for mathematical literacy that parallels scientific literacy and illustrates the interactions between and within the fundamental and derived senses (Table 3). People's knowledge about mathematics and problem solving interacts to help them find solutions for real-world problems and their emotional dispositions about certainty influence their thinking and reasoning. Furthermore, views about the nature of mathematics will influence the choice and use of mathematical terms and language since the metalanguage precisely represents the acceptable view of mathematics and common terms are used in uniquely mathematical ways.

Table 3. Interacting senses of mathematical literacy—Cognitive symbiosis
(Yore et al., 2007, p. 577)

Fundamental sense	Derived sense
Cognitive and Metacognitive Abilities	Understanding the Big Ideas, Strands, and Substrands of Mathematics
Mathematical Thinking and Quantitative Reasoning	Nature of Mathematics
Habits of Mind	Knowledge about Problem Solving
Language of Mathematics (including proofs as arguments)	Real-world Problems
Information Communication Technologies (ICT)	

Fundamental sense of mathematical literacy. The WNCP (2006) process standards (communication, connections, mental mathematics and estimation, problem solving, reasoning, technology, visualization) provided foundations for defining the cognitive, metacognitive, reasoning, habits of mind, language, and ICT abilities comprising fundamental literacy in mathematics. These standards identified the *cognitive* processes for constructing, connecting, and integrating understandings into coherent systems and the *metacognition* required for being aware of what, how, when, and where to use these processes and for planning, monitoring, regulating, and reflecting on the operations involved in problem solving (NCTM, 2000). The process standard of reasoning and proof involves *critical thinking* about what to believe and what to do in mathematics: "Develop and evaluate mathematical arguments and proofs. ... Select and use various types of reasoning and methods of proof." (NCTM, 2000, p. 402). *Habits of mind* toward doing mathematics and engaging the quantitative world includes beliefs, values, attitudes, and critical-response skills. "Teachers should consistently expect students to explain their ideas, to justify their solutions, and to persevere, ... to expect and ask for justifications and explanations, [while realizing that] demonstrating respect for students' ideas does not imply ... all ideas as reasonable or valid." (NCTM, 1991, pp. 57–58). Furthermore, students develop their mathematics self-efficacy, mathematics self-concept, and "confidence in their abilities to reason and justify their mathematical thinking" (WNCP, 2006, p. 8). Mathematics is a *sign system and distinctive discourse* that uses a variety of verbal languages, specific metalanguage, symbol systems, gestures, and representations that support the construction of understanding and communication of mathematics (NCTM, 2000). The communication and connections standards emphasize organizing and consolidating thinking; connecting diverse representations; analyzing and evaluating; and integrating, expressing, and reporting understandings. The representation standard involves selection, creation, translation, and applications of data displays, equations, models, and visuals to reveal patterns, interpret data, and transmit ideas. *ICT*, which should not be simply limited to computational tools, allow mathematicians, students, and users of mathematics to construct knowledge claims and understandings and apply mathematics, quantitative thinking, and statistical and data modelling techniques to create, compare, translate, and link multiple representations, to illustrate patterns and relationships, and to explain how components are connected and change (Partnership, 2004a).

Derived sense of mathematical literacy. The five NCTM (2000) *content standards* (number and operations, algebra, geometry, measurement, data analysis and probability) are regrouped and identified as four *strands/substrands*: number, pattern and relations (patterns, variables, equations), shape and space (measurement, 3-D objects and 2-D shapes, transformations), and statistics and probability (data analyses, chance, uncertainty) in the WNCP for mathematics (2006). The *nature of mathematics* as theoretical and applied disciplines attempt to search out, describe, and explain patterns and relationships of order, quantity, and shape amongst abstractions or real-world objects and events (AAAS, 1990). Mathematics and inherent processes are interwoven with science and technology and underpin actions in daily life, work, and culture (NCTM, 2000). *Problem solving* is a defining attribute of mathematics that involves identification of the problem, understanding influential factors and potential solutions, representing aspects of the problem space with abstractions, manipulating logically these abstractions according to established rules, and evaluating any resulting solutions or relationships against the problem conditions and mathematical assumptions and rules. Although mathematics is not bound by reality, relevance and *real-world problems* are central to applied mathematics and to making judgments about the real world and naturally occurring events.

Technological Literacy

The development of a parallel framework for technological literacy was necessitated by the inclusion of this goal in the Pacific CRYSTAL proposal, knowing that the construct was only partially articulated and implemented in K–12 schools in Canada. In British Columbia (BC) schools, this was apparent in the fragmented and unconnected curricular changes—informational skills involving ICT was changed from a stand-alone curriculum to integrated entries in the content areas (http://www.bced. gov.bc.ca/irp/te11_12/intro3.htm) and industrial arts and home economics to applied skills in automotive, construction, clothing, and food technologies (http://www. bced.gov.bc.ca/irp/welcome.php). The efforts to define technological literacy were made somewhat more difficult with the need to define technology with the broader context including computer science and engineering, to identify misconceptions about technology, and to differentiate between technology uses in science and mathematics as data collection and calculation aids and technology as way of solving problems.

Technological Literacy for All is "the ability to use, manage, and understand technology" (ITEA, 1996, p. 6), where (a) technology is defined as "human innovation in action" (p. 16), (b) engineering is "defined as design under constraint, ... and the most fundamental of these constraints is the laws of nature ... [while other] constraints include time, money, available materials, ergonomics, environmental regulations, manufacturability, reparability, and political considerations" (NAE, 2010, p. 6), and (c) computer science (or computing science) is defined as a field that studies information and computation. Computer science is often mistakenly linked to computers—the vacuum tube monsters of the 1960s, microelectronic versions of the 1970s, or today's PCs—when it is the study of computation and problems that includes a variety of disciplines devoted to computing and problem solving, such as algorithms, as well as the creating, organizing, displaying, and processing of information (see Carruthers et al., Chapter 6 this book). Computer science is in fact only secondarily connected to computers. Often, computer scientists are even asked to fix computers, which is comparable to asking a biologist to heal a person. Many of the fundamental computer-liberated conceptual aspects are clearly illustrated in *Computer Science Unplugged* (Bell, Witten, Fellows, Adams, & McKenzie, 2006).

Therefore, technology is taken here to represent a broad spectrum of studies and careers—inventor, technician, technologist, engineering assistant, computer programmer, professional engineer, computer scientist, and research engineer. The ITEA technological literacy rationale focuses on the "knowledge about the nature, behavior, power, and consequences of technology from a broad perspective" (1996, p. 1). The NAE (2002) stated, "[The] goal of technological literacy is to provide people with the tools to participate intelligently and thoughtfully in the world around them. ... As people gain confidence in their ability to ask questions and think critically about technological developments [and STSE issues generally], they are likely to participate more in making decisions" (pp. 3–4)—the central goal of Pacific CRYSTAL.

Technology has a rich history that predates science, having changed from the practical arts domain of craftspeople and inventors using intuition, apprenticed skills, and trial-and-error procedures to large organizations of professional technologists and networks of engineering science required to engage in complex problems and develop interdependent technologies (NAE, 2002). Woollacott (2009) developed taxonomies of engineering competencies taken as intellectual capacities, knowledge, skills, abilities, attitudes, and other characteristics required for skilful performance that enriches society, empowers people, and enhances economic and social development, which could provide a keystone for defining K–12 technological literacy. These "inter-related processes, knowledge, skills and attributes involved in engineering a technical system or product from its conception, through design, construction and implementation, through its operation and eventual life-end and disposal" (p. 268) are very much context and function related with adaptive attributes identified to allow effective movement between specific problem and work spaces. Furthermore, he recognized the importance of language, especially written language reflective of audiences and genres and the basic principle of constructivist approaches, to assess what learners know and then to use this information to design and deliver appropriate instruction.

The vague understanding of and lack of familiarity with technology have led to misconceptions, such as "technology is merely the application of science [and technological determinism that posits] technological developments [are] largely independent of human influence" (NAE, 2002, p. 51).

> Most people have very few direct, hands-on connections to technology, except as finished consumer goods. ... They are not aware that modern technology is the fruit of a complex interplay between many factors including science, engineering, politics, ethics and law. Another common misconception is that

technology is either all good or all bad rather than what people and society make it. They misunderstand that the purpose for which we use a technology may be good or bad, but not the technology itself. (NAE, 2002, pp. 5–6)

Technology and engineering, like science and mathematics, are processes—*verbs*— "human innovation in action" (ITEA, 1996, p. 16) and "design under constraints" (NAE, 2010, p. 6). However, people perceive them to be *nouns*—emphasizing the products (e.g., computers, cell phones and other microelectronic devices, bridges, cars, space shuttles, skyscrapers but unlikely stone tools, wheels, levers, cups, etc.)!

Gallup polls commissioned by ITEA (Rose & Dugger, 2002; Rose, Gallup, Dugger, & Starkweather, 2004) revealed that adults in the USA were interested but not well informed about technology. Comparisons of the two polls (2001 & 2004) indicated that Americans' opinions and beliefs were reasonably stable, they recognized the importance of technology, they valued technological literacy and K–12 technology education, their beliefs were heavily influenced by personal environments and experiences and recent microelectronic inventions and do not reflect the long history of technology and the complex infrastructure supporting technological innovations, and they demonstrated some gender- and age-related differences. Younger respondents expressed interest in knowing how technology works and believed they had influence in decisions about technology-related issues and applications. There is no reason to assume that Canadians' opinions and beliefs differ drastically from those reported by these Americans. However, the rapid changes within technology and present STSE issues will likely have changed the specifics identified by North American respondents today.

The science education reforms (AAAS, 1990, 1993; NRC, 1996) provide numerous mentions and links to technology, engineering, and design; however, they "do not add up to a comprehensive portrayal of the role of engineering [and technology] in scientific activities" (NAE, 2010, p. 24). There is no well-accepted or shared definition of technology literacy that reflects contemporary constructivist learning and the constructive, persuasive, and communicative roles of language in doing and learning technology; as well, there appears to be little progress made in achieving goals based on any of the definitions available. The NAE (2002) suggested that technological literacy is a range of general to elite competencies involving broad and essential understandings of the people-built environment and their place in this designed world, which "encompasses three interdependent dimensions— knowledge, ways of thinking and acting, and capabilities" (p. 3).

Sneider (2010) provided a summary of the big ideas in engineering as knowledge (design, human culture, contrast of science and technology), habits of mind or ways of thinking and acting (systems thinking, desire to encourage and support effective teamwork, concern for societal and environmental impacts), and skills or capacities (designing under constraint, using tools and materials, mathematical reasoning). Knowledge, along the limited–extensive dimension, involved the recognition of technology's pervasiveness; understanding basic engineering concepts, the relationships amongst people's histories, influences, and technology, and technology reflecting the values and culture of society; and familiarity with the nature and limitations of the design process, anticipated and unanticipated risks, trade-offs, and cost-benefit balance. The ways of thinking and acting, along the poorly–highly developed dimension, involved asking pertinent questions regarding the benefits and risks of technologies, seeking information about new technologies, and participating appropriately in decisions about the development and use of technology. The capabilities, along the low–high dimension, involved a range of ICT skills, identifying and fixing simple mechanical or technological problems, and applying basic mathematical concepts related to probability, scale, and estimation to make informed judgments about technological risks and benefits.

Technology education is varied across and within countries. It has been developed as a requirement in the Czech Republic, France, Italy, Japan, The Netherlands, Taiwan, and the United Kingdom (NAE, 2002). Design is a central theme of some programs (Illinois State University Center for Mathematics, Science, and Technology [IMaST], n.d.) and specific modules in elementary and middle schools in the USA (Biological Sciences Curriculum Study [BSCS], *Teaching Relevant Activities for Concepts and Skills* [TRACS], 2000; Lawrence Hall of Science, University of California Berkeley, *Full Options Science System* [FOSS], 2003; National Science Resources Center, *Science and Technology Concepts* [STC], 2009). Technology education in Canadian schools has been modified over the years, with the traditional business education, home economics, and industrial arts being refocused into applied skills with a strong technology influence.

In BC, the K–7 information technologies and skills were integrated into the content area curricula (BC Ministry of Education [MoE], 1996) while middle schools offer Technology 8 (MoE, 1995). The K–7 curricula focused on a specific set of cognitive, affective, and motor skills related to operating a device, achieving a task, locating, organizing and managing information, and problem solving with information technologies; however, they did not fully embrace the inherent features of the nature of technology, designs to extend people's capacities, and problem solving. The Grade 8 curriculum more completely reflects technological design and problem solving with specific learning outcomes related to self and society (solve problems that arise during the design process, identify practical problems in various contexts, collaboration, etc.), communications (concept sketches and final drawing, use various information sources to solve problems, develop 2-D and 3-D representations manually and with the assistance of graphic technologies, etc.), production (describe and use product design process, consider, specific and select materials based on requirements and characteristics, safe work habits, identify ways to minimize waste, etc.), control (design and construct controls, compare ways controls work, etc.), and energy and power (select energy transmission and conversion systems, identify how simple machines are used, etc.).

Yore (2010) synthesized these documents to develop a preliminary framework for general technological literacy—parallel to mathematical and scientific literacies—that would more fully identify the formal and informal expectations of students leaving the K–12 system and would address some of the NAE (2010) recommendations (Table 4). He built on earlier work (Ford et al., 1997) and existing technology education (not to be confused with educational technology) curricula to illustrate the critical features of the technological design process and

Table 4. Interacting senses of technological literacy—Cognitive symbiosis (Yore, 2010)

Fundamental sense	Derived sense
Cognitive and Metacognitive Abilities	Understanding the Big Ideas and Core Concepts
Critical and Creative Thinking	Nature of Technology
Habits of Mind	Technological Design
Technological Language (including Mathematics)	Designed World
Information Communication Technologies (ICT)	Relationships among Science, Technology, Society and Environment (STSE)

the abilities to use and manage these innovations. The abilities to use contemporary technological systems involves "much more than just knowledge about computers and their application [while management] involves insurance that all technological activities are efficient and appropriate [and understanding involves the synthesis of] information into new insights" (ITEA, 1996, p. 6). Grade-level expectations (e.g., K–2, 3–5, 6–8, 9–12) for some of these dimensions are specified by the benchmarks (AAAS, 1993; ITEA, 2007), ICT Literacy Maps (Partnership, 2004b), instructional resources packages (MoE, 1995, 1996), and assessment guides (ITEA, 2003). Caution is needed here, since there is very limited empirical evidence to justify these theoretical learning progressions.

Fundamental sense of technological literacy. Fundamental literacy in technology involves abilities, thinking, habits of mind, language (natural and mathematical), and ICT that allow people to design, produce, select, use, evaluate, and manage technological enterprises and innovations. Much of the fundamental sense of techno-logical literacy reflects the fundamental senses of mathematical and scientific literacies because of the close connections amongst the three disciplines.

Cognitive and metacognitive abilities Technology involves constructing under-standings and creating designs to meet or alleviate needs, solve problems, and extend human capacities. Technologically literate people must develop and demon-strate the "abilities to apply the design process, … maintain technological products and systems, … [and] assess the impact of products and systems" (ITEA, 2007, p. 113). These abilities involve identifying needs and opportunities, finding solutions, enacting design procedures, and building new innovations and solutions for reason-able problems. The cognitive processes may involve (a) creative insights (gestalts); (b) applying existing knowledge or prior solutions within unfamiliar contexts, accepted standards, existing constraints, and current limitations; and (c) testing and evaluating these designs to inform redesigns as required. Metacognition here involves the declarative (what), procedural (how), and conditional (when, where) knowledge and the real-time self-management or executive control (planning, monitoring, regulating) required to successfully design, test, evaluate, and redesign solutions (Bybee, 2010).

Critical and creative thinking. Thinking critically and creatively (asking pertinent questions regarding risks and benefits, assessing impact and consequences, seeking information, brainstorming alternatives, making decisions, etc.) is central to technology (ITEA, 2007; NAE, 2002). Deciding what to do or believe about a pressing problem or persistent need requires analytical thinking to identify the problem or need, relevant information, factors and skills, potential solutions and appropriate tests. Creating and considering alternative solutions from various perspectives requires using established solutions and others from 'outside the box' that reflect the identified criteria and constraints. They use systems thinking and nonroutine problem solving to make decisions regarding the design and applications of technologies involving a spectrum of qualitative–quantitative plausible reasoning (abduction, induction, deduction, etc.) and rational argumentation.

Habits of mind. Successful design and problem solving involve habits of mind (ways of acting, emotional dispositions, processes, manual skills, beliefs, attitudes, etc.) toward the technological enterprise, doing technology rather than listing products, and design procedure to create new products, systems, and environments. Technologically literate people have a balanced perspective involving scepticism, certainty, trust, self-efficacy, optimism, and willingness to seek solutions and view technology ethically and thoughtfully, being neither categorically antagonistic nor uncritical (AAAS, 1993; ITEA, 2007; NAE, 2002, 2010). They exhibit social skills (collaboration and individualism), adaptability, and rely on basic (observing, measuring, inferring, forecasting, estimating, predicting, classifying, visualizing, modelling, etc.) and complex (identifying needs and problems and deciding whether to address them; specifying criteria, limitations, and constraints; planning and applying design procedures, evaluating alternative designs and solutions, etc.) processes. They develop their manual capacities and craft skills to fashion plans, produce innovations, and maintain and manage technologies; use hand tools, power equipment, and technologies properly and safely; and troubleshoot systems to identify malfunctions, solutions, and redesigns (AAAS, 1993).

Technological language. Technologically literate people use natural and mathematical language abilities and strategies to communicate their innovations and solutions to diverse audiences; record, justify, and explain procedures, operations, and results; negotiate and construct shared solutions amongst collaborators; report findings; and persuade others of the validity of these solutions, ideas, and understandings. Some language tasks and strategies such as negotiations, representations, and arguments (backings, warrants, evidence, claims, counterclaims, and rebuttals) serve communicative, persuasive, and constructive functions. Communicative and persuasive aspects involve but are not limited to (AAAS, 1993):
- judge and indicate reasonableness of forecasts, estimations, measurements, and calculations and identify sources of disparities;
- keep understandable notebook of procedures, data, and designs to address ethical and proprietary issues; and

- use appropriate metalanguage, logical connectives, and terminology to describe designs, systems and subsystems, and relationships, and develop and deliver compelling arguments about these ideas.

Constructive aspects of language are less well articulated, but current research in disciplinary literacies and systemic functional linguistics provide insights into how language helps constitute understandings and construe meaning. These aspects involve but are not limited to:
- recognize the value of and use the knowledge construction cycle involving speaking, writing, and representing—compose, review, feedback, and revise;
- use and transform sketches, scale drawings, blueprints, diagrams, maps, pictures, data tables, charts, models, and other representations in making claims, constructing understanding, and developing explanations; and
- manipulate symbolic representations using established mathematical rules that produce other statements with the same relationship to locate mutual solutions within the established limitations and constraints.

Information communication technologies. ICT have changed how engineers, technologists, and technologically literate people go about doing technology, designing and understanding innovations, and informing and persuading themselves and others about these ideas. ICT allow people to design, model, test, and refine innovations without actually building the product, to produce prototypes and products using computer-assisted design or 3-D printing, collaborate at a distance by moving ideas not people, and share large databases to facilitate each others' work. ICT abilities involve but are not limited to (AAAS, 1993; Partnership, 2004a):
- understand, manage, and create effective oral, written, and multimedia communications and representations;
- use computers and other technologies to design, represent, model, and display data, ideas, solutions, and innovations;
- collect, select, summarize, and analyze data and information from multiple sources; and
- produce clear and secure records, calls for proposals, designs, and testing procedures while anticipating the need to establish proprietary rights and patents.

Derived sense of technological literacy. Like mathematical and scientific literacies, technological literacy involves knowledge about the big ideas and unifying concepts (called *core concepts* by ITEA, 2007, and *core ideas* by NAE, 2010), the nature of the discipline, the defining characteristic—design, the worlds produced by these efforts, and the relationship within and amongst technologies, science, society, and the environment. There is reasonable general agreement on these dimensions, but there is some level of disagreement on specifics (ITEA, 2007; NAE, 2002). Custer, Daugherty, and Meyer (2010) systematically reviewed curricula, philosophies, and standards and then held focus groups and conducted Delphi studies to identify 14 common conceptual foundations of K–12 engineering education: 11 were revealed by all 5 inputs, 2 were revealed by 4 of the 5 inputs, and 1 was revealed by 3 of the 5 inputs.

Understanding the big ideas and core concepts.   The core concepts in technology involve systems, resources, requirements, functionality, efficiency, optimization and trade off, processes, and controls (ITEA, 2007; NAE, 2010). Systems are building blocks for more complex systems and represent a way of thinking. Resources involve humans, materials, and technologies and their inherent qualities, availabilities, costs, and disposal risks. Requirements involve the criteria, physical laws, and constraints placed on a system, product, or setting. Optimization and trade-off are critical, on-going choices or exchanges in selecting resources, ranking requirements, designing and making products. Processes involve a "systematic sequence of actions used to combine resources to produce and output" innovations (ITEA, 2007, p. 33). Controls involve planned processes and evaluation–feedback loops to ensure that a product, service, or system meets established criteria and is performing as intended.

Nature of technology.   Nature of technology cannot be fully captured as an applied science although it is associated with science and mathematics. Technology predates science, it is found in various cultures without well-defined science traditions, and it is replete with examples of innovations that preceded the scientific understanding of the related science (keystones, crystal radios, kites, herbal medicines, etc.). "Technology is the modification of the natural environments in order to satisfy perceived human needs and wants" by means of design (ITEA, 2007, p. 7) and "extends human potential by allowing people to do things they could not otherwise do" (p. 22). Technologically literate students understand "the characteristics and scope of technology ... [and] relationships among technologies and the connections between technology and other fields of study" (p. 21). Sometimes, technology results in products with unintended outcomes and creates demands and opportunities for scientific and mathematical advances (AAAS, 1993).

Technological design.   Design methodology is the defining attribute and core problem-solving strategy of technology; it differs from scientific inquiry in that the design cycle identifies a need or problem, proposes solutions, tests the solution to get evaluative feedback, and proposes redesigns, refinements, or further solutions based on the feedback. Technological design is mission-driven and recursive involving (ITEA, 2007):

> [A] number of well-developed methods for discovering such solutions, all of which share certain common traits. First, the designers set out to meet certain design criteria, in essence, what the design is supposed to do. Second, the designers must work under certain constraints, such as time, money, and resources. Finally, the procedures or steps of the design process are interactive and can be performed in different sequences, depending upon the details of the particular design problem. Once designers develop a solution, they test it to discover its shortcomings, and then redesign it—over and over again. (p. 90)

Intuition, brainstorming, prior solutions, practical experiences, and engineering science interact within the design process in which trial-and-error is still recognized as worthwhile in a few situations. Cost, human, and procedural considerations of production, operations, maintenance, replacement, disposition, marketing, and sales are part of designing innovative devices and processes (AAAS, 1993). Risk analysis is an essential part of design and must consider public perceptions of technological, scientific, and psychological factors as well as safety considerations. Reduction of failure is addressed with performance testing that involves simulations, small-scale prototypes, mathematical models, analogous systems, and part–whole variations (ITEA, 2007).

Designed world. Today's world is a combination of the natural and people-built worlds. People must select, use, and manage various technologies: medical, energy and power, information and communication, transportation, manufacturing, construction, and agricultural and related biotechnologies (ITEA, 2007). Social and economic forces strongly influence the development, choice, and use of technological solutions—personal values, consumer acceptance, patent laws, availability of venture capital, federal/state/provincial regulations, support and taxes, media attention, and competition. Technological knowledge has proprietary features (patent, copyright, legal consideration of intellectual properties) and may require secrecy, which is a personal or employee responsibility. Decisions to develop, produce, or halt production of an innovation involve consideration of: alternatives; risks, costs, benefits, material and human resource limitations; and environmental issues. Human inventiveness in technological design has brought new risks and negative impacts as well as improvements to people and other species.

Relationships among Science, Technology, Society, and Environment.

> Technological progress often sparks advances [in technology, science, or mathematics] and sometimes can even create a whole new field of study. ... Conversely, technology borrows from and is influenced by many other areas. ... Science, [mathematics,] and technology are like conjoined [triplets]. While they have separate identities, they must remain inextricably connected in order to [flourish]. (ITEA, 2007, p. 44)

These interactions involve knowledge transfers and applications within, between, and amongst technologies, science, and mathematics that occur when a new user applies an existing idea in a different function or to different context.

"Technology has been called 'the engine of history' for the way in which its use drives changes in society; it influences cultural patterns, political movements, local and global economies, and everyday life" (ITEA, 2007, p. 56). Technological innovations are influenced by societal priorities and innovations (such as dynamite, oil exploration, hydroelectric dams, military devices, satellites, electronic communications, etc.) and influence societal actions. Explosives and mechanized warfare have allowed governments to impose their priorities on other governments. These encounters have been somewhat romanticized and were able to continue reasonably unaffected by public opinion until rapid video telecommunications started delivering the results of such actions to the public's dinnertime news.

Technology–environment influences can be positive or negative, direct or indirect, and slow or rapid. These issues involve how humans can devise technologies to conserve water, soil, and energy through such techniques as informed selecting, reusing, reducing, and recycling. "The entire lifecycle of a product must be taken into account before the product is created, from the materials and processes used in its production to its eventual disposal" (ITEA, 2007, p. 65). Decisions regarding the design and implementation of technologies involve the weighing of trade-offs between predicted positive and negative effects on the environment. Transfer of a technology from one context to another can cause changes and can affect effectiveness, risk-benefit, and consequences of established innovations (e.g., driftnet fishing, fish farming, recreational vehicles, etc.).

Lack of consideration for the environment has led to the most pressing STSE issues. Developing technologies for different cultures to satisfy their individual and shared needs, wants, and values are critical; however, it is necessary to think globally and act locally. The NAE (2002) stated:

> From a philosophical point of view, democratic principles imply that decisions affecting many people or the entire society should be made with as much public involvement as possible. ... Increased citizen participation would add legitimacy to decisions about technology and make it more likely that the public would accept those decisions. (p. 4)

The decision whether to develop a technology is influenced by societal opinions and demands in addition to corporate cultures (ITEA, 2007). Various factors (e.g., advertising, the strength of the economy, the goals of a company, and the latest fads) contribute to shaping the design or demand for various technologies. The easy and rapid flow of ideas associated with the digital age has allowed uncensored information that has changed and will continue to change local perspectives and generate demand for innovations.

CLOSING REMARKS

The SMT framework described in this chapter has the potential to illustrate how current reforms in science and mathematics could be revitalized by taking advantage of the powerful results in literacy and science education research and in disciplinary literacy generally. Furthermore, it could provide insights how technology, computer science, and engineering can be incorporated into the school curriculum. The current K–10 curriculum in most provinces and states is overcrowded and packed with excessive topics and courses. BC has tried to address this overcrowding by reducing the number of topics in K–7 to three in-depth units of study and to four units in Grades 8–10.

It appears as if there is no appetite to reduce existing subjects in the curriculum to make room for new subjects like technology, computer science, and engineering. This was the case with environmental education (EE) and science and technology (S&T 11) in the past. There has been some success with infusing EE into the K–10 social studies curriculum. The BC MoE has developed and provided several resources to promote environmental education in schools and support students under the Green Schools initiative (http://www.bced.gov.bc.ca/greenschools/). Environmental learning and experiences for sustainability course content, guides and curriculum maps for fundamental principles (complexity, aesthetics, responsibility and ethics) onto K–12 science, social studies, mathematics, language arts, and fine arts. The experience with S&T 11 has not been as positive. First, BC universities did not accept S&T 11 as a certified science course for postsecondary entry. Second, this excellent course was then assumed to be for nonacademic students; therefore, many of the interesting topics and STSE issues were not pursued with rigor.

It is unlikely that technology, computer science, and engineering will be accepted as new K–12 disciplines. Therefore, it appears that an infusion (embedding technology, computer science, and engineering standards in other disciplinary standards like science, mathematics, and social studies), mapping (identifying connections between the big ideas of technology, computer science, and engineering with important concepts in other disciplines standards like science, mathematics, and social studies), or repackaging parts of an existing course into interdisciplinary unit strategies will be the only possibilities to introduce technology, computer science, and engineering to students with some rigor.

The USA reports on engineering standards (NAE, 2010) and the draft science education standards (NRC, 2010) have highlighted the importance of science and technology. But both of these documents and the mathematics standards (NCTM, 2000) imply that technology and engineering standards should be integrated into science and mathematics and not to stand alone, as ITEA (2007) has suggested. Clearly, a first step for most countries would be to identify existing curricular resources that focus on engineering, technology, and computer science and are associated with standards. A second step would be to use the framework for scientific, mathematical, and technological literacies as a basic architecture to identify appropriate points for infusion and mapping commonalities. A number of such materials are available in some provinces, the United Kingdom, and the USA (see FOSS, STC, Insight, and TRAC series for self-contained modules on design, models, and other technology/engineering topics). Later in this book, the chapters on computer science applications and robotics (Carruthers et al., Chapter 6 this book; Francis Pelton & Pelton, Chapter 7 this book) will provide insights into Pacific CRYSTAL resources and projects.

REFERENCES

American Association for the Advancement of Science. (1990). *Science for all Americans: Project 2061*. New York: Oxford University Press.
American Association for the Advancement of Science. (1993). *Benchmarks for science literacy: Project 2061*. New York: Oxford University Press.
Anderson, J. O., Chiu, M.-H., & Yore, L. D. (2010). First cycle of PISA (2000–2006)—International perspectives on successes and challenges: Research and policy directions [Special issue]. *International Journal of Science and Mathematics Education, 8*(3), 373–388.
Bell, T., Witten, I. H., Fellows, M., Adams, R., & McKenzie, J. (2006). *Computer science unplugged. An enrichment and extension programme for primary-aged children* (teacher ed.). Retrieved from http://www.csunplugged.org/

Biological Sciences Curriculum Study. (2000). *Teaching relevant activities for concepts and skills (TRACS)* [Series]. Dubuque, IA: Kendall Hunt.

British Columbia Ministry of Education. (1995). *Technology education 8 to 10: Integrated resource package 1995.* Victoria, BC, Canada: Author.

British Columbia Ministry of Education. (1996). *Information technology K–7: Integrated resource package 1996.* Victoria, BC, Canada: Author.

Bybee, R. W. (2010). K–12 engineering education standards: Opportunities and barriers. In Committee on Standards for K–12 Engineering Education (Ed.), *Standards for K–12 engineering education?* (pp. 55–66). Washington, DC: The National Academies Press.

Council of Ministers of Education, Canada. (1997). *Common framework of science learning outcomes, K to 12: Pan-Canadian protocol for collaboration on school curriculum.* Retrieved from http://publications.cmec.ca/science/framework/

Custer, R. L., Daugherty, J. L., & Meyer, J. P. (2010). Formulating the conceptual base for secondary level engineering education: A review and synthesis. In Committee on Standards for K–12 Engineering Education (Ed.), *Standards for K–12 engineering education?* (pp. 67–80). Washington, DC: The National Academies Press.

Ford, C. L., Yore, L. D., & Anthony, R. J. (1997, March). *Reforms, visions, and standards: A cross-curricular view from an elementary school perspective.* Paper presented at the annual meeting of the National Association for Research in Science Teaching, Oak Brook, IL, USA. Retrieved from ERIC database. (ED406168)

Good, R. G., Shymansky, J. A., & Yore, L. D. (1999). Censorship in science and science education. In E. H. Brinkley (Ed.), *Caught off guard: Teachers rethinking censorship and controversy* (pp. 101–121). Boston: Allyn & Bacon.

Hand, B., Prain, V., & Yore, L. D. (2001). Sequential writing tasks' influence on science learning. In G. Rijlaarsdam (Series Ed.) & P. Tynjälä, L. Mason & K. Lonka (Eds.), *Writing as a learning tool: Integrating theory and practice* (Vol. 7 of Studies in Writing, pp. 105–129). Dordrecht, The Netherlands: Kluwer/Springer.

Hurd, P. D. (1958). Science literacy: Its meaning for American schools. *Educational Leadership, 16,* 13–16 & 52.

Illinois State University Center for Mathematics, Science, and Technology. (n.d.). *Integrated mathematics, science, and technology (IMaST) curriculum* [Series]. Carrollton, TX: Hewell.

International Technology Education Association. (1996). *Technology for all Americans: A rationale and structure for the study of technology.* Reston, VA: Author.

International Technology Education Association. (2003). *Advancing excellence in technological literacy: Student assessment, professional development, and program standards.* Reston, VA: Author.

International Technology Education Association. (2006). *Technological literacy for all: A rationale and structure for the study of technology* (2nd ed.). Reston, VA: Author.

International Technology Education Association. (2007). *Standards for technological literacy: Content for the study of technology* (3rd ed.). Reston, VA: Author.

Lawrence Hall of Science, University of California, Berkeley. (2003). *Full option science system (FOSS)* [Series]. Hudson, NH: Delta Education.

McEneaney, E. H. (2003). The worldwide cachet of scientific literacy. *Comparative Education Review, 47*(2), 217–237.

Moje, E. B. (2008). Foregrounding the disciplines in secondary literacy teaching and learning: A call for change. *Journal of Adolescent & Adult Literacy, 52*(2), 96–107.

National Science Resources Center. (2009). *Science and technology concepts (STC) program* [Series]. Burlington, NC: Carolina Biological Supply Company.

Norris, S. P., & Phillips, L. M. (2003). How literacy in its fundamental sense is central to scientific literacy. *Science Education, 87*(2), 224–240.

Organisation for Economic Co-operation and Development. (2003). *The PISA 2003 assessment framework: Mathematics, reading, science and problem solving knowledge and skills.* Paris, France: Author. Retrieved from http://www.oecd.org/dataoecd/46/14/33694881.pdf

Partnership for 21st Century Skills. (2004a). *Homepage*. Retrieved from http://www.p21.org/

Partnership for 21st Century Skills. (2004b). *ICT literacy maps*. Retrieved from http://www.p21.org/index.php?option=com_content&task=view&id=504&Itemid=185#ict

Roberts, D. A. (2007). Scientific literacy/science literacy. In S. K. Abell & N. G. Lederman (Eds.), *Handbook of research on science education* (pp. 729–780). Mahwah, NJ: Lawrence Erlbaum.

Rose, L. C., & Dugger, W. E., Jr. (2002). ITEA/Gallup poll reveals what Americans think about technology: A report of the survey conducted by the Gallup organization for the International Technology Education Association. *The Technology Teacher, 61*(6), (insert).

Rose, L. C., Gallup, A. M., Dugger, W. E., Jr., & Starkweather, K. N. (2004). The second installment of the ITEA/Gallup poll and what it reveals as to how Americans think about technology: A report of the second survey conducted by the Gallup Organization for the International Technology Education Association. *The Technology Teacher, 64*(1), (insert).

Shanahan, T., & Shanahan, C. (2008). Teaching disciplinary literacy to adolescents: Rethinking content-area literacy. *Harvard Educational Review, 78*(1), 40–59.

Shen, B. S. P. (1975). Science literacy: The public understanding of science. In S. B. Day (Ed.), *Communication of scientific information* (pp. 44–52). New York: S. Karger.

Sneider, C. (2010). A vision of engineering standards in terms of big ideas. In Committee on Standards for K-12 Engineering Education (Ed.), *Standards for K-12 engineering education?* (pp. 136–141). Washington, DC: The National Academies Press.

United States National Academy of Engineering. (2002). *Technically speaking: Why all Americans need to know more about technology* (G. Pearson & A. T. Young, Eds.). Committee on Technological Literacy, National Academy of Engineeering, & National Research Council. Washington, DC: The National Academies Press.

United States National Academy of Engineering. (2010). *Standards for K–12 engineering education?* Committee on Standards for K–12 Engineering Education. Washington, DC: The National Academies Press.

United States National Council of Teachers of Mathematics. (1991). *Professional standards for teaching mathematics*. Reston, VA: Author.

United States National Council of Teachers of Mathematics. (2000). *Principles and standards for school mathematics*. Reston, VA: Author.

United States National Research Council. (1996). *The national science education standards*. Washington, DC: The National Academies Press.

United States National Research Council. (2000). *Inquiry and the national science education standards: A guide for teaching and learning* (S. Olson & S. Loucks-Horsley, Eds.). Committee on Development of an Addendum to the National Science Education Standards on Scientific Inquiry. Washington, DC: The National Academies Press.

United States National Research Council. (2010). *A framework for science education* (H. Quinn & H. A. Schweingruber, Eds.) [Preliminary public draft]. Board on Science Education, Center for Education, Division of Behavioral and Social Sciences and Education. Washington, DC: The National Academies Press.

Western and Northern Canadian Protocol for Collaboration in Education. (2006). *The common curriculum framework for K–9 mathematics*. Retrieved from http://www.wncp.ca/english/subjectarea/mathematics/ccf.aspx

Woollacott, L. C. (2009). Taxonomies of engineering competencies and quality assurance in engineering education. In A. Patil & P. Gray (Eds.), *Engineering education quality assurance* (pp. 257–295). New York: Springer.

Yore, L. D. (2008). Science literacy for all students: Language, culture, and knowledge about nature and naturally occurring events [Special issue]. *L1—Educational Studies in Language and Literature, 8*(1), 5–21. Retrieved from http://l1.publication-archive.com/show?repository=1&article=213

Yore, L. D. (2009). Science literacy for all: More than a logo or rally flag! [Keynote address]. *Proceedings of the international science education conference 2009* (pp. 2393–2427). Singapore. Retrieved from http://www.nsse.nie.edu.sg/isec2009/downloads/

Yore, L. D. (2010, January 31). *Technology literacy* [Invited lecture]. Paper presented to the Academic Development Workshop at the University of the Witwatersrand, Johannesburg, South Africa.

Yore, L. D., Bisanz, G. L., & Hand, B. (2003). Examining the literacy component of science literacy: 25 years of language arts and science research. *International Journal of Science Education, 25*(6), 689–725.

Yore, L. D., & Hand, B. (2010). Epilogue: Plotting a research agenda for multiple representations, multiple modality, and multimodal representational competency [Special issue]. *Research in Science Education, 40*(1), 93–101.

Yore, L. D., Hand, B., & Florence, M. K. (2004). Scientists' views of science, models of writing, and science writing practices. *Journal of Research in Science Teaching, 41*(4), 338–369.

Yore, L. D., Pimm, D., & Tuan, H.-L. (Eds.). (2007). Language—An end and a means to mathematical literacy and scientific literacy [Special issue]. *International Journal of Science and Mathematics Education, 5*(4), 557–769.

Larry D. Yore
Department of Curriculum and Instruction
University of Victoria
Victoria, British Columbia, Canada

II. AUTHENTIC LEARNING—INFORMAL ENVIRONMENTS AND EXTRACURRICULAR SCIENCE, MATHEMATICS, AND TECHNOLOGY OPPORTUNITIES: ANCHORING AND BRIDGING REAL-WORLD, CULTURAL, AND SCHOOL EXPERIENCES

E. ANNE MARSHALL, FRANCIS L. GUENETTE, TANYA WARD,
TARA MORLEY, BREANNA LAWRENCE AND KATE FISHER

3. ADOLESCENTS' SCIENCE CAREER ASPIRATIONS EXPLORED THROUGH IDENTITY AND POSSIBLE SELVES

Choosing life and work pathways is a major developmental task for adolescents and young adults. In today's global information age, there is increasing importance placed on training in what has been termed the SMT disciplines—science, mathematics, and technology, where technology includes computer science and engineering. However, increasing, or even maintaining, enrolments in SMT-related courses and degrees at the senior secondary and postsecondary levels has continued to be a challenge (Lyons, 2006; Tilleczek & Lewco, 2001; Tytler, Symington, & Smith, 2009) Women and visible-minority students are particularly underrepresented in these disciplines (Hsu, Roth, Marshall, & Guenette, 2009; Mayer-Smith, Pedretti, & Woodrow, 2000). Educators and employers are calling for educational policies and practices that will help attract and retain more students in these areas.

Our research, conducted as part of the Pacific CRYSTAL Project, has focused on the career planning process, identity, and experiential learning of secondary school science students. Grounded in Social Cognitive Career Theory (SCCT) (Lent, Brown, & Hackett, 1996; 2000; Lent, Hackett, & Brown, 1999), our qualitative, longitudinal study has utilized the cognitive construct of *Possible Selves* (Markus & Nurius, 1986) as part of an in-depth exploration of adolescents' science-related identity and career goals. In this chapter, we describe our research with secondary school science students as well as the outcomes and implications for students, teachers, policy makers, and researchers. From the results of this research, our team has developed several Possible Selves exercises and tools that offer students concrete and engaging means to explore their work and educational aspirations as well as to assist them with decision making in this important planning process.

REVIEW OF SELECTED LITERATURE

Adolescent Career Choice Process

Making career and life decisions in secondary school is both an exciting and challenging experience for adolescents (Code, Bernes, Gunn, & Bardick, 2006; Turner & Lapan, 2002). On the one hand, young people express optimism with regard to their futures and have dreams of rewarding and fulfilling careers and of making

L. D. Yore et al (Eds.), Pacific CRYSTAL Centre for Science, Mathematics, and Technology Literacy: Lessons Learned, 47–65.

a difference in the world. On the other hand, the pressure to make career decisions, coupled with potential repercussions in the future, makes these decisions difficult for many students. Code and colleagues (2006) examined sources of adolescents' perceived discouragement about future career goals. They found that senior secondary students felt time was running out and that they were unprepared to make a decision of this magnitude. Their data revealed five main themes: concerns about training and education, overall security issues, levels of satisfaction, fear of failure, and anxiety related to career commitment.

Multiple factors contribute to successful career path development and decision making when transitioning from school to work or from school to postsecondary education (Bandura, 1993; Burkham, Lee, & Smerdon, 1997). One important factor in this process is the adolescent's self-concept. Research has shown that career development is related to a particular aspect of self concept that Bandura and others have termed *self-efficacy*; those students who feel more competent in a particular domain are more likely to engage in relevant career planning and decision-making activities (Bandura, 1993; Turner & Lapan, 2002; Wallace-Broscious, Serafica, & Osipow, 1994). Bandura (1997) discussed the growth of self-efficacy through adolescence and noted that "self-efficacy development can play a key role in setting the course" of the life paths (p. 177). He further asserted that "the task of choosing what lifeworks to pursue ... looms large during adolescence" (p. 184). In spite of the significance of youths' experiences, most examinations of self-efficacy, interest, and career choice have focused on college-age participants (Bieschke, 1991; Mau, 2003; Rottinghaus, Larson, & Borgen, 2003). It is long before their admission to postsecondary institutions, however, that students make important choices in secondary school that determine their options for postsecondary study. The confidence to explore the self in relation to the occupational world, to find educational and work-specific information, and to engage in self-directed vocational planning serves to facilitate successful adolescent career development and the achievement of aspirations.

Several authors have identified various methods of enhancing adolescents' career self-concept and increasing self-efficacy (Bandura, 1993; Cross & Markus, 1991; Mau, 2003; Wallace-Broscious et al., 1994), including participation in experiential learning opportunities (Bandura, 1993; Luzzo, Hasper, Albert, Bibby, & Martinelli, 1999). Experiential learning is defined as the process of actively engaging in an authentic experience, making discoveries, and experimenting with knowledge instead of simply hearing or reading about it from others (Kraft & Sakofs, 1988). In addition to increasing knowledge (Burkham et al., 1997; Powell & Wells, 2002; Tyler-Wood, Mortenson, Putney, & Cass, 2000) and promoting a deeper understanding of learning (Burkham et al., 1997), experiential learning has been found to facilitate career and educational decision making (Burkham et al., 1997; Martinez, 1992; Seymour, Hunter, Laursen, & Deantoni, 2004). Questions arise, however, regarding how these processes work in different fields of study (e.g., science versus arts disciplines).

Luzzo et al. (1999) found a significant relationship between mathematics and science self-efficacy measures and career choice interests and actions. Burkham et al.

(1997) found that students' lack of exposure to science can result in diminished knowledge and commitment to science. Classroom activities, promotion of interest in science, and encouragement of advanced study are important precursors to pursuing further science education and choosing science for a career. Martinez (1992) similarly found that the appeal of science experiments in school may be related to attitudes and future decisions regarding study and career choices. The more pro-longed exposure to the culture of science that is part of internships, co-op courses, and other experiential learning opportunities has been shown to enhance students' knowledge and skills in SMT subjects (Neville, 2008). As Correl (2004) pointed out, young people must have knowledge of a given career in order to develop aspirations toward it.

Social Cognitive Career Theory

Anchored in Bandura's (1986) general social cognitive theory, SCCT (Lent et al., 1996, 2000; Lent et al., 1999) is a social interaction view of career development that embraces constructivist assumptions about peoples' capacity to influence their devel-opment and surroundings (Mahoney & Patterson, 1992). SCCT focuses on several agentic or self-action variables and how these variables interact with environmental variables, such as social support and barriers in the context of career development (Lent et al., 1999). Three variables from Bandura's social cognitive theory—self-efficacy, outcome expectations, and personal goals—are the basic building blocks of career development and the central theoretical constructs of SCCT. Self-efficacy refers to people's beliefs about their capabilities (Bandura, 1986; Lent et al., 1996). It is not unitary, fixed, or decontexualized but is rather a dynamic set of self-beliefs, specific to particular contexts, that interact in a complex manner with other social, behavioural, and environmental factors. These beliefs are acquired and adapted through four main sources of information: personal performance accomplishments, vicarious learning, social persuasion, and physiological states and reactions. The most robust source of self-efficacy beliefs is personal mastery experience; failure experiences tend to diminish self-efficacy.

Outcome expectations are the second key variable in SCCT. They involve personal beliefs about and the imagined consequences of performing given behaviours. Outcome expectations include beliefs about extrinsic reinforcement, self-directed consequences, and outcomes derived from the process of performing a given activity (Lent et al., 1996).

The third key variable, goals, refers to people's determination to engage in a given activity or achieve specific objectives. Goal-setting is a critical mechanism through which people exercise personal control or agency. Goals help people organize, guide, sustain, and change their own behaviour.

General social cognitive theory posits a complex interplay between goals, self-efficacy, and outcome expectation. Goals are assumed to influence the development of self-efficacy while self-efficacy and outcome expectations, in turn, affect the goals that one selects and the effort expended in their pursuit (Bandura, 1986). However, these social cognitive variables do not arise in a vacuum, nor do they function alone in shaping vocational interests. SCCT is concerned with several other important personal and contextual influences (e.g., gender, race/ethnicity, family context, genetic endowment, physical health/disability, place, and socioeconomic status) and variables related to social cognitive processes and to the career development process (Lent et al., 1996). SCCT is particularly well-suited to this study's focus—the meaning-making and decision-making processes of young people in career planning.

Possible Selves

In a social–cognitive framework, self-knowledge becomes a key factor in one's ability to reflect on future directions while considering individual context. Markus and Nurius (1986) described one domain of self-knowledge as possible selves. These possible selves constitute a personalized form of self-concept that represents the hopes, dreams, and fears that individuals have had in the past and currently as well as those aspects of their selves in future. An individual's set of hoped-for, feared, and expected possible selves can be understood as "the cognitive manifestations of enduring goals, aspirations, motives, fears and threats ... [and can] provide the specific self-relevant form, meaning, organization, and direction to these dynamics" (Markus & Nurius, p. 954). They contend that self-knowledge or possible selves become important motivators to select future behaviours. Such selves are derived from a number of salient factors, including sociocultural and historical context, media influences, and social experiences. The construct of possible selves is particularly relevant to life and career development because people's work and educational aspirations are significantly influenced not only by personal variables but also by their social environmental context.

Several researchers have applied the concept of possible selves in exploring factors related to life and work choices (Cross & Markus, 1991; Fisher, 2010; Marshall, 2002; Marshall & Guenette, 2008b; Shepard & Marshall, 1999; Wai-Ling Packard & Nguyen, 2003). Lee and Oyserman (2007) suggested that, in order for possible selves to have an impact on outcomes, they must be "cued in relevant contexts, linked to strategies, and balanced, that is, include both possible selves to work toward and feared selves to strive away from" (p. 40). The feared self plays a particularly important role; it motivates individuals to partake in actions capable of preventing its occurrence in the future. It has been found that in considering hoped-for selves young people are able to identify actions necessary for avoiding feared selves (Shepard & Marshall, 1999). By exploring their possible selves, students become active participants in a meaning-making process that illuminates their hopes and fears for the future as well as specific concrete steps they are and can be taking to work toward their aspirations.

In the present study, possible selves mapping techniques were incorporated into semistructured interviews with adolescents to identify factors influencing career decision making and school-to-work transitions for adolescents interested in science-related fields. The research questions for the study were:
– How do secondary students describe their science identity and career aspirations?
– How do these students' self-views and aspirations change over time?

METHODOLOGY

Participants

The initial participants ($N = 13$) in the study at Time 1 were 16–17-year-olds enrolled in a Grade 11 biology career preparation program at an urban secondary school. Ethnic origins of the sample included Arab, Caucasian, East Asian, and South Asian cultures. As part of their career preparation program, students were required to participate in 100 hours of internship activities over 2 years; this included museum trips, assisting in laboratories, field work with naturalists, job shadowing medical practitioners, and other activities. All students participated in a 12-hr internship at a university science laboratory over three to four weeks between interviews at Time 1 and Time 2. As with all longitudinal studies, the sample declined over the 3 years; some participants were not available at interview time, some declined a follow-up interview, some had moved and could not be located. The total student interview sample is shown in Table 1.

Table 1. Total student interview sample

Time	Period	Number of participants
1	January of Grade 11	13 (11 F and 2 M)
2	May of Grade 11, postlaboratory	11 (9 F and 2 M)
3	May of Grade 12	6 (6 F)
4	August, 1 year post-Grade 12	4 (3 F and 1 M)

As part of the project, the biology career preparation teacher was interviewed at Times 1, 2, and 3; university laboratory researchers and graduate students were interviewed at Time 2. In this chapter, only student interview data are described and discussed. (For additional details regarding other elements of the study, including information on the development and applications of Possible Selves exercises and maps, see Hsu et al., 2009; Marshall & Guenette, 2008a, 2008b; Marshall, 2009; Roth, van Eijk, Hsu, Marshall, & Mazumder, 2009.)

Data Collection Methods

Semistructured interviews. Interviews were video-taped and lasted between 50 to 90 min. An interview guide was developed for each of the four data collection times. All interviews included initial general questions for rapport building (How have things been going? What's happening at school right now?), the Possible Selves Mapping Process (PSMP), and open-ended question prompts (Is there anything you would like to add? What stood out for you today?). Encouragers (mm-hmm. Tell me more about that) and open-ended questions (How did that turn out? What did you do next? Is there anything else to add to this list of hoped-for selves?) were used throughout the interviews to facilitate the conversation. Times 1 and 2 interviews included specific questions regarding the laboratory internship. Time 3 interviews focused more on future plans, including areas other than schooling. In the Time 4 interviews, participants were asked to reflect on the research process over the previous

3.5 years. All interviewers received training in general and PSMP interviewing skills and practiced with each other before interviewing participants.

Possible selves mapping process. The use of creative methods to engage youth participants in research is suggested by a number of researchers (Morrow & Richards, 1996; Punch, 2002). Over several years, our research team has developed and adapted different forms of visual data collection instruments that we have found to be effective in engaging participants (particularly youth) in qualitative interviews (Guenette & Marshall, 2009; Marshall, 2009). As Packard and Conway (2006) observed, "One major advantage of visual methods is that they are sensitive to non-textual, spatial forms of representation and participants are likely to find them a novel and creative form of expression" (p. 261). Based on a paper and pencil instrument (Cross & Markus, 1991), Shepard (1997) initially developed a mapping exercise utilizing the construct of Possible Selves; this exercise has been further revised and extended by our team in several studies (Guenette, Morley, & Marshall, 2007; Marshall, 2002; Marshall & Guenette, 2008b). In addition to the benefits of engagement and ease of construction, we have found that visual representations enable us to understand the complex and interrelated experiences of career development in a manner that would have been difficult to accomplish with self-report instruments or interviews alone. In this study, we utilized the PSMP developed specifically for this research and refined over the course of the project (Marshall & Guenette, 2008a). The 2008 version includes an illustrative DVD and accompanying manual for students and teachers.

The PSMP involves seven steps:
- Creating a Brainstorming Map of hoped-for and feared possible selves
- Grouping and naming these possible selves
- Debriefing the Brainstorm Map
- Identifying most hoped-for feared selves and expected selves
- Transferring brainstorm information to the Possible Selves Map
- "Things to do right now"—actions to achieve hoped-for selves and avoid feared selves
- Reviewing overall impressions, thoughts, and goals

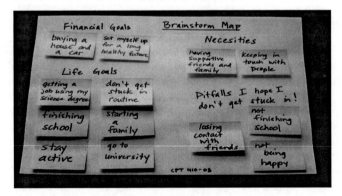

Figure 1. Brainstorming map.

Participants explain their choices and think aloud throughout the process. They use sheets of paper and coloured sticky notes that can be moved around for the Brainstorm Maps (Figure 1). Specific selves are transferred to the Possible Selves Maps (Figure 2), and participants then identify potential actions related to these selves. They are given copies of their maps to take with them for further reflection and as a concrete record of the interview.

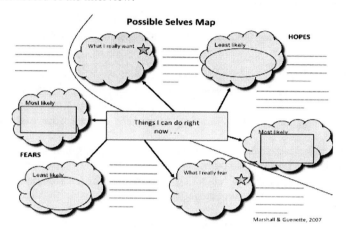

Figure 2. Possible selves map.

Data Collection Procedures

Observations and timeline. The study commenced with 22 hr of videotaped observations in the students' biology and career preparation classes in the fall semester 2006 of Grade 11 in order to gain an understanding of their school program context. Further observations were conducted during the students' university laboratory internship in the spring semester 2007 of Grade 11. As part of our interdisciplinary collaboration within the Pacific CRYSTAL Project, one graduate student utilized these and later observations and interview data as part of her doctoral research on science discourse (Hsu, 2008).

Interview – Time 1 Student participants were interviewed by graduate students in January 2007 of Grade 11, near the end of their first semester in the career preparation program. After initial discussion to provide background regarding career interests and to build rapport, students completed the PSMP. Additional questions focused on their experiences in the career preparation program and thoughts about the upcoming laboratory internship.

Laboratory Internship. In March 2007 of their Grade 11 year.

Interview – Time 2 After the laboratory internship, 11 participants were interviewed again. They were given interview summaries and their maps from Time 1. They completed the PSMP, adding any new hopes and fears, rearranging as needed, and explaining their choices. The students were asked how the laboratory experience had impacted their career choice and planning process.

Interview – Time 3   At the end of Grade 12 in 2008, 6 of the 11 Time 2 participants were available to be interviewed. After seeing Time 1 and 2 maps and interview summaries, they again completed the PSMP and were asked about their plans and intentions after graduation.

Interview – Time 4   Four students were available to be interviewed 1 year after completing Grade 12 in 2009 (one male had not been interviewed at Time 3).

Data Analysis

Analysis of the interview transcripts and maps was accomplished through multiple readings and iterative reflections on data themes and meanings (Guenette & Marshall, 2009; Marshall, 2009). The following steps were utilized after each round of interviews:

- Review video-taped interviews and make overall impression notes.
- Transcribe the interviews, adding further notes.
- First reading of transcripts, 'chunking' of complete ideas, assign tentative codes.
- First iteration of major data categories and specific content themes within transcripts.
- Read again; revise categories and themes, checking for consistency of coding.
- Highlight and colour-code transcripts by categories and themes; identify quotes.
- Read again; identify more specific subthemes within themes.
- Construct category and theme tables with corresponding quotes.
- Compare categories and themes across participants.

After the Time 4 analysis was completed, a reading across all four interviews was conducted for the four longitudinal participants. Overarching themes and subthemes were identified.

SUMMARY OF RESULTS

In this section, the research questions and data analysis summaries are presented. Tables of main data categories and more specific data content themes are included for each wave of interviews: Times 1 and 2, Time 3, and Time 4. Times 1 and 2 are presented together because the data categories and themes were very similar. Selected highlights from the data are described, with brief illustrative participant quotes *in italics*, due to space limitations.

Research Question for Times 1 and 2: How do Secondary Students describe their Science Identity and Career Aspirations Before and After an Authentic Laboratory Experience?

During Times 1 and 2, more than 50 interviews and observations were conducted with the participants in their classrooms and at the university laboratory. Data categories and themes identified across participants are presented in Table 2; highlights and participant quotes related to several data themes are described next.

Table 2. Interview analysis Times 1 and 2

Data category	Content theme
Identity related to career aspirations	Science careers
	Stereotypes about science
	Nonscience careers
	Hoped-for and feared selves
Influences on career decisions	Gender
	Supports and barriers
	Parental and family influences
	Other influences
Planning process	Planning for the future
	Knowledge
	Experiences and behaviours
Learning about science	Stereoypes about science
	Experiential learning

Science careers. Not surprisingly, all participants described specific goals and hoped-for selves in science fields: *Environmental engineer, Doctor, Marine biologist, Health service, Laboratory technician, Nurse.* While expressing an avid interest in biology and science, a few students shared hoped-for and feared selves that were unrelated to science, such as *Photographer, Lawyer, Actor,* and *Teacher.*

Hoped-for and feared selves. Students listed multiple hoped-for and feared selves in relation to future careers in science. Hoped-for selves categories were at times specific, for example, *Health science, Human health service, Medical doctor, Laboratory-work analysis.* At other times, the categories were quite broad, for example, *Involving mathematics, science, biology.* Some of the hoped-for career selves reflected deeply held values such as *A career that describes me, Doing something interesting, Helping the world.* The feared self categories focused on anticipated negative aspects of particular science work such as *Boring, Dangerous, Going nowhere.* Fears also related to issues of commitment: *Long hours away from family and friends, Years of schooling, Student debt.*

Stereotypes about science. When asked what scientists are like, one participant said, *Eccentric ... geeky ... pretty weird ... cooped up in a lab all day with a bunch of pig foetuses is pretty weird.* Other students described rather stereotypical views of scientists: *Absent-minded, Socially awkward, Looking like Albert Einstein.* After the laboratory experience, the students demonstrated a much more realistic and specific understanding of scientists: *It was really cool ... seeing how the scientists and the students worked through their experiments.... Now I know what they do.*

Parental and family influences. Parental and family influences contributed to both hoped-for and feared selves and career paths: *My mom really got me started on biology, My dad talked to me about Doctors without Borders, I watched my relatives who are doctors and that's way too much work—I want to have a life.* Talking with family members about options, as well as about the pros and cons of particular

55

science jobs, helped these students evaluate possibilities and establish priorities regarding future training and work.

Supports and barriers. The difficulty of making a decision at this stage of life represented a constraint for several students: *It's kind of hard to want to lock into choosing a career for the rest of your life when you're 17.* Students also felt decisions would affect the rest of their lives. *It's almost scary* [thinking about future career plans]. *They're* [decisions for the future] *so important. You can make one wrong move and you can't go back.*

Research Question for Time 3: How do Grade 12 Students describe their Science, Career, and Life Aspirations?

During this wave, follow-up interviews were conducted with 6 of the original 13 participants. Students were able to further reflect on their science career aspirations as they approached graduation. The data categories and content themes identified across the interviews are presented in Table 3, followed by some highlights of the themes from Time 3.

Table 3. Interview analysis Time 3

Data category	Content theme
Factors influencing career aspirations	Financial security
	Self efficacy
	Ideals and values
	Social influences
	Contextual influences
Planning process	Goals
	Maximizing success
Relationships	Family
	Balance

The participants were excited about their future options while being more aware near the end of Grade 12 that postsecondary education and the world of work would be more challenging than they had anticipated in Grade 11. There was more recognition that ideas about career and actual career choices could change over a work life. There was an acknowledgement that some of the hoped-for future selves generated at Time 2 were somewhat unrealistic, but these were still held as ideals of a future self. A few of the students regretted not having saved more money over the secondary school years as the real cost of postsecondary education was clearer at the end of Grade 12.

Financial security. As these students neared the end of secondary school, financial considerations appeared to be more salient: *University costs a lot ... I don't want to have money problems.* Some described conflicting thoughts: *I want to have a job that I can make good money at ...* yet ... *I don't want to take something just because it will make me a lot of money.*

Ideals and values. Students expressed their high ideals related to future careers mainly in the area of their desire to help others: *I like the helping part, helping people and making them better. I need to feel like, in my career, I am helping ... helping the world would be amazing. I want to count for something, having a big impact on something.*

Goals. During the PSMP part of the interview, participants were able to talk about what actions would help them to achieve their goals: *Well, if I study hard now I will have more choices about where to go for school ... maybe I'll get a big scholarship somewhere. I need to get some community type experience before I can apply to medical school.* They did sense the importance of the decisions they were making with regard to their futures: *This is a big deal ... I don't want to have any regrets later.* Yet, some were not too worried: *I have time to decide.*

Family. As they matured, the students seemed to put more emphasis on relationships with family and friends than when in Grade 11: *Well. I'll have to see ... because I do want to have kids and stuff. I'll need to get a good job so I can support my family.* They also acknowledged the time and commitment required in having a partner and children: *I don't want to work all the time like my mom had to ... I want to have time to enjoy things.*

Time 4: How do Beginning Postsecondary Students describe their Career and Life Aspirations?

Four participants were available to be interviewed 1 year after finishing Grade 12. Data categories and themes across participants are presented in Table 4.

A year after finishing secondary school, the participants were more difficult to locate. Only two were in postsecondary programs. Those who were interviewed at

Table 4. Interview analysis Time 4

Data category	Content theme
Factors influencing work aspirations	Influences
	Self-efficacy beliefs
	Ideals and values
	Financial security
	Career goals
	Finding meaning
Health and well-being	Happiness
	Self-care
	Healthy lifestyle
	Balance
Relationships	Relationships
	Family
	Peers
	Support

Time 4 described many goals and aspirations that were similar to previous times. Ideals and values, financial security, and finding meaning were still very important. Relationships and well-being were emphasized more strongly. Two new themes were identified and are briefly described.

Self-care. A new theme that was identified at Time 4 was self-care. A couple of participants were feeling pressured by multiple demands: *You know, it just seems like there is never enough time these days ... it's tough at times.* One participant had experienced health problems: *I just had to take time to take care of myself. Some of my plans just had to go on hold.*

Peers. Although friends had been mentioned before, participants spoke about the specific support they received from friends: *It's really important to me to have them there, you know ... I don't want to lose touch. I never thought I was really a social type but now it seems more important to me.*

Longitudinal Analysis from Time 1 to Time 4. How have Participants' Career and Life Aspirations Stayed the same or Changed Over the 3 Tears of the Study?

A longitudinal thematic analysis was conducted on the transcripts and maps of the four participants interviewed three or more times over the 3 years of the project. To distinguish this overarching longitudinal analysis from the preceding Times 1 to 4 analyses, the data analysis groupings have been called meta-themes and content elements and are presented in Table 5.

Table 5. Longitudinal analysis Times 1 to 4

Metatheme	Content element
Consistency over time	Career goals
	Life goals
	Hoped-for and feared selves
Changes in goals over time	Career choices refined
	Greater importance on relationships vs. careers
	Desire for overall happiness – balance
Influences on goals over time	Early career planning
	Experiential learning
	Life circumstances

Consistency over time. Looking back over the course of the study, all participants acknowledged consistency in their goals and possible selves. Upon being shown all her maps, one young woman commented: *Omigod, it's totally the same!* One participant was still committed to a career in environmental science; another had kept her interest in travelling; a third participant maintained her goal of a career in medicine, even though the specific field changed from dermatology to surgery or paediatrics. In terms of life goals, a desire for overall happiness and fulfillment was also important for everyone: *This whole thing* (map) *could be just "be happy."* A consistent feared-self for all was not being financially secure: *It's funny 'cause a lot of this stuff is the same, pretty much ... financial security.*

Changes in goals over time.   Not surprisingly, shifts in emphasis were evident from Grade 11 to after graduation. As one young woman commented: *I am starting to go more into life environmental technology ... so I have kinda almost branched off.* More than one participant acknowledged putting greater importance on maintaining relationships in both work and family contexts. Looking back, they also recognized a wish for balance in their lives: *I want to have time for both work and a family—not just working all the time.*

The career exploration and planning they did in Grades 10 and 11 encouraged these young men and women to think about what they wanted in their futures and to search out information about several possibilities: *We have been asked a lot of questions about our jobs, career, and stuff ... we have done a lot of projects. Yeah, I have pretty much researched all of these* [careers].

Influences on goals over time.   Experiential learning opportunities had clearly influenced the extent to which these young scientists could view themselves working in the field. For some students, these hands-on experiences reinforced their interest and commitment to a career; for example, one participant who had decided to become a paediatrician had volunteered in a hospital; another interested in biotechnology had done a co-op placement. For others, they became aware that a particular science career or work setting was not something they wanted to pursue: *I'd figured from that* [laboratory experience] *that I probably didn't want to be in a lab.*

Life circumstances had affected original educational and career plans for some. One young woman had to postpone postsecondary plans because she needed full-time employment to cover her current expenses. Another participant who struggled with a health issue realized that the typically intense course load in first and second year university science programs would be too much to handle at this time. Most commented that they had not thought much about back-up plans if their earlier goals were no longer attainable.

Overall, in looking back, the students could identify and articulate the experiences and influences that had shaped their pathways. Some could see the thematic or disciplinary continuity and links among their choices along the way: *You know, step by step I've been getting closer and closer to what I really want to do.* Others seemed to be moving toward greater diversity and increased options: *I want something that brings me more in contact with people and not the same thing all day. I'm not 100% certain what my end title will be ... the more I hear about things ... there are things you don't even know about, right ... so I don't have to decide right now.*

DISCUSSION

Most of the young people in this study maintained their *science identity* to some degree and their interest in science-related educational and career goals over the course of the study although their horizons had broadened over the 3 years. This could be expected, given that they had made a commitment in Grade 11 to a fairly demanding and focused biology career preparation program. However, at the end of Grade 12 and 1 year after, not all had enrolled in postsecondary science training or degree programs; and there had been a number of shifts in the interests and plans they had identified and developed in secondary school.

In Grade 12 and after, participants placed greater emphasis on relationships; participants were more aware of the *bigger life picture* and spoke of balance and life satisfaction. Moreover, these young people described a more practical and realistic view when articulating future plans. These findings are consistent with those of many career transition researchers (Burkham et al., 1997; Lent et al., 2000; Turner & Lapan, 2002). The emphasis on having a fulfilling job—one that would make a difference in the world and also pay well—was still prevalent, but a real awareness of the cost involved in postsecondary education slipped into the participants' maps and reflections. Some spoke of needing to be able to find the well-paying job that would make such a financial investment in education worthwhile. As noted by others (Code et al., 2006; Turner & Lapan, 2002), young people have dreams of rewarding and fulfilling careers but also feel concerned about making career decisions that could include potential repercussions in the future.

Similar to Arnett's (2004) research on emerging adults, young people in this study expressed optimism with regard to their futures. At the beginning, they did appear to feel some pressure to make the right choice and expressed some fears related to making a wrong or poor choice. This was similar to Code and colleagues' (2006) participants who felt that time was running out and experienced pressure to make a decision. However, anxiety seemed to decrease somewhat over time for the present participants. As they grew older, there appeared to be less emphasis on getting to the dream job than at the beginning of the study. New learning and life experience were providing more and new ideas, and the prevailing attitude was *I don't have to choose yet*. This shift highlights the importance of encouraging adolescents to remain open to career goal changes and new opportunities since relatively few students end up where they originally expected (Lent et al., 1996).

Experiential learning activities were clearly influential for these young people. Enhanced self-efficacy and increased science knowledge were significant outcomes of the university laboratory internship. This is consistent with research demonstrating the benefits of experiential learning opportunities (Neville, 2008; Roth et al., 2009). Participation in experiential learning opportunities has been found to enhance adolescents' career self-concept and increasing self-efficacy (Bandura, 1997; Luzzo et al., 1999). The experiences in the laboratory and elsewhere provided opportunities for them to engage with and practice science—not only to listen to or watch science. Burkham and colleagues (1997) suggested this promotes a deeper understanding of and better application of learning.

Correl (2004) posited that young people must have knowledge of a given career in order to develop aspirations toward it. Through the university laboratory and other hands-on science experiences, the participants had practical understandings of what some of the tasks of a career in science could include. The adolescents had the opportunity to explore their educational interests and abilities; previous research (Burkham et al., 1997; Martinez, 1992; Seymour et al., 2004) suggests experiential learning can facilitate career and educational decision-making. Martinez similarly found that the appeal of science experiments in school may be related to attitudes and future decisions regarding study and career choices.

The choice and career developmental processes described by the participants are consistent with the principles posited in SCCT. The students' interviews provided vivid and concrete examples of their self-action variables and how these interacted with and, in turn, were shaped by their environmental and social contexts. The findings provide support for continued emphasis on the central constructs of self-efficacy, expectations, and personal goals (Bandura, 1986) in career exploration and development resources and activities.

Applications

An important aspect of the research has been our commitment to community-based research partnerships with secondary schools and the importance of practical tools and solutions. This commitment has guided the development of a DVD resource and accompanying manual for teachers so they can use the PSMP in their classrooms (Marshall & Guenette, 2008a). These materials provide several individual and group options for middle and secondary school teachers to apply the Possible Selves concepts and techniques to help students explore and act upon their science (and other) career aspirations. Underserved and underrepresented groups should be prime foci for such applications to SMT-related disciplines and careers. Fisher (2010) attempted to use some ideas for Possible Selves to explore aboriginal students' secondary school mathematics experiences and their stories of opportunities and obstacles.

IMPLICATIONS

Research

Longitudinal studies are challenging but extremely valuable for theory and research. Following a group of secondary students over their key school-to-work/education transition years provided rich insight into career–life decision and planning processes. Given both the consistencies and the changes evident in all the participants, it is imperative that early career exploration in secondary school be revisited in order to help students integrate new ideas and experiences and extend their understanding of the potential implications for life and work choices and pathways.

With respect to methodology, the PSMP interviews provided rich and detailed data that we would not have obtained through surveys or even conventional inter-views. The PSMP provided participants with a unique opportunity to develop thoughts, ideas, and options before being asked to elaborate on their actual classroom, labora-tory internship, and other science-related experiences. The process facilitated engage-ment in and reflection on current hoped-for and feared future selves as well as on maps created previously. When participants construct images and explain their meaning, researchers are able to fill in gaps and spark further exploration and refinement of meaning. In the present study, bringing the visual map back to participants provided snapshots in time that facilitated further reflection on hopes, fears, and possible actions. The present investigation, along with Wai-Ling Packard and Nguyen's (2003) study with adolescent girls, appears to be the only research linking Possible Selves to youth science careers; more research is needed in this area.

Career Planning

The present research findings have implications for career education teachers and counsellors as well as for policy developers. The major theme of changes over time highlights the importance of planning and goal setting on young people's career planning. From the beginning of secondary school, counsellors, educators, and parents need to pay particular attention to students' goal-setting and decision-making skills and to assist them to assess the implications of their choices. Most postsecondary science programs for example, have particular prerequisite requirements for secondary mathematics courses. Helping students learn how to set and create steps for large and small goals is critical to successful career planning. Goal setting is also useful for other life issues, not just simply education and work. Demonstrating goal-setting strategies and following up on measurable steps is strongly recommended for counsellors and career educators working with youth or young adults on work–life issues. Our findings also underscore the importance of goal flexibility and having more than one option.

CONCLUDING THOUGHTS AND LESSONS LEARNED

Classroom activities, promotion of interest in science, and encouragement of advanced study are important precursors to choosing science for a career and pursuing further science education; however, they are not sufficient for a significant group of students. The findings from the present study emphasize that mentorship, experiential learning opportunities, and regular decision-oriented activities are critical elements in the career transition process.

Experiential learning opportunities enable students to see science in action: What do scientists do and how do they arrive at their particular work positions? How do you manage a laboratory, look after equipment, work on a team, and achieve goals? The potential of mentorship is underscored by the present research results demonstrating the importance of family influences, relationships, and experiential learning in authentic science setting (see Wright, Claxton, Williams, & Paul, Chapter 4 this book). When interacting with an adult scientist, students are able to observe and understand the connections among education, training, and skill development. Hands-on internships are ideal; however, conducting informational interviews or shadowing people in the workplace are also worthwhile. Preparation for these activities is particularly important, as is reflection afterward on the similarities and differences encountered.

Career exploration and development must include more than jobs and work. Values, relationships, and lifestyle preferences are closely connected to life decisions and satisfaction. The importance of fulfillment and making a difference in the world were strong motivators for several of the youth in the present study.

The skills and processes needed for setting goals, establishing priorities, and making decisions are vital in this time of transition to adulthood. Students should be encouraged to generate multiple plans and options and to be prepared for unexpected events. They are then less likely to feel discouraged or immobilized if their initial plan or preference does not work out.

Exploring science identity and possible selves over time would appear to facilitate adolescents' career transition process. Experiential learning and mentorship opportunities were seen to be particularly influential for enhancing self-efficacy and constructive decision-making skills. Teachers, career educators, counsellors, and parents are important supporters of and contributors to successful career transitions. Science educators in particular have a critical role to play in assisting young people to seek out information, experiences, and mentoring relationships that will help them make informed choices leading to rewarding careers in science.

REFERENCES

Arnett, J. J. (2004). *Emerging adulthood: The winding road from the late teens through the twenties.* New York: Oxford University Press.

Bandura, A. (1986). *Social foundations of thought and action: A social cognitive theory.* Englewood Cliffs, NJ: Prentice Hall.

Bandura, A. (1993). Perceived self-efficacy in cognitive development and functioning. *Educational Psychologist, 28*(2), 117–148.

Bandura, A. (1997). *Self-efficacy: The exercise of control.* New York: W. H. Freeman.

Bieschke, K. J. (1991). *A causal model of math/science career aspirations.* Unpublished doctoral dissertation, Michigan State University, East Lansing, Michigan, USA.

Burkham, D. T., Lee, V. E., & Smerdon, B. A. (1997). Gender and science learning early in high school: Subject matter and laboratory experiences. *American Educational Research Journal, 34*(2), 297–331.

Code, M. N., Bernes, K. B., Gunn, T. M., & Bardick, A. D. (2006). Adolescents' perceptions of career concern: Student discouragement in career development. *Canadian Journal of Counselling, 40*(3), 160–174.

Correl, S. J. (2004). Constraints into preferences: Gender, status, and emerging career aspirations. *American Sociological Review, 69*(1), 93–113.

Cross, S., & Markus, H. (1991). Possible selves across the life span. *Human Development, 34*(4), 230–255.

Fisher, K. (2010). *Aboriginal students' high school mathematics experiences: Stories of opportunities and obstacles.* Master's thesis, University of Victoria. Retrieved from http://hdl.handle.net/1828/3103

Guenette, F. L., & Marshall, E. A. (2009). Time line drawings: Enhancing participant voice in narrative interviews on sensitive topics. *International Journal of Qualitative Methodology, 8*, 85–92.

Guenette, F. L., Morley, T., & Marshall, E. A. (2007). Career experiences and choice processes for secondary school science students. In T. W. Pelton, G. Reis, & K. Moore (Eds.), *Proceedings of the University of Victoria Faculty of Education 2007 Connections Conference* (pp. 77–84).

Hsu, P.-L. (2008). *Understanding high school students' science internship: At the intersection of secondary school science and university science.* Doctoral dissertation, University of Victoria. Retrieved from http://hdl.handle.net/1828/1096

Hsu, P.-L., Roth, W.-M., Marshall, E. A., & Guenette, F. L. (2009). To be or not to be? Discursive resources for (dis)identifying with science-related careers. *Journal of Research in Science Teaching, 46*, 1114–1136.

Kraft, D., & Sakofs, M. (Eds.). (1988). *The theory of experiential education.* Boulder, CO: Association for Experiential Education.

Lee, S. J., & Oyserman, D. (2007). Reaching for the future: The education-focused possible selves of low-income mothers. In M. Rossiter (Ed.), *Possible selves and adult learning: Perspectives and potential* (pp. 39–49). San Francisco: Jossey-Bass.

Lent, R. W., Brown, S. D., & Hackett, G. (1996). Career development from a social cognitive perspective. In D. Brown & L. Brooks (Eds.), *Career choice and development* (3rd ed., pp. 373–421). San Francisco: Jossey-Bass.

Lent, R. W., Brown, S. D., & Hackett, G. (2000). Contextual supports and barriers to career choice: A social cognitive analysis. *Journal of Counseling Psychology, 47*, 36–49.

Lent, R. W., Hackett, G., & Brown, S. D. (1999). A social cognitive view of school-to-work transition. *Career Development Quarterly, 47*, 297–311.

Luzzo, D. A., Hasper, P., Albert, K. A., Bibby, M. A., & Martinelli, E. A. J. (1999). Effects of self-efficacy-enhancing interventions on the math/science self-efficacy and career interests, goals, and actions of career undecided college students. *Journal of Counseling Psychology, 46*(2), 233–243.

Lyons, T. (2006). The puzzle of falling enrolments in physics and chemistry courses: Putting some pieces together. *Research in Science Education, 36*, 285–311.

Mahoney, M. J., & Patterson, K. M. (1992). Changing theories of change: Recent developments in counseling. In S. D. Brown & R. W. Lent (Eds.), *Handbook of counselling psychology* (2nd ed., pp. 665–689). New York: Wiley.

Markus, H., & Nurius, P. (1986). Possible selves. *American Psychologist, 41*(9), 954–969.

Marshall, E. A. (2002). Life-career counselling issues for youth in coastal and rural communities. The impact of economic, social and environmental restructuring. *International Journal for the Advancement of Counselling, 24*, 69–87.

Marshall, E. A. (2009). Mapping approaches to phenomenological and narrative data analysis. *Encyclopaedia Journal of Phenomenology and Education, 25*(XIII), 9–24.

Marshall, E. A., & Guenette, F. L. (2008a). *Possible selves mapping process* [Unpublished manuscript & DVD resource]. Victoria, BC, Canada: University of Victoria. (Available from the authors)

Marshall, E. A., & Guenette, F. L. (2008b). *Possible selves: Concepts, applications, and implications for career practice and policy.* Paper presented at the National Career Development Association Conference, Washington, DC, USA.

Martinez, M. E. (1992). Interest enhancements to science experiments: Interactions with student gender. *Journal of Research in Science Teaching, 29*, 167–177.

Mau, W. (2003). Factors that influence persistence in science and engineering career aspirations. *Career Development Quarterly, 51*(3), 234–243.

Mayer-Smith, J., Pedretti, E., & Woodrow, J. (2000). Closing the gender gap in technology enriched science education: A case study. *Computers and Education, 25*, 51–63.

Morrow, V., & Richards, M. (1996). The ethics of social research with children: An overview. *Children and Society, 10*(2), 90–105.

Neville, A. J. (2008). Problem-based learning and medical education forty years on: A review of its effects on knowledge and clinical performance. *Medical Principles and Practice, 18*, 1–9.

Packard, B., & Conway, P. (2006). Methodological choice and its consequences for possible selves research. *Identity: An International Journal of Theory and Research, 6*(3), 251–271.

Powell, K., & Wells, M. (2002). The effectiveness of three experimental teaching approaches on student science learning in fifth-grade public school classrooms. *Journal of Environmental Education, 33*, 33–38.

Punch, S. (2002). Interviewing strategies with young people: The 'secretbox', stimulus material and task-based activities. *Children and Society, 16*, 45–56.

Roth, W.-M., van Eijk, M., Hsu, P.-L., Marshall, E. A., & Mazumder, A. (2009). What high school students learn during internships in biology laboratories. *American Biology Teacher*, *71*, 492–496.

Rottinghaus, P., Larson, L., & Borgen, F. (2003). The relation of self-efficacy and interests: A meta-analysis of 60 samples. *Journal of Vocational Behavior*, *62*, 221–236.

Seymour, E., Hunter, A., Laursen, S. L., & Deantoni, T. (2004). Establishing the benefits of research experience for undergraduates in the sciences: First findings from a three year study. *Science Education*, *79*(4), 437–473.

Shepard, B. (1997). *Adolescents' possible selves related to career and life planning decisions*. Unpublished doctoral dissertation, University of Victoria, Victoria, British Columbia, Canada.

Shepard, B., & Marshall, E. A. (1999). Possible selves mapping: Life-career exploration with young adolescents. *Canadian Journal of Counselling*, *33*(1), 37–54.

Tilleczek, K. C., & Lewco, J. H. (2001). Factors influencing the pursuit of health and science careers for Canadian adolescents in transition from school to work. *Journal of Youth Studies*, *4*(4), 415–428.

Turner, S., & Lapan, R. T. (2002). Career self-efficacy and perceptions of parent support in adolescent career development. *Career Development Quarterly*, *51*(1), 44–55.

Tyler-Wood, T., Mortenson, M., Putney, D., & Cass, M. A. (2000). An effective mathematics and science curriculum option for secondary gifted education. *Roeper Review*, *22*(4), 266–269.

Tytler, R., Symington, D., & Smith, C. (2011). A curriculum innovation framework for science, technology and mathematics education. *Research in Science Education*, *41*(1), 19–38.

Wai-Ling Packard, B., & Nguyen, D. (2003). Science career-related possible selves of adolescent girls: A longitudinal study. *Journal of Career Development*, *29*(40), 251–262.

Wallace-Broscious, A., Serafica, F. C., & Osipow, S. H. (1994). Adolescent career development: Relationships to self-concept and identity status. *Journal of Research on Adolescence*, *4*(1), 127–149.

E. Anne Marshall, Francis L. Guenette, Tanya Ward, Tara Morley
and Breanna Lawrence
Department of Educational Psychology and Leadership

Kate Fisher
Department of Curriculum and Instruction
University of Victoria
Victoria, British Columbia, Canada

NIKKI WRIGHT, EARL CLAXTON, JR., LEWIS WILLIAMS
AND TAMMY PAUL

4. GIVING VOICE TO SCIENCE FROM
TWO PERSPECTIVES

A Case Study

SNIT☐E☐ (pronounced *sneakwith*) is SENĆOŦEN for *The Place of the Blue Grouse*, a special place to WSÁNEĆ [Saanich] First Nations communities on the Saanich Peninsula, north of Victoria, British Columbia (BC). (The alphabet for the SENĆOŦEN language was developed by David Elliott, Sr., and can be studied at the website for the First Peoples Cultural Foundation http://www.fpcf.ca/.) Part of this traditional territory was utilized for hunting, fishing, shellfish gathering, and sacred ceremony; SNIT☐E☐ was historically considered a safe settlement during the winter months. WSÁNEĆ Elders remember ceremonies and SENĆOŦEN names for the abundant plant life in what is now known as Gowlland Tod Provincial Park, which surrounds Tod Inlet and borders the Butchart Gardens, a world-renown botanical tourist attraction. It is this authentic science, technology, society, and environment (STSE) setting that serves as the context for a community-based, ethno-botanical program involving six First Nations members over the course of 5 years. (In the following, *LINDY*, *EDWARD*, and *TOM* are pseudonyms given to the First Nations program participants.)

The program increased the capacity of First Nations youth to enter into science-related careers—both traditional indigenous and western science—and increased understanding of how traditional knowledge has been and is presently used in The Place of the Blue Grouse (Figure 1). This chapter describes the evolution of the program, some of its challenges, and its significance in the larger community.

The SNIT☐E☐ program had its roots in ecological restoration. In 2000, eelgrass shoots (*Zostera marina*) were transplanted in an inlet known to many as Tod Inlet, a small embayment within Saanich Inlet in the southwestern Salish Sea, the traditional territory of the WSÁNEĆ First Nations. The SeaChange Marine Conservation Society, a not-for-profit organization, was the lead in the eelgrass project. The intent was to give back some of the rich diverse habitats lost in the inlet through industrial practices. Over time, native plant restoration extended into the park lands surrounding the inlet.

The early stages of the project were successful in reintroducing terrestrial and marine native plants to protect resident aquatic and nonaquatic organisms just below the international botanical gardens within a provincial park. BC Parks (part of the

L. D. Yore et al (Eds.), Pacific CRYSTAL Centre for Science, Mathematics, and Technology
Literacy: Lessons Learned, 67–82.

provincial Ministry of the Environment), the Tsartlip First Nation, the federal Department of Fisheries and Oceans, community volunteers, and local businesses formed the matrix for the restoration.

> We had a connection to that land. The land doesn't belong to us, we belong to the land. We are the caretakers of that place. *EDWARD*

Figure 1. S NIT□E□.

The Place of the Blue Grouse was central to the WSÁNEĆ people's life for thousands of years. It served as a limestone quarry and cement plant in the late 19th and early 20th centuries. Restoring the inlet to health provides excellent authentic opportunities for First Nations and non-First Nations students to be a part of a living, breathing body of knowledge known as traditional ecological knowledge and wisdom (TEKW). It also offers opportunities for an integration between indigenous ways of knowing and practice with technology and western science—botany, biology, ecology, oceanography, and chemistry.

To capitalize on these authentic border crossings between TEKW and western knowledge about nature, SeaChange Marine Conservation Society (hereafter called SeaChange), WSÁNEĆ First Nations, and Pacific CRYSTAL formed a community-based research and development program that funded part-time internships for First Nations individuals. Community-based meant that the participating communities shared in the establishment or maintenance of partnerships, shared the responsibility for setting the research and development agenda, funding, and the establishment of outcomes and documentation of successes and challenges. The codirectors of Pacific CRYSTAL deferred to SeaChange and First Nations on the research, development, and reporting activities.

This chapter is a mutually developed publication of the 5-year project; it focuses on the overall capacity-building and programmatic outcomes resulting in successful internships for several young First Nations members, the recruitment and development of First Nations community educators, a successful place-based nature studies and ethnobotanical tours program, and summer internships for First Nations secondary school students. This case study illustrates ways that community-based partnerships can give voice to First Nations people as they negotiate the crossing of borders between TEKW and science cultures and can serve as models for others. It is also a case study of place-based environmental education that involved relevant experiences to enhance motivation and learning.

BACKGROUND

SNIT☐E☐ nourishes a reciprocal relationship—enriching the programs offered by a community not-for-profit organization by giving voice to First Nations knowledge to a wider population that seems eager to hear them. As plants depend upon good soil, nutrients, and sunlight, so too the foundation for partnerships require trust, mutual respect, and perseverance. For the First Nations interns, the program gave opportunities for them to learn from their Elders (knowledge keepers) and ways to formally communicate that rich body of knowing to a wider audience while simultaneously learning about botany, soil science, water analysis, and biology.

Providing opportunities for indigenous peoples to voluntarily explore and experience science and technology, achieve science and technology literacy, access science- and technology-related careers, and utilize these perspectives to consider STSE issues were the central goals of the Pacific CRYSTAL Project. Making these goals accessible and achievable for underserved and underrepresented populations have been perplexing problems worldwide. Many indigenous students are alienated by their school science experiences and thereby disengage academic studies, drop out of formal schooling, and develop nonproductive science, mathematics, and technology identities.

Snively and Corsiglia (1996) stated, "Acknowledging the contributions of multicultural science ... [is] a necessary step in enabling students to recognize and learn from groups outside the dominant culture" (p. 743). Thus, teaching science from a cross-cultural perspective can be more inclusive to students from various cultures and can promote intercultural understanding.

> Although early European explorers described the northwest coast as untouched wilderness, in fact, the aboriginal peoples did have an impact on the landscape through selective harvesting of trees and controlled burning. Coastal people burned selected woods and meadowlands to maintain open conditions and promote the growth of desired plants including berries, nuts, root vegetables and forage plants for deer and other game. (Pojar & MacKinnon, 1994, p. 21)

Examples of incorporating indigenous ways of knowing into science learning can be found world-wide. In Aotearoa New Zealand, a parallel science education program, *Putaiao*, for Māori students utilized indigenous worldviews, ways of knowing, identities, concept labels, and examples to address the colonized science curriculum of the English-speaking schools (McKinley & Keegan, 2008). The National Science Council of Taiwan has funded several research and development projects to address indigenous students' learning, classroom practices, and instructional resources. A research team recently produced a collection of indigenous artefacts to supplement school and teacher education programs (Guo, 2008). These artefacts have been placed on public display at regional historical and technology museums to increase public awareness of indigenous cultures, knowledge about nature, and ways of knowing before utilizing them as instructional resources. Gadicke (2005) under a Columbia River Trust grant accessed, documented, and developed science and technology ideas related to water that could be embedded in the BC K–7 science curricula for schools located in the Columbia River Basin. These projects illustrate the power of such approaches, the difficulty in accessing place-based examples of traditional knowledge and technologies, and potential entry opportunities that indigenous artefacts provide for formal science, mathematics, and technology instruction.

Indigenous peoples and some religious groups worldwide have not fully embraced western science because its underlying assumptions do not align with their cultural and personal beliefs about nature and naturally occurring events. The philosophy of scientific knowledge has two main areas of consideration: ontology and epistemology (Yore, 2008). The ontological considerations focus on the kind of entities that can properly figure into scientific theories, principles, and claims about reality and the limitations that these entities place on the knowledge system. The epistemological considerations analyze and evaluate the conceptual networks and methods employed in studying nature and naturally occurring events. These considerations revealed general concepts and methods common to all scientific inquiries and the specific concepts and methods that distinguish specific domains within the discipline. TEKW about nature and naturally occurring events are based on similar, rigorous ways of knowing and updating knowledge (Snively & Williams, 2008); but they differ in their underlying ontological assumptions in that TEKW includes integrated world-views and causality involving spiritualism, mysticism, and physical causes.

The lack of agreement and convergence in cultural studies of knowledge about nature and naturally occurring events illustrates the foolishness of assimilation and the difficulties in border crossing for science and TEKW systems that focus primarily on scientific approaches rather than technological literacy and constructivist approaches (Aikenhead, 2006; Chinn, Hand, & Yore, 2008; McKinley, 2007; McKinley & Keegan, 2008). If science is defined as searching, describing, and explaining patterns of events in the natural universe (Good, Shymansky, & Yore, 1999), then scientific approaches fail to produce agreement and consensus beyond the epistemological levels of searching and describing. Once deliberations address the ontological dimensions of metaphysics, explanations, and fundamental causal elements, then western science and other forms of knowledge about nature and naturally occurring events clash. The ontological assumptions about western science set it apart from many religious and traditional knowledge systems about nature and naturally occurring events (United States National Research Council, 1996).

However, technology (e.g., engineering, medicine, etc.)—as designs that adapt the environment to alleviate or meet the needs of people—and ethnobotany—the study of traditional medicinal, technological, and dietary uses of plants—have much more in common across cultures; and the ontological differences are not as obvious. In fact, modern technology represented by a range of practitioners (e.g., inventors, technicians, engineers, researchers) still value and recognize trial-and-error design approaches found in most cultures. The scientific inquiry and technology design (commonly known as R&D) epistemologies are similar across western, eastern, and traditional ways of knowing. Likewise, ethnobotany and other hybridized sciences have cross-cultural similarities. The quality of exploration, thinking, inquiry, description, and representation are similar across cultural attempts to search out and describe patterns of events in the natural universe and can inform many contemporary scientific investigations (Yore, Florence, Pearson, & Weaver, 2006). These insights help achieve culturally sensitive curricula that encourage explorations and two-way transitions between cultures while respecting the difficulties with acculturation into a science discourse community for some people (Stephens, 2000).

METHOD

This autobiographic study of the community-based SNIT□E□ project involved interpretations and reflections on experiences and artefacts. The first author composed the preliminary text based on her interpretations of the events, successes, and challenges of the 5-year project as well as her interpretations of early studies of the project. She attempted to document critical events over its duration to capture important issues and changes that were not detected by the other studies. Once this draft document was completed, it was shared with the other authors as an informant check and with a trusted Pacific CRYSTAL colleague. The discussions clarified and confirmed some interpretations and modified others. The results reported in this chapter are the shared understandings and assertions about the context, program, education, field studies, restoration, challenges, and significance.

CONTEXT

Place-based education is significant in indigenous studies. TEKW tends to impart ungeneralized knowledge about nature and naturally occurring events in a specific geographic location. These insights cannot, and should not, be separated from the cultural history of the people constructing the knowledge. Therefore, the cultural–ecological context of SNIT□E□ is critical to provide a sense of place for this community-based R&D project.

SNIT□E□ has been a place of safety for the WSÁNEĆ people over the last several thousand years. The land, forests, and waters have provided many essential materials and food. The Western Red Cedar tree provided bark for clothing, logs for totems and canoes, and planks and boughs for housing. Many terrestrial plants served as medicines and foodstuffs. The stream and ocean provided edible aquatic plants and seafood.

The WSÁNEĆ people have a long and rich history based on the oral tradition of storytelling; only recently have they developed a written language to preserve these stories and knowledge. The preservation of the TEKW associated with SNIT□E□ is only partially complete. Much of the oral histories and TEKW are held by a few Elders in their 80s and 90s, which makes this project a temporal priority.

THE SNIT☐E☐ PROGRAM

Three WSÁNEĆ members interned with SeaChange, a not-for-profit environmental organization with a focus on marine and watershed education, conservation, and restoration. The initial stage of the program prepared them for scientific investigations of the water and sediment of Tod Inlet and supported them in acquiring leadership skills for leading ethnobotanical tours for the public. These natural history walks explain the traditional uses of local plants for food, medicines, and tools by the WSÁNEĆ people. As the interns' confidence and skills increased, they mentored three secondary school students in the summer of 2009. Over the 5 years, internships became part-time staff positions in SeaChange.

The goals of the SNIT☐E☐ program are twofold: To increase the capacity of First Nations youth to enter into science-related careers—both traditional indigenous and western science—and to increase understanding of how TEKW has been and is presently used in The Place of the Blue Grouse. SeaChange facilitated by bridging scientific knowledge from two perspectives for the ultimate goal of cultural and ecological restoration of SNIT☐E☐.

SeaChange has had a 12-year history with SNIT☐E☐ in a very engaged partnership with the staff of BC Parks (Ministry of Environment). We worked together to restore the underwater marine wildlife habitat in Tod Inlet. In 2000, 1,800 eelgrass shoots (*Zostera marina*) were installed subtidally—with the expectation that it would create a meadow for fish, crabs, seastars, and birds in which to forage and find shelter (Figure 2). Eelgrass beds were historically abundant in the inlet; however, because of historical industrial uses further up the watershed (e.g., cement plant, farming, and solid waste landfill), much had disappeared over time. BC Parks helped with permits, signage, and encouragement.

After the transplant, BC Parks became less empowered to continue the support because of changes mandated by the provincial government. Therefore, SeaChange took on more responsibilities to steward the area, which led to several opportunities to promote public awareness of environmental best practices. In 2004, SeaChange was honoured to work with two Elders, John Elliott of the Tsartlip community and

Figure 2. Crab in an eelgrass bed (Photo: Jamie Smith).

Earl Claxton, Sr., of the Tsawout First Nations, on a Youth in Science Careers project, which revealed the rich history of the Saanich Inlet from a First Nations perspective. In 2006, SeaChange collaborated with Tye Swallow, an educator in the Saanich Adult Education Centre, and Marie Cooper, Elder of the Tsartlip community and member of the Saanich Indian School Board (SISB), to formulate a place-based education course. Interviews with members of the WSÁNEĆ people, in preparation for the course, revealed that knowledge is of most worth when it is associated with land and its significant elements; that is, SENĆOŦEN language and place names; WSÁNEĆ history, teachings, stories, ceremonies, and their sense of belonging and identity. Elders in oral cultures are carriers of that knowledge. A pilot curriculum project, ÁLE□ENEC [homeland] Place Studies, was created and delivered by the SISB in May and June 2006.

The purpose of this experiential project was the development of a sense of place (location within the cultural–historical context) and how we learn to understand the land as teacher. ÁLE□ENEC centred on culturally significant places (place-names) within WSÁNEĆ territory. Experiences were culturally and ecologically informed through Elders, community guest speakers from environmental organizations and restoration projects focused on the SENĆOŦEN language and place names, outdoor education experiences supplemented with various aboriginal and other readings, class discussions, and student reflective journals. The literacy tasks utilized both English and SENĆOŦEN languages in the speaking, listening, reading, writing, and representing tasks to support students' understanding. The highlight and culminating activity of the course was a 5-day kayaking trip through traditional territory.

> *TOM* taught the children how to root plant cuttings today. We cut some dogwood, thimbleberry, honeysuckle and picked some wild strawberry runners. Some of the boys caught a lizard on the rocks. Beautiful little creature. (from the journal of an ÁLE□ENEC participant during a visit to S̲NIT□E□)

The ÁLE□ENEC program documented TEKW and specific place names or regions, which included traditional and recent histories and current and future uses. Two individuals (*TOM* and *LINDY*) from ÁLE□ENEC expressed interest in participating with SeaChange in researching the cultural uses of plants in S̲NIT□E□.

> What drew me toward this were the plants. I started off being trained as a horticulturalist, and then it was my biology teacher, Chris, who told me about the ÁLE□ENEC course, and I found out not all plants are created equally (*laughter*). If I was going to work with plants, I should be focused in on working with native plants. It was in the ÁLE□ENEC class that I learned that. *TOM*

Shortly thereafter, a community-based research and development project was formed amongst the WSÁNEĆ people, SeaChange, and Pacific CRYSTAL (a Natural Sciences and Engineering Research Council, Canada [NSERC] funded project) to continue these efforts. SeaChange, *TOM*, and *LINDY* worked together to expand the ecological restoration and place-based education program in S̲NIT□E□. The purpose was to restore the cultural and ecological health of this very beautiful place that held a deeply rich cultural history.

I started working with the plants, and *LINDY* started learning more of the history of the area, because of her family ties and being close to the Lands Management person over here [Tsartlip territory]. Then we went to see Marie Cooper [Tsartlip Elder] for things we could copy to make up a First Nations display for the Nature Float so it is more of a complete history of down there. Before that, we had the settlers' history and the more recent restoration history. Then we got into the water quality testing with the BC Conservation Corps that really cemented the fact that we need to hybridize the program, using both the science and the traditional ecological knowledge. *TOM*

Having seed money to fund the two interns who expressed interest in leadership and careers in science was the start of what was called Internships in Environmental Technology. The beginning stages included planning sessions, interviews, and onsite visits with biologists who make their living from scientific fieldwork. *LINDY* and *TOM* began testing water quality in Tod Creek and Inlet on a regular basis. They monitored salinity, turbidity, temperature, and oxygen at five sites every 2 weeks. They designed the educational poster for the Tod Inlet Nature Float, a floating houseboat that serves as an educational centre in the inlet during the summer months. They wanted the public to know about The Place of the Blue Grouse from a First Nations perspective.

From the beginning, in tradition of true community-based R&D, the group has worked as a team, with *TOM* and *LINDY* having a strong voice as to the type of activities they wanted to undertake to bring First Nations perspectives back into SNIT☐E☐. To that end, they conducted ethnobotany tours, demonstrated the impacts of nonpoint pollution on the 3-D model of the Tod Creek watershed, removed invasive plants, and installed native plants with community volunteers.

SeaChange had attempted to transplant eelgrass in sites closer to the mouth of Tod Creek after its first successful transplant in 2000. After one growing season, however, these more recent transplants failed. It seemed more was at work than poor light availability due to sedimentation in the water. Discussions with *TOM*, *LINDY*, and others led to the speculation that heavy metals and other toxics might be the cause for failure. Therefore, it was arranged with the University of Victoria Water Quality Laboratory to test sediment and shellfish tissues for pollutants. The test results sparked interest across the indigenous and regional environmental education communities and led to a workshop on toxic pollutants in the marine environment.

These monitoring, restoration, and education efforts continued until the early spring of 2007. At that point, with additional money from the Victoria Native Friendship Centre, *EDWARD*, an established Tsawout community educator, came aboard to provide expertise in cultural and historical perspectives of the area. *EDWARD* also served as the resident resource in the oral tradition of storytelling and many traditional technologies and artefacts of his people. *LINDY* receded into the background with school and family responsibilities taking front stage for her.

The interns' interests and needs dictated the course of study and actions. The formal and informal education activities, research, conference presentations, and field experiences offered them opportunities to enhance their TEKW and western science understandings, develop leadership skills, explore careers in science, and identify the needs within their communities (Tsartlip and Tsawout) for reclaiming their harvesting practices and traditions in SNIT□E□. TEKW promotes a world-view that includes long-term resource management, ecological connections, survival skills, culture, and respect that has been recognized more as an important source of verifiable scientific and ecological knowledge by the Government of Canada and around the world (Johnson, 1992).

Reflecting on the research and development within the SNIT□E□ program revealed common themes. The three major components to the program are education, field studies, and restoration.

Education

Elementary and middle schools on the Saanich Peninsula and in Victoria, the Vancouver Island University (Nanaimo, BC), the University of Victoria, the LAU, WELNEW Tribal School (including professional development sessions with their teachers), four WSÁNEĆ tribal communities, and the public participated in the nature tours and talks about SNIT□E□. SeaChange has used a 3-D watershed model of the Tod Creek area, field and school saltwater aquaria, the Tod Inlet Nature Float (Figure 3), planting events and, more recently, traditional pit cooks to complement the tours. The educational interactive walks have had a deep influence on children, teachers, and the wider audience of Victoria as indicated by the feedback received since the program started. Bridging the past with the present is an ongoing theme:

> *How did you build your knowledge base about plants?* I started to become more interested in First Nations' names for these plants and how they got those names. I started to collect stories about those plants, and they started to become more meaningful to me. I started to become more connected to my late grandmother, who was very knowledgeable about plants, and she would very proudly show me the plants she had planted on reserve over at Tsawout. I felt the connection with my grandmother and I was continuing the knowledge she held. I felt good about what I was doing, and still do. *EDWARD*

The education experience for all participants involved a hands-on approach with the support of a knowledgeable leader. Programs on site and on the beach facing the Tsartlip community with classes from LAU, WELNEW Tribal School involved elementary school students in hands-on activities with sea life, including species living in eelgrass habitats. Marine animals were collected and placed in the school's seaquarium (saltwater aquarium) and then monitored and maintained by students, teachers, and SeaChange volunteers.

> Even though [western science and traditional knowledge] may seem quite different fields, they are fairly similar in that there are procedures or protocols you need to follow, and they are fairly similar protocols too. … Water quality testing: there is a set measurement, chemicals to be able to tell you what is in it; and the way I was thinking of it, there are set measurements in traditional ecological knowledge in terms of harvesting something without destroying it. A good example of that is the knowledge of being able to strip cedar bark without harming the tree, or the knowledge of the camas and being able to

understand that it takes more acidic soil and human interaction with those bulbs to get the bulbs we desire for consumption. *TOM*

Figure 3. Tod Inlet nature float.

Education activities at the Tod Inlet Nature Float involved water monitoring activities during the summer, such as salinity, temperature, and pH testing. A federally funded subsidy allowed one intern to staff the Nature Float for two consecutive summers. He conducted ethnobotanical tours and presented cultural history information to the hundreds of visitors of all ages who visited the Nature Float. The goal of this program is to raise awareness of the cultural and ecological biodiversity of the surrounding lands and waters of SṈIT□E□.

Do you think the messages you are giving are having an effect on the people to whom you address your words? Yeah, they come back the following year and have said that to me—that what I was able to bring to them, to teach them both from the scientific and the traditional ecological standpoints, and being able to use both of those tools to complement each other, rather than using one tool to verify the other one. It is better to use them to complement each other because it makes the information, for me, more complete, more trustworthy. … We have essentially become, in my opinion, translators for the academic and science side of things to the greater public. *TOM*

Cultures Connecting to Place is an environmental field program initiated in June 2009 and continuing in 2010. Elementary school children visit SNIT□E□ for a day to investigate the mouth of Tod Creek in small boats; explore the woods with *EDWARD*, making plant artefacts as they learn about the plants and their ecology; and learn about water quality and its relation to eelgrass from the dock of the Nature Float.

Field Studies

The research, development, and education aspects of the SNIT□E□ program created field studies in which TEKW and western science hybridized into a perspective emphasizing a place-based perspective of the environment in a cultural–historical context. With assistance from the NSERC-Industrial Research Chair's Water Quality Laboratory at the University of Victoria, water, sediment, and shellfish tissue samples from three sites in Tod Inlet were analyzed for heavy metals, PCBs, herbicides or pesticides, and volatiles. This authentic research provides information to assist with the long-term plans for the restoration of SN̲IT☐E☐.

Lindy and Tom participated in the water-quality analyses to enhance their conceptual and procedural knowledge about chemistry and qualitative and quantitative analyses. The data from both the water quality testing and the sediment/tissue sampling were part of public presentations to the local community to raise awareness of nonpoint pollution within Tod Inlet and land practices that have long-term effects on the inlet's marine life and ecology. Table 1 highlights those contaminants that exceeded criteria set by the provincial and federal governments.

Table 1. Contaminants in marine sediments from Tod Inlet
as measured by atomic spectroscopy

Drinking water laboratory		D70610	D70615	D70617
Sampling date		11/6/2006	11/6/2006	11/6/2006
Sediment site number		Site 1–1	Site 2–2	Site 3–2
Metals measured by inductively coupled plasma mass spectroscopy (ICPMS)	Criteria (mg/Kg)	sediment	sediment	sediment
Arsenic (As)	33	7.57	5.04	2.71
Cadmium (Cd)	5	**10**	**10**	**9**
Chromium (Cr)	52.3	**71.9**	16.3	9
Copper (Cu)	70	**9,260**	**18,700**	**13,200**
Lead (Pb)	30.2	**41.6**	13.4	6.38
Mercury (Hg)	0.15	**0.3**	0.07	0.02
Nickel (Ni)	30	9.7	8.3	6.8
Zinc (Zn)	120	91.1	48.2	29.4

Note. Numbers in bold are those in excess of the approved criteria from BC Ministry of Environment, Lands, and Parks 1995 and Environment Canada 1994.

The blasting for the limestone quarry that today is Butchart Gardens chased the blue grouse away. Scientists now tell us the settlers must have dumped heavy metals into the water at SN̲IT☐E☐ [and other toxins have] leached from the landfill at Hartland. Development and septic systems throughout the watershed continue to flow down here with their pollution. All the silt from agriculture and development that flows out the stream has changed the nature of this place. I have also been told that the inlet at SN̲IT☐E☐ is a moonscape below the surface; there is no life. All the pesticides and herbicides from the Butchart Gardens and their summertime entertainment continue to pollute and keep away animals that might return. On the weekends in summer there are hundreds of pleasure boats here. Not pumping sewage into these waters is still optional for them. How is this possible! How is this possible when we know that the causes of this problem are clear? The clams, herring, salmon, and crabs that were once plentiful are no longer able to live here. (SISB & Elliott, 2008, p. 15)

The finding of heavy metals, pesticides, and herbicides in both the sediment and the tissues of oysters and clams initiated a 3-day workshop attended by 35 professional field scientists entitled Impacts of Metals and Toxic Organic Chemicals on Aquatic

Ecosystems and Human Health led by Dr. Fran Solomon, an environmental biologist from the University of British Columbia Mining Studies Institute. The purpose of the course was to increase the knowledge of conservationists and other environmental professionals about the workshop topic as well as to promote interorganizational and interdisciplinary collaboration in developing and implementing pollution prevention and cleanup actions in the saltwater bays and freshwater bodies of Vancouver Island.

Restoration

Because of its long-term relationship with the Ministry of Environment (BC Parks), SeaChange is permitted to work in Gowlland Tod Provincial Park for educational and restoration purposes. SeaChange at times has succeeded in bridge-relationships between BC Parks and the Saanich First Nation communities. The common goal is the long-term commitment of First Nations, community volunteers, and SeaChange staff to the restoration of native plants as well as eelgrass. These relationships, built over time, are founded on hard and honest work toward shared goals and insights from both traditional and western science and are mutually beneficial.

In 2006, SeaChange interns and staff worked with six members of the BC Conservation Corps who laboured diligently within SNIT□E□ to remove invasive plants. They then created a Native Plant Installation Plan for 12 sites. The plan is being followed throughout consecutive planting seasons (fall to early spring). Each season, the First Nations interns (now SeaChange staff), with the SeaChange volunteer coordinator, orient and train community volunteers to assist with invasive plant removals and native plant installations. This ongoing program has involved many classes from the Restoration of Natural Systems and Environmental Studies Program at the University of Victoria as well as groups such as the local Girl Guides, the LAU, WELNEW Tribal School, Saanich and Victoria School Districts' elementary and middle schools, and the general public.

Restoration of eelgrass has slowed as the sediment analysis results showed that the limiting factors preventing success were much more complex than water quality issues alone. Restored beds further away from the mouth of Tod Creek are expanding with more shoots installed as budgets allow. Education has taken the place of restoration in the area closer to the creek until a long-term restoration strategy is undertaken.

One way that cultural restoration is occurring is through pit cooks in SNIT□E□ and other sites of the WSÁNEĆ territory:

> One of the first field trips [with the secondary school youth interns] was the pit cook with the Pauquachin. We assisted with the festivities set for that day. It was an excellent day because we got to meet members of the community, young and old, eat traditional foods from Saanich, and eat in the traditional manner. The students really liked the idea of assisting with a pit cook; they never had seen one before—digging the hole, cooking the fish and clams, getting it out, serving it. The connection with food with the Saanich people is very important. Feasting is a big part of the Saanich people. Get together, eat, and then discuss things afterwards. *EDWARD*

CHALLENGES OF HYBRIDIZING WORLDVIEWS

The beginnings of this successful program were borne from the relationships established between SeaChange and Elders John Elliott and Earl Claxton, Sr., in 2004 while working on a youth-oriented science careers project. Both Elders opened the lens of perception of what it means to live next to indigenous communities with thousands of years of history on the salt waters of the Saanich Inlet and the Salish Sea. Social justice issues were an ongoing theme in that story and continue into the present. "How is this possible when we know that the causes of this problem are clear? The clams, herring, salmon, and crabs that were once plentiful are no longer able to live here." (SISB & Elliott, 2008, p. 15). These Elders opened the doors to planning for the future together when clams, oysters, crabs, and plentiful fish would once more populate Tod Inlet for harvesting by First Nations.

The problems of integrating western science and TEKW to solve restoration issues are at once complex and simple. The complexity lies in the social world of damaged relationships over millennia, bureaucracy (rules and regulations of a provincial park designation), changing land use practices stemming from agricultural, development, and industrial habits further upstream, and the slowness at which integrated TEKW and western science curricula have been incorporated into school systems. The problem's simplicity lies in the ecological damage occurring over a hundred years. Most likely, the answer to the restoration of SNIT☐E☐ lies with capping the marine substrate and rebuilding the foundations for a healthy marine system while clearing the watershed's upper reaches of invasive plants and installing native ones. The ecological solutions are straightforward in the end.

The hybridization of scientific western approaches and traditional indigenous knowledge and practices could be used to resolve the ecological damage to SNIT☐E☐ and address historical ecological injustices; the social construct with which the hybridization happens is problematical. The first step is encouraging students and adults to experience SNIT☐E☐ firsthand and to take responsibility for its healing. In working together, whether by tying eelgrass shoots to metal washers as preparation for a transplant or digging the heavy clay with shovels to plant sword ferns on a steep slope, relationships begin to take root. One of the social slopes that may become too slippery to manoeuvre, however, is not with the relationships forming within the restoration community but the one between the scientific and restoration communities.

When perusing the available literature on the subject of integrating these two scientific perspectives, the first author noticed time and again how subtly but assuredly one worldview overshadows the other. To be successful, seems to be the message, First Nations students need to complete curricula well steeped in western science paradigms. The authors would argue that it is timely to re-examine this premise and with fresh eyes enter into a dialogue with First Nations communities about motivations for the pursuit of scientific careers.

One way to succeed would be to bring young people into projects as interns with the goal of bringing back First Nations cultural and ecological integrity, with TEKW a centrepiece in the work.

The plain fact is that the planet does not need more "successful" people. But it does desperately need more peacemakers, healers, restorers, storytellers, and lovers of every shape and form. It needs people who live well in their places. It needs people of moral courage willing to join the fight to make the world habitable and humane. And these needs have little to do with success as our culture has defined it. (Orr, 1991, para. 15)

Over time, we have cultivated a relationship of trust and respect amongst the partners and participants in this community-based R&D project. The needs and desires of Tom, Edward, and Lindy have, for the most part, dictated our next steps and priorities in developing an effective cultural and environmental restoration and education program. When Tom and Lindy spent time in the water quality laboratory at the University of Victoria and witnessed the scientific analysis of the water, sediment, and shellfish tissue samples, it was a one-way border crossing. They did not have an opportunity for a two-way crossing with the laboratory scientists in which their perspective was honoured and respectfully engaged. When the data came out of the high-priced technologies, there was little support for the practical considerations of what these data were telling us about the health of the inlet or about the next steps in resolving the problems.

We showed Bayside Middle School how to make a native garden and actually had the students go out and harvest those plants to be put in that garden. That was done so that they can make that reconnection with nature as there is a lot of disconnect from nature amongst students, not only First Nations but with all students of any heritage. That is the biggest reason we wanted to make it extremely inclusive, because we don't want to leave anybody behind [emphasis added by the first author]. Also, it makes it that much better because these visitors are not going home anytime soon, so we'd better start teaching them. (laughter)

[Now you have broken this, will] you help us fix this? (*laughter*) There is this phenomena worldwide looking to First Nations to fix it—you can see it as a common thread that indigenous people say, of course you want to give it back to us now that it is broken. We have been talking to you a long time that what you are doing is wrong, and what you are doing is not assisting the whole practice by any stretch of the imagination. ... Indigenous people know that the people asking for the help are not the ones who initiated this whole thing. The people are not reacting in a negative way. We need to be thankful that they actually stopped and are not actually falling over the cliff—this is just before. (*laughter*) TOM

Significance of SNIT□E□ for the Larger Community

The way I picture it—and it is slowly evolving this way—is that we are going to create pockets of SNIT□E□ but for other territories ... we are cultivating and propagating more knowledge keepers. These knowledge keepers coming after us have a passion for acquiring this knowledge—not strictly academic; doing it because we want to do it, which is a bit different, makes it more enjoyable and more personable to one's self. TOM

Over the 5 years of the project, this internship program created many ripples in the surrounding communities of the Saanich Inlet, the Gulf Islands, and Vancouver Island. *TOM* and *EDWARD* have initiated native plant gardening projects with middle school students and have given numerous presentations in schools, community centres, universities, and Band Councils:

> We started off working with the elementary grades at the Tribal School—just a few classes. Then the number of teachers increased because they have family, and they went back home and told their family, and some of their family members work in different schools, and they became interested. Then we started to do professional development days and invited the teachers down for a tour. It is more like the traditional manner of it being spoken and spoken about a lot. It is an excellent program. *TOM*

Many nongovernmental and not-for-profit agencies have developed effective *game-changing* programs on short-term, small-scale, R&D projects like the SṈIT☐E☐ program. Public awareness of science and the use of authentic science, mathematics, and technology programs as springboards for further academic studies and career awareness are much needed, especially for underserved and underrepresented people like indigenous students. However, funding agencies are not willing to support such programs for longer terms and do not realize the exponential costs, efforts, and logistics of scaling effective single-site programs to multiple sites involving different partners.

We have tried to illustrate how cascading leadership and internships can help concerned participants build leadership capacity for future environmental restoration efforts with a balanced approach between two world paradigms.

> We do not know the plan the creator has for us. He made all nations of people, and he brought non-First Nations people here. There must be a reason. We need to work together. We have come to this point in time when the general society is starting to understand that, in living in this place, it might be helpful to begin understanding a fundamental spiritual belief. We call this ÍY, NEUEL or living in harmony with one another, being good to one another. We all belong to the land. We do not own it. We all need to have a good place to live, and we all need to learn how to live together. This relationship requires more than talk. We all talk and perhaps we are starting to listen but what have we done? AXE☐ is a word that implies that to say something is to do something, and encompasses much of our traditional beliefs and values. We all have a lot to say but more to do. (SISB & Elliott, 2008, p. 17)

REFERENCES

Aikenhead, G. S. (2006). *Science education for everyday life: Evidence-based practice*. New York: Teachers College Press.

Chinn, P. W. U., Hand, B., & Yore, L. D. (2008). Culture, language, knowledge about nature and naturally occurring events, and science literacy for all: She says, he says, they say [Special issue]. *L1— Educational Studies in Language and Literature*, *8*(1), 149–171. Retrieved from http://l1.publication-archive.com/show?repository=1&article=220

Gadicke, J. M. (2005). *Integrating aboriginal knowledge into the elementary science curriculum*. Unpublished masters of education project, University of Victoria, Victoria, British Columbia, Canada.

Good, R. G., Shymansky, J. A., & Yore, L. D. (1999). Censorship in science and science education. In E. H. Brinkley (Ed.), *Caught off guard: Teachers rethinking censorship and controversy* (pp. 101–121). Boston: Allyn & Bacon.

Guo, C.-J. (2008). Science learning in the contexts of culture and language practices: Taiwanese perspective. *L1—Educational Studies of Language and Literacy*, *8*(1), 95–107. Retrieved from http://l1. publication-archive.com/show?repository=1&article=217

Johnson, M. (Ed.). (1992). *Lore: Capturing traditional environmental knowledge*. Hay River, NWT, Canada: International Development Research Centre.

McKinley, E. (2007). Post colonialism, indigenous students, and science education. In S. K. Abell & N. G. Lederman (Eds.), *Handbook of research on science education* (pp. 199–226). Mahwah, NJ: Lawrence Erlbaum.

McKinley, E., & Keegan, P. J. (2008). Curriculum and language in Aotearoa New Zealand: From science to Putaiao. *L1—Educational Studies of Language and Literacy*, *8*(1), 135–147. Retrieved from http://l1.publication-archive.com/public?fn=enter&repository=1&article=219

Orr, D. W. (1991, Winter). What is education for? Six myths about the foundations of modern education and six new principles to replace them. *In Context*, (27), 52.

Pojar, J., & MacKinnon, A. (1994). *Plants of coastal British Columbia*. Vancouver, BC, Canada: Lone Pine.

Saanich Indian School Board & Elliott, J. (2008). *S̲NIT̲E̲: Learning from a traditional place*. Unpublished manuscript.

Snively, G. J., & Corsiglia, J. (1996). Pre-service teachers explore traditional ecological knowledge in a science methods class. *Proceedings of the annual international conference of the Association for the Education of Teachers in Science* (pp. 721–767). Cincinnati, OH.

Snively, G. J., & Williams, L. B. (2008). "Coming to know": Weaving Aboriginal and western science knowledge, language, and literacy into the science classroom. *L1—Educational Studies of Language and Literacy*, *8*(1), 109–133. Retrieved from http://l1.publication-archive.com/public?fn=enter&repository=1&article=218

Stephens, S. (2000). *Handbook for culturally responsive science curriculum*. Fairbanks, AK: Alaska Native Knowledge Network.

United States National Research Council. (1996). *The national science education standards*. Washington, DC: The National Academies Press.

Yore, L. D. (2008). Science literacy for all students: Language, culture, and knowledge about nature and naturally occurring events [Special Issue]. *L1—Educational Studies of Language and Literacy*, *8*(1), 5–21. Retrieved from http://l1.publication-archive.com/show?repository=1&article=213

Yore, L. D., Florence, M. K., Pearson, T. W., & Weaver, A. J. (2006). Written discourse in scientific communities: A conversation with two scientists about their views of science, use of language, role of writing in doing science, and compatibility between their epistemic views and language. *International Journal of Science Education*, *28*(2/3), 109–141.

Nikki Wright
SeaChange Marine Conservation Society
Brentwood Bay, British Columbia, Canada

Earl Claxton, Jr., and Lewis Williams
Tsawout First Nation

Tammy Paul
Tsartlip First Nation

DAVID B. ZANDVLIET, MARY HOLMES
AND MATTHIAS STARZNER

5. SEAQUARIA IN SCHOOLS

*Participatory Approaches in the Evaluation of an Exemplary
Environmental Education Program*

Aquatic habitats, both freshwater and marine, are an essential part of British
Columbia's defining character. Yet many people living here rarely appreciate
the true value of the natural wealth at their doorsteps, do not know how to
contribute to its well-being, and are unaware of how their activities affect
their surrounding lands, streams, rivers, and ocean. ... Improved public awareness and action are essential in ensuring that BC's aquatic ecosystems will be
maintained for future generations. (WestWind SeaLab Supplies [WSS] &
World Fisheries Trust [WFT], 2008, p. 9)

Seaquaria in Schools is a British Columbia-based environmental education (EE)
program that fosters science and environmental learning through children's hands-
on experiences with marine organisms in a school setting, the supply of a chilled
seawater aquarium, and the provision of a variety of local, live marine organisms.
Seaquaria in Schools is also a successful partnership involving nongovernmental
agencies, schools, universities, and local communities. Throughout the project, professional development workshops and action research efforts funded by the Pacific
CRYSTAL Project helped to enliven this community of practice in which partners
actively participated in setting agendas, developing educational goals, and contributing to ongoing program evaluation efforts. This chapter reports on the results of
two case studies: a qualitative participatory evaluation project and a participatory
action research project. Both studies highlight the need to develop both participatory
and inclusive models for program evaluation and to relate these closely to the stated
needs and goals of program proponents.

BACKGROUND

Environmental education involves some of the most pressing science, technology,
society, and environment (STSE) issues facing people today. Scientific, mathematical,
and technological literate citizens and politicians must be prepared to participate in the
public debate about these STSE issues to reach informed and sustainable decisions,
solutions, and policies (see Yore, Chapter 2 this book). Pacific CRYSTAL has attempted to address these pressing issues in a number of projects. Understanding the context,
background, and theoretical influences is also important in addressing such efforts.

*L. D. Yore et al (Eds.), Pacific CRYSTAL Centre for Science, Mathematics, and Technology
Literacy: Lessons Learned, 83–97.*

Program Context

Seaquaria in Schools is a nonprofit program whose goal is to stimulate integrated marine and ecosystem education in schools and communities; it was developed through extensive partnerships and collaboration with informal educators, teachers, community activists, and university academics. The program targets diverse learners of all ages, extends learning to the real world, and provides increased leadership opportunities (WSS & WFT, 2008). A variety of programs specific to elementary, middle, and secondary schools have been developed. The program includes cross-curricular and outreach materials developed and shared among a network of informal educators, teachers, and school administrators. According to the educator's guide, the key processes for a Seaquaria program are:
- Participative learning: students and teachers learning together
- Teachers modelling learning processes
- Peer-teaching
- Research & enquiry vs. Rote learning
- Interdisciplinary and integrated learning
- Fostering a positive school-wide learning atmosphere
- Building linkages to local field, environmental and community programs. (WSS & WFT, 2008, p. 5)

To achieve these goals, the program places chilled saltwater aquaria in schools and provides real-life examples of captivating, ever-changing, marine ecosystems with a variety of live marine specimens. As students observe and care for these model eco-systems and participate in hands-on activities, they can build an understanding and respect for the organisms and develop integrated stewardship skills. In the process, it is anticipated that these aquaria foster a passion for learning and critical thinking in students.

The Seaquaria in Schools program (hereafter called Seaquaria) aims to provide for a type of science education that goes beyond written materials, preserved specimens, and books. As students work hands on and interactively with local creatures in the classroom and on a long-term basis, they learn about the environment, science, nature, and the role of stewardship. Seaquaria has potential as a tool for multidisciplinary teaching and for bridging school-based and field programs. The program is most unique because it (the seaquarium) becomes a permanent fixture in the school. "It is a window into the natural world around us that is only limited by our imaginations in how we can connect it to the school curriculum, community initiatives and our students' day to day lives." (WSS & WFT, 2008, p. 9).

Environmental Learning in British Columbia

Seaquaria, while potentially being an example of innovative science instruction also aims to be an exemplar of place-based EE practices. The British Columbia Ministry of Education (BC MoE) published a curriculum framework for environmental learning entitled *Environmental Learning and Experience* (BC MoE, 2007). Among its many principles, the document relates that direct experiences form an important part of learning for children. It emphasizes the interdisciplinary nature of environmental learning utilizing the lenses of *complexity*, *aesthetics*, *responsibility*, and *ethics* to examine the curriculum in interdisciplinary ways by mapping EE goals onto established discipline-specific curricula and to develop in students an ethic of care.

Many jurisdictions provide environmental topics only cursory attention in mainstream curricula (Smith & Williams, 1999). For environmental learning to have any kind of effect, its concepts and approaches need to take a central position in schools. Hutchison (2004) described three general approaches to conducting environmental learning: a *supplemental* approach in which teachers are provided with curricular materials they may use in addition to regular teaching; an *infusionist* approach in which environmental themes are integrated into curricular topics (usually in science or social studies programs); and an *intensive experience* approach in which students participate in short, outdoor, immersive trips and experiences. In the supplemental approach, the curricular materials are self-contained and require limited knowledge or preparation on the part of the teacher. In the infusionist approach, the environment becomes the organizing concepts for an interdisciplinary curriculum—the premise being that all education is environmental education (Orr, 1994).

Seaquaria uses the environment as an organizing theme for both the intensive and infusionist approaches. This stems from the belief that sustainability education is not subject matter to be treated separately in curriculum but is interconnected with everything we do as human beings (MoE, 2007). It is anticipated that an interdisciplinary approach to teaching about the aquatic environment will support students in understanding how their actions affect the environment at both local and global levels. Working to integrate environmental learning within all subject areas (especially science) promotes this change in attitude by providing students with opportunities to experience and investigate the relationships linking individuals, societies, and natural surroundings. Education *about*, *in*, and *for* the environment provides students with opportunities to learn about the functioning of natural systems, identify their beliefs and opinions, consider a range of views, and ultimately make informed and responsible choices for themselves, their families, and communities.

Conceptual Framework

Owing to the interdisciplinary nature of this research, the conceptual framework for this study is informed by four areas: evaluation research, learning environment theory, action research, and place-based education. Together, these perspectives informed the methods employed in the study and engendered a process of participatory action research that eventually led to the development of the evaluation protocols used in the two case studies described here.

Participatory evaluation. Fitzpatrick, Sanders, and Worthen (2006) identified five distinct approaches to evaluation: objective-oriented, management-oriented, consumer-oriented, expertise-oriented, and participant-oriented approaches. Variations on the participant-oriented approach were selected for this research effort because that approach responds to the needs of participants in a collaborative program while having the advantages of inductive reasoning, multiplicity of data, emergent planning, and acknowledgement of multiple rather than single realities. Participatory approaches can also use description and judgment to provide background, justification, and description of a program of study while listing and recording intended antecedents, transactions, and outcomes. These approaches can also explicitly state standards and record judgments.

There are several ways to increase participant voices during an evaluation process. One methodology that has been successfully used in EE evaluation is participatory evaluation (McDuff & Jacobson, 2001). While participatory evaluation is generally understood to involve a high degree of stakeholder participation in the evaluation process, it is a broad term that has been defined differently by scholars in different disciplines (McDuff & Jacobson, 2001; Quintanilla & Packard, 2002). McDuff and Jacobson (2001) suggested that participatory evaluation involves stakeholders in the design and evaluation process. Cousins and Earl (1995) defined participatory evaluation as a process that involves having an expert train "key organizational personnel" in evaluation research (p. 8). A participatory qualitative evaluation approach was used in Case Study 1.

Learning environments. Learning environment studies seek to describe educational contexts and to identify relationships among subject matter (curriculum), teaching practices, and environmental variables (Fraser, 1998; Jamieson, 2003; Oblinger, 2006). The study of learning environments is an established field of academic inquiry now prevalent within elementary, secondary, and postsecondary research; it focuses on participant perceptions of the learning environment fostered by an educational program. Disciplines exploring this relationship between the environment and learning include science education (Fraser, 1998) and EE (Zandvliet, 2007). Learning environment studies can acknowledge and account for both the physical and social realm in which learning occurs (Temple, 2007) and how these socioenvironmental conditions influence the process and experience of learning (Strange & Banning, 2001). A quantitative learning environments approach was adopted for Case Study 2.

Action research. The case studies presented in this chapter are both forms of action research. Action research is understood to be a disciplined form of inquiry that is based upon a collaborative, democratic, and participatory process that seeks not only to research but also to inspire action (Cohen, Manion, & Morrison, 2000; Kemmis & Wilkinson, 1998). Our objective in applying such an approach was to be involved in a process that facilitates change. We wanted to implement processes that are relevant, useful, and of value for small organizations and their program participants. Cohen et al. (2000) described action research as a "powerful tool for change and improvement at a local level" (p. 226). Furthermore, action research often focuses on understanding and changing institutional culture and society.

Classroom-based action research challenges the conventional research paradigm; "action research is not done on people ... [it] involves research by people on their own work, to help them improve what they do, including how they work with and for others" (Kemmis & Wilkinson, 1998, p. 21). This attribute is particularly applicable to programs such as Seaquaria because it seeks to work with students, educators, and teachers and leave an immediate legacy of insight and change.

In response to the call for evidence-based practices in both informal science education and EE (Hussar, Schwartz, Bioselle, & Noam, 2008; Thomson & Hoffman, 2003; United States National Science Foundation, 2008), action research can provide a credible process that features systems that other researchers will be able to understand, augment, and debate. Further, because it is defined as a "flexible, situationally responsive methodology that offers rigour, authenticity and voice," it is ideal to help build a bridge between academic research and grassroots community initiatives (Cohen et al., 2000, p. 241).

Commitment to an action research methodology holds researchers to an accountable, participatory, democratic process that not only seeks to foster change but also provides opportunities for reflection on the process as it unfolds, while making it a strong basis for developing and understanding the evaluation process for the multiple stakeholders and for the youth that these programs hope to engage. Importantly, action research can utilize both qualitative and quantitative methodologies that have the potential to identify and explain relationships within the case context.

Place-based environmental education experiences. The notion of a place-based education has been well described by Sobel (1993, 1996), and related ideas have been expanded upon by others (Gruenewald, 2003; Hutchison, 2004; Orr, 1992, 1994; Woodhouse & Knapp, 2000). The difficulty in describing exactly what would constitute a place-based education becomes clouded partly due to the multiple and interdisciplinary nature of the literature where this notion seems to reside. Gruenewald (2003) posited that the idea of place-based learning connects theories of experiential learning, contextual learning, problem-based learning, constructivism, outdoor education, indigenous education, and EE. In arguing for what he described as a critical pedagogy of place, Gruenewald suggested that educational concern for local space— community in the broad sense—is sometimes overshadowed by both the discourse of accountability and by the discourse of economic competitiveness to which it is linked. An ecological framework would seek to discard this one-sided view of progress by taking as its first assumption education *about* and *for* defined communities. Place-based education denotes an emphasis on the inescapable embeddedness of humans and their technologies in natural systems. Rather than seeing nature as *other*, this ecological view of education involves the practice of viewing humans as one part of the natural world and human societies and cultures as an outgrowth of interactions between species and particular places (see Smith & Williams, 1999). This view of education is evident in the following case studies.

CASE STUDY 1: PARTICIPATORY EVALUATION THROUGH
A STAKEHOLDER WORKSHOP

Method

This case study describes the findings from a 2-hr educational workshop held with 17 diverse stakeholders related to Seaquaria in three Greater Victoria School Districts. The workshop included program educators, teachers, principals, school trustees, representatives from Pacific CRYSTAL, volunteers, and several secondary school students. Participants were recruited by e-mail and word of mouth by the Seaquaria program director and staff. During the workshop, a series of activities designed specifically for the evaluation process were conducted and included the following themes: identifying a common vision, taking stock of the successes and challenges, and planning for the future (Starzner, 2010).

First, participants identified a common vision or mission statement through a brainstorming exercise. Throughout this exercise, all participants had a chance to hear one another's understanding of the current vision or mission statement; and a dialogue ensued to determine a common vision, which was intended to allow individuals with different capacities in the program to understand the thoughts and positions of others.

Second, participants were invited to take stock. This portion of the workshop involved inventorying all the activities or opportunities that the program provided or created. Individuals were then asked to assign values to entries on the inventory list using a 'sticky dot' voting system where specific colours were used to rate the success of each activity or opportunity. Participants were invited to explain their ratings, with the expectation that the dialogue would lead to further understandings and discussion of the successes and challenges.

Third, participants began planning for the future. They used the results of the taking-stock activity to identify goals and strengths and weaknesses for each activity or opportunity. The facilitator asked the participants to collectively identify what strategies, revisions to current activities, and additional activities were needed to accomplish the program goals.

Data Analysis and Evaluation

The audio-recorded participation, observer notes, and workshop activity outcomes of these participatory processes were later transcribed, coded, and analyzed. Wherever possible, preliminary results were reviewed by the participants themselves as an informant check, with the researcher then analyzing these data to identify themes, trends, commonalities, differences, areas of strength, and areas needing improvement.

Results

The results from the coding and interpretation were grouped into major findings and supplemental themes. The major findings related to the program's vision and future.

Defining a vision. After initial introductions, the workshop group completed a brainstorming exercise to define a collective vision for the Seaquaria program. After approximately 15 min, the group had identified 26 distinct words and phrases, such as joint learning, engagement, hands-on experience, direct interaction, mentoring, and a vehicle for education. When the group felt that they had exhausted their list, they were asked to define a collective vision, that is, one that they could agree upon for the duration of the workshop. One participant said, *To me, it's the last one, the 'vehicle for education' that sort of captures all the others.* Heads began to nod around the room. Another participant stated:

> To me ideally, the [Seaquaria program] is not environmental education but it's a way of doing education, so somehow getting away from those silos and looking at it as a vehicle of education ... using the environment to provide an education in a holistic fashion.

Charting the journey to understand the destination. The workshop then focused on what the participants thought was most important by taking stock of the program and ranking ideas in the inventory list. The group identified 25 distinct themes or areas of importance. Once the list was established, participants were instructed to vote for the five topics that meant the most to them or the ones that they considered to be the most important.

Upon completion of the voting, the results were tallied and the top eight categories were selected for further discussion. Participants then considered how well the program was accomplishing each task by scoring each on a 10-point scale (1 = very poorly ... 10 = excellently). Some participants scored individual topics very differently, and the contrast amongst these outliers (highest and lowest ratings of a topic) provided an immediate source of discussion within the group. Table 1 provides the average scores for participants' ratings. These topics formed the basis for the various themes that emerged for the interpretation. In an effort to be concise, we describe only the five top-ranked themes in detail.

Table 1. Results of Seaquaria in schools educators' workshop topic scoring

Topic / Area of importance	Average rating
Positive experiences	8.4
Observations – Hands-on learning	8.1
Learning about complexity	7.9
Seaquaria becomes a special place in the school: focal point	7.9
Hooks vulnerable kids	7.8
Flexibility for curriculum use	7.8
Commitment to sharing learning: mentoring, lifelong learning, etc.	6.5
Fosters volunteerism / employment	6.7

Note. Topic scores are not intended to give a statistical evaluation but to provide a basis for comparison and discussion.

Theme 1: Positive experiences Connecting students to a positive learning experience received the highest average rating. Despite Victoria's close proximity to the ocean, participants often expressed that reconnecting students to a positive learning experience is a key role for Seaquaria. A student participant stated:

> Except for this program, it's not really being taught anywhere else. I mean I've lived on the ocean my whole life ... and I had no idea. ... I knew there was a red rock crab and ... a Dungeness crab, but that's it, that's all I knew. But now I go [to the ocean] and I'm like, oh, that's what it is and I can name it and I can show my parents ... I mean they didn't know it and neither did I.

One teacher had observed that students in her school had organically interacted with the seaquarium and she thought this was a key experience. She stated, *It doesn't require a teacher telling them to do it for them to enjoy it ... it's right there and* [they] *can initiate self involvement ... it just happens.* Another teacher said that at her Grade 8–12 school the seaquarium is located in the secondary area of the school and that she often:

> [catches] teenagers just sitting there and staring at it, and I think the value of it is absolutely indescribable ... it is a positive interaction with nature in a comfortable space ... a space they are familiar with ... and they are interacting with the natural world ... it's acquiring a sense of place, of natural place in a familiar environment.

Theme 2: Making observations and learning about complexity   The second and third rated characteristics dealt with observations during hands-on activities stimulating higher-order thinking about how these observations are related to one another and to other factors. An elementary teacher stated, *If you are watching a goldfish tank, there's not much going on in your mind really. If you are watching the seaquarium, there's a lot going on.* Workshop participants felt strongly about the observation opportunities offered by Seaquaria.

One key element was to encourage teachers to use the program as a stepping-stone for field trips to local or regional sites. One secondary school student shared that trips to the ocean to observe marine organisms were essential to her marine learning. She said, *You learn so much more just by spending a few hours* [at the ocean] *than you would by cramming for five hours at home ... it's having observations firsthand—it just helps so much more.* A classmate emphasized the importance of being provided with hands-on classroom learning opportunities for marine observations and explained such observations are important:

> They are your own observations, as opposed to reading it in a textbook and it saying 'this person observed this' ... you are observing it so you can write down 'this is what I saw' ... it's much more hands on, it's much more enjoyable.

The students also provided insight into the seaquarium's value as an unstructured learning experience:

> I went to [a local middle school] and that tank is like, everybody sits there at lunch and everybody knows the creatures and you name the creatures that are in there. ... It was so much fun ... you are observing it and you don't have to report back to your teacher and say 'this is what the textbook told me.'

Several teachers had observed similar informal learning opportunities, including an elementary teacher who shared that in the *seaquarium there's so much interdependency, that's the complexity and the surprising thing is that the kids always know what's going on and what is dependent on everything else.*

Theme 3: Engaging vulnerable kids and providing a tranquil place   The fourth and fifth rated characteristics converged to focus on students and space in which the seaquarium provides a tranquil place for vulnerable or at-risk students to observe, think, daydream, or be quiet. The placement and physical presence of the seaquarium provides a distractor or psychological respite for many children.

During the workshop, several educators told stories about how the seaquarium hooked vulnerable students. This topic is closely related with the notion that it provides a special place in a school. Participants felt that the seaquarium created a tranquil place that can be used as a staging point to deal with behavioural issues or to prevent their escalation. Having the seaquarium located in a central area was identified as being key to allowing widespread access and providing students the opportunity to spend time there before school and during their lunch break. In many schools, the seaquarium is located in the main foyer so that not only the students but also parents and school visitors can benefit from it. One elementary school principal further explained that in her school the seaquarium had become *the outer office.* She overheard students talking in front of the seaquarium, *What do you think the sea cucumber would be doing right now if it felt like you feel?* She noted that in her role as principal:

> Children ... are generally coming to me because they need calming down or they need help to solve a problem or something, and they stop when they get to the tank and by the time they get to me they have had time to decompress, process their own problem, and I have very little to do with the solution and they are headed back.

That sense of calming was also noticed by another teacher who shared that, when he first arranged for the seaquarium to be built in his school, he really hoped that it would not only be a focal point for the school but that it would also act as a *place of peace and tranquility.* He observed, *it was amazing; it would be a place where people sit around and do whatever it is they do.*

Theme 4: Flexibility for curriculum use Participants expressed that the wide range of curriculum connections and interdisciplinary opportunities that Seaquaria presented was integral to the program's success (sixth rated characteristic). One teacher enthusiastically shared that you can do lessons *in almost every area of the curriculum, there's art, drama, social studies, science, personal responsibilities. So it's very integrated and it can be integrated into the curriculum for any grade and into a whole variety of subject areas.* A secondary school student added that the previous day her class had participated in a canoe trip on the Gorge Waterway and learned about the Songhees Nation and the importance of plants and marine life to their culture. While the participants demonstrated that Seaquaria could be easily integrated into the curriculum, they also identified clear barriers to doing so, which included the physical location of the seaquarium, curricular restraints, and time pressures. Another secondary school student commented on the time pressure placed on teachers and students; she shared that during elementary and middle school there had been a lot more time for random observations of the seaquarium. She recalled that in middle school *there was so much interest and you would always talk about* [the seaquarium] *when you passed it but once you get to high school you are booked.* The first student added, *We don't have enough time to just like take a few minutes and see it for ourselves, we just have to keep on studying, I wish that would be different.*

Theme 5: Fostering volunteer and employment opportunities Perhaps the most successful dialogue among the program educators, program developers, teachers, and students took place around this combined topic (seventh and eighth rated characteristics) involving volunteerism and employment opportunities. As one student commented, *I think there is a definite difference between what the students thought was important and what the adults and teachers thought was important. I think the volunteering was definitely important for us.* A program director later expressed that as an organization *we've always struggled with what to do with high schools* and offered that the dialogue surrounding inspiring volunteer and employment opportunities had *created a new kind of window* for him. He suggested that, if they looked at how Seaquaria can foster those opportunities, they could depart somewhat from feeling like they have to create a special class around the seaquarium. Central to these discussions were stories shared by students. One student explained how she *started volunteering a lot with Oceans Day and finally I got a job and I've had a job ever since, and looking back on it, it all kinda started there.* Other teachers relayed the important role that Seaquaria played in exposing students to potential career options. In fact, because of her involvement with the program, one student stated that she now *wanted to become a marine biologist.*

CASE 2: THE LEARNING ENVIRONMENT IN A SEAQUARIA CLASSROOM

Method

The research for the second case study used an action research approach involving a quantitative one group pretest-posttest methodology (Holmes, 2010). This case of one intact classroom of Grade 4 students (conducted by a classroom teacher) used a quasi-experimental design with a group of 21 students completing a learning environment instrument: the Place-based Learning and Constructivist Environment Survey (PLACES; Zandvliet, 2007). A version of this instrument was adapted for elementary classrooms and administered as a pretest and posttest to the intervention of Seaquaria in one elementary teacher's classroom.

Earlier studies utilizing the PLACES instrument (Zandvliet, 2007) observed several trends in the data:
– Student expectations around the learning environment in place-based EE settings are often higher than for other settings.
– Differences among student perceptions on most scales between preferred and actual forms of the survey for place-based EE settings are often smaller (less significant) than in other settings (students perceive these environments as more closely meeting their expectations).
– Students' perceptions of the actual environment for place-based EE settings tend to be lower than those for their preferred environment (these differences, though small, may initiate inquiry and action research on the part of individual teachers).

In this case, the participating teacher investigated the following points using an action research approach. Research questions for Case Study 2 were: How does the integrated approach to learning using the Seaquaria program affect the classroom learning environment as measured by the PLACES instrument? Will the program's hands-on activities and firsthand (direct) experiences with marine life improve the learning environment as perceived by the students in this class?

The teacher's implementation of Seaquaria for this classroom environment included small groups of students taking responsibility to observe and monitor the microecosystem of the seaquarium each day (e.g., measuring salinity, temperature, air and water flow, and recording observations of interest). Integrated lessons connected the science and social studies curricula to the seaquarium. Students in pairs or small groups created a *Seaquarium Charter of Rights and Freedoms* that integrated social studies, social responsibility, and science ideas. Weekly neighbourhood walks provided a terrestrial comparison to the marine environment. This addition provided students with more regular field opportunities to enrich their understanding of their local environment. In one activity, students created a research poster of their back-yard or marine neighbours. A culminating field trip to the beach provided an opportunity for children to share their accumulated knowledge with their parents in which the children answered many of the adults' questions.

Data Collection

The primary tool for data collection in this study was the PLACES instrument (Zandvliet, 2007) to document students' perceptions of the learning environment. "Few fields in education can boast the existence of such a rich array of validated and robust instruments which have been used in so many research applications." (Fraser, 1998, p. 8). It is from this rich array that the PLACES instrument for element-ary students was designed; there are eight scales in the Preferred and Actual forms of the instrument. Specifically, the scales measuring important attributes for environ-mental pedagogy (e.g., environmental integration or relevance) are included in the questionnaire in an effort to describe and explain associations with environments that emphasize place-based and constructivist approaches. Design of the instrument reflected participant-oriented approaches; for example, a series of focus groups over a 4-month period resulted in a consensus around eight constructs that were deemed most important to place-based and environmental educators and, therefore, included in the instrument (Zandvliet, 2007).

Data Analysis and Results

The students' responses to the PLACES questionnaire were analyzed using the SPSS program to verify the reliability of each of the 8 scales. Consistent with earlier studies, the mean responses based on the data for each scale of the preferred form of the questionnaire were rated consistently higher than responses on the actual form although in many cases the differences were small (Figure 1).

A paired-samples statistical comparison of the actual and preferred perceptions on the 8 dimensions revealed that for the scales of Relevance/Integration (RI), Critical Voice (CV), Student Negotiation (SN), Student Investigation (SI), Group Cohesive-ness (GC), Open Endedness (OE), and Environmental Interaction (EI) the ratings

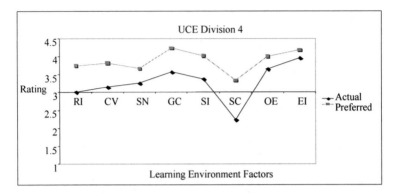

Figure 1. Student class means for scores on 8 scales on the PLACES instrument.

Note. Axis scale is drawn at 3 (neutral) for Likert scale responses.

on the preferred and actual forms indicated no statistically significant differences. This is consistent with trends in other PLACES research (Zandvliet, 2007). The exception to this trend was for the Shared Control (SC) scale where the difference was significant ($p = .003$). One interpretation for this finding is that the program's intervention might have accounted for the difference in the students' perceptions. However, since an actual form of the questionnaire was not administered prior to the investigation, it is not clear that this perception can be attributed to the program or other contextual factors in the program. For example, an actual form preintervention may have revealed a lower perception of SC than was measured postintervention. However, as presented, a comparison of preferred and actual environments shows SC as the only negatively rated aspect in this learning environment.

During the investigation, the teacher puzzled with how to balance human inquiry with children as free agents to follow their own interests and guide them in setting self-determined goals (Glassman, 2001) and with students meeting the prescribed learning outcomes. Themes in the reflective journal she kept revealed other contextual impacts on the classroom learning environment, for example, school community, student/teacher interaction factors, home/school factors, curricular and pedagogical influences. *This year ... some of the spark is missing ... a strong 'clique' of students who are interested in 'fashion' consumerism/brand recognition/socializing vs. school activities* (Reflective Journal, page 58). Perhaps the gap was too great between the expressed goals and students' experiences. Or conversely, perhaps in the push to cover material and promote a more responsive interaction with their environment, the teacher–investigator tried to move the students too far and they responded with resistance. Also, it may be that while the students say they prefer shared control, when it comes to taking on some of the responsibility to enact shared control, they are less willing. In subsequent administrations of the PLACES instrument at this school, other teachers have consistently seen SC as the lowest rated score.

Interpretation. In terms of participatory action research, the culmination of this learning environment study in a Seaquaria classroom is only the beginning of an action research agenda that is continually evolving at this school. In subsequent action research, teachers administered the preferred form of PLACES; then after the children were accustomed to daily classroom routines, they administered the actual form. A program of inquiry that examined the differences between the two forms ensued; teachers then designed various actions in terms of classroom interventions to address the perceived needs (i.e., detected differences between preferred and actual perceptions of classroom environment) of their students. Fraser (1998) made suggestions for research design using participant-oriented investigations, wherein participants use a five-step approach consisting of assessment, feedback, reflection and discussion, intervention, and reassessment.

In our subsequent studies, teachers collected other information from students' journal entries looking at quality, quantity, and engagement of writing in relation to daily entries compared to entries on days when more engaging, hands-on, experiential lessons occurred. We plan to incorporate the use of other data collection tools: teacher–researcher and student journals; photographs; tape and video recordings of highly motivational activities and discussions afterwards. We plan to measure the quality of student questioning and knowledge or scientific process skills pre- and postintervention. A wider range of data collection tools used in conjunction with the PLACES survey will serve to inform teaching practice through these enhanced and participatory forms of action research.

DISCUSSION AND CONCLUSIONS

We developed our research methodologies for the reported case studies based on an understanding that Seaquaria in Schools is both a science education program and an EE program. Within this interdisciplinary context, we sought to evaluate in part *if* and *how* the program fostered ecoliteracy through a place-based approach to curriculum and how it influenced the learning environment of students. However, our results show the program to be either a unique context for science education or, as various stakeholders identified, a vehicle for education that promoted social learning of various kinds. In many ways, the adoption of experiential EE programs helps to foster more positive learning environments for students. The interplay of these science and EE aspects are worthy of focused future investigation.

The qualitative evaluation (Case Study 1) revealed a number of strengths related to the development of ecoliteracy and ecological citizenship in Seaquaria. In particular, students gave high marks to the program with respect to the opportunity it presents for observing animals. Both students and teachers cited examples of how it fosters care of and compassion for living things. Students and teachers shared stories of how the complex environment allowed them the opportunity to begin to understand the relationships between organisms in the ecosystem and to develop their observational skills. The observation of complex marine relationships within the seaquarium was considered to have a calming effect on frustrated or angry students. Lastly, the observation and relationship opportunities provided a platform for discussion about anger and behavioural issues of at-risk students.

The community-based learning model advocated by Seaquaria ensures that both students and teachers are actively involved; this is acutely evident in the quantitative learning environments study (Case Study 2). This model of learning can potentially foster a more democratic learning environment and allow both students and teachers enhanced learning opportunities. It also has the possibility to develop positive, productive learning environments where students are more engaged in the lessons while learning other important social and developmental skills. Other learning environment studies within science education have shown positive learning environments to be predictive of student outcomes, such as attitude and cognition (Fraser, 1998). Importantly, the combination of qualitative and quantitative approaches used here— combined with the participatory approach to action research fostered by these studies—have yielded key insights into the workings of Seaquaria.

One of the greatest strengths of Seaquaria is the physical presence and ease of accessibility of the seaquarium throughout the school year and the inherent and ever-changing relationships of the organisms. However, students involved in all aspects of this research placed a clear importance on being outside the school and with having direct experiences in nature coupled with Seaquaria experiences. This may suggest that students place greater value on *place*—their outdoor contextual learning experiences—than on indoor marine education. While it is understood that one intention of the Seaquaria in Schools program is to act as a stepping-stone for such outdoor learning, we believe the conclusions of this study further support that contextual outdoor learning is essential and valued by learners. In an era of restrictive school schedules, increased liability concerns, and curriculum pressures, it is important to remember that classroom programs cannot and should not replace opportunities for true hands-on learning in the natural environment.

REFERENCES

British Columbia Ministry of Education. (2007). *Environmental learning and experience: An interdisciplinary guide and video clips for teachers.* Victoria, BC, Canada: Author.

Cohen, L., Manion, L., & Morrison, K. (2000). *Research methods in education* (5th ed.). London, England: Routledge Falmer.

Cousins, J. B., & Earl, L. M. (1995). *Participatory evaluation in education: Studies in evaluation use and organizational learning.* London, England: Falmer Press.

Fitzpatrick, J. L., Sanders, J. R., & Worthen, B. R. (2004). *Program evaluation alternative approaches and practical guidelines.* Toronto, ON, Canada: Pearson.

Fraser, B. J. (1998). Classroom environment instruments: Development, validity and applications. *Learning Environments Research, 1,* 7–34.

Glassman, M. (2001). Dewey and Vygotsky: Society, experience, and inquiry in educational practice. *Educational Researcher, 30*(4), 3–14.

Gruenewald, D. (2003). The best of both worlds: A critical pedagogy of place. *Educational Researcher, 32*(4), 3–12.

Holmes, M. (2010). *Gently down the stream: Reflections on a Seaquarium journey.* Unpublished master's thesis, University of British Columbia, Vancouver, BC, Canada.

Hussar, K., Schwartz, S., Boiselle, E., & Noam, G. G. (2008). *Towards a systematic evidence-base for science in out-of-school time: The role of assessment.* Cambridge, MA: Harvard University & McLean Hospital.

Hutchison, D. (2004). *A natural history of place in education.* New York: Teachers College Press.

Jamieson, P. (2003). Designing more effective on-campus teaching and learning spaces: A role for academic developers. *International Journal for Academic Development, 8*(1/2), 119–133.

Kemmis, S., & Wilkinson, M. (1998). Participatory action research and the study of practice. In B. Atweh, S. Kemmis, & P. Weeks (Eds.), *Action research in practice: Partnerships for social justice in education* (pp. 21–36). London, England: Routledge.

McDuff, M. D., & Jacobson, S. K. (2001). Participatory evaluation of environmental education: Stakeholder assessment of the Wildlife Clubs of Kenya. *International Journal of Geographical and Environmental Education, 10*(2), 14–35.

Oblinger, D. G. (2006). Space as a change agent. In D. G. Oblinger (Ed.), *Learning spaces* (pp. 13.1–13.11). Retrieved from http://www.educause.edu/learningspacesch1

Orr, D. W. (1992). *Ecological literacy: Education and the transition to a postmodern world.* Albany, NY: State University of New York Press.

Orr, D. W. (1994). *Earth in mind.* Washington, DC: Island Press.

Quintanilla, G., & Packard, T. (2002). A participatory evaluation of an inner-city science enrichment program. *Evaluation and Program Planning, 25*(1), 15–22.

Smith, G. A., & Williams, D. R. (1999). *Ecological education in action: On weaving education, culture and the environment.* Albany, NY: State University of New York Press.

Sobel, D. (1993). *Children's special places.* Tucson, AZ: Zephyr Press.

Sobel, D. (1996). *Beyond ecophobia: Reclaiming the heart in nature education.* Great Barrington, MA: Orion Society.

Starzner, M. (2010). *Listening to kids: Developing and inclusive evaluation process for environmental education.* Unpublished master's thesis, Royal Roads University, Victoria, British Columbia, Canada.

Strange, C., & Banning, J. (2001). *Educating by design: Creating campus environments that work.* San Francisco: Jossey-Bass.

Temple, P. (2007). Learning spaces for the 21st century: A review of the literature. *The Higher Education Academy,* 1–79.

Thomson, G., & Hoffman, J. (2003). *Measuring the success of environmental education programs.* Calgary, AB, Canada: Canadian Parks and Wilderness Society.

United States National Science Foundation. (2008). *Framework for evaluating impacts of informal science education projects.* Washington, DC: Author.

WestWind SeaLab Supplies & World Fisheries Trust. (2008). *Seaquaria in schools: An educator's guidebook and manual.* Retrieved from http://www.worldfish.org/images-pdfs/Projects/Seaquaria/Seaq%20Manual%20%2011%20Feb.pdf

Woodhouse, J. L., & Knapp, C. E. (2000). *Place-based curriculum and instruction: Outdoor and environmental education approaches.* Retrieved from ERIC database. (ED448012)

Zandvliet, D. B. (2007, November). *Learning environments for environmental education.* Paper presented at the annual meeting of the Australian Association for Research in Education, Fremantle, Australia.

David B. Zandvliet
Faculty of Education
Simon Fraser University
Burnaby, British Columbia, Canada

Mary Holmes
Pacific Heights Elementary School
Surrey School District
Surrey, British Columbia, Canada

Matthias Starzner
Royal Roads University
Victoria, British Columbia, Canada

SARAH CARRUTHERS, TODD M. MILFORD, YVONNE COADY,
CELINA GIBBS, KATHERINE GUNION AND ULRIKE STEGE

6. TEACHING PROBLEM SOLVING AND COMPUTER SCIENCE IN THE SCHOOLS

Concepts and Assessment

Computer science is no more about computers than astronomy is about telescopes. (Dijkstra, n.d.)

Computer Science Education (CSEd) is a young field that is comprised of numerous established disciplines, such as science, mathematics, education, and psychology. Fincher and Petre (2004) in their seminal text on CSEd suggested that moving the discipline toward independence would require that researchers ask questions that may only be answered through computer science. Because of CSEd's relative youth, it is common for researchers in this problem space to look to other disciplines for theory to help answer research questions. This chapter outlines pilot studies that exposed middle school students (11 to 13-year-olds) to a series of new and unique hands-on curricula associated with numerous fundamental concepts in Computer Science (CS). We hypothesized that through experiences for youth with activities such as those outlined here the number of students who understand the concepts covered and who might potentially pursue CS in postsecondary education will increase. In this chapter, the curriculum, classroom experiences, preliminary (largely descriptive and qualitative) results, and next steps in our research are discussed.

The importance of attracting students to the discipline of CS is well recognized (Carter, 2006; Flakener, Sooriamurthi, & Michalewicz, 2010; Klein, 2006; Slonim, Scully, & McAllister, 2008; Zweben, 2008). There is a severe shortage of individuals pursuing CS at the postsecondary level—the essential pipeline issue. Since the CS industry's peak around 2000–2001, CS departments in universities and colleges across Canada have experienced declining enrolment (Slonim et al., 2008). At the same time, CS graduates have emerged into a job market with a higher projected demand level than the average in other areas (1.9% vs. 0.7%) and a higher percentage making above \$50,000 annually compared to other occupations (52% vs. 31.1%; Service Canada, 2011).

While it appears that this trend of declining enrolment may be reversing in the USA, the same is not yet certain in Canada (Zweben, 2008). However, there continues to be concern with enrolment in CS at the postsecondary level. Thus, attracting more students to the CS discipline will potentially improve enrolment and retention in postsecondary CS programs and increase the number of graduates and will more

L. D. Yore et al (Eds.), Pacific CRYSTAL Centre for Science, Mathematics, and Technology Literacy: Lessons Learned, 99–112.

closely match industry's needs. It is hypothesized that this enrolment concern is the result of a perception of a decreased number of jobs in the industry, inaccurate perceptions of what computer scientists do, and general unfamiliarity with the content of the discipline (Carter, 2006; Klein, 2006). However, Flakener et al. (2010) take this idea further to suggest that this is even more serious as "today's marketplace needs more skilled graduates capable of solving real problems of innovation in a changing environment" (p. 20). What they believe is missing from the majority of CS curricula is a focus on developing problem-solving skills. To address this concern, we have focused our research interests on the teaching of problem-solving skills.

There are many approaches to addressing the pipeline issue and to improving enrolment and retention in CS programs, including informing students about CS and better preparing students before they enter undergraduate programs (Slonim et al., 2008). This solution would address both the pipeline issue and the mainline issue of seeking to improve citizens' general CS understanding (Yore, Chapter 2 this book). Various strategies for improving elementary, middle, and secondary school CS education are suggested, including supporting CS teacher education and improving curriculum by better defining what constitutes the CS knowledge base (Goode, 2008). While these efforts are laudable, elementary mathematics and science curricula should also be examined to identify where elements of CS can be infused to support these subjects before secondary school, a seemingly appropriate strategy for this highly interdisciplinary area. As in all fields, we should constantly reflect upon and re-evaluate what we are teaching. By strengthening the foundation of CSEd, we will have a more educated student body around the fundamental CS concepts as well as one that better understands how CS fits into society (i.e., an understanding of what computer scientists do).

ELEMENTARY SCHOOL COMPUTER SCIENCE

The question is whether or not CS should be taught in elementary schools. The current prescribed elementary school curriculum is overcrowded and continues to expand with requests to add new disciplines (e.g., environmental education, engineering design, etc.; see Yore, Chapter 2 this book) while instructional time in the school year is not increasing. At the 2010 Western Canadian Conference on Computer Science Education in Kelowna, British Columbia (BC), critics of the introduction of CSEd in elementary classrooms pointed out that, while students today ride in automobiles, they are not taught automotive mechanics in elementary classrooms and, therefore, being surrounded by computational devices, computers, and other information communication technologies does not imply that they need to be taught CS. However, while the elementary science curriculum in Canada does not contain automotive mechanics, it does include units in physics and chemistry—the fundamental sciences that allow us to understand how and why automobiles work. Similarly, elementary students ought to be able to learn some foundational elements of how and why computers work as well as the use of CS to facilitate problem solving. Carruthers (2010a) noted that most youth currently use technological devices on a daily, if not hourly, basis; communication via cell phones or instant messenger programs on laptops and desktops are examples. Internet access via mobile devices is on the rise, and mobile phone use is overtaking traditional phone networks worldwide. These changes in technology use happen rapidly and have implications for personal privacy protection (e.g., Facebook[C]). Basic CSEd, integrated into today's curriculum, can be the basis for understanding how these technologies work, how this may be possible (Carruthers, 2010b; Romanow, Stege, Agah St. Pierre, & Ross, 2008).

Perhaps even more important, CSEd has broad benefits. Beyond being simply an intellectual pursuit, CSEd teaches problem solving, supports and connects to other sciences and disciplines, can be engaging for different types of learners, and can lead to many career paths other than software developers or designers. *A Model Curriculum for K–12 Computer Science* (United States Computer Science Teachers Association [CSTA], 2006) stated that, "Professionals in every discipline—from art and entertainment, to communications and health care, to factory workers, small business owners, and retail store staff—need to understand computing to be globally competitive in their fields." (p. 11). Giving young students an understanding of basic CS and nurturing an interest in the field is beneficial not only for students who go on to pursue a major or career in CS (pipeline goal) but also for all students (mainline citizenship goal). Further, "Basic computer science education can provide world citizens with the tools and knowledge necessary to make informed decisions about how to use technology, and how to share information" (Carruthers, 2010a, p. 7).

THREE CORE CONCEPTS IN COMPUTER SCIENCE

For each of the three studies detailed below, we selected a CS core concept: concurrency, recursion, and graph theory. These concepts are in line with those identified as required in the model K–12 CS curriculum (CSTA, 2006). Each concept plays an important role in basic problem solving and, once learned, enriches students' general problem-solving skill set. Further, all play an important role in algorithm development and programming. These studies are presented in the order in which they were conceptualized and conducted. The collaboration between Computer Science and Education was established midway through both the concurrency and recursion studies and was only fully involved in all aspects of design, implementation, and analysis of the graph theory study. This increased collaboration will be reflected as the reader moves through the studies; we are excited about the future possibilities this collaboration holds.

Our approach to presenting the CS concepts in the three studies is decidedly constructivist (Yore & Van der Flier-Keller, Chapter 1 this book). We accepted the idea of constructivism in our program design that views individuals as actively involved in constructing knowledge for themselves (Schunk, 2000). The core concept of constructivism is that knowledge is built by learners rather than simply transmitted among persons. In Education, there is increasing understanding and acceptance of the value in students working together to construct meaning about subject matter, resulting in student groups constructing more complex understanding of a topic than any single student could do alone (Ormond, Saklofske, Schwean, Harrison, & Andrews, 2006). In all activities, the students were provided with materials with which they could become actively engaged through manipulation and social interaction. Some of the ways we sought to aid students to construct their knowledge base was through experimenting with challenging activities, negotiating in small groups, encouraging the presentation of individual and group ideas to others, and emphasizing conceptual understanding by focusing on a few core topics then exploring them in detail. We did this by using authentic activities and resources, promoting dialogue with peers in the sessions, and creating a community of learners to aid in learning.

METHOD

We used a lesson study design to explore and improve the teaching and instructional resources (Bell, Witten, Fellows, Adams, & McKenzie, 2006). The lessons focused on an important CS concept related to problem solving that did not necessarily require computer technologies. The preliminary lessons were taught to a target group or intact class of elementary school students. Observations and field notes of the instruction, students' actions, and outcomes were used to document the initial teaching and learning. These data were interpreted to make inferences about lesson effectiveness and improvements needed regarding the students' actions, understanding, and use of the CS concepts. Lessons were modified to address the strengths and weaknesses identified in the first cycle of lesson study. However, in this chapter, we report only the preliminary lesson design and study results.

Lesson Study 1: Concurrency

Concurrency may be best described as acting together either as events, circumstances, or agents. In CS, concurrency describes a property of systems: several computations executed simultaneously while potentially interacting with each other. These computations may happen on the same processor or on separate processors. Concurrency has achieved more importance with the arrival of a new era of programming where developers must consider the subtleties of concurrency inherent in modern many-core architectures. This calls for a revamp of the area, ranging from fundamental pedagogical processes to software development tools. An observed problem with teaching, learning, and using concurrency is that corresponding real-world scenarios, commonly leveraged in pedagogical practices, contain implicit relationships that are difficult to explicitly anticipate in complex code-bases. In our study on the concept of concurrency, we observed students' abilities to come up with both valid and creative solutions to the assigned problems addressing these issues. We highlight three activities and various students' solution approaches to investigate ways to introduce key concepts to Grade 7 students (Gunion, 2009).

All three activities used real-world scenarios or a storyline style approach. The first activity, the dishwashing scenario, is about two people washing a set of dishes: a stack of dirty dishes needs to be cleaned, dried, and put away. The second activity, the movie ticket scenario, involves two people and two ticket queues: two friends wishing to purchase nonrefundable tickets for a popular movie at a theatre with two long queues. The movie theatre has two cashiers—each positioned in such a way that people in the two different queues cannot see each other. The movie has begun and the students need to decide if they will split up to try to buy tickets. The third activity, the dining philosophers' scenario, is an altered version of the classic pedagogical, concurrency scenario of the dining philosophers: here, five knights are sitting at a round table with a single fork between each two neighbours. Each knight requires the acquisition of two forks in order to eat. Students were asked to come up with solutions to manage the forks shared between the knights.

Each scenario allows a range of concurrency to be introduced within the possible solutions for completing the activity. While different strategies for solving the problem(s) introduce different levels of complexity in executing a solution, the core activity remained the same. We refer to the general notion of tasks associated with each activity as *computation*. With the introduction of multiple students participating in each activity, some level of *communication* between individuals was required while solving the activities' problem. The following subsections indicate the ways in which computation tasks and communication play out within the solution space defined by the students for each scenario. We studied the two core concepts of communication and computation individually as well as their interaction, *concept overlap*. Further, we discuss some of the associated consequences encountered when concurrency is introduced.

Scenario 1: Dishwashing.   Although the students proposed a variety of solutions for distributing the work, the core task remained the same with differing communication levels in each case.

Computation   The subtasks of washing a dish, drying a dish, and putting a dish away—for all of the dishes in the stack—were immediately identified by all students as core elements of computation. All of these subtasks can be considered small, distinct pieces of computation that combine to make up the larger complete task.

Communication   The exact communication between participants in this scenario is solution-dependent. In general, students identified a visual communication mechanism that would occur between participants as one person handing off a dish to the next person. While the concrete hand-off point varied, the idea that one person must complete a portion of the task before the next person can receive that dish prescribed a partial ordering of the subtasks.

Concept overlap   Although students seemed to immediately recognize elements of computation and distinguish them from elements of the communication process, both concepts are tightly coupled; namely, the act of completing one computation is a form of communication to a partner.

Scenario 2: Movie Tickets.   This scenario is a slightly concocted problem in which communication is limited by lack of visual contact between the queues. Students had to come up with solutions that involved sticking together or splitting up while considering the consequences of each.

Computation The computation in this scenario is simply the act of purchasing a ticket. Depending on the solution, multiple tickets can be bought by one person or a single ticket by each person.

Communication Communication was necessary in cases where students decided the quickest way to get tickets was to split up. They soon realized the associated consequence of possibly buying too many tickets. This required them to consider creative ways to communicate beyond subtle visual cues.

Concept overlap The overlap between computation and communication in this scenario is solution-dependent. In the case of students using two ticket queues, computation can be performed at the two ticket booths but this introduces the need for communication. In the case of the students staying together in one queue, communication is not necessary; however, the concurrency is sacrificed.

Scenario 3: Dining Philosophers. The students discussed whether a time exists when every knight can eat to avoid starvation. At any one time, a knight either eats—requiring access to the forks on their left and right at the same time—or thinks.

Computation The tasks are the actions of eating and thinking—although attempting to acquire a fork is arguably a subtask as well. However, this task is considered a second priority task.

Communication Communication is aided by the visual cue of a fork being available for use by a knight wishing to transition from thinking to eating. This communication of one participant attempting to acquire a fork from two adjacent participants is required to allow a knight to eat.

Concept overlap Similar to the dishwashing scenario, visual cues (e.g., an adjacent knight releasing or acquiring a resource) prescribed an ordering such that the end of one subtask could trigger the beginning of another although this was not a precondition for the subtask. Students encountered classic CS concurrency issues (e.g., race conditions, deadlock, starvation, etc.) through role playing and devised multiple strategies for managing the shared resource to facilitate each participant's ability to eat. Each strategy required some form of communication between participants based on the computation (e.g., eating, thinking) patterns.

The three pedagogical activities in Lesson Study 1 helped identify common ways in which these students thought about problems associated with concurrency. In each case, students immediately identified tasks or subtasks and coupled them with the often implicit communication mechanisms, including visual cues.

Lesson Study 2: Recursion

Recursion (Goodrich & Tamassia, 2002; Grimaldi, 1998) is a mathematical concept as well as a CS programming construct that can serve as a problem-solving strategy.

It is a method commonly used to approach and solve numerous problems (e.g., searching and sorting tasks) and consists of defining functions where the function being defined is called within its own definition until a stop condition (i.e., base case) is met. Recursion is observed in the built and natural worlds (Briggs, 1992); for example, virtual advertisements such as the Borax Soap Box (http://piscines-apollo.com/images/borax_box.jpg), a picture within a picture often referred to as the Droste effect. This common occurrence of recursion within day-to-day experiences of many people, including the middle school students in this study, adds to the appeal, relevance, and application of the concept.

Because of its ubiquity and usefulness, recursion is usually taught in its most basic form in the first 2 years of programming (Hsin, 2008). When and how to teach recursion has long been a topic of debate within CS because it is both central in the discipline and thought to be difficult to learn and comprehend (Haberman & Averbuch, 2002). Once recursion is understood, it may be applied to many traditional CS problems. There is a rich literature base documenting efforts to improve the teaching of recursion at the elementary CS level. Some CSEd researchers have suggested that (a) expanding the instructional approach toward a nontraditional, more active and inclusive one would be worthwhile and (b) providing outreach activities beyond university classes would have the added benefit of appealing to nontraditional and underrepresented populations in CS (Ford, 1982; Goode, 2008). This approach to instruction guided our lesson study.

We conducted a pilot study with students in an after-school program (SPARCS, http://outreach.cs.uvic.ca/) that sought information on an appropriate and successful set of engaging hands-on lessons in recursion for a small (n = 9) group of Grades 6–8 students aged 11 to 13 years (Gunion, 2009; Gunion, Milford, & Stege, 2009a, 2009b). We focused on three basic types of recursion: head recursion, tail recursion, and divide and conquer. The activities designed to teach recursion investigated a combination of kinaesthetic learning and programming activities. These activities were similar to those used by Bell et al. (2006) and involved hands-on, problem-solving, group activities focused on CS basics without the direct use of technology, called *unplugged*. A series of weekly unplugged activities was developed to convey the mental models needed, building upon topics that were covered in the previous weeks. Each lesson attempted to explore at least one of the main questions: Can students (a) recognize recursion, (b) understand recursion, and (c) develop a more positive attitude toward CS and recursion? Furthermore, students were asked to solve programming activities in the LOGO-based language (MicroWorlds EX, 2010) to deepen and apply their understanding of recursion in a programming context.

Using a variety of data collection tools (i.e., clickers, written answers, video and audio recordings), the pilot study results found middle school students increasing their recognition of recursion and enjoyment of these activities and, in some cases, their ability to problem solve with recursion improved. We were able to show on this small scale that exposing these students, long before they find themselves in first year university CS, may ease the challenge that both students and instructors face when covering this topic. Furthermore, after being introduced to similar concepts in ways that foster enjoyment and interest, we may find more and better suited undergraduates studying CS at university—an outcome that would benefit the students, the university, and society.

Lesson Study 3: Graph Theory

One important area based in theoretical CS is graph theory. Graphs—not to be confused with the more commonly known bar or line graphs—are a mathematical construct that can be used to model relationships and connections. A graph is a set of vertices and a set of edges. Vertices (typically indicated by a dot or circle) can be connected by edges (represented by lines) to indicate a relationship or connection between them. An evolutionary tree is an example of a graph, where species are represented by vertices and evolutionary connections are represented by edges. Another example is a road map, where roads connect cities and towns (see Carruthers, 2010c, for more examples).

Graph theory has its origins in the historical Seven Bridges of Königsberg Problem proposed by Leonard Euler in 1735. Parts of the city of Königsberg (including two islands) are divided by a river and connected by seven bridges (Figure 1 left). The question posed is: Is there a way to walk through the city and cross every bridge only once? This problem can be modeled as a graph with the distinct land masses (the two islands and the mainland on either side of the river) represented by vertices and the bridges as edges (Figure 1 right).

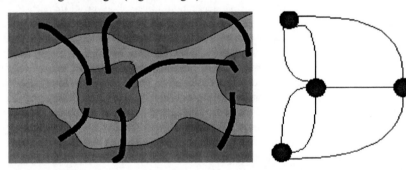

*Figure 1. Euler's problem of the seven bridges of Königsberg
and a graph model of same (Carruthers, 2010a).*

Graph theory investigates properties of graphs such as paths, cycles, topology, and connectivity. Graphs are used to represent data structures in computer programs. For example, file systems that navigate and search for files on a computer are often modeled as a graph, where files and folders are represented by vertices and edges indicate the hierarchy or an *is in* relationship—a file is in a folder that in turn is in another folder. Findings in theoretical CS lead to better, more efficient methods for accessing and manipulating files and folders in these file systems. This connection between data structures and graph theory is important and is an example of one of the many ways in which a sound understanding of theoretical CS can lead to better programmers and more user-friendly computer programs. Like many other areas of theoretical CS, graph theory has connections to other disciplines including biology (modelling habitat and migration patterns) and sociology (analysis of social networks). Using graph theory in problem solving is particularly important. Relational graphs provide a means to distil a problem, highlighting only the relevant information. Extracting relevant data from a problem is fundamental to successful problem solving.

In a recent pilot study investigating the impact of graph theory instruction in Grade 6 mathematics classes, students were taught the basics of graph theory, including how to correctly construct a graph, and how to abstract a problem to a graph representation (Carruthers, 2010a; Carruthers, Milford, Pelton, & Stege, 2010). Participants learned the basics of graph theory and, on certain types of problems, to adopt graphs as a problem-solving strategy. Additionally, for some students, there was a positive association between the use of graphs in solving problems and the correctness of these solutions. Once students learn to apply graphs to represent the information in problems, they can potentially learn to apply algorithms to solve problems.

DISCUSSION

Reflections across the three lesson studies revealed limitations and concerns, informed our research approach, and identified future research questions and studies. The following sections will address these reflections.

Limitations and Concerns

We have been able to draw a few ongoing lessons from these early explorations into interdisciplinary collaboration. For example, when working with teachers and students in actual classrooms, the attrition rate is much larger than anticipated, which likely stems from demands on teachers' time and the overcrowded school day. The addition of other researchers to assist in the classroom would eliminate some of the factors that lowered the overall numbers. Further, research ethics requirements have increased the demands on researchers and may have negative effects on students and parents being willing to participate in research studies. Clearly, classroom-based research requires collaboration and trust amongst researchers, teachers, students, and parents (Anthony et al., 2009). We believe that to broaden these interdisciplinary collaborations from Education and Computer Science into other areas (e.g., psychology and applied statistics) may prove fruitful and improve the validity of this research.

Computer Science Education

An understanding of technology, the role it plays in society, and how to use it responsibly are important components of education today. In addition to supporting learning in general, CS students learn a number of important skills, including problem solving, algorithmic thinking, and logical reasoning (CSTA, 2006). The integration of CS topics into mathematics classes has the potential to support a number of processes; for example, visual abstractions common in computer science can support the communication process; logical reasoning is a fundamental component of the reasoning process; and problem solving, an integral CS skill, is fundamental to many aspects of learning. CS is a broad subject, comprised of many different specialized areas of study; a key step in evaluating its teachability in elementary classrooms is determining appropriate CS topics. Niman (1975) identified graph theory as a potential topic for elementary school instruction due to its versatility in visually representing ideas and its application to puzzles.

Just as important as an understanding of technology is ensuring that future CSEd research has a sound theoretical and practical foundation. If existing publications are indicative of the current state of CSEd research, then researchers in this area should select studies upon which to base their work with caution. Randolph, Julnes, Sulinen, and Lehman (2008) noted a number of shortcomings and flaws found in CSEd research publications, including flaws in reporting the elements recommended by the American Psychological Association, problems with sampling of participants and self-selection, and a lack of validity and reliability of measures. They also noted that many of the studies analyzed used research designs that suffer from weak internal validity.

With this constructive criticism in mind, our research group chose a collaborative approach in designing and deploying research studies. We addressed some of these concerns about individual studies by a planned research agenda that evolves from individual lesson studies that explore appropriateness, to sequential lesson studies that develop valid and reliable measures and documentation procedures, and further to experimental designs that investigate cause–effect relationships using proper inter- pretation techniques for the data. Recognizing that as computer scientists we are not experts in the field of human research, we have made connections and found collaborators in the field of education research. Equally important, we keep in mind that human research studies almost invariably fail to conform exactly to theoretical plans (i.e., working within the educational system with students and teachers can prove 'messy'). Faced with improperly implemented testing procedures and partici- pant attrition, researchers ought to be flexible and need to be adaptable. Ultimately, just because a study deviated from the intended design, this does not mean that no valuable information can result.

As an example of this approach, we cite our recent study on the impact of graph theory instruction in Grade 6 mathematics classes (Carruthers, 2010a). We chose to use a contingency table analysis for the nominal and ordinal data (i.e., the quality of a graph drawn by participants in the experimental groups to which they were assigned). While perhaps less well known than analysis techniques for continuous (i.e., ratio or interval) data, contingency table analysis can be a useful way to investi- gate possible associations between variables (e.g., whether or not a graph was drawn pre- and postintervention) as well as associations between an intervention or outside influence and variables. Categorical data are quite common in educational research and these data can be either ordinal or nominal, with each type requiring different analysis techniques.

For our study, the resulting data were ordinal in nature; that is, there was a sense of order to the values for the type of picture that participants drew as part of their solution to the problems: 0 for no picture, 1 for a nongraph picture, and 2 for a graph (vertices and edges). As the intervention taught how to use graphs to solve problems, drawing a graph was considered better than a nongraph picture that in turn was better than no picture at all. We were interested in whether or not there might be a higher incidence of the use of graphs following graph theory instruction. This type of association can be evaluated using McNemar's test of association (Elliot & Woodward, 2007). Since we are essentially measuring two separate readings of the same characteristic, it is expected that the measurements would be similar to some extent; therefore, it is not necessarily meaningful to determine if the variables are independent. However, if there is an outside force that might influence one measurement more than the other (in this case, an intervention), then there might be a shift in the counts. The McNemar test of association can indicate whether the observed shift is significantly different from the probability of no association.

This analysis technique usually requires minimum cell counts of 5; unfortunately, our small data set ($N = 9$) rendered it unusable. Reduced participation rates, particularly in the control groups (those not engaged in the intervention lessons on graph theory), combined with improperly administered posttests resulted in descriptive data tables with much reduced cell counts in the final data. In some cases, data sets were limited to less than 10 data points total; so it was impossible to expect a minimum cell count of 5 in a 2x2 or 3x3 matrix, which precluded the intended statistical analysis techniques. This meant that high or low p-values associated with the measures were suspect and no measure of significance could be given. Significance indicates the probability of test statistics occurring by chance. Normally, a significance value greater than .05 would suggest rejection of the experimental hypothesis; however, this does not mean that the null hypothesis is true. The null hypothesis is one of no effect; however, all a nonsignificant result indicates is that the effect is not big enough to be anything other than a chance finding—it does not indicate that the effect is zero. Cohen (1990) pointed out that a nonsignificant result should never be—despite that it often is—interpreted as no relationship between variables.

Rather than being deterred by the fact that we were unable to claim significance, we chose instead to treat the results as exploratory in nature. Trends and patterns that emerged from the data, while not necessarily significant, could still be indicative of a possible effect and hint at places that may be worthy of further investigation. What is essential is to carefully account for and report any deviations from the intended research methodology and analysis procedures. Readers of research studies need to be informed of the reasons for post hoc changes in analysis or methodology, and future studies should be able to learn from the mistakes of others in order to improve practices and refine research designs. We believe that adherence to these practices by both ourselves and other researchers in the field will contribute to addressing concerns around internal validity.

Future Research

It is widely assumed that collaboration in research is desirable and that it should be encouraged (Katz & Martin, 1997). Canada, through its Natural Sciences and Engineering Research Council, has demonstrated interest in the notion of research collaboration via Pacific CRYSTAL, of which all the contributors to this book are a part. Katz and Martin (1997) identified several factors that motivate collaboration: funding agencies' need to save money, the growing availability and falling (real) cost of transport and communication, the desire for intellectual interactions with other scientists, the need for a division of labour in more specialized or capital-intensive areas of science, the requirements of interdisciplinary research, and govern-ment encouragement of international and cross-sectoral collaboration. Many of these reasons motivated our research through Pacific CRYSTAL in general and the Education/Computer Science collaboration specifically.

Educational research can be generally defined as the formal, systematic application of the appropriate scientific method (i.e., quantitative, qualitative, mixed method) to the study of educational problems. Educational research findings are important because they shape and influence teacher education programs and help define the intellectual context within which all involved in education work. However, there is criticism of the quality of research in the field (i.e., its partisan nature, methodo-logical shortcomings, nonempirical approaches, 'great thinkers' adulation, and lack of relevance to practice, policy, or theoretical approaches) serious enough to raise both concerns and misgivings (Tooley & Darby, 1998). A major advantage to our collabo-ration across disciplines is that some, if not all, of these concerns and misgivings have been addressed.

With the three pilot studies reported in this chapter, we have restarted an investiga-tion on the possibility of teaching basic CS concepts earlier in students' schooling. Our future research plans include expanding on the studies to test the preliminary but promising findings for the three concepts as well as increasing the list of core concepts and problem-solving techniques applicable to elementary, middle, and secondary school students. Besides understanding what concept or technique can be taught in which grade and at what level, we are interested in long-term consequences of CSEd; that is, does teaching CS concepts early address the mainline goal for citizens and the pipeline goal of CS students and careers? What is the best time to start with CSEd and at what level? Does CSEd improve students' decision making regarding career choices? Does CSEd improve the quality of CS students? Does CSEd increase the number of CS students in postsecondary institutions to a level that satisfies the supply–demand ratio? Does CSEd improve general problem-solving capabilities? Does CSEd ensure more responsible use of social networking tools on the Internet?

Of course, the path to understanding the long-term consequences is not easy. How can we best realize the teaching of CSEd in K–12? We believe that an inter-disciplinary and cross-disciplinary approach is the most promising and is possible in a rather seamless way. CS activities include many prescribed learning outcomes from K–12 curricula (see a discussion on this topic by Romanow et al., 2008, for BC) from basically all disciplines. Many activities, if prepared carefully, are easily approachable (a great example is the ongoing *Computer Science Unplugged* by Bell et al., 2006) not just for the students but also for the CS-inexperienced teacher. Commitment from governments and school districts for including CSEd as a priority into curricula could make this possible (see BC's environmental education guide, http://www.bced.gov.bc.ca/environment_ed/). We believe that a better education in CS in K–12 does not just educate better citizens (mainline goal) and increase the number of students in CS programs at universities and colleges—we believe it will attract a student population better suited to the discipline (pipeline goal).

REFERENCES

Anthony, R. J., Yore, L. D., Coll, R. K., Dillon, J., Chiu, M.-H., Fakudze, C., et al. (2009). Research ethics boards and gold standard(s) in literacy and science education research. In M. C. Shelley II, L. D. Yore, & B. Hand (Eds.), *Quality research in literacy and science education: International perspectives and gold standards* (pp. 511–557). Dordrecht, The Netherlands: Springer.

Bell, T., Witten, I. H., Fellows, M., Adams, R., & McKenzie, J. (2006). *Computer science unplugged. An enrichment and extension programme for primary-aged children* (teacher ed.). Retrieved from http://www.csunplugged.org/

Briggs, J. (1992). *Fractals: The patterns of chaos.* New York: Touchstone.

Carruthers, S. (2010a). *Grasping graphs.* Master's thesis, University of Victoria. Retrieved from http://hdl.handle.net/1828/3193

Carruthers, S. (2010b). *An interdisciplinary guide for K–8 computer science (CS) education* [Poster]. Presented at the 41st ACM Technical Symposium on Computer Science Education (SIGCSE'10), Milwaukee, WI, USA.

Carruthers, S. (2010c). *Relational graphs: What are they?* [DVD]. Presented at the 41st ACM Technical Symposium on Computer Science Education (SIGCSE'10), Milwaukee, WI, USA.

Carruthers, S., Milford, T. M., Pelton, T. W., & Stege, U. (2010). Moving K–7 computer science instruction into the information age. In *Proceedings of the 15th Western Canadian Conference for Computing Education (WCCCE'10)* (pp. 1–5).

Carter, L. (2006). Why students with an apparent aptitude for computer science don't choose to major in computer science. In *Proceedings of the 37th SIGCSE Technical Symposium on Computer Science Education (SIGCSE'06)* (pp. 27–31).

Cohen, J. (1990). Things I have learned (so far). *American Psychologist, 45*(12), 1304–1321.

Dijkstra, E. W. (n.d.). Retrieved from Wikipedia, the Free Encyclopedia: http://en.wikipedia.org/wiki/Edsger_W._Dijkstra

Elliot, A. C., & Woodward, W. A. (2007). *Statistical analysis quick reference guide with SPSS examples.* Thousand Oaks, CA: Sage.

Fincher, S., & Petre, M. (2004). *Computer science education research.* London, England: Routledge Falmer.

Flakener, N., Sooriamurthi, R., & Michalewicz, Z. (2010). Puzzle based learning for engineering and computer science. *IEEE Computer Society, 43*(4), 20–28.

Ford, G. (1982). A framework for teaching recursion. *SIGCSE Bulletin, 14*(2), 32–39.

Goode, J. (2008). Increasing diversity in K–12 computer science: Strategies from the field. In *Proceedings of the 39th SIGCSE Technical Symposium on Computer Science Education (SIGCSE'08)* (pp. 362–366).

Goodrich, M. T., & Tamassia, R. (2002). *Algorithm design: Foundations, analysis and internet examples.* New York: Wiley.

Grimaldi, R. P. (1998). *Discrete mathematics* (4th ed.). Reading, MA: Addison-Wesley.

Gunion, K. (2009). *FUNdamentals of CS: Designing and evaluating computer science activities for kids.* Master's thesis, University of Victoria. Retrieved from http://hdl.handle.net/1828/2750

Gunion, K., Milford, T. M., & Stege, U. (2009a). Curing recursion aversion. In *Proceedings of the 14th ACM SIGCSE Conference on Innovation and Technology in Computer Science Education (ItiCSE'09)* (pp. 124–128).

Gunion, K., Milford, T. M., & Stege, U. (2009b). The paradigm recursion. *Journal of Problem Solving, 2*(2), 142–172.

Haberman, B., & Averbuch, H. (2002). The case of base cases: Why are they so difficult to recognize? Student difficulties with recursion. *SIGCSE Bulletin, 34*(3), 84–88.

Hsin, W. (2008). Teaching recursion using recursion graphs. *Journal of Computing Sciences in Colleges, 23*(4), 217–222.

Katz, J. S., & Martin, B. R. (1997). What is research collaboration? *Research Policy, 26*(1), 1–18.

Klein, A. (2006). K–12 education shrinking future college graduate population in computer studies. *Journal of Computing Sciences in Colleges, 21*(4), 32–34.

MicroWorlds EX [Computer software]. (2010). Retrieved from http://www.microworlds.com/solutions/mwex.html

Niman, J. (1975). Graph theory in the elementary school. *Educational Studies in Mathematics, 6*(2), 351–373.

Ormond, J. E., Saklofske, D. H., Schwean, V. L., Harrison, G. L., & Andrews, J. J. W. (2006). *Principles of educational psychology* (2nd Canadian ed.). Toronto, ON, Canada: Pearson Education.

Randolph, J., Julnes, G., Sulinen, E., & Lehman S. (2008). A methodological review of computer science education research. *Journal of Information Technology Education, 7*(1), 135–162.

Romanow, H., Stege, U., Agah St Pierre, A., & Ross, L. (2008). *Increasing accessibility: Teaching children important computer science concepts without sacrificing conventional subjects of study.* Presented at the 13th Western Canadian Conference on Computing Education (WCCCE'08). Retrieved from http://outreach.cs.uvic.ca/2008WCCCE.pdf

Schunk, D. H. (2000). *Learning theories: An educational perspective* (3rd ed.). Upper Saddle River, NJ: Merrill.

Service Canada. (2011). *Computer programmers and interactive media developers.* Retrieved from http://www.servicecanada.gc.ca/eng/qc/job_futures/statistics/2174.shtml

Slonim, J., Scully, S., & McAllister, M. (2008). Crossroads for Canadian CS enrollment: What should be done to reverse falling CS enrollment in the Canadian education system? *Communications of the ACM, 51*(10), 66–70.

Tooley, J., & Darby, D. (1998). *Educational research - A critique.* London, England: Office for Standards in Education. Retrieved from http://www.ofsted.gov.uk/Ofsted-home/Publications-and-research/Browse-all-by/Education/Leadership/Governance/Educational-research-a-critique-the-Tooley-report

United States Computer Science Teachers Association. (2006). *A model curriculum for K–12 computer science: Final report of the ACM task force curriculum committee* (2nd ed.). New York: Author.

Zweben, S. (2008). *Computing degree and enrolment trends from the 2007–2008 CRA Taulbee Survey: Undergraduate enrolment in computer science trends higher; doctoral production continues at peak levels.* Washington, DC: Computing Research Association. Retrieved from http://archive.cra.org/taulbee/CRATaulbeeReport-StudentEnrollment-07-08.pdf

Sarah Carruthers, Yvonne Coady, Celina Gibbs, Katherine Gunion and Ulrike Stege
Department of Computer Science

Todd M. Milford
Department of Educational Psychology
University of Victoria
Victoria, British Columbia, Canada

LESLEE FRANCIS PELTON AND TIMOTHY W. PELTON

7. OUTREACH WORKSHOPS, APPLICATIONS, AND RESOURCES

Helping Teachers to Climb Over the Science, Mathematics, and Technology Threshold by Engaging their Classes

Many elementary and middle school teachers' confidence and competence with respect to science, mathematics, and technology (SMT) topics and effective information communication technology (ICT) use in support of student learning is limited. This is often an echo of sparse opportunities to experience authentic, meaningful, SMT-related activities and effective technology use in their own educational experiences (K–university). In the Pacific CRYSTAL Project, technology, which emphasizes design to adapt the environment to address or alleviate problems, is taken to include engineering and computer science (see Yore, Chapter 2 this book). Negative attitudes and anxiety toward SMT topics affect the way teachers view their abilities in mathematics and science and influence the choices they make as teachers (Ellsworth & Buss, 2000; Hancock & Gallard, 2004; Plourde, 2002; Tobin, Tippins, & Gallard, 1994). Thus, the issue of how to alter teachers' beliefs and attitudes toward science and mathematics is of considerable interest (Plourde, 2002). We believe that this limited confidence results in the underrepresentation of these topics and tools in the classroom and the avoidance of problem-based learning (PBL) activities.

BACKGROUND

A recent survey of professionals from groups traditionally underrepresented in SMT-related careers (i.e., female and minority chemists and chemical engineers) identified factors influencing their career choice (Bayer Corporation, 2010). Those responding to the survey reported that their science teachers played a larger role than parents and others in inspiring their interest in science—70% at the elementary level and 88% at the high school level, compared to 46–54% for parents. These SMT professionals reported that an inspiring or dedicated teacher was a significant positive factor in encouraging them to pursue a career in a SMT-related field. This is a particular concern as many elementary and middle school teachers come from groups identified as underrepresented in the SMT areas. Their lack of experience and comfort teaching SMT topics reduces the likelihood they will be the catalyst in motivating students to pursue further SMT-related studies. Advice that survey respondents offered to precollegiate teachers to foster SMT studies included

L. D. Yore et al (Eds.), Pacific CRYSTAL Centre for Science, Mathematics, and Technology Literacy: Lessons Learned, 113–129.

encouraging and supporting an interest in and passion for science, offering more hands-on science experiences to students, teaching without bias, and ensuring their own proficiency in science and science education.

Current international standards in both science and mathematics promote constructivist learning environments that allow students to explore these topics through authentic contexts and relevant problem-based activities (United States National Council of Teachers of Mathematics [NCTM], 1989, 2000; United States National Research Council, 1996). The ideal of constructivism involves providing learners with opportunities to explore and make sense of the world around them. Papert's theory of constructionism is similar; it also points to giving learners the opportunity to create or build something—something that they are engaged with, something that challenges them appropriately, and something that is rewarding in both the process and the product (Resnick, 2008). Constructionism complements constructivism with the addition of the notion of authentic hands-on activities supporting engagement and learning (Papert, 1993, 1980). If we expect teachers to teach mathematics and science using constructivist- and constructionist-based approaches and to include more hands-on experiences for students, then we need to prepare them by allowing them to experience such activities themselves. We believe that by providing teachers with opportunities and support as they offer students more authentic and engaging SMT-related, PBL experiences we help both groups build a better understanding of these topics. We believe that ICT is much more than presentation tools—chalk or white boards, overhead projectors, PowerPoint™ presentations, and data projectors; these technologies provide powerful opportunities to engage students with relevant challenges, interpret experiences, and construct understandings. We address three interrelated problems in our work.

First, there are many new, innovative, and effective ICT that can be used to support and encourage learning and mastery in SMT areas; however, its adoption in schools is slow, and many learning opportunities—and students!—are being lost. Although we could wait several years for the natural progression of technology adoption, many ICT can be put to good use much earlier in the cycle.

Second, teachers have limited time to explore new ICT. Unless some tool or process is explicitly brought to their attention and shown to be effective and efficient in helping students learn SMT concepts and processes in normal classroom conditions, they are unlikely to attempt to master it and apply it in their teaching. Teachers need to have opportunities to see ICT's potential for promoting student success before they will fully engage with them. They need to be helped over the threshold of each technology (e.g., costs, knowledge, skills, fear, vision of potential, etc.) and be satisfied that the friction associated with the technology is manageable (e.g., ongoing costs, time with students, educational utility, etc.) (Pelton & Francis Pelton, 2008). Successful experiences with school-based PBL activities will promote further application, exploration, and sharing with other teachers.

Third, there are too many ICT for any individual interested teacher to review and explore fully. Innovators and early adopters, both teachers and educational researchers, already explore the potential of these technologies and share results in the evidence-based practice literature. We seek to build a mechanism to improve the efficiency of this knowledge transfer in which the next generation of teachers—either the ready majority or the early majority—is exposed to and provided with opportunities to adopt practical, vetted activities to teach SMT curricular objectives using these effective technologies.

This chapter describes our Pacific CRYSTAL Project work with teachers to promote authentic SMT-related activities in the classroom. We have supported these activities in two ways: outreach workshops and enriched mathematics classes. Outreach workshops make SMT topics more accessible to teachers by modelling the successful use of effective pedagogies, appropriate technologies, and authentic PBL activities with their students. Enriched classes promote scientific and mathematical literacy of students by integrating specifically designed laboratories, demonstrations, and projects into mathematics courses for Grades 9–12. We describe four types of PBL outreach workshops: robotics, comics, geotrekking, and audience response systems (aka clickers) as well as the enriched mathematics courses.

ROBOTICS

One SMT outreach initiative that we have undertaken provides authentic PBL experiences using LEGO® robotics. Children are introduced to basic robot design principles and introductory programming for the LEGO MINDSTORMS® robots (LEGO Group, 2010). We support schools that want to continue with an ongoing robotics program through promotion and coordination of the Vancouver Island Regional *FIRST®* LEGO League (FLL®). The FLL is a PBL program integrating SMT for children aged 9–14 years who design and build robots using the MINDSTORMS kits and then program the robots to complete various challenges (see http://usfirst. org/roboticsprograms/fll/). Each year, student teams complete an FLL Challenge comprised of four components: team work, robot design, robot challenge (programming the robot to complete a series of challenges), and a presentation on the science theme for the year. We support schools in two ways: through the loan of the MINDSTORMS kits (acquired with a University of Victoria Constructivist Education Resources Network grant) and through provision of University of Victoria preservice teachers (supported by the University's work-study program and Pacific CRYSTAL) and faculty as mentors to the school teams.

We begin with a meeting for the preservice teachers where they are introduced to the FLL program and are challenged to build a robot using the MINDSTORMS kit. Building their own robot allows the preservice teachers to experience the same excitement, struggles, creativity, and learning as the students they will be helping. The preservice teachers are engaged and motivated to learn because they know they will be applying their learning in a real setting. They are also able to understand the benefits of a hands-on, PBL task through their experience with the task and are prepared for the support their students will need.

Next, the preservice teachers are introduced to the FLL Challenge and assigned as the expert to support the classroom teacher/school liaison and to mentor the FLL students on programming, research, or robot design. They help students prepare by presenting mini-challenges for them to complete as a team. The highlight for all involved is attending the FLL qualifying tournament where the students put their challenge solutions to the test, competing with other teams for the opportunity to move on to the provincial competition.

Participating in the LEGO robotics program was motivating and satisfying for the classroom teachers ($n \sim 4$), preservice teachers ($n \sim 8$), students ($n \sim 80$), and authors. Students gained experience with an engaging PBL activity, and teachers increased their confidence and desire to incorporate such activities in their teaching. Written comments from students focused on the engaging nature of the tasks, the opportunity to work collaboratively to do problem solving, the opportunity to experiment and try new things, the open-ended nature of the challenges, and the ongoing aspects of the program. Students liked the fact the program was not a 'one-shot' activity. We have experienced a steady increase in demand for the program over the 4 years of the outreach workshops and supported FLL teams. The main limitation on expansion of the program is the availability of sufficient preservice teacher volunteers to serve as mentors. Our experience is that engaging preservice teachers enhances and expands their repertoire with SMT topics and appropriately using technology to support PBL; in addition, they provide needed support for in-service teachers to become more confident with both the technology and the content.

COMICS

Comics creatively and concisely combine visual and textual components. Comics have evolved into a more efficient and stimulating tool for transmitting information in this multimedia age than either visual art or literature alone. Many educators are discovering the benefits of this powerful format for communicating information and presenting engaging challenges. Several studies describe innovative projects in which students create comics to develop literacy skills, challenge misconceptions, or communicate their understanding of a topic (Bitz, 2004; Francis Pelton, Pelton, & Moore, 2007b; International Reading Association & United States National Council of Teachers of English, 2011; Kornbluth, 2004; Millard, 2003; Morrison, Bryan, & Chilcoat, 2002; Naylor & Keogh, 1999; Vega & Schnackenberg, 2004; Wax, 2002; Wright & Sherman, 1999).

Comics can be used effectively to support students in an active learning process whereby they reflect upon, express, and discuss their understandings and views through the creation of comics. Students creating comics promotes literacy and higher-level thinking and writing skills as well as supports the acquisition and sharing of essential processes such as making connections, problem solving, reasoning, representation, and communication (NCTM, 2000). In addition, comic story development enhances their skills in creative writing, storyline development, various fine arts, graphic design, document layout, and computer literacy. This is consistent with Papert's (1993) suggestion that some of the most powerful learning occurs when individuals design or create things that are meaningful to them or to those around them.

Technology and software have further enhanced the appeal and possibilities for student-generated comics. Comic Life (Plasq, 2009–2011) is an accessible, comic-processing software program that is akin in relative capabilities to a word processing program. It is both low threshold—teachers and students can begin using it with ease—and low friction—easy to use with respect to preparation, process, and production (Pelton & Francis Pelton, 2006). Students transform their ideas and images (e.g., photographs, etc.) into comic creations consisting of a series of frames that express a message, idea, or problem solution. The user interface is intuitive, intelligible, and friendly; even the sound effects are meaningful and helpful.

This application's potential to support education through student engagement and success is high. By using a comic processor to express and explore their understandings, students engage in the creative and critical aspects of making a comic without the excessive wordsmithing load associated with setting the context or concerns about their drawing and penmanship skills associated with the visual representation of their ideas. Instead, and most importantly, students can focus on the message and thus increase the likelihood of satisfactorily communicating their ideas.

We have been using comics with elementary and middle school students for 4 years. Students work with peers to create a storyboard for an assigned mathematical topic, then find or develop appropriate images or props to support their storyline, and finally develop a comic with text bubbles to teach someone else about their topic. We analyze the comics for evidence of student understandings and misconceptions related to the mathematical concepts. Although data analysis of the comics themselves is currently underway, we have learned some lessons about the most effective way to integrate a comic creation activity into the classroom. We recommend that students be guided and supported in their early creative endeavours so that they see the comic creation task as an effective problem-solving, reasoning, representing, and communicating process. We recommend that students be guided to select or be challenged with goals that match their mastery level.

The software's ease of use makes most of the procedural aspects of comic creation simple, allowing students to focus on the content rather than the software's features. By scaffolding students through this process, we lead them to generate interesting, accurate, and pleasing learning artefacts and ensure that they begin with success. We recommend the following series of lessons, with the first four done in the classroom:

- Examine sample comics to identify communication elements and create awareness of the medium's potential.
- Discuss and demonstrate the problem-solving process with an authentic comic design activity.
- Demonstrate the functional potential of the software by creating the comic.
- Engage students in the planning portion of the problem-solving process where they create and revise their storyboards for a curricular topic they have already mastered (otherwise concepts presented in their comics may be incomplete or erroneous).
- Create a finished comic in the computer laboratory using the software.

As part of this process, students are introduced to the four-step problem-solving cycle (Polya, 1957). Specifically, we provide them with the following procedure and reflective guidance:

- *Understand what it is you are explaining.* Think about what you want to share. Make sure that you have a clear and correct understanding of what it is you are trying to show.
- *Plan.* Make some notes about ideas that will help to explain your understanding of the central issue, related information, and real context for your example. Do not worry about including jokes or making it funny but keep a record of quirky ideas if you have them. Create a storyboard and sketch what you want to say; try to keep it to 6 or 8 frames. Remember your audience. Identify resources that will help you create a comic that matches your storyboard. Look through the sample comics that provide examples of the sequence and content progression. Think about how you might represent some of the characters in your story (e.g., a picture of you, a puppet, a drawing).
- *Carry out your plan.* In the laboratory, set up your page of frames, capture the images (import previously collected photos or real-time capture of poses or drawings), position and adjust the images and frames, add text, embellish, and polish. Revise your plan when things do not work.
- *Be reflective.* Keep looking back through all stages of this process. Does everything make sense? What other ideas do you have? What might you do next?

We leave it to the classroom teacher to support the students as they engage in the planning process and to provide feedback on the storyboards for content and clarity. We suggest that students provide peer-feedback on other students' storyboards and early versions of their comics as a way to share understandings and creative ideas and as a metacognitive check to confirm that the ideas presented are clear, complete, and accurate. Finally, a debriefing activity is a gallery walk that allows students to share their final comic with their peers and their views on the strengths and weaknesses of each presentation. This activity provides opportunities for peer-assessment, self-assessment, and reflection that consolidates, elaborates, and reinforces understanding of mathematical concepts.

We have included three examples of comics created with Comic Life software to illustrate the learning cycle. Evaporating and Condensing H_2O (Figure 1) is a comic that we constructed to share with students before they begin their comic creation process. It uses cropped elements from two pictures and an imaginary dialogue to support learners as they build their understanding of water and water vapour in everyday life. Pizza Buffet (Figure 2) was constructed jointly with students to demonstrate the planning and creation cycle for comics. We began by presenting the concept of comparing fractions and then brainstormed possible scenarios and storylines to compare two fractions. This comic used the software's capture-image feature to import the photographic images of student actors and the hand-drawn images. Lollipops (Figure 3) is an example of a student-generated comic demonstrating the use of a number line to solve a percent problem. Again, students used both a combination of photographic and hand-drawn images to demonstrate the mathematics concepts that form the basis of their story.

Figure 3. Lollipops.

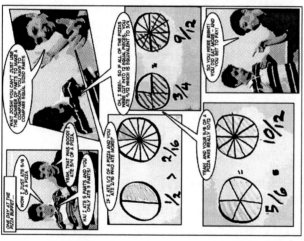

Figure 2. Pizza buffet.

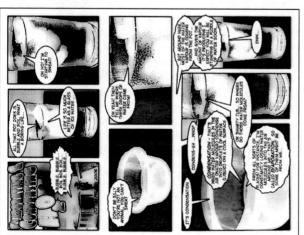

Figure 1. Evaporating and condensing H_2O.

Qualitative responses from students and teachers have been very positive about the comic workshops. The following teacher comment is typical of the many received:

> I think that the students learned that math can be fun! I had a few students tell me that it was the best math lesson ever. They need those kinds of lessons. A lot of students don't look forward to math class and it's these kinds of projects that can make it more engaging for students. ... You can see that they were evidently able to on their own create an example of a real-life situation where a math concept was applicable to a real-life situation that is of interest to them. As a result, they were much more engaged. I think that they also learned the importance of problem solving and thinking ahead. They learned how to devise a plan and think things through, put their ideas in sequential order.

There is growing evidence supporting the use of comics to enhance communication and learning (Bitz, 2004; Ezarik, 2003; Millard, 2003; Morrison et al., 2002; Ujiie & Krashen, 1996; Versaci, 2001; Wright & Sherman, 1999). Creating comics can support literacy development, critical thinking, problem solving, and creative classroom activities (Yore, Chapter 2 this book). Technology enables students to focus on the critical and creative aspects associated with constructing a comic to communicate conceptual understanding while eliminating many of the more time-consuming and tedious elements of the task. This marriage of multimedia repre-sentations with technology is a happy one, and we believe that its inclusion in teachers' toolkits can have a significant positive impact on student learning.

GEOTREKKING

Geocaching is a civilized treasure-hunting activity enjoyed by enthusiasts all over the world (http://www.geocaching.com/). It engages participants of all ages in an activity that may involve physical exercise, mental challenges, learning opportunities, shared experiences, and even solitude (Chavez, Schneider, & Powell, 2004; Hauser, 2003; Lary, 2004). When compared to other hide-and-seek types of activities (e.g., waymarking, letterboxing, etc.), geocaching's distinguishing feature is the use of the Global Positioning System (GPS) and GPS receiving devices to locate caches—a hidden container ranging in size from 3x1x1 cm to 30x30x50 cm, usually containing a log boo and possibly additional information or tradable items—according to latitude and longitude (Lat/Long) coordinates (Stern, 2004).

Geotrekking expands upon the educational potential of geocaching by using enjoyable physical and mental activity to support student mastery of specific cur-ricular objectives and to engage students in meaningful PBL challenges. In a geotrek, the teacher designs a collection of geocaches (traditional, virtual, or online through Google Earth™) to provide clues, resources, and scaffolding to support students as they work toward their learning goals individually or as a group (Pelton, Francis Pelton, & Moore, 2007). By engaging students in authentic and purposeful activities in real-world contexts, geotrekking supports improvement in their attitudes toward related subjects and promotes an increase in engagement, learning, and transfer (Baker & White, 2003).

Geotrekking may be seen as an instructional design model that promotes the integrated fundamental and derived components of geographical, mathematical, cultural, scientific, and technological literacies (Yore, Chapter 2 this book):
- Understanding the *where* and *why there* issues with respect to the Earth and its natural and cultural features.
- Ability to deal with the quantitative aspects of life and to evaluate and accept or reject mathematical statements of others as well as the skills and foundational concepts to support effective reasoning and problem solving.
- Ability to converse fluently in the idioms, allusions, and informal contexts that create and constitute a culture.
- Knowledge about, and ability to apply, technology in everyday life.
- Emotional disposition, skill, and knowledge that support learning, problem solving, and communicating with respect to society.

By interweaving meaningful PBL challenges (Jonassen & Rohrer-Murphy, 1999; Kolodner et al., 2003) with appropriate authentic and contrived learning resources (i.e., caches) and by multimodal engagements (e.g., visual, aural, kinaesthetic), teachers can add variety to their educational programs and meet a broader range of student interests. A geotrekking activity will typically focus on activities that support particular learning objectives; it may include an overarching challenge or group of challenges and a collection of traditional, virtual, or online geocaches. The geocaches provide students with an integrated collection of relevant learning opportunities and appropriate scaffolding.

Geotrekking.net (2006) is a website that has been established as a resource for educators interested in developing or sharing educational geotreks. It provides descriptions of the various types of geotreks and sample geotreks for various topics. Other resources available on the website include definitions and background information on Lat/Long, GPS use, teacher instructions, and templates to help persons interested in developing geotreks. It also includes a section where educators may share the geotreks that they have developed.

We define three types of geotreks: portable, fixed location, and Google Earth (GE). As geotreks are developed by and shared with teachers, preservice teachers, students, and others, they may be revised, expanded, or otherwise transformed into derivative geotreks. Transformations depend upon the type of resources needed (i.e., location, features unique to the site, and geocaches presented) and the imagination of the creators.

Portable Geotreks

Portable geotreks are designed to help students discover, develop, or review a collection of concepts or skills that can be easily transposed to other suitable locations. Generally, the location will be a schoolyard or convenient park where students have sufficient space with limited forest canopy and building obstructions of the GPS signal to address the challenges.

Some portable geotreks may be cacheless. Such geotreks typically require a suitable place for student groups to work as they identify convenient temporary waypoints (i.e., points of reference entered into a GPS device) and carry out experiments to gather data and information needed to achieve the intended goals or work out a solution to the challenge. Other geotreks may require the teacher or supporting volunteer to set up temporary caches, either traditional or virtual. These geocaches might take the form of a stake driven into the ground, a telephone pole, a fire hydrant, or any other convenient feature of the landscape. The geocache instructions may include directions to examine an attached label (temporary or permanent) for a clue, observe a feature visible from that spot (near or distant), open a container and retrieve some resource, evidence or reward, or use some implement provided (e.g., clinometer) to accomplish a task that will support them in their trek.

An example in mathematics education would be for secondary students to apply their knowledge of trigonometry. Students can calculate the area of any polygonal region by breaking the region into triangles then finding the distance between three waypoints, the angles and height using trigonometry (i.e., Law of Cosines & Sine), and the area of the triangle. Another portable geotrek that supports the integration of mathematics, history, and geography challenges the students to explore the nature of Lat/Long and the relationship of this coordinate system with the metric system.

Fixed-location Geotreks

Fixed-location geotreks are designed to lead groups of students through or around a place of interest (e.g., park, monument, city block, etc.), to discover important features, and to engage in challenges and problem-solving activities. Although fixed-location geotreks are not directly portable, they can be used as models and exemplars to support the development of similar geotreks for other places.

Some fixed-location geotreks may be cacheless—having only the range or boundaries specified so that the students can explore, observe, and log the features of some particularly informative natural or cultural site. Other fixed-location geotreks will have real or virtual geocaches that are designed to provide information or resources. Examples of a real geocache might be a box containing a tool that supports the examination of a feature at a particular location, a document that explains how to make observations or decipher the meaning of an artefact or local feature, a resource that presents a new skill to support understanding, or a mini-challenge where the physical context provides the necessary resources. Each of these geocaches can be thought of as being 'just-in-time-and-place' resources that support learning in a context where it is most efficient and useful.

We have used a fixed-location geotrek on campus to provide preservice teachers with a contextual activity on fractions. Over a 30–60 min period, they visit and explore a series of waypoints where they sketch, compare, and describe familiar fractional relationships that they walk by everyday (concrete, pictorial, or symbolic). The activity provides an opportunity to experience hands-on, engaging activities that can easily be modified for use with their future students.

Google Earth Geotreks

GE geotreks are virtual geotreks that are accomplished on a computer using Google Earth. A GE geotrek typically includes a goal or set of challenges supported by a collection of resources and GE geocaches. GE is an Internet-based tool that maps satellite imagery and other information onto a virtual globe that can be manipulated. Because GE may be augmented with privately created collections of marked locations, labels, location-specific data or images, and links to additional content on the web, many geotrekking challenges can be partially or completely presented on a computer (Google, 2011). GE geotrekking may be a practical alternative when weather, time, or other resources (e.g., GPS units) are limited or unavailable. GE geotreks can cover large or distant geographical areas and thereby support activities and learning outcomes that may not be practically addressed within the context of portable or fixed-location geotreks.

GE interlinks a manipulable globe of satellite reference imagery with the dynamic display of the cursor's Lat/Long location and an optional grid display. This allows GE geotrek designers to easily scan, locate, and place geocaches and provides a meaningful mechanism for students to explore geographic features and search for geocaches. By using this tool in authentic ways, students may build a strong sense of earth-scale and Lat/Long coordinate understanding. The GE measure tool provides a mechanism to measure the length of a line or a path (sequence of selected locations) on the Earth using either metric or customary units; it also allows participants to measure distances with a level of accuracy similar to handheld GPS devices.

GE geotrek designers can create geocaches as a series or web of placemarks and image overlays—located within a very small range or scattered across the globe—for students to search for, zoom in on, and examine. One example highlights aircraft flight paths and distance between originating and destination cities. Students are given authentic data on the cost of flights from one location to another. After measuring the distance between these cities, they determine the cost per kilometre. Students observe that the average cost per km decreases as the distance increases and reflect upon the reasons for the variations (e.g., airport charges, take-off, head and tail winds, etc.). An extension of this geotrek provides a schedule of flights and a table of time zones and challenges students to find the average speed of flights from their airport to various destinations within and between time zones (Pelton et al., 2007).

AUDIENCE RESPONSE SYSTEMS

Audience response systems—often referred to as clickers—support enhanced communication in the classroom by allowing the teacher to collect and analyze responses to questions from every student through handheld wireless response units with minimal interruption of individual or small group negotiations (Pelton & Francis Pelton, 2005; Pelton, Francis Pelton, & Epp, 2009). This system can help teachers transform traditional passive learning lessons into PBL activities and engaging discussions with all students actively participating. Teachers can use clickers to support student engagement, encourage participation, allow anonymity in the exploration of sensitive topics, and facilitate formative assessment (Francis Pelton & Pelton, 2006).

The typical use of clickers in a learning environment involves some or all of the following steps: (a) introduce challenge topic or problem, (b) provide participants with information or context, (c) invite participants to elaborate or discuss a challenge, (d) present a multiple-choice question related to a challenge (objective or subjective, single or multiple correct answers), (e) collect student responses through clicker technology, (f) invite students to predict outcomes, (g) display results, (h) engage class in a discussion on the response distribution, and (i) challenge students to convince their neighbour to support a revote (depending on response distribution). Although most of the research on audience response systems has focused on their use in larger (30–250 students) classes, they can be effective in small (as few as 15 students) classes (Draper & Brown, 2004; Francis Pelton & Pelton, 2006; Guthrie & Carlin, 2004; Pelton & Francis Pelton, 2005; Pelton et al., 2009; Pelton, Francis Pelton, & Sanseverino, 2008).

Few preservice teachers have participated in classrooms using clickers; because many early adopters of this technology are still learning to use these devices, even fewer still have experienced the full potential of clickers. We demonstrate the effective use of clickers in content and methodology courses for preservice teachers and graduate courses for inservice teachers by (a) introducing the technology, (b) describing the use and benefits of clickers in education, (c) discussing the efficacy of their application in a particular class, and (d) asking the teachers to reflect on potential uses in their classrooms (Pelton & Francis Pelton, 2005).

We offer to share the clicker technology with our students by allowing them to use the devices for a day or a week during their practicum. To support this process, we work with them to develop a plan for creating a presentation and then coteach an initial lesson in their practicum classroom. Our experiences in this outreach activity have been very positive. Preservice teachers are keen to test these new technologies in a supportive environment and to include them in their professional toolkit. Students in the classroom consistently respond very well, which boosts the preservice teacher's self-esteem and confidence. One group of Grade 11 students that were using the clickers at 2:55 p.m. on a sunny June afternoon chimed, *Can't we do more clicker questions?* when the teacher said it was time to get ready to go home.

ENRICHED MATHEMATICS

The enriched mathematics project began by combining three secondary mathematics courses into a single course offered over a school year (Willers, 2005). Because of the overlap or continuation of prescribed learning outcomes in the combined course, less time was required for review of previously learned topics. This time provided opportunities for the introduction of alternate assignments and teaching strategies. All of these enrichment activities were designed to promote the NCTM (1989) process strand (problem solving, reasoning, communication, connections, and representation).

The first course developed, Enriched Mathematics 10/11, combined the content of Principles of Mathematics 10, Principles of Mathematics 11, and Applications

of Mathematics 11. Integrated projects and laboratories included in the first year of the course offering were:
- Terminal Velocity Laboratory (equations of lines)
- Pendulum Laboratory (radicals)
- Jailbreak Project (radicals)
- Exponential Decay (exponential growth and decay)
- Projectile Motion Laboratory (quadratic functions)
- Famous Mathematicians PowerPoint
- Trinomial Multiplication Project

Projects and laboratories included in the second year of the course were:
- Ohm's Law (linear equations)
- Kirchoff's Law (linear systems)
- Boolean Algebra and Cellular Automata (logic and reasoning)
- Parabolic Motion Laboratory (quadratic functions, quadratic regression, graphing)
- Robotics Project (problem solving, linear equations, proportional reasoning)
- Linear Regression Analysis

An example of a typical course activity is the Terminal Velocity Laboratory in which student pairs collected and analyzed data to discover the relationship between surface area and velocity. Students began with an 11x11 in. piece of paper (121 in.^{2}) that they dropped 10 times from a constant height. One partner dropped the paper while the other recorded the time it took to reach the floor. Students then folded in the corners of the paper to make a 7.8x7.8 in. (60.5 in.^{2}) square and repeated the experiment. The corners were folded in four more times, each time halving the paper's area. Students then calculated the mean time for the paper to drop for each area, graphed their results, and performed a regression analysis to find a line of best fit for their data.

Evaluation of the Enriched Mathematics project was based on in-class observations (videotaped), student products from the enriched activities, achievement test scores, questionnaire responses, and student interviews. Observation of the activities showed a high level of student engagement and cooperative interaction. When students were surveyed about their reasons for taking and reactions to the course, the most frequently cited reasons were that they enjoyed mathematics, liked the fact that they would have mathematics the whole year, got credit for three courses in two course blocks, would have advanced placement, enjoyed a challenge, and liked having applications included in the course (Francis Pelton, Pelton, & Moore, 2007a).

Students said that they got more out of the course because of the laboratories, it was more interesting than regular mathematics classes, it was much clearer and simpler to follow and *better than just having something drilled into your head.* When students were offered the opportunity to discuss the activities that had the most impact, they almost always chose the ones that were the most interactive and hands-on (e.g., robotics and the terminal velocity, pendulum, and parabolic motion laboratories). Comments included:

I enjoyed the robotics because it allowed us to get out of the classroom and play with the robots and the computers. We had to adjust the program as we encountered problems, and the sheets we filled out using our data allowed us to learn how to apply linear equations instead of learning from a textbook.

It worked well because I learned that equipment is never the same. (Robotics)

It was easy to visually see the time differences and how different things [a]ffected the falling paper. (Terminal Velocity Laboratory)

Was a very interesting lab. I learned you have a greater chance of living if you are free falling by making yourself bigger. (Terminal Velocity Laboratory)

I thoroughly enjoyed this lab as we got to use our mathematical knowledge in a hands-on way. (Pendulum Laboratory)

All of the students were keen to recommend the course to others. This is significant as the class was developed for regular mathematics students, not for students in an honours or gifted program. Several students had struggled with mathematics in the past; in fact, three of them anticipated that they would fail the course and need to repeat it. Of note, however, is that 26 of the 30 students (86.7%) intended to continue on to Principles of Mathematics 12 and that 13 students intended to take calculus. On average, only 36% of the total secondary school population in British Columbia enrol in Principles of Mathematics 12. Participation in the enriched mathematics course was significantly related to the students' achievement; their average score was 10 points above the average on the provincial examination for the Principles of Mathematics 10 course that year. These Grade 10 and 11 students had the added benefit of an entire year of mathematics instruction that included the Principles of Mathematics 11 and Applications of Mathematics 11 course content.

The enriched mathematics course supports the position that we have advocated in this chapter: Hands-on PBL is engaging, supports student understanding, and encourages further participation in SMT-related courses. The success of this course showed the need for such courses and led to the development of an Enriched Mathematics 9/10 course (combining Mathematics 9 and Applications of Mathematics 10). Both courses continue to be very popular at the school.

CLOSING REMARKS

The last few years have seen a surge in interest in North America to incorporate more SMT topics and activities in the K–12 curriculum. In order for this to happen, not only will the curriculum need to provide opportunities for infusion of SMT-related topics but teachers will need to be comfortable with both the content and teaching strategies. Both constructivist and constructionist approaches to teaching and learning provide ideal learning environments for SMT topics. PBL activities encourage exploration in authentic environments and support students in their developing understanding of SMT generally.

Many educators, particularly those in elementary and middle schools, lack the experience and motivation to incorporate SMT activities into their teaching. Teacher educators need to support both preservice and inservice K–12 teachers so that they can develop the needed knowledge of and confidence with SMT content.

For inservice teachers, we offered outreach workshops in comic creation to communicate understandings of SMT topics, geotrekking to engage students in authentic, just-in-time-and-place learning activities, and robotics to demonstrate an integrated approach to SMT. Each workshop models effective strategies, activities, and technologies in teachers' classrooms with their students. This designed approach gives the teachers a hand up and over the technology–content threshold and demonstrates to them that the friction associated with these new activities is manageable.

We incorporated SMT activities—comic communication, interactive problem discussions and discovery learning with audience response systems, and explorations with geotrekking—into our preservice teacher education classes. Optional workshops of a similar nature were offered to all preservice teachers both in the topics listed above and in robotics challenges. These activities provided experience, understanding, and knowledge of SMT content and teaching strategies for the new generation of K–12 educators. This two-pronged approach is designed to increase the experience, confidence, and competence of both preservice and inservice teachers with respect to SMT topics and PBL activities. With this knowledge and experience, more teachers will be comfortable integrating SMT in their regular instructional units.

REFERENCES

Baker, T. R., & White, S. H. (2003). The effects of GIS on students' attitudes, self-efficacy, and achievement in middle school science classrooms. *Journal of Geography, 102*, 243–254.

Bayer Corporation. (2010, March). *Bayer facts of science education XIV: Female and minority chemists and chemical engineers speak about diversity and underrepresentation in STEM*. Pittsburgh, PA: Author. Retrieved from http://bayerfactsofscience.online-pressroom.com/

Bitz, M. (2004). The comic book project: Forging alternative pathways to literacy. *Journal of Adolescent & Adult Literacy, 47*(7), 574–586.

Chavez, D. J., Schneider, I., & Powell, T. (2004). The social-psychology of a technology driven outdoor trend: Geocaching in the USA. In *Proceedings of 4th annual Hawaii international conference on social sciences* (pp. 583–594). Retrieved from http://www.hicsocial.org/SOC04.pdf

Draper, S. W., & Brown, M. I. (2004). Increasing interactivity in lectures using an electronic voting system. *Journal of Computer Assisted Learning, 20*, 81–94.

Ellsworth, J. Z., & Buss, A. (2000). Autobiographical stories from preservice elementary mathematics and science students: Implications for K–16 teaching. *School Science and Mathematics, 100*(7), 355–364.

Ezarik, M. (2003, April). *The latest developments in math, science, language arts and social studies: Comics in the classroom*. District Administration. Retrieved from http://www.districtadministration.com/viewarticle.aspx?articleid=842

Francis Pelton, L., & Pelton, T. W. (2006). Selected and constructed response systems in mathematics classrooms. In D. Banks (Ed.), *Audience response systems in higher education: Applications and cases* (pp. 175–186). Hershey, PA: Idea Group.

Francis Pelton, L., Pelton, T. W., & Moore, K. (2007a, May). *Integration of laboratory activities, demonstrations, and projects in enriched mathematics 9–12 courses to foster science and mathematics literacy*. Paper presented at the XXXVth annual conference of the Canadian Society for the Study of Education, Saskatoon, Saskatchewan.

Francis Pelton, L., Pelton, T. W., & Moore, K. (2007b). Learning by communicating concepts through comics. In R. Carlsen, K. McFerrin, J. Price, R. Weber, & D. A. Willis (Eds.), *Proceedings of Society for Information Technology and Teacher Education International Conference 2007* (pp. 1974–1981). Chesapeake, VA: Association for the Advancement of Computing in Education (AACE).

Geotrekking. (2006). *Homepage*. Retrieved from http://geotrekking.net/

Google. (2011). *Google Earth™ for educators website*. Retrieved from http://www.google.com/earth/educators/

Guthrie, R. W., & Carlin, A. (2004). Waking the dead: Using interactive technology to engage passive listeners in the classroom. In *Proceedings of the 10th Americas conference on information systems*. Retrieved from http://www.mhhe.com/cps/docs/CPSWP_WakindDead082003.pdf

Hancock, E. S., & Gallard, A. J. (2004). Preservice science teachers' beliefs about teaching and learning: The influence of K–12 field experiences. *Journal of Science Teacher Education, 15*(4), 281–291.

Hauser, S. G. (2003, March 19). Pinpoint GPS spawns a global treasure hunt. *The Wall Street Journal*, p. A.20.

International Reading Association & United States National Council of Teachers of English. (2011). *Comic creator on read write think homepage*. Retrieved from http://www.readwritethink.org/classroom-resources/student-interactives/comic-creator-30021.html

Jonassen, D. H., & Rohrer-Murphy, L. (1999). Activity theory as a framework for designing constructivist learning environments. *Educational Technology Research and Development, 47*(1), 61–79.

Kolodner, J. L., Camp, P. J., Crismond, D., Fasse, B., Gray, J., Holbrook, J., et al. (2003). Problem-based learning meets case-based reasoning in the middle-school science classroom: Putting learning by design™ into practice. *Journal of the Learning Sciences, 12*(4), 495–547.

Kornbluth, J. (2004, November/December). Comics, hot rods, hip hop: Nine innovative teachers show how to score a slam-dunk with today's kids. *Scholastic Instructor*. Retrieved from http://teacher.scholastic.com/products/instructor/Nov04_hiphop.htm

Lary, L. M. (2004). Hide and seek: GPS and geocaching in the classroom. *Learning & Leading with Technology, 31*(6), 14–18.

LEGO Group. (2010). *11+ LEGO® MINDSTORMS® Education™ website*. Retrieved from http://education.lego.com/en-gb/preschool-and-school/secondary-11-18/11plus-lego-mindstorms-education/

Millard, E. (2003). Towards a literacy of fusion: New times, new teaching and learning? *Reading, 37*(1), 3–8.

Morrison, T. G., Bryan, G., & Chilcoat, G. W. (2002). Using student-generated comic books in the classroom. *Journal of Adolescent & Adult Literacy, 45*(8), 758–767.

Naylor, S., & Keogh, B. (1999). Constructivism in the classroom: Theory into practice. *Journal of Science Teacher Education, 10*(2), 93–106.

Papert, S. (1980). *Mindstorms*. New York: Basic Books.

Papert, S. (1993). *The children's machine: Rethinking school in the age of the computer*. New York: Basic Books.

Pelton, T. W., & Francis Pelton, L. (2005). Helping students learn with classroom response systems. In C. Crawford, et al. (Eds.), *Proceedings of society for information technology and teacher education international conference 2005* (pp. 1554–1559). Chesapeake, VA: AACE.

Pelton, T. W., & Francis Pelton, L. (2006). Product review: Comic life deluxe. *Leading and Learning with Technology, 34*(1), 40–41.

Pelton, T. W., & Francis Pelton, L. (2008). Technology outreach workshops: Helping teachers to climb over the technology threshold by engaging their classes. In K. McFerrin, R. Weber, R. Carlsen, & D. A. Willis (Eds.), *Proceedings of society for information technology and teacher education international conference 2008* (pp. 4273–4278). Chesapeake, VA: AACE.

Pelton, T. W., Francis Pelton, L., & Epp, B. (2009). Clickers supporting teaching, teacher education, educational research and teacher development. In I. Gibson, R. Weber, K. McFerrin, R. Carlsen, & D. A. Willis (Eds.), *Proceedings of society for information technology & teacher education international conference 2009* (pp. 1065–1070). Chesapeake, VA: AACE.

Pelton, T. W., Francis Pelton, L., & Moore, K. (2007). Geotrekking: Connecting education to the real world. In R. Carlsen, K. McFerrin, J. Price, R. Weber, & D. A. Willis (Eds.), *Proceedings of society for information technology and teacher education international conference 2007* (pp. 2082–2088). Chesapeake, VA: AACE.

Pelton, T. W., Francis Pelton, L., & Sanseverino, M. (2008). Clicker lessons: Assessing and addressing student responses to audience response systems. In J. Raffoul (Ed.), *Collected essays on learning and teaching* (Vol. 1, pp. 85–92). Windsor, ON, Canada: Society for Teaching and Learning in Higher Education.

Plasq. (2009–2011). *Comic life (Version 1.3)* [Computer software]. Retrieved from http://plasq.com/products/comiclife/win

Plourde, L. A. (2002). The influence of student teaching on preservice elementary teacher's science self-efficacy and outcome expectancy beliefs. *Journal of Instructional Psychology, 29*(4), 245–253.

Polya, G. (1957). *How to solve it: A new aspect of mathematical method* (2nd ed.). Princeton, NJ: Princeton University Press.

Resnick, M. (2008). *Falling in love with Seymour's ideas.* Retrieved from http://llk.media.mit.edu/papers/AERA-seymour-final.pdf

Riggs, I. M. (1991, April). *Gender differences in primary science teacher-efficacy.* Paper presented at the annual meeting of the American Educational Research Association, Chicago, IL, USA.

Stern, D. P. (2004). *Latitude and longitude.* Retrieved from http://www-istp.gsfc.nasa.gov/stargaze/Slatlong.htm

Tobin, K., Tippins, D. J., & Gallard, A. J. (1994). Research on instructional strategies for teaching science. In D. L. Gabel (Ed.), *Handbook of research on science teaching and learning* (pp. 45–49). New York: Macmillan.

Ujiie, J., & Krashen, S. D. (1996). Comic book reading, reading enjoyment, and pleasure reading among middle class and chapter 1 middle school students. *Reading Improvement, 33*(1), 51–54.

United States National Council of Teachers of Mathematics. (1989). *Curriculum and evaluation standards.* Reston, VA: Author.

United States National Council of Teachers of Mathematics. (2000). *Principles and standards for school mathematics.* Reston, VA: Author.

United States National Research Council. (1996). *The national science education standards.* Washington, DC: The National Academies Press.

Vega, E. S., & Schnackenberg, H. L. (2004, October). *Integrating technology, art, and writing: Creating comic books as an interdisciplinary learning experience.* Paper presented at the 27th conference of the Association for Educational Communications and Technology, Chicago, IL, USA.

Versaci, R. (2001). How comic books can change the way our students see literature: One teacher's perspective. *The English Journal, 91*(2), 61–67.

Wax, E. (2002, May 17). Back to the drawing board: Once-banned comic books now a teaching tool. *The Washington Post,* p. B01.

Willers, M. (2005). *Enriched mathematics 10/11: Focus on the NCTM process standards.* Unpublished master's thesis, University of Victoria, Victoria, British Columbia, Canada.

Wright, G., & Sherman, R. (1999). Let's create a comic strip. *Reading Improvement, 36*(2), 66–72.

Leslee Francis Pelton and Timothy W. Pelton
Department of Curriculum and Instruction
University of Victoria
Victoria, British Columbia, Canada

III. MOVING TESTED IDEAS INTO CLASSROOMS

CHRISTINE D. TIPPETT AND ROBERT J. ANTHONY

8. EXPLICIT LITERACY INSTRUCTION EMBEDDED IN MIDDLE SCHOOL SCIENCE CLASSROOMS

*A Community-based Professional Development Project
to Enhance Scientific Literacy*

The *Explicit Literacy Instruction Embedded in Middle School Science Classrooms* project was initiated in the spring of 2005 at the request of a small group of teachers from two middle schools in a Victoria, British Columbia (BC), school district that had French immersion and English programs of instruction in Grades 6, 7, and 8. A third middle school joined the project later. Part of the motivation was that the school district was implementing the new K–7 and Grade 8 provincial science curricula (BC Ministry of Education [MoE], 2005, 2006) and the schools' had recently selected and purchased textbooks.

There were expressions of commitment to collaboration from teachers, school and district administrators, and Pacific CRYSTAL researchers that called for a community-based, emergent research and development approach to this project. A community-based approach would collectively identify needs and opportunities, design solutions, evaluate and revise solutions, and provide funding for the required instructional resources and teachers' professional learning opportunities. Such flexibility would enable university researchers and collaborators from the field to adapt and take advantage of case study opportunities throughout the project (Anthony, Tippett, & Yore, 2010). The overarching purpose of the project was to develop, field-test, refine, and eventually disseminate research and field-based activities that would integrate literacy strategies in the context of the ongoing science instruction to enhance teachers' pedagogical content knowledge and students' science literacy (Yore, Chapter 2 this book).

The community-based project has several dimensions that were within the shared authority and responsibility of the participants: school district, schools, teachers, university, Pacific CRYSTAL, and researchers. The first dimension was ongoing assessment of needs through measures of student beliefs, attitudes, and strategies in relation to science literacy, school-wide assessments of reading and writing performance, and the observations and comments of participating teachers. The second dimension, design of instructional options, arose from the identification of research-based options related to the identified needs in published research. The third dimension was the implementation and evaluation of these classroom-level solutions within the opportunities provided by the prescribed curricula, available instructional resources, school priorities, and classroom contexts, which were conducted through

L. D. Yore et al (Eds.), Pacific CRYSTAL Centre for Science, Mathematics, and Technology
Literacy: Lessons Learned, 133–148.

embedded case studies of classroom practices and teacher reflections. This design was to serve the goals of participating teachers and university researchers to systematically inform the professional development agenda to improve science literacy instruction.

OVERVIEW AND SUMMARY

The organization of this 5-year project centred on a series of workshops. Each series included discussion of the multimodal character of scientific discourse and the roles of oral and written discourse in doing and learning science; a variety of discipline-specific literacy strategies that reflected the nature of science and the research evidence behind each strategy was also presented. Participants had opportunities to discuss implementation of the strategies and to share ideas about embedding the strategies into their classroom science curriculum. Discussion of classroom applications and evaluative feedback on implementation were a part of each workshop. The strategy workshop activities included demonstration lessons, team teaching, and working sessions where teams of teachers collaborated in the creation of instructional resources. Due to the collaborative nature of the project, the workshop schedule reflected teachers' interests and students' needs. Over the first 2 years of the project, responsibility for the delivery of professional development workshops did shift from teachers to researchers in response to the preferences expressed by the group. However, later the leadership shifted back to the teachers as part of the community-based, cascading leadership model designed to leave a legacy of science advocates (lead teachers) in these three middle schools. The selection of workshop topics and activities remained the outcome of discussion with participants.

Participating teachers were generalists who taught a variety of subjects in addition to science. None were specialists who taught only science, and only a rare few had university degrees in science. During the project, the focus and number of participants fluctuated (see Table 1) as a result of "competing priorities within the school districts and schools, retirements, maternity leaves, staffing changes, and the relocation of one school" (Anthony et al., 2010, p. 55). Participation in the workshops changed from an open invitation to teachers to drop in whenever they chose to come, to a year-long commitment to participate in all workshop sessions in Year 4, and to broad dissemination in Y5 involving at least two potential lead teachers from each middle school (Van der Flier-Keller, Anthony, Tippett, & Stege, 2010).

Y1 began late in the school year; therefore, activities were limited to providing a background for interested teachers and exploring aspects of science literacy and the role of language as a cognitive tool in science. This formed a nucleus of participating teachers who developed a tentative agenda of priority areas for the next year's workshops. At the first workshop in the fall of Y2, participating teachers from both English and French immersion streams were shown a summary of opportunities for embedding literacy strategies into the science curriculum and textbooks. Pacific CRYSTAL researchers developed the summary by classifying the instructional procedures presented in the two new textbook series (*BC Science 6, 7,* and *8*, McGraw-Hill Ryerson, 2004, 2005, 2006a; *Science Probe*, Nelson Education, 2005a, 2005b, 2006) into a descriptive framework for science literacy activities adapted from the

Science Theme Sets™ (National Geographic School Publishing, 2008). Later, the French immersion teachers developed a parallel framework for the French science textbook (*Sciences 6, 7,* and *8 Colombie Britannique*, McGraw-Hill Ryerson, 2006b, 2006c, 2006d). This writing–reading and representing–viewing framework was based on four aspects of literacy activities that should be familiar to teachers. As the project progressed, oracy was added as the fifth dimension in order to reflect provincial and school goals and to emphasize the importance of discussion in constructing understanding of science concepts. An example of the application of this framework is shown in Table 2.

Table 1. Overview of 5-year middle school science literacy project

Y1 – Exploring the problem space	– Problem clarified and potential collaborations identified by school administrators, teachers, and Pacific CRYSTAL personnel
	– Professional development topics initiated by teachers
	– Researchers as observers and facilitators
Y2 and Y3 – Building a repertoire	– Responsibility for professional development topics shifted to Pacific CRYSTAL personnel
	– Approximately 25 different teachers attended 14 workshops
	– Demonstration lessons, frequent classroom presence by researchers
Y4 – Developing lead teachers	– 10 teacher advocates created a curriculum resource
	– Case studies of classroom implementation, adaptation and refinement of strategies
Y5 – Disseminating resources	– Instructional resource manual edited and published during summer months
	– Lead teachers provide workshops (two at each middle school) to 75 other teachers as part of the schools' professional development program

In order to gain a better understanding of the range of instructional activities that were supported by the new textbooks and curriculum, the Pacific CRYSTAL team catalogued the teaching suggestions from the new textbooks into the categories of the Working Framework for Explicit Literacy Instruction and linked some suggestions to specific examples in the National Geographic Science Theme Sets. This categorization revealed literacy areas where the texts included a variety of suggested activities as well as areas where few strategies were listed. Participating teachers were invited to use this overview of teaching suggestions along with their personal preferences to identify specific instructional strategies for subsequent workshops; for example, visual literacy strategies were the focus of several Y2 workshops. The selected strategies emphasized the nature of science—concept mapping, reading and creating labelled diagrams, and creating informational posters. Along with negotiating strategies to include in the Y2 workshops, teachers expressed a desire for support with assessing students' multimedia work and, in particular, for assessing informational posters (Anthony et al., 2010).

Table 2. Working framework for explicit literacy instruction in middle school science

Vocabulary/ concept development	Reading comprehension strategies	Visual literacy	Science reading and writing genres	Oracy
– Topic-specific concept words – Greek and Latin roots – Concept mapping	– Determining importance – Synthesizing – Visualizing – Making connections – Questioning – Inferring	– Labelled diagram – Labelled photograph – Cross-section – Flow diagram – Cutaway diagram – Graphs – Posters	– Information brochure – Posters and PowerPoints – Explanation – Cause-effect – Problem-solution – Encyclo-paedia entry	– Argumentation – Small group discussion

Teachers from the third middle school joined the project in Y3, which required some review of Y2 workshops with these new participants. The professional development activities focused on multimedia representations and included writing-in-science genres, using reading strategies such as THIEVES (a prereading strategy that sets the purpose for reading using an easily remembered acronym in which students learn how to *steal* information from the **T**itle, **H**eadings, **I**ntroduction, **E**very first sentence, **V**isuals/**V**ocabulary, **E**nd-of-chapter questions, and **S**ummary before reading the entire text selection; Manz, 2002), constructing graphs, creating informational brochures, designing posters and PowerPoint® presentations, investigating the functions of visual representations (Carney & Levin, 2002), and developing rubrics for science assessment and strategy proficiency.

The initial goal of this project was to facilitate the shift of leadership from the Pacific CRYSTAL researchers to the participating teachers—a cascading leadership model. During Y4, participation in the workshops was limited to lead teachers willing to consider becoming professional development facilitators in Y5. The planning of Y4 workshop activities shifted to include grade-level working groups that purposefully embedded the literacy activities previously demonstrated at Y2 and Y3 workshops into authentic science units to be taught in their classrooms (three for Grades 6 and 7 and four for Grade 8, as prescribed by the provincial curricula).

There were also new instructional strategies included in Y4 workshops such as Foldables® (3-D graphic organizers that include both written and visual information; Zike, 2001) and formal argumentation (i.e., data, backings, warrants, evidence, claims, counterclaims, rebuttals). The sequence and focus of the professional development workshops that were offered throughout the project are shown in Appendix A. Of particular note is the summer institute between Y4 and Y5, where lead teachers met to prepare an instructional resource (Tippett et al., 2009) to be shared with all content area middle school teachers in the district through a series of teacher-led workshops in Y5.

Due to the collaborative nature of the project, the workshop agendas were regularly adjusted to reflect teachers' interests and students' perceived needs. The community-based design assured a balance between (a) the researchers' initial focus on science inquiry approaches, learning cycles, and specific literacy strategies and (b) the teachers' focus on selecting a repertoire of individual strategies that they perceived to be the most promising and practical within the constraints of their classrooms. As topics and strategies were selected for workshops, the participating teachers and Pacific CRYSTAL leaders reviewed and revised the summary of instructional strategies that were represented in the framework (Table 2) introduced in Y2 and updated throughout. This framework served as both a record of strategies that were available and a reminder of literacy areas that were not as fully represented. The orientation was to try to achieve balance across science literacy categories. The engineering design of the project (i.e., ongoing assessment of needs, designing solutions, evaluating and revising solutions) meant that the agenda and solutions reflected the real needs of students and generalist teachers and were constrained by the realities of classrooms, instructional schedules, and funding. Some priorities of the university participants (e.g., inquiry teaching approach, science-specific strategies, the learning cycle) were not enacted by the community, and other strategies (e.g., Foldables, PowerPoints) were embraced and implemented by the participating teachers.

Classroom observations and teacher interviews suggested that participating teachers were moving toward a literacy-infused science program (Tippett, Yore, & Anthony, 2008): As Teacher C said, *Not one of us has a science background, although many of us have literacy backgrounds, and as a result of this project we can use our expertise to enhance our science instruction.* Classroom observations and teachers' self-reports indicated that some literacy strategies presented at professional development workshops were appropriate for use in science (and other subject areas) and were adaptable for students with a range of learning needs at all middle school grade levels (6, 7, & 8). Focus group results indicated that the collaborative partnership between teachers and researchers had enriched and enhanced science instruction. One teacher reported, *It's mutually beneficial to students and teachers because we are able to collaboratively plan and share ideas to enhance our units.* (Van der Flier-Keller et al., 2010).

RESULTS

This project was evaluated by a series of reflections, teacher interviews, and case studies (Tippett, in progress). The reflections were conducted and reported as part of the ongoing annual evaluations of the Pacific CRYSTAL Project while the teacher interviews and case studies were part of the doctoral research of the first author.

Reflections on Professional Development

From its inception, this project has been conducted with deliberate emphasis on high levels of collaboration and facilitation among peers and research professionals.

This orientation not only accords with the personal orientation of the participants but also reflects the qualities that are cited as fundamental to effective professional development, particularly for science teachers (Cochran-Smith & Lytle, 1999; Hutchins, Arbaugh, Abell, Marra, & Lee, 2008; Loucks-Horsley, Love, Stiles, Mundry, & Hewson, 2003). These features provide a backdrop from which to examine the qualities and challenges of professional development that were demonstrated in this project.

Loucks-Horsley et al. (2003) described five key features of professional development for science teachers; the first is *aligning and implementing curriculum*. This feature is exemplified at several places in the project. Early on, teachers had the opportunity to explore the instructional characteristics of the newly authorized curriculum and textbooks by aligning the texts with the working framework (Table 2). This descriptive framework, based on a theoretically sound model of science literacy and a successful instructional resource, situated the innovative strategies and other teaching supports provided through the workshops within a coherent and consistent frame of reference and articulated a structure for identifying areas for further development. Such an overarching framework served to avoid the sense of 'one-shot' workshops for those teachers who participated in some but not other workshops because the framework served to link the strategies that were presented and connect those strategies to the ultimate goal—enhanced science literacy. In addition to the demonstration of instructional strategies, teachers had the opportunity to meet together in grade-level groups to design new units aligned to the new curriculum that could replace units from the former curriculum.

Collaborative structures are a second feature of effective professional development identified by Loucks-Horsley et al. (2003). This feature is evident not only in the development and delivery of the school-based workshops but also in the logistical and financial collaboration. All workshops were held in district schools and during regular school hours. The significant cost of release time for participating teachers, which was not fundable by the Pacific CRYSTAL grant, could have been a major impediment. However, through the dedicated collaboration of all stakeholders, the project was able to proceed. For example, in the initial stages the school district and the district teachers' association provided funding. Such financial support reflects the high value that the school district, its administrators, and the teachers placed on the workshops. Additional funding for teacher release time was later provided by grants from the University of Victoria Vice-President Research, the Dean of the Faculty of Education, and CER-Net (the Constructivist Education Resources Network is a fund created by private donors to support research through the Faculty of Education).

Participating teachers demonstrated an especially high commitment to this collaborative project. Their commitment was demonstrated as they facilitated a plan to share a single Teacher-on-Call (TOC) to allow two teachers to attend workshops. This was accomplished by offering each workshop in two sessions, one overlapping the lunch hour and the other extending the normal workday. Through this arrangement, one participant would attend the first session and another the second session, and they would share a single TOC thereby substantially reducing the cost of teacher release time. Teacher commitment to the project extended to travel arrangements; there are considerable distances between the three middle schools. Teachers volunteered to share the travel time and cost in order to participate in the project. This commitment and collaboration was in part due to the teachers' belief in the value and authenticity of the professional learning provided; that is, planning and developing instructional units and assessments for science would be good for their students and good for them. They viewed the Pacific CRYSTAL researchers as having both theoretical and practical expertise with extensive research and school experience. The classroom teachers and university researchers saw the first author as 'one of their own' as she was a member of both the practicing teacher and academic communities, which greatly facilitated the collaborative nature of the project.

The project afforded teachers time to inquire about their practice by allowing them to be removed from their classroom's daily demands for brief, but repeated and connected, opportunities to reflect on the third attribute of effective professional development: *articulate the tacit knowledge embedded in their experiences* (Loucks-Horsley et al., 2003). The format of the workshops included reporting back on classroom experiences with strategies that had been introduced; this often included reports of variations and innovations devised by the teachers along with examples of student work to document and illustrate assessment potentials. This context allowed teachers to integrate content and pedagogical knowledge about the target science concepts and literacy strategies into pedagogical content knowledge about disciplinary literacy in science. In addition, the Y4 workshops included working sessions by grade-level teams that developed exemplary teaching units. Although each team included a Pacific CRYSTAL researcher, the discussion and decisions about content were collegial and devoid of an expert/acolyte distinction. One might speculate that after 3 years of interaction any deference to the authority of the researchers or acquiescence resulting from perceived power differential in this collaboration had dissipated.

The fourth feature identified by Loucks-Horsley et al. (2003) is *teaching experience*. This project featured guided teaching experience through teaching simulations, modelling, and demonstration lessons in the context of the workshops and middle school classrooms. Teachers actively adapted and expanded the strategies that had been modelled at the workshops in their classrooms. Uncertainties arising after the workshops were addressed by invitations to the project staff to conduct demonstration lessons in one of the participating teachers' classrooms. These teaching experiences and the innovations vastly expanded the power and potential of the workshop strategies. For example, teacher participants had been using visual representations in their classrooms, primarily in the form of posters, but expressed interest in developing better assessment procedures for these visual displays. The project team responded by developing a draft assessment rubric and a PowerPoint slide set for classroom use to demonstrate the qualities of the criteria featured in the rubric. These assessment ideas were demonstrated at a subsequent workshop and, through discussion, improvements to the rubric and slide set were suggested. From this point, the participating teachers experimented with the criteria of the rubric with other visual representations in the context of a variety of subject areas. Teachers reported back examples of new assessment rubrics, such as a PowerPoint criteria, and expansion of poster representations by embedding mixed-media Foldables (another workshop topic) and, most diverse of all, informational brochures (Tippett et al., 2008). Key to these extensions of the initial workshop demonstrations was the classroom experimentation and innovation by participating teachers that empowered participants to adapt, and not just simply adopt, these robust strategies.

Loucks-Horsley et al. (2003) identified *a legacy of professional development materials and mechanisms* as the fifth essential characteristic. The print and digital materials that were produced for the workshops will have a persistent presence in the district. In addition, Science Theme Sets (National Geographic, 2008) were purchased for each participating school. These sets provided examples of opportunities for embedding explicit literacy activities into existing science programs and were used extensively as model material in workshops. It is anticipated that the *Handbook* (Tippett et al., 2009) that emerged from the grade-level lesson writing teams in Y4 and the lead-teacher writing team in Y5 will serve as the most prominent material—not only for the close connection between these materials and the curriculum in the classroom but also as a demonstration of the practical potential for close collaboration between university researchers and teachers in the field.

In summary, this community-based research and development project was envisioned as an engineering project, rather than a research inquiry, where all participants shared the responsibility for identifying problems, creating and verifying solutions, and disseminating evidence-based practices. The structure, responsibility, and agenda of the project needed to be dynamic and responsive, reacting quickly to constraints, feedback, successes, and challenges—much like a recursive engineering design. The initial expectation that teachers in the field and university resource personnel would participate as full and equal partners throughout the project was reconsidered and revised as it progressed and when participating teachers requested the university partners to take greater responsibility for suggesting and directing the workshop agendas. However in the final years, lead teachers were in the forefront of directing the development of the resource handbook and offering workshops to colleagues. The researchers did not consider imposing any particular structure onto the professional development workshops that dominated this project. Rather, the choice was to consult and, most importantly, to collaborate to ensure that the expertise, experience, and expectations of teachers and researchers would maximize the potential benefit for middle school students to achieve higher levels of science literacy. It is only in hindsight that we are able to reflect on the five characteristics of effective professional development for science teachers outlined by Loucks-Horsley et al. (2003). In doing so, we are encouraged but not surprised to realize that the features of professional development that emerged from this collaborative process exemplify these optimal features.

Teacher Interviews and Case Studies

Classroom observations and teacher interviews suggest that participating teachers did believe that they were better able to identify opportunities and strategies for infusing science literacy activities into their classroom science program (Tippett et al., 2008). Classroom observations from individual case studies and teachers' self-reports revealed that a number of teachers were making use of science literacy strategies presented at the workshops in other curricular areas. Although the focus of this project was squarely on literacy in science, there are indications that the outcomes included enrichment in other unanticipated parts of the curriculum (Van der Flier-Keller et al., 2010).

Lead teachers arose as advocates for the value of participating in their schools. These teachers, who often had more experience with a particular grade or topic or who had more confidence in their ability to teach science, became increasingly involved in the project and in Y5 directed the professional development activities. In Y2, Y3 and Y4, lead teachers acted as mentors by providing encouragement and day-to-day support for colleagues who were beginning to implement science literacy strategies. Through demonstration lessons conducted by the researchers at the workshops and in participating teachers' classrooms, the university partners were able to contribute to the implementation of science literacy strategies (e.g., concept mapping, creating informational brochures) and support teacher-initiated innovations (e.g., Foldables, CSI Chemistry, science fair projects). This in-class professional development allowed teachers to observe specific literacy, knowledge construction, and metacognitive strategies while assessing classroom management needs. Researchers team-taught in classrooms to provide scaffolding for teachers attempting to implement unfamiliar instructional approaches. In addition, researchers developed teaching resources such as PowerPoint presentations for classroom use (e.g., how to create informational posters).

At each workshop, teachers were invited to report on their experiences trying out the strategies that had been suggested and to share samples of student work. During the Y5 summer writing workshop, a small survey of lead teachers was conducted (Appendix B). A summary of the responses is reported in Table 3. The limited sample size cannot be taken as representative of all participants, but it does point to some factors that influenced the substantial variation in the uptake of particular strategies. Some strategies were tried repeatedly while others were hardly attempted at all. It is not possible to identify what contributed to this. It might be assumed that strategies regarded as more effective would have been tried more often, but this is not consistently the case. For example, the ABCDarium is little used but regarded as highly effective, while labelled diagrams were used quite often and yet not regarded as highly effective.

The culminating contribution of this project was the creation of the *Handbook of Strategies for Developing Literacy across the Curriculum* (Tippett et al., 2009). Each teacher who participated in the summer workshop that resulted in the creation of this resource had an opportunity to implement, reflect on, and revise a number of literacy strategies that had been presented during the then 4 years of the project. During the summer writing workshop, the teachers discussed the benefits and challenges of those strategies that a majority of them rated as high in effectiveness. The group also considered the cross-curricular applicability of each strategy because strategies selected for demonstration in the workshops were chosen for their relevance

Table 3. Summary of strategy uptake

Strategy	n^a	Avg. no. times used[b]	Rank (usage)[c]	Avg. effectiveness[d]	Rank (effectiveness)
THIEVES	6	3.83	1.5	2.50	2
Concept maps	6	1.83	5.0	1.67	8
Argumentation	5	1.50	6.5	2.00	5
Foldables®	6	3.83	1.5	2.17	4
Brochures or posters	6	1.50	6.5	n/a	
Brochures	4	0.67		1.75	7
Posters	5	0.83		2.50	2
Vocabulary	6	2.33	4.0	n/a	
Foldables	4	1.33	7.5	2.50	2
Interpretation	3	0.50		2.33	3
ABCDarium	2	0.33		3.00	1
Other	6	1.33	7.5		
Labelled diagrams	6	3.17	3.0	1.80	6

[a] Total number of teachers surveyed = 6; n = number who reported using a particular strategy.

[b] Number of times used = 0 to 5; average calculated by dividing total times used by 6.

[c] Ties indicated by an intermediate rank (i.e., a tie for 1 is indicated as 1.5 for each).

[d] Effectiveness = low (1.0), average (2.0), or high (3.0); average calculated by dividing the sum of effectiveness ratings by the number rating the strategy.

to science education. Additional considerations included school and district goals, ease of implementation, and the teachers' estimates of the probable effectiveness of the strategy for increasing science literacy for all students. Identifying the six strategies or techniques that were included in the resource *Handbook* turned out to be less contentious than anticipated. Teachers had a very high level of agreement about including a particular strategy or not. There were no instances of a significant divergence of opinion.

The teaching strategies agreed upon were: THIEVES (Manz, 2002), vocabulary acquisition, Foldables (Zike, 2001), argumentation, informational brochures and posters, and concept mapping. These strategies are generic and can likely be applied with slight modification in language arts, mathematics, and social studies (Shanahan & Shanahan, 2008). The *Handbook* was composed of three parts:

- *Part 1*: A guide containing descriptions, rationales, key features/functions, connections to science goals, ideas for implementations, cross-curricular connections, interactive whiteboard connections, ideas for assessment, student samples, related articles, blackline masters, and references for each of the six strategies.
- *Part 2*: Sample instructional frameworks for Grades 6, 7, and 8 science units that illustrate some ways in which these literacy strategies could be incorporated along with other science activities to meet the Prescribed Learning Outcomes

contained in the *Science K to 7: Integrated Resource Package* (MoE, 2005) and *Science 8: Integrated Resource Package* (MoE, 2006).

- *Part 3*: A CD containing Parts 1 and 2 in electronic form, along with full-colour examples of student samples. The CD also included articles about the strategies and the PowerPoint slide sets that had been developed for classroom use. All blackline masters included on the CD were formatted so that they could be adapted to suit particular activities and/or students or used with technology such as inter-active whiteboards.

Challenges Facing Community-based Professional Development

The teacher participants in this project demonstrated powerful commitment to engaging in the enhancement of their science teaching classroom practices. The effectiveness of the outcomes attests to the level of commitment. The experiences of this project revealed some features that critically influence such community-based professional development. Previous studies of best practices for teacher professional development are quite clear that there needs to be time set aside for teachers to devote their attention to reflecting on their own practice and setting goals for changing practices (Cochran-Smith & Lytle, 1999; Hutchins et al., 2008; Loucks-Horsley et al., 2003).

In the face of such a well-attested characteristic of effective teacher development, there was no point in undertaking a project that did not include plans for teacher release time in order to focus intently on personal practices. Unfortunately, the conditions on expenditures from the national funding agency (Natural Sciences and Engineering Research Council, Canada) for Pacific CRYSTAL did not permit paying for teacher release time. Thus, from its inception, this project was burdened with the logistical task of securing resources to provide this essential release time. There was great enthusiasm for the project from teachers and administration in the school district, and our partners (University of Victoria, CER-Net, and local teachers association) were willing to transform this personal support into several contributions of resources for release time. The scramble for release time occupied the project team in each of the 5 years of the project. Through the contributions of many partners combined with more than a little 'good luck,' the necessary release time was financed and the prospects for successful outcomes of the project greatly enhanced. None-theless, the uncertainty about funded release time was an encumbrance on long-term planning as well as project presentation.

The reporting back by teachers at each workshop, along with classroom obser-vations and survey results, demonstrated that the material selected for presentation had influenced classroom practice. Each strategy selected for inclusion in the work-shops was identified through consultation with participants about their perceived needs and in relation to curricular goals and available published research about the strategy's effectiveness. Some strategies, such as informational brochures, were widely taken up and further developed by a large proportion of participants. Other strategies, such as concept mapping, were less extensively adopted. The factors that contribute to the uptake of some strategies but not others remain unclear.

CLOSING REMARKS

As this project reached its end, it was tempting to speculate on its legacy. There are a number of material contributions that will remain: the print and digital resource materials that were distributed and modelled at each of the workshops and especially the *Handbook* (Tippett et al., 2009). The personnel legacy is more difficult to predict. It was heartening to see the emergence of a team of lead teachers from each school. The project afforded these teachers a context in which to interact and to develop and express their leadership. The lead teachers took an increasingly prominent role as the project progressed. In the final year, the production of the resource handbook and the presentation of the school-wide workshops were primarily in the hands of the lead teachers. After the presentation of the highly successful workshops offered at each participating school, but open to all teachers in the district, there was an invitation to the lead teachers to present at a multidistrict professional conference. On this occasion, none of the lead teachers accepted the invitation and it fell to a university team member to conduct the sessions. There is some uncertainty as to whether the cascading leadership model actually worked as intended and if the lead teachers will continue their advocacy role beyond the framework that was provided by the Explicit Literacy Instruction Embedded in Middle School Science Classrooms project.

REFERENCES

Anthony, R. J., Tippett, C. D., & Yore, L. D. (2010). Pacific CRYSTAL project: Explicit literacy instruction embedded in middle school science classrooms [Special issue]. *Research in Science Education, 40*(1), 45–64.

British Columbia Ministry of Education. (2005). *Science K to 7: Integrated resource package 2005.* Victoria, BC, Canada: Author.

British Columbia Ministry of Education. (2006). *Science Grade 8: Integrated resource package 2006.* Victoria, BC, Canada: Author.

Carney, R. N., & Levin, J. R. (2002). Pictorial illustrations *still* improve students' learning from text. *Educational Psychological Review, 14*(1), 5–26.

Cochran-Smith, M., & Lytle, S. L. (1999). Relationships of knowledge and practice: Teacher learning in communities. *Review of Research in Education, 24*(1), 249–305.

Hutchins, K., Arbaugh, F., Abell, S., Marra, R., & Lee, M. (2008). A consumer guide to professional development. *Science Scope, 31*(8), 16–19.

Loucks-Horsley, S., Love, N., Stiles, K. E., Mundry, S., & Hewson, P. W. (2003). *Designing professional development for teachers of science and mathematics* (2nd ed.). Thousand Oaks, CA: Corwin.

Manz, S. L. (2002). A strategy for previewing textbooks: Teaching readers to become THIEVES. *The Reading Teacher, 55*, 434–435.

McGraw-Hill Ryerson. (2004). *BC Science 7.* Toronto, ON, Canada: Author.

McGraw-Hill Ryerson. (2005). *BC Science 6.* Toronto, ON, Canada: Author.

McGraw-Hill Ryerson. (2006a). *BC Science 8.* Toronto, ON, Canada: Author.

McGraw-Hill Ryerson. (2006b). *Sciences 6 Colombie Britannique.* Toronto, ON, Canada: Author.

McGraw-Hill Ryerson. (2006c). *Sciences 7 Colombie Britannique.* Toronto, ON, Canada: Author.

McGraw-Hill Ryerson. (2006d). *Sciences 8 Colombie Britannique.* Toronto, ON, Canada: Author.

National Geographic School Publishing. (2008). *Science theme sets™: Differentiated instruction at its best.* Des Moines, IA: Hampton-Brown.

Nelson Education. (2005a). *BC Science Probe 6.* Toronto, ON, Canada: Author.

Nelson Education. (2005b). *BC Science Probe 7*. Toronto, ON, Canada: Author.

Nelson Education. (2006). *BC Science Probe 8*. Toronto, ON, Canada: Author.

Shanahan, T., & Shanahan, C. (2008). Teaching disciplinary literacy to adolescents: Rethinking content-area literacy. *Harvard Educational Review, 78*(1), 40–59.

Tippett, C. D. (in progress). *Exploring middle school students' representational competence in science: Development and verification of a framework for learning with visual representations*. Doctoral dissertation, University of Victoria, Victoria, British Columbia, Canada.

Tippett, C. D., Yore, L. D., & Anthony, R. J. (2008). Creating brochures: An authentic writing task for representing understanding in middle school science. In *Proceedings of the 9th Nordic research symposium on science education* (pp. 46–51). Reykjavik, Iceland.

Tippett, C. D., Evans, L., Johnson, S., Makuch, M., McNee, D., Robillard, C., et al. (2009). *Handbook of strategies for developing literacy across the curriculum*. Victoria, BC, Canada: Pacific CRYSTAL. (available from first author)

Van der Flier-Keller, E., Anthony, R. J., Tippett, C. D., & Stege, U. (2010, January). *The outcomes of large-scale professional development in science education: Pacific CRYSTAL*. Paper presented at the annual international conference of the Association for Science Teacher Education, Sacramento, CA, USA.

Zike, D. (2001). *Dinah Zike's big book of science for middle school and high school*. San Antonio, TX: Dinah-Might Adventures.

Christine D. Tippett and Robert J. Anthony
Department of Curriculum and Instruction
University of Victoria
Victoria, British Columbia, Canada

APPENDIX A

The Sequence and Focus of Professional Development Activities

Session	Focus	Activity	Intended outcomes
Year 1 (2005–2006): Exploring the Problem Space			
Workshop 1	Information	The literacy component of science literacy	Generate interest in the project and recruit participants
Workshop 2	Information	Language as a cognitive tool	Develop understanding of theories of language and reading
Workshop 3	Information	Feedback on the process and workshops	Project planning and prepare of an agenda for Year 2
Year 2 (2006–2007): Building a Repertoire			
Workshop 4	Information	Project review	Establish procedures for quantitative data collection Set goals for upcoming workshops
Workshop 5	Information	Identify literacy foci in textbooks	Generate a list of science literacy strategies to be explored in upcoming workshops
Workshop 6	Vocabulary/ concepts	Concept mapping	Use concept maps to assess pre- and postunit understanding of science concepts
Workshop 7	Information (district wide)	*Learning Odyssey* PowerPoint presentation	Develop understanding of the interaction of fundamental and derived science literacy
Workshop 8	Visual literacy	Emphasize visual representations	Read and create labelled photographs and flow diagrams
Workshop 9	Visual literacy Genre writing	Create posters and PowerPoint presentations	Develop alternative methods to assess understanding of science concepts
Year 3 (2007–2008): Building a Repertoire			
Workshop 10	Genre writing	Guided inquiry with pillbugs	Use inquiry as a springboard into writing a variety of science genres: argument, description, instructions, and explanation
Workshop 11	Reading comprehension Genre writing	THIEVES Informational brochures	Use a prereading strategy to improve comprehension Integrate visual and print elements Develop confidence implementing a common science genre

Workshop 12	Visual literacy	Functions of visual elements	Identify functions of visual elements Use functions to create visuals that enhance understanding
Workshop 13	Visual literacy	Assessment of visual elements	Establish criteria and develop rubrics for diagrams, tables, graphs, etc.
Workshop 14	Genre writing	Unification of rubrics for informational genres	Establish a framework for assessing a range of multimodal informational genres (e.g., posters, PowerPoint presentations, brochures)

Year 4 (2008–2009): Developing Lead Teachers

Workshop 15	Vocabulary/ concepts Visual literacy Reading comprehension	Foldables	Introduce a teaching strategy (using Foldables) that uses visual and written information Incorporate Foldables into unit planning
Workshop 16	Oracy	Argumentation (I)	Develop understanding of the aspects of argumentation
Workshop 17	Oracy	Argumentation (II)	Incorporate argumentation into mandated units
Workshop 18	Vocabulary acquisition Genre writing	Sharing of strategies Mystery powders	Establish a repertoire of vocabulary-acquisition strategies Identify aspects of laboratory reports

Year 5 (2009–2010): Developing and Disseminating Resources

Summer Planning Sessions	Literacy strategies with cross-curricular utility	Create a resource for district-wide dissemination	Select strategies and determine format of presentation Finish purposeful embedding of strategies in science units
Presentation Day 1	School A School B School C	THIEVES Vocabulary acquisition Foldables	Present three literacy strategies in an interactive school-based workshop for content area teachers
Presentation Day 2	School A School B School C	Argumentation Informational brochures and posters Concept mapping	Present three literacy strategies in an interactive school-based workshop for content area teachers
District-wide K–12 Conference		Foldables Informational brochures and posters THIEVES Argumentation	Present literacy strategies to a wider audience (more schools and extended grade range)

APPENDIX B

Strategy Implementation Survey

Pacific CRYSTAL Literacy Strategies in Middle School Science
Strategy Implementation Survey (2008-2009)

Name: _____   School/Grade: _____

Class Description: _____

_____

_____

Literacy Strategy	Number of times used	Effectiveness	Comments and Suggestions
THIEVES	0 – 1 – 2 – 3 – 4 – 5	low – average – high	
Concept Maps	0 – 1 – 2 – 3 – 4 – 5	low – average – high	
Argumentation	0 – 1 – 2 – 3 – 4 – 5	low – average – high	
Foldables	0 – 1 – 2 – 3 – 4 – 5	low – average – high	
Brochures	0 – 1 – 2 – 3 – 4 – 5	low – average – high	
Posters	0 – 1 – 2 – 3 – 4 – 5	low – average – high	

Literacy Strategy	Number of times used	Effectiveness	Comments and Suggestions
Vocab: _____	0 – 1 – 2 – 3 – 4 – 5	low – average – high	
Vocab: _____	0 – 1 – 2 – 3 – 4 – 5	low – average – high	
Vocab: _____	0 – 1 – 2 – 3 – 4 – 5	low – average – high	
Labelled Diagrams	0 – 1 – 2 – 3 – 4 – 5	low – average – high	
Cross-sections	0 – 1 – 2 – 3 – 4 – 5	low – average – high	
Flow charts	0 – 1 – 2 – 3 – 4 – 5	low – average – high	
Other: _____	0 – 1 – 2 – 3 – 4 – 5	low – average – high	
Other: _____	0 – 1 – 2 – 3 – 4 – 5	low – average – high	
Other: _____	0 – 1 – 2 – 3 – 4 – 5	low – average – high	

SUSAN M. TEED, DAVID B. ZANDVLIET
AND CARLOS GUSTAVO A. ORMOND

9. ENHANCING SCIENCE EDUCATION THROUGH AN ONLINE REPOSITORY OF CONTROVERSIAL, SOCIOSCIENTIFIC NEWS STORIES

Scientific literacy involves the engagement of authentic science, technology, and environment issues by applying scientific knowledge and fundamental literacy (Yore, Chapter 2 this book). This project and its series of studies explored how students and teachers responded to an innovative instructional resource—*Science Times*—designed on contemporary and controversial issues. The importance of this effort is to establish relevance for science and environmental education by using contemporary, local news issues to challenge students and the related teaching approach to critically engage students. Case studies of the resource and teaching approaches are used to document student and teacher learning and reactions.

Science Times (ST; 2011), first and foremost, represents a proactive response by teachers to the call for current, authentic news stories in science. It was born out of our frustration with the rate at which science in textbooks becomes outdated, the limiting perspective of science that is often conveyed to students, and the apparent lack of relevance of a traditional science education to students' everyday lives. From its beginning, our project attempted to reflect the changing nature of science and the implications these changes have for society, especially in an age when socio-scientific issues (SSI) inundate the media (Reis & Galvão, 2004). It is our contention that students require certain skills to make sense of the world around them, specifically, the ability to recognize and understand the issues they face, identify key stakeholders, appreciate the multiple perspectives accompanying each issue, demonstrate open- and fair-mindedness when formulating an opinion, and make reasoned judgments based on ethical principles.

The structure of this chapter, like the ST Project, employs an autoethnographic reporting style in which "researchers constitute their own object of research so that the knowing subject and the research object become one" (Roth, 2005, p. 109). This has been achieved by juxtaposing a conversation that takes place between the researchers looking back on their experiences during the project with four detailed case descriptions that capture the essence of these experiences and the literature that supports it.

L. D. Yore et al (Eds.), Pacific CRYSTAL Centre for Science, Mathematics, and Technology Literacy: Lessons Learned, 149–163.

BACKGROUND

What are Socioscientific Issues?

SSI education is issue-based education where issues in scientific content are examined in their social, environmental, cultural, moral, legal, and personal context. SSI education differs from science, technology, society, and environment (STSE) education in a number of ways. Ratcliffe and Grace (2003) provided a comprehensive list of descriptors referring to the nature of SSI; a partial list includes:
- have a basis in science
- involve forming opinions
- deal with incomplete information due to nature of science (NOS) issues
- address local, national, and global dimensions of society and politics
- involve cost-benefit analyses in which risks interact with values
- involve values and ethical reasoning.

Abd-El-Khalick (2003) articulated the nature of SSI, describing the issues as ill-defined, multidisciplinary, heuristic, value-laden, and constrained by missing knowledge. He compared SSI to STSE issues, which are fully defined, driven by available and focused disciplinary knowledge, algorithmic, and objectively oriented and engaging the right procedures that often result in a single right/wrong answer. Zeidler, Sadler, Simmons, and Howes (2005) argued that SSI is not just a context for curriculum, like STSE, which can be ignored or used only marginally when introducing scientific content. SSI is a pedagogical strategy that stimulates and promotes moral and ethical development along with understanding the science–society interdependency. An important point to clarify is that SSI education recognizes the personal beliefs of the student when examining issues instead of the removed objectivity of STSE.

Conceptual Frameworks

The conceptual framework for SSI education suggested by Zeidler et al. (2005) addresses four socioscientific elements of pedagogical importance: discourse issues, cultural issues, case-based issues, and NOS issues. These issues can be thought of as entry points into the science curriculum that inform pedagogy in science education and as topics to guide implementation of SSI in the classroom. Furthermore, these issues contribute to personal cognitive and moral development that leads to functional scientific literacy. This proposed framework encourages further research in each area and addresses many of the issues raised with STSE education.

Interestingly, another conceptual framework has been proposed. Levinson's (2006) epistemological framework includes three categories: reasonable disagreements, communicative virtues, and narrative or logico-scientific modes of thought. He argues for the term *reasonable disagreements*, rather than controversial issues, and that they incorporate moral and social values. Communicative virtues include those that are necessary for having conversations addressing reasonable disagreements and across differences. The modes of thought are distinct ways of thinking that can be reflected in reasoning about reasonable disagreements. Narrative modes of thought seek to interpret logico-scientific modes of thought. Levinson expressed this framework using different vocabulary; however, his three categories are quite similar to the four components of Zeidler et al. (2005). Reasonable disagreements are similar to case-based issues. Communicative virtues arguably are the same as discourse issues, and modes of thought are similar to cultural issues. Zeidler et al. go beyond Levinson by including a fourth issue, NOS, when approaching SSI education. Also, they do not attempt to categorize the possible facets of each issue; rather, they provide an umbrella term under which all voices, reasoning patterns, and cases fall.

Challenges and Limitations to SSI Education

It can be said that SSI education suffers from the same problems as environmental education. These problems, or challenges to the implementation of issue-based curricula, have been well articulated. Stevenson (2007) argued that there is a discourse–reality gap between the language and pedagogies surrounding environmental issues that was not being reconciled with the current standards of classroom practice. As well, the traditional role of schools, teacher pedagogy, teacher attitudes, and the need to maintain authority have hindered the inclusion of environmental issues. Therefore, it can be posited that challenges to environmental education are the same as those facing SSI education.

As research continues on SSI education, one area of interest is implementation. Will educators employ issue-based education in their classrooms? Bringing SSI into the classroom is challenging and requires an awareness of NOS issues and epistemological considerations; both involve reflective practice and potentially forfeit the teacher's authority role (Abd-El-Khalick, 2003). It remains to be seen how these issues are dealt with by educators and how successful SSI education can be in the long term. This then is the focus of our research as part of the Pacific CRYSTAL project—and particularly around the development of a purposeful SSI resource for teachers.

CONTEXT AND METHODS

When the Pacific CRYSTAL Project began in 2005, *Science Times* was conceptualized as a 1-page article featuring current events in science with an accompanying student activity sheet. The editor subscribed to over 50 online science news feeds and then selected stories according to the following criteria: an issue that students find relevant, involves multiple stakeholders, and no clear solution to the problem. Each story was edited to produce three versions accommodating basic, intermediate, and advanced reading levels. Since then and while maintaining its original mandate, ST has grown into a collaborative of partners from the science education community (e.g., science centres, teachers, schools, and school districts); and it has moved to an online delivery model (http://sciencetimes.ca/) in both of Canada's official languages (English, French), with plans for a Spanish version. Most importantly and as this chapter will illustrate, it has sparked the development of a unique pedagogical approach that disrupts the traditional power structure in science classrooms by empowering students to engage in open-ended discussions about controversial SSI.

The research for the following four case studies and dialogue has been collected over the period 2007–2010. Three cases were conducted at an island community school in which one of the authors is a local researcher assisting with the execution of the school's environmental action plan. This is noteworthy because it afforded the project a special status that is not normally granted to outsiders. As a result, the staff welcomed and participated in the study. Two other elements included in the research pertain to each coauthors' interest in sharing the resource and teaching strategy with a broader spectrum of educators.

The data connected to the ST Project are presented in several ways. In the first two descriptive studies, ST is a resource that is used with several elementary school classes. In the third case, ST inspires an approach to controversy but does not actually act as the content source for it. The final case study considers the use and application of ST pedagogy with secondary school teachers.

The data for these studies were collected as video recordings, interviews, and personal accounts. These data are presented in chronological order to show the temporal developments from one case to the next. For each case description, they are introduced and summarized then given a more detailed commentary. Coauthors are identified by their first names.

Case 1: An Emerging Pedagogical Approach to the Resource Science Times

Two classes of Grades 6/7 students ($N \sim 60$) and their teachers file into the school library. To create an atmosphere of sharing, they are invited to sit in a circle. One teacher is proactive and uses the age-old classroom management technique of having the students sit boy-girl. Today, Susan tells the group that she is conducting some research into the feasibility of using biodegradable plastic in this island community. She adds that she has come from Simon Fraser University to spend an hour or so with them to learn their position on an environmental issue highlighted in the latest article of ST.

In preparation for the discussion, students were asked to read a 1-page news story presenting an issue involving biodegradable plastic that their teacher downloaded from the ST website. During this lesson, Susan will invite them to actively participate in a discussion so that they may develop their abilities "to express an opinion on important social and ethical issues with which they will increasingly be confronted" (Millar & Osborne, 1998, p. 9). If she is successful, students will engage in the conversation, despite the facts that they may not be familiar with the issue, she is a stranger, and they may not fully understand the science behind the making of biodegradable plastic.

The discussion begins with the question: What is considered newsworthy in the article? This is an excellent way to begin the conversation, especially in this case where Susan does not know the students. This approach is important because it allows a teacher to ascertain (a) the students' background knowledge of the topic and (b) what concepts may require further explanation before beginning the discussion.

In practice, this technique also can serve as an informal reading comprehension check regarding the language and terminology in the news story.

This experience is important because it is the first time in which teachers of this community school will be exposed to ST. They will observe and possibly engage in a demonstration lesson of an unusual, pedagogical approach to using this news resource in the classroom. According to Susan's experience, it is during firsthand experiences that teachers witness the powerful exchanges that can take place within a facilitated dialogue with students, which is the most effective way to share the resource. However, this is not an easy task for teachers; two common complaints by teachers that are often reported when considering the inclusion of SSI activities are lack of adequate training and lack of time (Hermann, 2008). It is our expectation that, once these teachers see how highly engaged their students become and the pedagogical practices used to stimulate debate (argumentation) and manage participation, they will become supporters of the resource and be more inclined to add this technique to their teaching repertoire.

Perhaps the most significant aspect of this question-led, facilitated process is the idea that it has the potential to invert the power dynamic from teacher as *knowledge bearer* to teacher as *information gatherer* or, in more popular terms, the "guide on the side, not the sage on the stage" (Christenson, Horn, & Johnson, 2008, p. 39). The task of the teacher is to conduct an inquiry into the students' positions on the issues found in the news story. However, there is a key element that is required to carry out this task successfully: The teacher must begin by adopting an unpopular, uncommon, or fringe position in the controversy.

In today's scenario, Susan is urging students to embrace the idea of biodegradable plastic because she has guessed that they will be more inclined to take the opposing position of avoiding plastics because they lead to pollution.

SUSAN: Now might be a good time to explain why taking the unpopular position is critical to setting the stage for this teaching strategy. David, how did you first start using this approach?

DAVID: Well, I remember that it became important because often participants will not appear to have an opinion even about the most pressing scientific issues of the day. ... The reasons for this are complex. A few years ago, I presented an issue about mad-cow [BSE] disease to a group of teachers at a local science conference using *Science Times*. To my concern, initially many seemed indifferent to the question as to how many or whether or not cattle should be culled in response to the outbreak ... my sense was that many felt it was unsafe to voice an opinion and this frustrated and surprised me.

SUSAN: So what did you do to get participants more engaged with the topic?

DAVID: Well, in my customary style, I used a bit of dry humour and then adopted a 'Hindu' perspective on the issue—stating that not one cow should be harmed and that we had no business eating cows anyway—that it was unethical. ... That really proved to be a fringe position—the conference was in Alberta—and that really opened up the conversation as people began to react strongly to my tongue-in-cheek position ... I think it worked because it opened up the possibility to critique me as the speaker and to probe the issue a bit more.

In our experience, if a teacher does not have a strong sense of the students' positions in advance, the teacher can simply poll the students at the beginning of the discussion. It is not as important how strongly the teacher stands by a particular viewpoint as it is to convey a sense of indecision around the issue. In this case, as students question the impact and effects of biodegradable plastic on the environment and grow confident in their positions, Susan tells them that she is feeling rather confused by their very compelling arguments. She tries to expose them to different views as impartially as possible so that the students realize that arriving at and defending their opinion is the primary goal of this exercise, which Hand (2008) calls "teaching something as controversial" (p. 213).

Teaching to the controversy opens up the complexity of the issue and the variety of other perspectives, which might be important in considering societal implications. Once this dynamic has been created, it is important to model an inquiry disposition. Susan does this through a constant flow of questions that she poses to the students in an attempt to help them uncover what is fact and fiction in the news story, who the stakeholders are, and what questions they need to have answered in order to make sense of the issues. She encourages them to identify with others' viewpoints regarding ethical positions so they might attain a more pluralistic perspective (Bainer, 1985). Due to the complex nature of the issue, students soon see that there are many factors to be considered when examining a controversial topic. Based on her exchanges with the group today, Susan challenges with the assertion that cleaner beaches in a community that benefits from tourism would make biodegradable plastics a valid technology and perhaps one worth exploring.

By presenting the news story in such an open-ended manner, students who usually feel compelled to adopt the teacher's position experience a sense of disequilibrium. On one hand, they have come to accept what the teacher says at face value or fact, but now they are confronted with information that makes them wonder what they should believe. It is at this moment that they must re-evaluate the question at hand and decide for themselves which position to take. One way to explain students' disengagement with science would be to consider the lack of cognitive dissonance they experience in the classroom. Festinger (1957) stated, if they are not undergoing psychological discomfort, "there would be no motivation ... to seek out new or additional information" (p. 127). Our assertion is that SSI approaches might provide this type of cognitive dissonance for students.

Susan took steps to make the classroom environment safe for everyone to voice their perspective by taking the unpopular or fringe position. It became evident that students were comfortable expressing their thoughts and reactions to the issue. Interestingly, without realizing that this is part of an unconventional teaching strategy, one teacher observing the demonstration lesson soon joined the students in challenging the notion of embracing biodegradable plastic.

SUSAN: I think this example really shows how students and even teachers can become motivated to address a topic when it is meaningful and relevant to them. I truly believe more teachers would bring controversial issues into their classrooms if they could see how engaging it can be for students.

DAVID: Okay Susan, what do you think makes controversy such a powerful teaching tool? And why did you get so excited about getting involved with *Science Times* when I first asked you?

SUSAN: Well, I could not answer your first question without telling you about my early days of teaching science methodology courses at the University. I was working with a group of preservice teachers who had just come from a system where transmission of knowledge through lectures was the principal teaching strategy. No matter how hard I tried, I could not seem to generate any worthwhile discussions about how effectively or ineffectively we educate kids in science. Most of the group seemed quite satisfied with their education and were surprised to learn that fewer than 15% of secondary school students ever go on to study science. So I had to resort to drastic measures. It occurred to me that the only way I might be able to shake up these students with their tunnel vision would be to show them a video (Schneps, 1989) in which an 'A' student who answers all of the standard test questions about the cause of the seasons with complete success soon reveals some very fascinating, nonscientific interpretations (misconceptions) of the Earth's orbit when asked some probing questions. As the video concluded, on the board I wrote, "Can we really teach anyone anything?" It was during the discussion that followed when I realized the true power of controversy.

Case 2: An Elementary Teacher Volunteers to Teach Using Science Times

Shortly after the first ST presentation at the research school, STEVE (a pseudonym), a teacher who witnessed the first lesson (Case 1), expresses interest in trying out the pedagogy. He says that he is intrigued with the approach and would like to try it with Grades 4 and 5 students. He inquires about the articles: where to find them, what support materials are available, and whether or not there is anything he should know before he sets out to lead 60 students on this adventure.

Despite offers to help him prepare, the only thing STEVE says he requires is the address of the ST website with the stories. Independently, he selects a story, maps out a 40-min lesson, and weaves together innovations and ideas that reflect his personal teaching style. For example, he organizes the students into cooperative groups of four and instructs them to divide the following tasks: captain, writer, reader, and speaker. He also introduces a hand-gauge signal in which the students indicate their response to a comment or question by moving their thumb in the appropriate direction. The students have 24 hrs to read the story. By providing resources in advance, teachers can ensure students who are not able to participate in more spontaneous discussions have time to process and reflect on the information, thereby leading to a richer dialogue. For introverts especially, this and small group discussions can come as a great relief (Burruss & Kaenzig, 1999).

STEVE opens with the question: *What is* new *to you in this article?* He then invites students to talk amongst themselves in their cooperative group and report back a few minutes later. As each speaker shares their group's responses, the other 59 students listen respectfully, indicating 'that's new to me' with a thumbs-up or 'I knew that already' with a thumb horizontal to the ground. Speakers take turns calling on each other, and STEVE ensures that all groups contribute.

The second step Steve includes, consistent with the ST approach, is taking the unpopular position. In this instance, he opposes wind energy because of its danger to birds, bats, and other flying creatures. To further provoke the conversation, he proposes that oil and gas are a much safer alternative. Students quickly voice concerns about global warming, pollution, oil spills, and the additional threats to humans and the environment. Clearly, wind power is the better choice in these students' minds, and the obvious next step is to make it safer for animals.

However, if STEVE is to be fully convinced, he must first see some designs of safe wind turbines that would eliminate any chance of birds being killed. He asks the writers to assist their group members to brainstorm and invent an effective wind turbine. The lesson concludes with a student volunteer who draws her group's design on the board and explains how it will protect birds and bats while providing environmentally friendly energy. STEVE offers some parting words: *I'd really like to thank you because I think I have a much better idea about using wind turbines in a safe manner.*

SUSAN: There are a few reasons why I think STEVE was really successful using this approach. In order to take this leap with several Grade 4/5 classes, he showed that he is not afraid to take risks. He must have felt engaged and intrigued during his own experience as a participant to make the offer in the first place. But perhaps the more important quality STEVE possesses that a teacher must have in order to use this method with confidence is a willingness to let go of control and empower the students to take the lead. So, in answer to your earlier question, these are also the reasons why I got excited about *Science Times*. I could see the potential that this resource has to stimulate these kinds of experiences for kids and possibly even change the way that teachers approach science education. I thought that if we could get these controversial news stories into classrooms there would be a greater chance of engaging students in science and making it more relevant and meaningful for them.

DAVID: Wait! I'm having an epiphany. I'm thinking about the elements that would have to be in place for this teaching strategy to work. You would need open-endedness about curriculum and would need to allow students a critical voice and shared control of their classroom routines. These are constructivist ideas about pedagogy that you would have to subscribe to. Further, the radical notion that knowledge is conjecturable—you would have to believe that too. Well, in this research school we have been working to develop a place-based and constructivist pedagogy in teachers ... and the SSI approach seems to foster this effectively. In our discussions with teachers, using environmental issues like these allow us to have an open-ended aspect to the curriculum ... opening up some of the content to local interpretation [by students and teachers]. Allowing students to adopt a critical voice in the classroom is key as well; students must feel comfortable in questioning ... even challenging the teacher. Finally, some notion of sharing [curricular] control with the students about where a topic might go—these are all key ideas or principles in our evolving pedagogy using SSI.

Case 3: Taking the Pedagogy One Step Further

One benefit of the Pacific CRYSTAL Project was the opportunity to learn about other innovative science, mathematics, and technology activities as well as engineering and environmental education (Chapters 4, 5, 6, 7, & 13 this book). Of particular interest was Seaquaria in Schools (Zandvliet, Holmes, & Starzner, Chapter 5 this book), a project by a Pacific CRYSTAL partner/researcher to get marine aquaria full of native sea creatures into local schools. It seemed only logical that the community school in which Carlos and David conducted their research should have one; the school's staff and administrators agreed. Before long, classes were circling the seaquarium in the front hallway, studying its ocean creatures, and observing with fascination what lay below the waters surrounding their island—until one fateful day during the winter school break when the seaquarium's circulation pump malfunctioned.

David, being an island resident, was able to go to the school and deal with the situation. It was clear that the only thing that could be done was to release the organisms back into the ocean, at least while someone sorted out the technical challenges. In the meantime, Carlos and David began to hear from teachers that some students had generated a petition to release the animals and get rid of the seaquarium.

One teacher in support of the seaquarium went to David and Carlos to discuss the issue. Together they decided to view the emerging controversy as if it were a ST story and apply the same teaching strategy. They recognized the powerful potential of this cognitive conflict that had spurred the students to action and wanted to help them process it. In Piagetian terms, the new situation did not fit with their current cognitive schema creating a sense of disequilibrium. "In trying to overcome disequilibrium—here perturbations, errors, mistakes, confusions—the student reorganizes with more insight and on a higher level than previously attained" (Doll, 1993, pp. 82–83). What follows is a brief summary of what transpired in this impromptu lesson that capitalized on the opportunity afforded by the seaquarium malfunction when the students returned to school in January.

Taking advantage of opportunity as a need to know. The seaquarium malfunction was a potential controversy that provided real local context in which to apply the ST pedagogy. Using the essential components of the pedagogy (e.g., problematic issue, controversy, multiple perspectives, and fringe opinion), Carlos and David enacted the following lesson.

Carlos is about to say something. The students become quiet to listen. He looks upset. He turns to look at David and says in an angry voice, *I'm really mad about the fact that you made the decision to put the animals back in the ocean without talking to me first.* David replies, *I came to the conclusion while you were away that I find it ethically wrong to have animals taken out of their habitat and placed in an aquarium. Besides, I had no idea it would upset you so much and I figured you didn't want to be disturbed over the holidays.* The students look on, some in disbelief. They must be asking themselves: Who is right? Carlos or David?

Carlos answers back, *How did you suddenly change your mind? We should have discussed this. I am upset that you did this without consulting me and the rest of the students.* David turns to the students and asks, *Well, let's ask them now. Did I do the right thing? Is it okay to have the seaquarium in the school, or should we leave the animals in their natural habitat?* Hands fly up. Most of the students have something to say. There is a flurry of comments and questions: Were all of the animals still alive? Maybe we shouldn't keep creatures in the seaquarium. Where did you let them go? Let's just get a new one and find some more animals. Why does the seaquarium need a pump in the first place?

The entire conversation lasts about an hour. It seems as though half of the students want to reconsider having the seaquarium. They express concerns about a repeat incident: What if it happens again over the summer when no one is around to fix the pump? On the other side are those students in favour of keeping the seaquarium. They begin suggesting ways to avoid such a mishap; maybe there are some creatures that would make better aquarium dwellers and others that should be left in the ocean. The conversation concludes, and everyone agrees that the next step should be to conduct an inquiry into the most appropriate creatures for the seaquarium.

> SUSAN: It was pretty amazing what happened during this discussion. Instead of starting with a *Science Times* article, you started with a real scenario but applied the same strategy. It shows how powerful controversy can be to inspire critical and creative thinking in students. The fact that 9- and 10-year-olds are debating the merits of keeping animals in captivity—and by the way this continued for days afterward—speaks to the magic that can be sparked with a little planning and an authentic situation.

> DAVID: I think the epiphany I had here was that by personalizing the seaquarium situation to Carlos and me we made it a personal conflict rather than an abstract one, which is why I believe it was so powerful for the students of this grade level. I believe this was also developmentally appropriate—situating the controversy as one between two people—rather than as a societal one— I thought that the issue might be too difficult or abstract for Grade 4's to understand ... but this approach seemed to work.

Case 4: Using Humour to Approach Sensitive, Controversial Issues

Science conferences provide an excellent opportunity to share ST with others. So far, these public forums have been the most effective way to expose a large group of educators to both the resource and teaching strategy. The following is a typical description of the workshop we have presented at conferences:

> *Science Times* is a news source that provides students with up-to-date information about breaking, controversial stories related to science, technology, and environmental issues. Join us as we demonstrate how we use these news articles (written for three reading levels) to challenge students' attitudes about science while promoting scientific literacy. (Zandvliet & Teed, 2010)

As the 30 attendees arrive to the workshop described above, they are presented with a 1-page printout of the story entitled *Robotic Surgery*, which tells the benefits of using a robot to repair a valve during heart surgery. If they turn the sheet over, they will find the same story written for a different reading level. Later, we advise them to prepare the handouts in this way so that their students can select the side that is most comfortable for them.

David and Susan have prepared for this workshop in two ways: They have determined what they believe the unpopular position will be, and they have taken opposing sides on the matter. Once the audience (in this example, mainly secondary school science teachers) has had time to read the story, David explains that instead of going over the resource upfront we will demonstrate how it might be used first and then debrief later. Next, he poses the question: What is considered newsworthy in the article? A sprinkling of answers comes from the audience: *It was interesting that surgeons will have to develop a whole new set of skills. I've never heard of the technique called the 'American Correction'. My husband just had heart surgery and will have to have it again in 20 years—it made me wonder what kind of processes will be around then.*

Respectfully, David acknowledges the group's contributions and declares, *When I read this article, I just wanted to jump for joy because I love technology. I like video games. I was thinking that maybe they would even let me try this out because I have really good hand-eye coordination.* As you have probably guessed, David and Susan anticipate that the audience may not be so quick to jump on the technology bandwagon and that this is likely an unpopular fringe position. David says, *Wouldn't you like to try to do an open-heart surgery using this technique? I would really love to hear what you think about this.* Someone in the group questions the cost of the surgery: *If it's expensive, who would actually have access to the technology?* Another person challenges the reliability of the software program, citing personal experiences of frustration using the Internet and various word processing programs. Susan wonders what would happen if something failed; who would be at fault, the doctor or the robot? A moment later, a woman points out that decreased hospital care and costs and shorter recoveries would result from robotic surgery compared to the lengthy recuperation that follows repairing a breastbone. Another gentleman sitting in the back says he would go with the robot, and he would hope that the doctor grew up playing video games because his skills would be that much better. He adds that we could train a whole bunch of doctors quicker if they have grown up playing hand-eye coordination style games. Then someone chimes in, *Doctors won't have to have any social skills to be able to interact with their patients* and the crowd bursts into laughter. The woman who had mentioned her husband's open-heart surgery says that she thinks he probably would have opted for the robotic surgery because of the invasive nature of cutting through his sternum in the current method.

Yet, despite all this support for the technology, David suddenly announces that he feels totally confused and now finds himself leaning away from technology. Susan responds by stating that she feels compelled to reconsider her position due to the strong arguments in favour of technology. She remarks that computer simulations might be a great way to engage students in science, especially since one of the struggles facing science teachers is being able to provide equipment and authentic experiences.

At this point, David announces that we will now end the discussion portion of our presentation and commence the debriefing process. He begins by summarizing the types of arguments people used to defend their various positions throughout the discourse: people expressed personal values, scientific and technological advancements, economics as well as social and ethical issues. He points out that these all emerged spontaneously from the discussion, adding that when we do this with students, an important part of the debrief is to actually analyze the controversy— not with the intention of resolving it but to summarize why it is a controversy, what makes it authentic, and what are all the perspectives brought to bear in a controversy that deepens the discussion. *The first time I did this with a Grade 8 science class, I didn't do the debrief; and there was almost a fistfight in the hallway between two people with opposing viewpoints. That's how engaging this experience can be for kids*, recalls David.

At the core of this technique is a pedagogy that involves carefully constructing activities that address SSI, which encourage the development of scientific literacy by reflecting authentic, open-ended problems that occur in life (Zeidler & Sadler, 2008). These are up-to-date news stories that need to be resolved, not canned issues where we already know the answer. As a result, it is safe to have a range of viewpoints on the issue. And, unlike what is often conveyed in traditional science lessons, there is not one right answer.

One way that David demonstrates a sense of open-mindedness is by playfully interacting with the ideas from the audience as well as challenging his own statements. For example, midway through the conversation he proclaims, *I thought I knew how I felt about this issue but now I'm beginning to have serious doubts*. In this way, he models that as we are confronted with new advances in science and technology, it is only natural to have doubts and questions.

Another aspect that emerges from this approach is the need for further research. In other words, students may discover that they need to know more about a certain topic before they can really take a position on an issue. In our case, questions requiring more investigation included: How robust is the software used in robotic surgery? Is the doctor in the same room or performing the surgery across a network? How does robotic surgery work? These questions act as an authentic springboard into inquiry, especially since they have been student generated. When students see that their questions become the basis of follow-up assignments, they have more connection and conviction to pursue the answers.

Finally, there are two techniques in this method that teachers employ. First, they engage students in a process that is empowering. Second, if that occurs, they facilitate a conversation that has the potential to gain momentum as students begin expressing ideas. Teachers generally choose not to subject themselves to the risks of introducing controversies when it is far safer to maintain the status quo (Sanjakdar, 2005). When it looks like an eruption might take place, one effective strategy is to ask the students to step back and answer this question: What is it about us humans that make us feel so strongly about these issues? By doing this, students must become observers of those behaviours demonstrated when people are highly engaged with a topic. This brings awareness to the emotionality that often accompanies controversial SSI. It also allows students to see that personal values play a key role in the way people respond to emotionally charged topics.

SUSAN: I got a good feeling from most of the people in the audience about our presentation although a few were hard to read. I think for some people what we are proposing is really radical. They may be thinking that this would be a nice activity to try in some spare time but I'm not sure if they can see applying it to their regular teaching—perhaps because they don't see the connection to the curriculum.

DAVID: It's true. We really are asking people to move away from the traditional teaching model. And not only do they have to talk about the science but they need to address the social, economic, and environmental elements as well. In order to use this approach, you have to be open to different positions. And you have to be culturally sensitive because some students may have opposing moral and ethical viewpoints.

SUSAN: But that's the beauty of switching sides. You can't cling too tightly to any one position. Not only does it prevent you from showing your own biases, but it also makes the students wonder what you're up to. That's how you create the cognitive dissonance!

Cross-case Analysis

Each case description illuminates one or more aspects of the learning that took place for the coauthors during the Pacific CRYSTAL Project. In Case 1, the emerging pedagogical approach, it seems evident that the model works very well with Grades 6/7 students. In fact, it was so effective that it inspired one teacher to volunteer to lead a ST lesson with Grades 4/5 students. By observing his presentation of a controversial issue (Case 2), one could begin to imagine how teachers might personalize and innovate the approach to make it work best for them. However, he did preserve and reinforce the importance of our three basic elements: opening question (What is new for you?), adopting the unpopular or fringe position at the onset, and changing (modelling) different viewpoints partway through the lesson. These cases illustrate the essential elements and how robust the approach is to modification and personalization made by teachers as they enact the approach in different contexts.

Case 3 illustrates the opportunistic aspect of capitalizing on the need to know and just-in-time delivery of the teaching approach that, when authentic situations replace ST news stories, the technique still works. In fact, it seems appropriate to use this approach to facilitate science-related as well as other conflicts that may occur at school or in the community. It also highlights the importance of personalizing the controversy, particularly for young people, so that the conversation is rich and meaningful for them. Secondary school students can benefit by a sense of immediacy as well, but they will likely be more able to handle abstract concepts with a higher level of complexity than younger students.

When presenting this pedagogical approach to secondary school teachers, who can be critical of innovative techniques as in Case 4, several observations can be made. First, like their students they enjoy humour and its ability to bring levity to a serious conversation. Second, they can see the merit of using controversial SSI in their classrooms and acknowledge the power it has to engage participants. However, they express reticence about their own ability to carry off such a presentation and wonder what would happen if the discussion gets too intense. This should come as no surprise because, as Doll (1993) might say, it signifies the perturbations that are necessary to reorganize and advance their own thinking. If this is their first experience addressing potentially sensitive issues, they may decide that they require further training.

CONCLUSIONS

There is no doubt that now more than ever students require the skills to face the ever-changing world in which they live. It is the intent of the Science Times Project to enable students to gain valuable insights into the potential social and ethical implications of current science and technological advancements. The use of ST news stories allows teachers to challenge students' attitudes toward and beliefs about science while promoting scientific literacy through discussion. Choosing stories that are open-ended in nature empowers students to think critically and creatively about socioscientific issues. Furthermore, members of the so-called *net generation* are ready to be presented with options; they do not want to be taken for granted, and they enjoy challenges.

As part of the Pacific CRYSTAL initiative, we were able to follow the development of ST as a teaching tool and accompanying pedagogy. We learned that teachers are more comfortable using the teaching strategy once they experience it firsthand, and we discovered that its impacts can be memorable and long lasting. What we have not ascertained is to what degree teachers will incorporate Science Times into their toolkit. This prompts the question: What further resources, professional development, or support do teachers require so that they see the inclusion of socioscientific events as mandatory in the preparation of scientifically literate students instead of a fun activity that might only be done in some spare time?

REFERENCES

Abd-El-Khalick, F. (2003). Socioscientific issues in pre-college science classrooms. In D. L. Zeidler (Ed.), *The role of moral reasoning on socioscientific issues and discourse in science education* (pp. 41–61). Dordrecht, The Netherlands: Kluwer.

Bainer, D. (1985). What to do when people disagree: Addressing ideational pluralism in science classes. *Science Education, 69*(2), 171–183.

Burruss, J. D., & Kaenzig, L. (1999). Introversion: The often forgotten factor impacting the gifted. *Virginia Association for the Gifted Newsletter, 21*(1). Retrieved from http://www.sengifted.org/articles_social/BurrussKaenzig_IntroversionTheOftenForgotten.shtml

Christensen, C. M., Horn, M. B., & Johnson, C. W. (2008). *Disrupting class: How disruptive innovation will change the way the world learns.* Toronto, ON, Canada: McGraw-Hill.

Doll, W. E. (1993). *A post-modern perspective on curriculum.* New York: Teachers College Press.

Festinger, L. (1957). *A theory of cognitive dissonance.* Stanford, CA: Stanford University Press.

Hand, M. (2008). What should we teach as controversial? A defense of the epistemic criterion. *Educational Theory, 58*, 213–228.

Hermann, R. S. (2008). Evolution as a controversial issue: A review of instructional approaches. *Science & Education, 17*, 1011–1032.

Levinson, R. (2006). Towards a theoretical framework for teaching controversial socio-scientific issues. *International Journal of Science Education, 28*(10), 1201–1224.

Millar, R., & Osborne, J. (Eds.). (1998). *Beyond 2000: Science education for the future.* London, England: King's College London School of Education.

Ratcliffe, M., & Grace, M. (2003). *Science education for citizenship: Teaching socioscientific issues.* Berkshire, England: Open University Press.

Reis, P., & Galvão, C. (2004). Socio-scientific controversies and students' conceptions about scientists. *International Journal of Science Education, 26*, 1621–1633.

Roth, W.-M. (Ed.). (2005). *Auto/biography and auto/ethnography: Praxis of research method.* Rotterdam, The Netherlands: Sense.

Sanjakdar, F. (2005, November–December). *Controversy in our classrooms: Problems, perspectives and possibilities.* Presented at the annual conference of the Australian Association for Research in Education, Parramatta, Australia.

Schneps, M. (1989). *A private universe* [Video]. Santa Monica, CA: Pyramid Film & Video.

Science Times. (2011). *Homepage.* Retrieved from http://sciencetimes.ca/

Stevenson, R. B. (2007). Schooling and environmental education: Contradictions in purpose and practice. *Environmental Education Research, 13*(2), 139–153.

Zandvliet, D. B., & Teed, S. (2010, March). *Science Times: A free online resource for teachers.* Paper presented at annual conference of Catalyst, Kelowna, BC, Canada.

Zeidler, D. L., & Sadler, T. D. (2008). The role of moral reasoning in argumentation: Conscience, character, and care. In S. Erduran & M. P. Jiménez-Aleixandre (Eds.), *Argumentation in science education* (pp. 201–216). New York: Springer.

Zeidler, D. L., Sadler, T. D., Simmons, M. L., & Howes, E. V. (2005). Beyond STS: A research-based framework for socioscientific issue education. *Science Education, 89*, 357–377.

Susan M. Teed, David B. Zandvliet and Carlos Gustavo A. Ormond
Faculty of Education
Simon Fraser University
Burnaby, British Columbia, Canada

EILEEN VAN DER FLIER-KELLER, DAVID W. BLADES
AND TODD M. MILFORD

10. PROMOTING EARTH SCIENCE TEACHING AND LEARNING

Inquiry-based Activities and Resources Anchoring Teacher Professional Development and Education

Science is a fundamental underpinning for society. Earth Science, which studies the way in which the natural world works as a system, is a key element in our understanding of natural processes and is, therefore, critical to how society responds to many important issues. More specifically, Earth Science (ES) deals with the finding and sustainable use of natural resources (e.g., water, soils, energy, and minerals) that are limited, precious, and relied upon to sustain our existence on the planet. ES also addresses the prediction and remediation of natural hazards such as earthquakes, volcanoes, and mass wasting. Understanding the complexity of the Earth's systems and appreciation for how the Earth has changed over time will inform our responses to current issues of global change, such as increasing global temperatures, melting ice, sea-level changes, and extinctions.

BACKGROUND

ES plays a unique role in the sciences in that it is highly interdisciplinary, utilizing all of the sciences to understand the complex operations and processes in the Earth's systems. While observations and experiments taken in the field are important, so are laboratory experiments and complex computer models. ES is strongly connected with the aesthetic enjoyment of the natural world where humans go to recreate, relax, and experience joy and pleasure—whether it be green spaces in cities or parks featuring mountains, plains, rivers, glaciers, or coastlines. This chapter outlines the authors' efforts to address the role of ES instruction in the K–12 school system in British Columbia (BC). We outline our efforts to enhance and enrich the teaching of ES in schools through a two-pronged approach: teacher professional development and innovative approaches to teacher education.

Earth Science in the School Curriculum

In spite of the relevance of ES to society, there is less focus on it in the BC school curriculum, particularly at the senior levels, compared to physics, chemistry, and biology. The interdisciplinary make-up of ES has the potential to tie together many

L. D. Yore et al (Eds.), Pacific CRYSTAL Centre for Science, Mathematics, and Technology Literacy: Lessons Learned, 165–183.

different disciplines and offer personal relevance to students at all ages. Many ES topics, however, are prescribed in the K–10 BC general science curriculum and Instructional Resource Packages (IRP). These topics include soil and water in Grade 2, weather in Grade 4, resources in Grade 5, extreme environments in Grade 6, Earth's crust in Grade 7 (BC Ministry of Education [MoE], 2005), water systems on Earth in Grade 8 science (MoE, 2006a), and energy transfers in natural systems in Grade 10 science (MoE, 2008). In addition, many ES topics are prescribed in the social studies curriculum; for example, physical features and natural resources of Canada in Grade 5, major world geographic and political features in Grade 6, and natural disasters in Grade 7 (MoE, 2006b).

In the senior secondary school years, Earth Science 11 and Geology 12 courses exist; however, these courses are offered in a limited number of schools. Between 2000 and 2005, approximately 8,000, 13,000, and 18,000 students per year took the Grade 12 physics, chemistry, and biology examinations, respectively. Over the same period, less than 2,000 students per year took the Geology 12 examination (Van der Flier-Keller, 2007). In addition, in 2004/05, both the mean provincial examination scores and pass rates for Geology 12 (62% & 79%, respectively) were lower than those for Physics 12 (72% & 90%, respectively), Chemistry 12 (71% & 90%, respectively), and Biology 12 (68% & 83%, respectively).

Earth Science in Schools

Some of the motivation for designing and implementing procedures to increase students' understanding of and interest in ES came about as a result of the first author's experiences with teacher attitudes toward teaching ES when her children attended school (circa 1991–2008). During this time, several teachers explicitly stated at parent-teacher meetings that they would not be teaching the required ES portion of the curriculum of the specific grade in question. A variety of reasons were given including lack of background and interest in ES (for many of these teachers, their science background was primarily in biology). Additional feedback from teachers who subsequently attended ES workshops suggests that the lack of appropriate ES classroom resources (e.g., labelled rock kits, fossil samples, maps, etc.), lack of ES background, and issues with funding and waivers for field trips were other major impediments to teaching ES in the elementary school grades. This is by no means an indictment of those who work as teachers in the BC school system; these comments only provide context and motivation for the work outlined in this chapter.

In fact, the resistance to teaching ES identified by BC teachers is corroborated by studies, including Jenkins (2000) who noted insecurity regarding teaching ES among English and Welsh teachers at having to teach beyond the science specializations in which they were educated. King (2001) stated, "without a proper background or 'feel' for an area of science, it is difficult to teach about it in a way that demonstrates its background, scope, importance, ramifications, links to other areas of science, or the way in which scientific investigations in that area are conducted" (p. 645). He noted, "Since most UK teacher education institutions do not have an Earth science specialist on their staff, students receive little input in this area during their teacher education, and so are generally unprepared for their teaching of NCS [National Curriculum for Science] earth science" (p. 643). Perhaps in consequence, King suggested that, based on a survey of 164 UK science teachers, the content of practical, investigational, and field work in ES courses in UK schools is low.

Student perceptions of their secondary school ES experiences—identified in a 2005 survey of students graduating from BC schools and enrolled in a first year university ES course (Van der Flier-Keller, 2007) are reflected in the following comments: ES was not emphasized very heavily and had low status compared to chemistry and physics; 'Academic' students were encouraged to take chemistry, physics, and biology; The other sciences were definitely more of a focus; Senior ES courses are often considered to be 'rocks for jocks'. In addition, written comments identified the small amount of time spent on the subject, a lack of enthusiasm by teachers, and the boring teaching methods as key factors that negatively affected their enjoyment and interest in ES in secondary school.

Teacher Professional Development in Earth Science

Watters and Ginns (2000) noted, "at the core of making science meaningful for children are the actions and initiatives of classroom teachers" (p. 301). Further, Fensham (2008) stated, "the fundamental factor in the improvement of students' learning in science and technology is the quality (knowledge, skills and enthusiasm) of their teachers" (p. 39). Based on this recognition of the key role of teachers in student learning about science, it follows that supporting teachers in teaching ES through good quality professional development should be of highest priority. Teachers themselves have expressed a strong interest in professional development support for ES teaching (e.g., King, 2001). The need for and interest in ES professional development is particularly acute when new ES curricula are introduced or when ES topics become examinable.

Professional development is not just important in ES; it is widely recognized as a critical part of a teachers' professional career. The USA's *National Science Education Standards* (United States National Research Council [NRC], 1996) state:

> Becoming an effective science teacher is a continuous process that stretches from preservice experiences in undergraduate years to the end of a professional career. Science has a rapidly changing knowledge base and expanding relevance to societal issues, and teachers will need ongoing opportunities to build their understanding and ability. Teachers also must have opportunities to develop understanding of how students with diverse interests, abilities, and experiences make sense of scientific ideas and what a teacher does to support and guide all students. And teachers require the opportunity to study and engage in research on science teaching and learning, and to share with colleagues what they have learned. (p. 55)

Given that ES appears to not be taught well in some schools—if at all—and given the assumed importance of professional development of preservice and inservice teachers for the effective teaching of ES, we developed a project to examine the role such professional development might play in the academic success of students enrolled in the Education Laboratory section of EOS 120 and if this constructivist-based experience and associated resources would effectively support these preservice teachers in delivering ES during and following their teacher education program.

Effective Teacher Professional Development

The goal of effective continuing professional development for teachers is to support teaching and learning in the classroom. Researchers (e.g., Adey, Landau, Hewitt, & Hewitt, 2003; Day, 1999; Guskey, 2000; Joyce & Showers, 1988; Lydon & King, 2009) generally agree that the major characteristics of effective professional development include:

- provision of new knowledge, ideas, and skills that are relevant to the needs of the teacher (e.g., linked to the curriculum, direct benefit in the classroom, etc.)
- delivery in a content-appropriate manner by a skilled practitioner
- a collaborative and sustained approach
- provision of opportunities for discussion and exploration with colleagues
- a chance to experiment and reflect, away from the pressures of the classroom
- provision of coaching
- support by school management.

Four outcomes of professional development were identified by Joyce and Showers (1988): knowledge or awareness, changes in attitude, development of skills, and transfer of training and control. Harland and Kinder (1997) discussed different order outcomes: third-order (lowest impact) deal with materials, information, and awareness. Second-order outcomes are based on motivation, affect, and institutional change while first-order outcomes comprise knowledge, skills, and change in attitude. However, there is general consensus that, if some of the seven elements of professional development are not present, the effectiveness will be reduced, "possibly to nil" (Lydon & King, 2009, p. 67).

Considerable teacher professional development takes place in informal learning environments (see Yore & Van der Flier-Keller, Chapter 1 this book). Fenichel and Schweingruber (2010) suggested that:

> ... teacher professional development offered by informal science institutions should adhere to the following criteria:
> - goals need to be defined clearly and need to be attainable;
> - programs should be developed in collaboration with teachers and schools to ensure the applicability and usefulness of the strategies offered (conduct a needs assessment);
> - programs ought to aim beyond the immediate professional development experience and focus on implementation in the classroom, with attention to fidelity of implementation while allowing teachers to adjust to their specific situation;
> - professional development experiences need to allow teachers to learn from one another, share experiences, and model new strategies; and
> - online offerings need to include "practice at school" and follow-up support should be provided. (p. 181)

These criteria are remarkably similar to those discussed in the broader professional development literature and provided the template from which we explored this issue with practicing and preservice teachers through the Pacific CRYSTAL Project at the University of Victoria from 2005 to 2010.

Professional Development in Earth Science

There are many models globally for ES teacher professional development. For example, in the UK the Earth Science Education Unit developed and provided 90-min workshops to entire secondary school science departments (Lydon & King, 2009). In Canada, locally developed ES workshops that were monetarily supported by EdGEO facilitated the provision of resource packages (e.g., rock and fossil kits, activity manuals, etc.) for teachers to take with them for classroom use (Van der Flier-Keller, Clinton, & Haidl, 2009). In the USA, the *Earth Science by Design Handbook for Professional Developers* (McWilliams et al., 2006), which was based on *Understanding by Design* (Wiggins & McTighe, 2005), was designed to improve science teachers' knowledge by implementing inquiry-based pedagogy using web-based visualizations of Earth processes. These workshops examine the teaching, learning, and development of curriculum-based understanding of the big ideas in Earth system science. Another USA professional development program focusing on the Earth systems approach, provided through the Earth System Science Education Alliance (http://esseacourses.strategies.org/) developed a series of online, inquiry-based courses to provide content knowledge and tools to support teachers in incorporating Earth system science into their curricula.

PACIFIC CRYSTAL TEACHER PROFESSIONAL DEVELOPMENT IN EARTH SCIENCE

A recent model for offering ES teacher professional development was provided through Pacific CRYSTAL: stand-alone workshops and a special laboratory section for EOS 120. The ES workshops were developed by professional geoscientists with feedback from practicing teachers; the interdisciplinary ES workshops were developed by the first author in collaboration with a biologist and an environmental scientist with feedback from inservice and preservice teachers. While the workshops were designed as one-time events, many teachers attended several workshops, often coming back year after year.

Workshops were held on province-wide professional development days, at school district professional development conferences, interdisciplinary conferences, provincial science teacher conferences, and national conferences (e.g., Geological Association of Canada) and nongovernmental organization (NGO) teacher conferences (e.g., Mitchell Odyssey). Workshops ranged in duration from 1 hr to 1.5 days, including a field trip. Activities were based on a constructivist learning model (i.e., people learn best by actively constructing their own understanding based on prior knowledge, concurrent experience, and sociocultural interactions) and were classroom tested prior to the workshops. Between 6 and 12 classroom workshops were held per year (2005–2010). In addition, a lesson study approach was used with the activities and workshops where the content, delivery, and approach were modified and improved in response to teacher feedback. The intended workshop outcomes included increasing teacher confidence in teaching ES, developing more positive attitudes toward and enthusiasm for ES, and improving knowledge and understanding of key ideas in ES. The workshops were designed to provide support in specific areas of the science curriculum around which teachers had expressed a need for professional development, while highlighting "the 'Big Ideas' and supporting concepts" of ES as outlined in the *Earth Science Literacy Principles* (Earth Science Literacy Initiative, 2009, para. 1). Topics and curricular links are shown in Table 1.

Table 1. Earth science (ES) teacher professional development topics by grade level

Topic	BC science grade level (ES)	Collaboration or impetus
Grade 10 ES	10	Introduction of provincial Grade 10 science examination
Earth history fossils and the stories rocks tell	7, 10, 11, 12	
Plate tectonics, earthquakes, and volcanoes	6, 7, 10, 11, 12	
ES and society: Resources, hazards, and global change	4, 5, 7	
Geological journey	7–12	CBC Learning (Canadian Broadcasting Corporation, 2007)
What on earth is in our stuff: Nonrenewable resources & BC	5	BC Ministry of Energy, Mines, & Petroleum Resources
Wet and wild: Water systems, weathering, and erosion	2, 8	
Interdisciplinary ES & biology: Soils	2	Pacific CRYSTAL & Kelly Nordin
Interdisciplinary ES & biology: Nearshore marine ecology and evolution	Biology 9, 10, 11	Pacific CRYSTAL & Seaquaria in Schools Project

Design of Workshops

Key features of the ES workshops, which met effective professional development requirements (Lydon & King, 2009), are as follows:

Provision of new knowledge, ideas, and skills relevant to the needs of the teacher

- Direct teacher participation in constructivist based hands-on activities, experiments, literacy activities, field trips as well as discussions, question sessions, and brainstorming.
- Directly relevant to the practical and pedagogical classroom needs of teachers, meeting curriculum requirements through workshop content and practice with concepts, activities, and discussions. Workshops also met teacher needs for inspiration and a boost to science enthusiasm.

- Promotion of hands-on curriculum activities and experiments in line with ES practice.
- Classroom resources, such as rock and fossil kits, provided to support the transfer of hands-on learning activities and ideas into the classroom.

Delivery in a content-appropriate manner by a skilled practitioner

- Leaders are skilled practitioners, a combination of experienced ES-savvy teachers and professional Earth scientists, who can address both ES content or knowledge issues and classroom applications. The hands-on, field-based approach is content appropriate, modelling how ES is done in practice.

Collaborative and sustained

- Inherently collaborative given the mix of practitioners; in addition, teachers collaborate amongst themselves to share applications, approaches, and what works and does not work.
- One-time events; however, ongoing opportunities are advertised through teacher professional development networks so that teachers may attend multiple workshops as they require and choose.

Provides teachers with opportunities for discussion and exploration with colleagues

- Promote small group discussion among teachers both during activities, which are done in groups of 3–5, and in dedicated discussion time.
- Leader-scaffolded discussions are an important part of workshops enabling transfer of ideas, suggestions, and comments between the larger groups of participants.
- Participants are encouraged to link with the wider ES education community through membership in the Canadian Geoscience Education Network (n.d.). This network facilitates interaction between teachers and practicing Earth scientists and provides opportunities for ongoing professional development.

Involves experimentation and reflection, away from the pressures of the classroom

- Typically held on professional development days at a centrally located venue, often a large school, so that most participants are away from their normal environments and everyday pressures.
- Activities are designed to incorporate experimentation as well as reflection, both in small and larger groups.

Provision of coaching

- Modelling plays an important role; the active participation of teachers in all of the workshop tasks and activities (e.g., role-playing, experiments, etc.) provides many opportunities for one-on-one support and discussion, both in terms of ES content and teaching approaches.

Supported by school management

- Invited by school board professional development coordinators, often cosponsored by individual schools, reflecting support by the school system and school management. Teacher leaders are supported in this role by their school administration.

Classroom Resources

While the development of ES understanding and teaching practice through hands-on activities, peer collaboration, discussion, and modelling good pedagogy were important aspects of the workshops, the provision and use of good-quality, appropriate classroom resources were considered key components. Availability of resources was deemed critical to successful constructivist teaching, especially since teachers have cited this as a barrier to teaching ES. Local resources—including the *South Vancouver Island Earth Science Fun Guide* (Van der Flier-Keller, 1998), *A Field Guide to the Identification of Pebbles* (Van der Flier-Keller, 2005), and *Geoscape Victoria* (Yorath, Kung, & Franklin, 2002)—were important for relevance and place-based examples and contexts. In addition to these resources, the teachers received relevant rock and fossil kits, books, posters, and manuals containing activity descriptions and lesson plans.

Workshop Evaluation Methods and Results

The workshops were evaluated using a short survey (EdGEO evaluation) completed by teachers at the end of each session. Additional comments were provided by workshop, NGO, and other conference organizers. The evaluation goals, as part of the lesson study design, were to determine what the teachers considered useful or not and elicit suggestions to facilitate iterative change and workshop improvement. In addition, remarks about the activities, resources, and approaches were requested. Analysis of the responses indicated that they were overwhelmingly positive. On a 7-point scale (0 = poor … 6 = outstanding), teachers evaluated the workshops as primarily outstanding (6) or excellent (5). Feedback was collected and analyzed for content, revealing five main aspects (sample comments are included to illustrate the theme):

Workshop approach: Wow!! How much more practical could a workshop be—I can now teach a science unit that I've had so much difficulty with before (Grade 2/3 teacher). Excellent information, interesting presentation, hands-on, applicable. Things I can take back to my classroom to show and use. I found this so helpful for my ES unit (Grade 7/8 teacher). Excellent demonstrations and materials. Strategies to help students to understand these concepts were outstanding (Grades 6–10 teacher). Hands-on/real life problem solving. Nice to be in the place of our students for a change. Need more specialized workshops like this one (Grade 11/12 teacher).

Active involvement: She had us engaged in hands-on activities. It was a wonderful session. Hands-on, resources, meaningful activities for kids, fascinating (Grade 6 teacher).

Links to the curriculum: Hands-on strategies/examples to teach/show my students the material/curriculum (Grades 6–10 teacher).

Classroom resources: Very practical resources and ideas I can't wait to try in a classroom. Excellent information, demonstrations, and take-home goodies

(Grades 6–10 teacher). Excellent visuals and demos—very useable. Thank you for the materials. I really enjoyed this and will be using your demos THIS WEEK in EarthSci 11 (Grade 10/11 teacher).

Inspiration: Excellent presentation, great materials. Thank you very much; you've really inspired me (Grades 10–12 teacher). Having neither taught the curriculum strand "Rocks and Minerals" nor distinctly studied it, my initial expectations on the subject were low and of little excitement. After experiencing the lessons prior to and the journey on our 'rock walk', I have a new-found appreciation and energy for the subject (Grade 5/6 teacher).

A school district professional development conference organizer (from a location where we offered two workshops) commented: *In short, you've made a difference to many of our teachers—and that's what good professional development is all about.*

Expanding from Teacher Professional Development to Teacher Education

Working with practicing teachers in the ES workshops indicated that ES was not only de-emphasized in their initial teacher education program and science curricula, but that there was also a disconnect between how ES was being taught in university content courses and how it should be taught to elementary, middle, and secondary school students. We recognized that "[e]xtensive rethinking of how teachers are prepared before they begin teaching and as they continue teaching—and as science changes—is critical to improving K–8 science education" (NRC, 2007, pp. 1–2). This requires coordinated efforts by the Faculty of Science and the Faculty of Education to ensure consistent expectations are established and demonstrated in the science content and science pedagogy courses in the university program. Adopting these integrative approaches will more likely lead to potential teachers adopting an informed pedagogical understanding of teaching ES. As one preservice teacher commented, *Let's make good teachers now as opposed to fixing them later.* For the authors, the logical step forward in engaging teachers in ES was to expand the practicing teacher professional development approach to include similar opportunities for preservice teachers.

With the support of Pacific CRYSTAL, the EdGEO National Teacher Workshop Program, and the University of Victoria (School of Earth and Ocean Sciences, Learning and Teaching Centre, and the Department of Curriculum and Instruction), a program was designed and implemented building on lessons learned from teacher workshops and integrating them into the teacher education program. The outcome was the development of a new laboratory section in an ES course commonly taken by preservice education students as part of their Bachelor of Education degree to partially satisfy the laboratory science requirement. The research project to develop and evaluate the effectiveness of this *Education Laboratory* is a unique collaboration between the Faculties of Science and Education. Expanding into the realm of teacher education is an unusual step for science departments and is additional evidence of the success and impact of the research network encouraged and facilitated by the Pacific CRYSTAL Project (Fenichel & Schweingruber, 2010).

The Education Laboratory in EOS 120

EOS 120 is a university science course entitled Introduction to the Earth System II. This 1-term (4 months) course includes lecture and laboratory components and is offered by the Faculty of Science. The Education Laboratory (EdLab) is one of several laboratory sections (all with the same content) to reinforce the lecture material and provide practical experience with the course objectives. Piloted over 3 years (2005–2007), the EdLab is now an ongoing part of the EOS 120 course. Regular laboratory sections consist of 12 3-hr sessions; the EdLab has an additional preliminary teaching tutorial in which constructivist teaching methods, the basis for all succeeding laboratory activities, are introduced. The EdLab was distinct from regular laboratory sections in that the approach was to present the course materials, with resources, transferable to the K–10 classroom and curriculum. The same ES concepts as the other laboratory sections were taught, but a teaching strategy grounded in constructivist pedagogies advocating an inquiry approach was adopted. In particular, this section sought to develop learning experiences that reflected those advocated by the science methods courses in the Faculty of Education on the premises that aspiring teachers should learn from these approaches as early as possible and that science content and pedagogy should be aligned. Every class activity was considered from the perspective of modelling effective teaching practice and giving students ideas for lesson planning and resources for teaching.

Pre-Education students were provided opportunities to model, experience, and practice a wide range of teaching methods, including the EDU (Explore, Discuss, Understand) modified learning cycle (Blades, 2000, 2001); hands-on activities; demonstrations; think–pair–share; student-generated representations (e.g., classification charts, diagrams, etc.); role playing; language arts links (e.g., fortunately/ unfortunately stories, rock obituaries, etc.); experiments; peer teaching; lesson planning; jigsaw discovery; concept mapping; group work; discussions; and field trips.

Distinct from regular laboratory sections, there was minimal lecturing and use of worksheets. The dedicated laboratory manual provided activity instructions, background information, and EDU sheets with sample questions to assist in skill development for leading teacher-scaffolded discussions at different stages of the activity. The capacity of the EdLab is 20 students per year; they are screened based on their interest in teaching and proximity to time of application and entry into the teacher education program. Following the approach for the ES professional development workshops, resources were provided to these students for use in their future classrooms, including rock kit (26 samples), mineral kit (20 samples), fossil kit (11 samples), books, posters, colour overheads, and activity blackline masters.

RESEARCH DESIGN

The EdLab was the focus of an evaluation study conducted over the fall of 2005, 2006, and 2007. It consisted of two major groups: EOS 120 students in regular laboratory sections ($n = 421$) representing 88% of the students enrolled and pre-Education students in the EdLab sections ($n = 60$) representing 22% of the students. Several aspiring teachers in EOS 120 were not able to be accommodated in the EdLab and thus enrolled in another section composed of regular students. The numbers of students were reasonably consistent, with 135 in the regular sections and 20 in the education section in 2005, 142 and 20 (respectively) in 2006, and 144 and 20 (respectively) in 2007. Students' ages were collected as categorical data and ranged from 16 to over 40 years. Overall, 53% were in the 16–20 range, 26% in the 21–25 range, 4% in the 26–30 range, and 5% in the >31 group (approximately 10% did not report their age). Additionally, 51% of the sample was female and 37% was male (again, approximately 10% did not report their gender).

Procedure

Ethical approval for this study was secured through the Human Research Ethics Board (HREB) at the University of Victoria. The study employed a mixed method (Patton, 1990) of quantitative and qualitative data toward gaining a rich understanding of the impact of the special laboratory section, both in terms of the understanding of and attitudes toward ES. None of the information on study participants was made available to the researchers until after submission of term grades for each year as per the HREB requirements. The data collection tools used over the 3-year study are described next.

Surveys. Pre- and postlaboratory surveys were completed by all EOS 120 students regardless of laboratory section. Surveys included demographic information (i.e., dichotomous gender, age range), information about their ES secondary school experiences (i.e., dichotomous for if they attended school in BC, Likert scale for ES class experiences), an attitude toward ES question, and 20 multiple-choice knowledge questions based on common misconceptions about ES (same on pre and post). These data were used to document gains in attitude and knowledge between the students in the EdLab and regular laboratory sections. The surveys were given at the beginning and end of term, each time without prior notice so that the knowledge–question results represented long-term knowledge as opposed to last-minute cramming. Content validity of the knowledge questions was verified by the instructors; both are tenured faculty in Earth Science and Science Education. Reliability of the content test was explored using a Cronbach □ analysis that revealed an internal consistency coefficient of 0.53 amongst the 20 items. Furthermore, the means of the pretest (11.8) and posttest (13.7) were significantly different ($p < .001$), thereby lending support to the sensitivity of the content items.

Interviews. Student group interviews were conducted at the end of the term but prior to the final examination for the EdLab and a regular section (taught by the same teaching assistant) for comparison.

Course grades. Student grades (laboratory, lecture midterm and final examinations) were analyzed for comparisons of overall achievement in the EOS 120 course.

RESULTS

The results of the evaluation study are reported in order of the global question of performance to more specific, detailed performance. Course grades are used to address the normative values of the Faculty of Science and the Faculty of Education in which most judgments are based on grade point average. The knowledge, attitude, and perception results are more specific to the ES education community.

Achievement in Earth Science – Course Grades

EOS 120 student grades over the 3-year pilot study were analyzed as indicators of understanding of ES concepts. Results for all years for laboratory, lecture, and final grades for both cohorts of students are provided in Table 2. Students in the EdLab scored better in their laboratory grades than their peers in the regular sections while performances in lecture and final grades were mixed but generally favoured the EdLab students.

Achievement in Understanding of Earth Science – Survey Questions

All students in this study completed a 20-question, selected-response test addressing common misconceptions as part of the pre- and postlaboratory surveys. A series of Wilcoxon signed-rank tests was conducted on all scores in all laboratory sections across all 3 years of the study on these content knowledge questions. Wilcoxon was selected as these data did not meet parametric assumptions of normality; the analysis is simply a count of the number of differences that are positive and negative and then making decisions based upon these counts (Elliot & Woodward, 2007). The Wilcoxon signed-rank test results (Table 3) indicate the number of scores on the posttest that improved over the number of students taking both tests. The significance is based upon a Z score and subsequent p value with $\square$ set at .05 (a Bonferroni adjustment was added to the interpretation to accommodate for inflated Type 1 error). According to this output, there was a significant increase in students' scores on the content test for five of the six sections (only the 2006 EdLab section was not significantly different from zero). Effect sizes tended to be in the medium range for the regular group and high for the education group.

Table 3. Output for Wilcoxon signed-rank tests

Group	2005	2006	2007
Regular	66/108; $Z = -3.84$; $p < .001, r = -.37$	70/117; $Z = -3.52$; $p < .001, r = -.33$	87/128; $Z = -5.64$; $p < .001, r = -.49$
Education	16/20; $Z = -3.37$; $p = .001, r = -.76$	11/18; $Z = -2.34$; $p = .019^*, r = -.55$	17/18; $Z = -3.64$; $p < .001, r = -.86$

* Nonsignificant difference with Bonferroni adjusted $\square$.

Of the 20 questions, 7 were identified as being most sensitive to instruction (Q1—age of the planet, Q2—date life recorded on the planet, Q5—human and dinosaur coexistence, Q7—earthquakes in BC, Q8—Vancouver Island plate name, Q11—soil formation, Q12—ground and surface water system). The results of these questions for both groups across all 3 years are presented in Table 4. Inspection of these results revealed that Q7, Q8, and Q11 offered the lowest pretest performances and, therefore, the potential for improvement. The aggregated data across all years revealed two patterns. First, there is an identified increase in the percentage per-formance for the EdLab group on all three questions while the performance for the regular group was mixed (Q8, performance decreased on the posttest). Second, the absolute posttest performances of the EdLab group were higher than the regular group while their pretest performances were either lower or equal to the regular group. For example, the EdLab group changed by a percentage of +15, +10, and +12 for the three questions, respectively, while the regular group changed by a percentage score of +8, –4, and +8. There appeared to be a positive influence of instruction on the correction of misconceptions across the entire study, and this influence was greater for the EdLab group.

Attitude toward Earth Science

This section addresses the pretest and posttest answers to students' attitude toward ES to explore any change following instruction. Data were collected on students' responses measured on a 5-point Likert scale (1 = strongly disagree … 5 = strongly agree) to the question: *Do you feel the study of Earth Science is relevant to society?* These results are presented in Table 5. Initial interpretations and comparisons of these data show that students generally agreed that ES was a topic relevant to society with little difference observed either across the years or between the EdLab and regular laboratory sections.

Given this pattern of relationship, the data were aggregated across all three groups and a McNemar's test was performed on each group to determine if student impressions of the relevance to society changed significantly after instruction. McNemar's test is designed for the analysis of paired dichotomous categorical variables much like a paired *t*-test for quantitative data (Elliot & Woodward, 2007). Using McNemar's test, no significant change was found for students being more likely to feel ES was more relevant if they were in the EdLab section ($p = 0.31$); however, students were significantly more likely to feel ES was more relevant if they were from the regular group ($p = 0.04$).

Finally, considerable data were collected from student interviews, written reflections, and evaluations. Although all data have not been fully analyzed for content, some themes are evident upon initial observation. For example, EdLab students generally and overwhelmingly commented on their increased comfort level and enjoyment of ES following the course. Sample comments include: *I was scared of this course, as a science course coming from an Arts background, but now I feel comfortable and confident to teach ES. I enjoyed it. I would take another science*

Table 2. Laboratory, lecture, and final grades (mean, standard deviation, number) for education and regular students enrolled in EOS 120 in 2005, 2006, and 2007

Laboratory	M	SD	N	Lecture	M	SD	N	Final	M	SD	N
2005 Regular	40.5	3.4	150	2005 Regular	30.3	6.9	150	2005 Regular	70.8	9.1	150
2005 Education	43.4	1.5	20	2005 Education	32.4	7.1	20	2005 Education	75.8	8.0	20
2006 Regular	39.5	3.3	114	2006 Regular	35.2	6.4	114	2006 Regular	74.8	8.8	114
2006 Education	43.4	1.5	18	2006 Education	34.6	8.1	18	2006 Education	74.5	11.3	18
2007 Regular	40.5	3.5	132	2007 Regular	30.1	6.5	132	2007 Regular	70.0	10.1	132
2007 Education	41.5	2.8	20	2007 Education	30.9	5.8	20	2007 Education	72.3	8.4	20

Table 4. Percentage correct for pre- and posttest student responses to select questions on common misconceptions

Question	2005		2006		2007	
	Regular (n = 118)	Education (n = 20)	Regular (n = 115)	Education (n = 18)	Regular (n = 134)	Education (n = 17)
Pre #1	98	100	99	100	99	100
Post #1	100	100	99	100	98	100
Pre #2	99	100	99	100	97	94
Post #2	99	100	100	93	98	100
Pre #5	95	85	96	94	88	100
Post #5	95	95	95	100	95	100
Pre #7	28	20	20	17	21	41
Post #7	31	40	28	23	33	38
Pre #8	56	78	50	41	30	12
Post #8	60	70	34	43	34	42
Pre #11	68	80	59	56	59	61
Post #11	73	85	65	79	72	67
Pre #12	85	80	77	83	83	89
Post #12	89	90	91	79	87	89

Table 5. Number and (percentage) pre- and posttest perceptions of the relevance of the study of earth science to society

	2005 Education		2005 Regular		2006 Education		2006 Regular		2007 Education		2007 Regular	
	Pre	Post	Pre	Post	Pre	Post	Pre	Post	Pre	Post	Pre	Post
SD	0 (0)	1 (5)	1 (1)	4 (3.3)	0 (0)	0 (0)	2 (2)	0 (0)	0 (0)	1 (5.5)	1 (1)	1 (1)
D	1 (5)	0 (0)	5 (4)	6 (5)	0 (0)	1 (5.5)	2 (2)	3 (3)	0 (0)	0 (0)	0 (0)	3 (2)
N	8 (40)	7 (35)	15 (12.5)	11 (9)	0 (0)	0 (0)	12 (10.5)	6 (5)	1 (5.5)	0 (0)	7 (5)	13 (10)
A	4 (20)	7 (35)	52 (43.5)	35 (35)	7 (39)	6 (33)	43 (37)	41 (35.5)	4 (22)	4 (22)	61 (45.5)	52 (39)
SA	7 (35)	5 (25)	47 (39)	53 (44)	9 (50)	9 (50)	55 (48)	65 (56.5)	1 (48)	13 (72)	63 (47)	60 (45)

Note. SD = Strongly disagree; D = Disagree; N = Neutral; A = Agree; SA = Strongly agree.

course now—I am much more confident about science in general. This class and especially this lab, has definitely made me more confident and enthusiastic about the teaching of ES to young children. Additionally, students commented on how much more relevant this class seemed once they had completed the experience: *I didn't see it [ES] as very important in my life, but I've changed my view now that I see the environment isn't necessarily set in stone. I have previously taken EOS 110 and wasn't too excited about this class initially but with the fun, interactive lab experience and Dr. Eileen's lectures, I became interested in the course. ... The lab was more than just sitting, listening and writing. It involved working together as a team, activities which made learning fun, I think which was key. Earth science is the most interesting science there is, relevant!*

SUMMARY, CONCLUSIONS, AND LESSONS LEARNED

It has been argued here that, due to the fundamental role Earth Science plays in promoting an understanding of the way the natural world works as a system and in aiding society to respond to important and current issues, there should be an increased role for ES in the BC education system. In fact, data collected by Van der Flier-Keller (2007) on first year ES students who had graduated from BC secondary schools showed that ES was not as highly emphasized as the more traditional sciences (i.e., biology, chemistry, physics) and that it was often awarded lower status by both teachers and students.

In an effort to address some of the misunderstandings and beliefs of low importance and low relevance toward ES, this chapter has outlined a series of procedures that were designed and implemented within the Pacific CRYSTAL Project. Following the suggested outcomes for professional development by authors such as Joyce and Showers (1988), Harland and Kinder (1997), and Fenichel and Schweingruber (2010), numerous ES professional development workshops were offered each year to empower teachers in their teaching of ES. These workshops were developed by professional geoscientists with feedback from teachers and were jointly led with professional scientists and experienced teachers.

The evidence of the positive effects of the professional development workshops was overwhelming. Participating teachers evaluated the workshops as primarily outstanding or excellent. In addition, they spoke of a new and renewed confidence and an increased interest in and a desire to bring these ES ideas to their students. Obviously, capturing the enthusiasm of teachers just after a workshop is much different than having them take these ideas and implementing them in their class-rooms. The literature is full of suggestions that transference is less than assured. However, this overall finding does suggest that workshops offering hands-on, constructivist-type activities—where participants are actively involved and leaving with increased enthusiasm toward ES and physical materials for classroom use—is an important step in improving ES classroom instruction.

In addition to the professional development opportunities for current teachers, a new laboratory section was developed for a first year ES course over the 2005–2007 academic years. This course was chosen because it is often taken by preservice

Education students as a science prerequisite course for their teaching degree. The EdLab is distinct in that it presents course material using constructivist-based activities and resources that are linked and transferable to the K–10 classroom. This EdLab section was the focus of a 3-year study that measured understanding of ES concepts, common misconceptions, and attitudes toward ES. Overall, findings indicated that (a) the EdLab section outperformed the regular one; (b) misconceptions were correctly addressed for both sections, with the EdLab performing slightly better in a few areas; and (c) students in the regular laboratory sections after instruction believed that ES was more relevant to society. The evidence of effects for the EdLab group, although not overwhelmingly positive, does point to a clear and consistent trend indicating the instruction for this population following a constructivist hands-on design was effective in improving conceptual understanding, correcting misconceptions, and increasing attitudes toward the relevance of ES. A key point here may be that students in the EdLab section scored as well if not better than those in the other sections while being exposed to innovative and pedagogically sound instructional practices that have the potential to influence their interactions with students as they progress to becoming teachers.

As is always the case with research, this overview of the Pacific CRYSTAL work in ES raises many questions. We wonder, for example, if the workshops for teachers led to increased instruction in ES in their classrooms. We intend to study if the EOS 120 course experience encourages the teaching of science, and especially ES, in the practice of new teachers who enrolled in this course. We intend to continue studying the effects of the EdLab section on student understanding of ES and especially wish to study in more detail attitude development. While there is clearly more research needed, the studies reported in this chapter offer insights into some potentially positive areas of intervention for improving the delivery and understanding of Earth Science in the BC education system; they help to articulate additional questions more precisely as well as offer further research hypotheses that can lead us in new and different directions of inquiry. Moreover, it has given us a glimpse of what can be achieved by allying ourselves with those who work as teachers in the educational system in British Columbia.

REFERENCES

Adey, P. W., Landau, N., Hewitt, G., & Hewitt, J. (2003). *The professional development of teachers: Practice and theory.* Dordrecht, The Netherlands: Kluwer.

Blades, D. W. (2000). *Constructivism in the science classroom.* Toronto, ON, Canada: Pearson Education.

Blades, D. W. (2001). *Student preconceptions.* In C. Booth, et al. (Eds.), *Science in action 7 & 8: Teachers' resource package* (pp. 38–40). Toronto, ON, Canada: Addison-Wesley.

British Columbia Ministry of Education. (2005). *Science K to 7: Sciences integrated resource package 2005.* Victoria, BC, Canada: Author.

British Columbia Ministry of Education. (2006a). *Science Grade 8: Integrated resource package 2006.* Victoria, BC, Canada: Author.

British Columbia Ministry of Education. (2006b). *Social studies 10: Integrated resource package 2006.* Victoria, BC: Author.

British Columbia Ministry of Education. (2008). *Science Grade 10: Integrated resource package 2008*. Victoria, BC, Canada: Author.

Canadian Broadcasting Corporation. (2007). *Geologic journey: Teacher resource guide*. Toronto, ON, Canada: CBC Learning. Retrieved from http://www.cbc.ca/geologic/teachersguide/GeologicJourney TRG.pdf

Canadian Geoscience Education Network. (n.d.) *Homepage*. Retrieved from http://www.geoscience. ca/cgen

Day, C. (1999). *Developing teachers: The challenges of lifelong learning*. London, England: Routledge Falmer.

Earth Science Literacy Initiative. (2009). *Earth science literacy principles: The big ideas and supporting concepts of earth science*. Retrieved from http://www.earthscienceliteracy.org/index.html

Elliot, A. C., & Woodward, W. A. (2007). *Statistical analysis quick reference guide with SPSS examples*. Thousand Oaks, CA: Sage.

Fenichel, M., & Schweingruber, H. A. (2010). *Surrounded by science: Learning science in informal environments*. Board on Science Education, Center for Education, Division of Behavioral and Social Sciences and Education. Washington, DC: The National Academies Press.

Fensham, P. J. (2008). *Science education policy-making: Eleven emerging issues*. Paris, France: UNESCO.

Guskey, T. R. (2000). *Evaluating professional development*. Thousand Oaks, CA: Corwin.

Harland, J., & Kinder, K. (1997). Teachers' continuing professional development: Framing a model of outcomes. *British Journal of In-service Education, 23*, 71–84.

Jenkins, E. W. (2000). The impact of the national curriculum on secondary school science teaching in England and Wales. *International Journal of Science Education, 22*, 325–336.

Joyce, B., & Showers, B. (1988). *Student achievement through staff development*. New York: Longman.

King, C. (2001). The response of teachers to new subject areas in a national science curriculum: The case of the Earth science component. *Science Education, 85*, 636–664.

Lydon, S., & King, C. (2009). Can a single, short continuing professional development workshop cause change in the classroom? *Professional Development in Education, 35*(1), 63–82.

McWilliams, H., McAuliffe, C., Lockwood, J., Larsen, J., Ledley, T., Rosenberg, M., et al. (2006). *Earth science by design: Handbook for professional developers*. Cambridge, MA: TERC & American Geological Institute.

Patton, M. Q. (1990). *Qualitative evaluation and research methods* (2nd ed.). Newbury Park, CA: Sage.

United States National Research Council. (1996). *The national science education standards*. Washington, DC: The National Academies Press.

United States National Research Council. (2007). *Taking science to school: Learning and teaching science in grades K–8* (R. A. Duschl, H. A. Schweingruber, & A. W. Shouse, Eds.). Board on Science Education, Center for Education, Division of Behavioral and Social Sciences and Education. Washington, DC: The National Academies Press.

Van der Flier-Keller, E. (1998). *South Vancouver Island earth science fun guide*. Calgary, AB, Canada: Bare Bones.

Van der Flier-Keller, E. (2006). *A field guide to the identification of pebbles*. Madeira Park, BC, Canada: Harbour.

Van der Flier-Keller, E. (2007). Geoscience in British Columbia high schools: Understanding the student experience—university student retrospectives. In *Abstracts of the 2007 GAC-MAC annual meeting* (Vol. 32, pp. 83–84).

Van der Flier-Keller, E., Clinton, L., & Haidl, F. (2009). EdGEO: Helping teachers teach earth science. *Geoscience Canada, 36*, 133–138.

Watters, J. J., & Ginns, I. S. (2000). Developing motivation to teach elementary science: Effect of collaborative and authentic learning practices in preservice education. *Journal of Science Teacher Education, 11*(4), 301–321.

Wiggins, G., & McTighe, J. (2005). *Understanding by design* (expanded 2nd ed.). Alexandria, VA: Association for Supervision and Curriculum Development.

Yorath, C., Kung, R., & Franklin, R. (2002). *Geoscape Victoria.* Geological Survey of Canada, Miscellaneous Report #74. Retrieved from http://geoscape.nrcan.gc.ca/victoria/index_e.php

Eileen Van der Flier-Keller
School of Earth and Ocean Sciences

David W. Blades
Department of Curriculum and Instruction

Todd M. Milford
Department of Educational Psychology and Leadership
University of Victoria
Victoria, British Columbia, Canada

IV. KNOWLEDGE TRANSFER, SYSTEMIC IMPLEMENTATION, AND BUILDING LEADERSHIP CAPACITY

TODD M. MILFORD, JOHN O. ANDERSON AND JIESU LUO

11. MODELLING OF LARGE-SCALE PISA ASSESSMENT DATA

Science and Mathematics Literacy

Information on student success in formal education as indicated by student scores on tests of academic achievement, by graduation rates, and by employment statistics is often reported in the form of school and country rankings—the so-called *league tables*. These rankings are often reported in terms of mean performance on achievement tests to make a political statement rather than to inform public policy or instruction decisions (Shelley, 2009). The results typically show that some schools and some countries perform better than others in the different skill areas and at different grades. In some public reports (e.g., Cowley & Easton, 2008), schools are ranked in terms of student results on these tests—often by aggregating results across subject areas—in an attempt to monitor system quality. Typically, some schools show consistently above, below, or at-average performance across all areas and grades whereas other schools have varied performance in comparison with their provincial or national counterparts. The publication of these rankings is often misinterpreted to mean that variation in student performance is solely due to school effects.

The Programme for International Student Assessment (PISA) is one such large-scale assessment that is often used to report such school and country rankings. PISA has been developed by the Organisation for Economic Co-operation and Development (OECD) to provide participating countries with internationally comparative mean literacy scores in reading, mathematics, and science for students nearing the end of compulsory schooling. What makes PISA more useful in providing policy-relevant information on educational performance is the additional collection and analysis of student-level and school-level background information (e.g., social background and school organization). PISA can go beyond the simple ranking of nations to look at the results—not as causal or directional—but as outcomes of schooling that nations should take seriously because they have implications for competence levels of individuals and subsequent populations.

Most information related to human endeavours is complex; in order to understand educational performance at the school level, information in the form of test results needs to go beyond simple rankings of schools to consider the underlying context of factors and situations. These factors potentially include home, family, and community characteristics such as number of parents in the home, number of children in

L. D. Yore et al (Eds.), Pacific CRYSTAL Centre for Science, Mathematics, and Technology Literacy: Lessons Learned, 187–201.

the home, income levels of the home, educational backgrounds of parents, or employment rates in the community.

The understanding of empirical relationships between student, home, and school correlates of learning outcomes is not well developed. There is a dearth of meaning and understanding that can be attributed to the scores and statistics in relation to educational policy and practice. To attain this understanding, we need better knowledge of the relationships among achievement measures and student, home, and school characteristics. Only through identifying those characteristics that are consistently and strongly related to student achievement and are accessible to policy can we suggest potential places of meaningful intervention. For example, if we can establish that student motivation is positively related to achievement and if we can influence levels of student motivation by instructional intervention, then modifications to educational policy and practice to enhance student motivation would be reasonable.

Additionally, a persistent positive relationship between the socioeconomic status (SES) of students and achievement has been shown to exist in many important learning outcomes (Nonoyama-Tarumi, 2008; Wilms, 2004). However, direct intervention in modifying student SES is not feasible and so direct policy intervention is unreasonable. But there may be ways in which the effects of student-level SES can be moderated through educational interventions, and it has been shown in some schools and in some countries that there is a near-zero relationship between SES and achievement. By identifying those school characteristics with high levels of achievement and equity in terms of SES and by contrasting them to schools with relatively low equity (a strong relationship between SES and achievement), we could identify pathways to school improvement by moderating the effects of SES.

The relationships between school system traits and the outcomes of schooling are of basic interest and significance to the educational policy community (Yore, Anderson, & Chiu, 2010). The logic to this interest lies in what may be termed the path of policy influence (Kennedy, 1999a): Those elements of public schooling that are accessible to policy makers (e.g., funding, certification qualifications of professional staff, curriculum, nature and extent of instructional support and supervision, provision of opportunities for professional development, school organizational structure) should show some influence over the key consequences of schooling (e.g., student learning, graduation rates, ease of entry into the labour market). However, many assumptions and hypothesized relationships about educational outcomes and policy-sensitive factors lack evidentiary support. The empirical investigations associated with school effectiveness often take the form of studies of the pattern of correlation between educational indicators such as expenditures (school resource inputs) and test scores (student learning achievement outcomes). The field has a history of equivocal findings (e.g., Greenwald, Hedges, & Laine, 1996a, 1996b; Hanushek, 1996).

Educational indicator models have several potential uses that range from a simple description of the educational system to the development of cause–effect models to inform policy decisions (Camilli & Firestone, 1999). Much of the work done with educational indicators has adopted a production function model of description

(Bryk & Hermanson, 1993) in which system inputs (e.g., funding and human resources) interact with schooling processes to result in outcomes, particularly student achievement. This modelling has been premised on the utility of student performance results in the monitoring of schools, evaluation of programs, formulation of policy, and implementation of school change. But as Lindblom (1968, 1990) has pointed out, the desire for models of complex social systems to have an instrumental use remains an elusive dream. Such models are likely to be, at best, enlightening, allowing incrementally expanding understandings of complex and dynamic systems such as public schools (Kennedy, 1999b). In order for these indicator models to have an enlightenment function and to expand understandings of educational systems, the analyses and models must be of a school-relevant and long-term nature, have to be clearly communicated to a broad and varied audience, and must inform discussion initiated and sustained over a period of time. It seems unlikely that one model will suffice. Variation is to be anticipated: one school to another, one province to another, one grade to another, one achievement database to another.

From this discussion, the question arises: Where can we find empirical evidence to direct our investigations toward the identification and description of policy-relevant associations among student, home, and school characteristics and the achievement of valued learning outcomes? Large-scale assessment programs can provide such information. For example, educational jurisdictions in Canada have a long history of collecting information about student achievement of learning outcomes, funding inputs, and—to a lesser extent—student, school, and home characteristics. At the provincial level, most provinces assess student achievement at selected grades in selected subject areas annually. At the national level, Canada has the recently developed *Pan-Canadian Assessment Program* (PCAP, formerly the *School Achievement Indicators Program*) that assesses 13-year-olds in reading, writing, mathematics, and science (Council of Ministers of Education, Canada [CMEC], 2008). Canada is also an active participant in international studies of student achievement such as the Trends in Mathematics and Science Study (TIMSS; United States National Center for Educational Statistics, n.d.), the International Adult Literacy Survey (IALS; Statistics Canada, 2010), and PISA (OECD, n.d.). These data are potentially rich sources of information directly related to the performance and quality of schools in the nations involved. The challenge is to access, analyze, and interpret the information in meaningful ways so as to inform our understanding of the interactions of individual and school factors that result in educational outcomes.

SECONDARY DATA ANALYSIS

Basing research on the analysis and modelling of data that has been collected by others is termed secondary data analysis (SDA). It is a form of research generally encouraged by the originators of large-scale assessment programs and has several distinct advantages. The data generated are generally of high quality in that the test and survey instruments have been carefully designed and developed to yield reliable information on clearly described variables. The sampling procedures used for test and survey administration are well designed to yield representative sampling of populations of interest. Since the data have already been collected and organized into data sets that are available to researchers, the costs associated with data collection have been met by the originating agency.

There are a number of limitations associated with SDA. A fundamental limitation is the definition and operationalisation of variables. The originating agency (the OECD in the case of PISA) has predefined the variables (e.g., the nature of achievement being measured or the way in which student self-concept or school climate is defined), and these definitions cannot be changed by the SDA researcher even if they are not exact matches to what variables are desired in the analysis to be conducted. Likewise, the sample of respondents is predetermined—in the case of PISA, 15-year-olds in schools and their teachers and principals are sampled. Although not confined to SDA but characteristic of large-scale multivariate studies, missing data are generally an issue that has to be addressed and tends to reduce the power of analyses conducted (Rogers, Anderson, Klinger, & Dawber, 2006). Lastly, an additional limitation of large-scale studies is that results are in the form of general patterns and relationships that apply to a large group of individuals, with substantial variation at the individual student level. As a consequence, SDA reporting needs to clearly describe the limits on application, especially with regard to implications for instructional practices.

HIERARCHICAL LINEAR MODELLING

The analyses of large data sets often involve the development of statistical models to identify, describe, and possibly explain relationships among important variables. A contemporary approach widely used in education is multilevel modelling or hierarchical linear modelling (HLM). HLM is a regression-based analysis that explicitly incorporates the hierarchical structure common to many educational data sets, that is, students nested within schools within countries (Raudenbush & Bryk, 2002). The data required for these analyses consist of both achievement (performance) and personal measures of students (level 1) and measures of school traits for each school (level 2) attended by the students (Anderson, Lin, Treagust, Ross, & Yore, 2007; Anderson, Milford, & Ross, 2009).

At level 1, HLM allows us to describe the linear relationships of achievement to student characteristics such as gender, SES, motivation, and attitude toward self or school. This can be represented as the familiar regression equation, for example, modelling mathematics achievement (math for student i in school j) with student gender, SES, and motivation:

$$\text{Math}_{ij} = \beta_{0j} + \beta_{1j}\text{Gender}_i + \beta_{2j}\text{SES}_i + \beta_{3j}\text{Motivation}_i + \text{error}_{1j} \qquad (1)$$

where each student's mathematics score is modelled as the intercept (β_{0j}—roughly similar to the mean mathematics score with the effects of student gender, SES, and motivation removed—in this case for each of j schools) plus the weight (β_{1j}) associated with gender plus the weighted (β_{2j}) SES-level for that student plus the weighted (β_{3j}) motivation score plus individual error. However, the j subscript tells the reader that a different level-1 model is being estimated for each j level-2 unit (schools). Each school in Equation 1 will have a different average mathematics score (β_{0j}) and a different gender (β_{1j}), SES (β_{2j}), and motivation (β_{3j}) effect on the mathematics score. These are termed the level-2 models (Equation 2). For example, in modelling the intercept (β_{0j}—which can be thought of as the conditioned school mean mathematics scores), not only is school variation in the intercept modelled (the error term—$error_{0j}$) but also school-level traits, such as school size and an index of teacher morale, can be incorporated into the equation:

$$\beta_{0j} = \gamma_{00} + \gamma_{01}\text{School Size}_j + \gamma_{02}\text{Teacher Morale}_j + error_{0j} \tag{2}$$

Here the school intercept is modeled with a level-2 intercept (γ_{00}—which is constant for all schools in the data set) plus, in this example, a weighted (γ_{01}) measure of school size plus a weighted (γ_{02}) measure of teacher morale plus a school-level error term. This models the average school mathematics score as a function of the overall average mathematics score, school size, and teacher morale. HLM then tests the significance of the residual error variation in school mean mathematics scores (the intercepts or β_{0j}'s) once mathematics achievement has been conditioned on school size and teacher morale. If the error variance is significant, it can be interpreted to mean that there is still significant variation in the average school scores after conditioning on school size and teacher morale, whereas a nonsignificant error variance term suggests that, once school size and teacher morale are accounted for, there is no significant variation in mean scores one school to another.

Likewise, the gender, SES, and motivation slopes or gradients in the student-level Equation 1 can be modelled with school-level variables. This modelling of slopes is something that is unique to multilevel modelling: the modelling of relationships. For example, it may be that at the student level (level-1) SES is significantly and positively related to mathematics achievement. HLM analysis explicitly estimates and evaluates these relationships for each school and in doing so provides the researcher with the opportunity to model the school slope variation with school traits. For example (Equation 3), if the SES slopes (β_{2j} in Equation 1) vary significantly across schools, they can be modelled with school traits such as measures of school academic focus or teacher morale:

$$\beta_{2j} = \gamma_{20} + \gamma_{21}\text{Academic Focus}_j + \gamma_{22}\text{Teacher Morale}_j + error_{2j} \tag{3}$$

Another fundamental outcome of HLM analyses is the intraclass correlation co-efficient (ICC) generated by running an unconditioned model or the "null model" (Raudenbush & Bryk, 2002, p. 24). The intraclass correlation estimates the variance component at the student and school levels and can be interpreted as the proportion of variance at the school level in relation to the total variance (Luke, 2004). Thus, it offers an indication of the amount of variance that can be potentially reduced in subsequent models of school effects. The results from PISA 2003 (Table 1) show that on average 35% of the variance in mathematics literacy achievement can be attributed to schools.

Table 1. Intraclass correlation coefficients (ICC) for PISA 2003—
Mathematics literacy

Country	Correlation	Country	Correlation
The Netherlands	0.626	Greece	0.363
Hungary	0.586	**Mean**	**0.345**
Germany	0.581	Portugal	0.341
Belgium	0.562	Switzerland	0.334
Turkey	0.560	Luxembourg	0.317
Austria	0.553	Russian Federation	0.307
Japan	0.537	USA	0.263
Slovak Republic	0.533	United Kingdom	0.223
Italy	0.527	Latvia	0.223
Czech Republic	0.523	Australia	0.212
Hong Kong–China	0.471	Spain	0.196
France	0.459	Macao–China	0.185
Indonesia	0.454	New Zealand	0.180
Brazil	0.445	Ireland	0.171
Uruguay	0.433	Canada	0.168
Tunisia	0.426	Denmark	0.132
Liechtenstein	0.418	Poland	0.127
Korea	0.415	Sweden	0.108
Mexico	0.388	Norway	0.070
Thailand	0.374	Finland	0.048
Yugoslavia	0.364	Iceland	0.042

The proportion of variance in achievement that can be attributed to schools at the international level varies widely from one country to another. The variation in ICC suggests structural differences in the ways school characteristics are related to student performance. For example, the ICC ranges from 4% for schools in Iceland to over 60% for The Netherlands. Although both Iceland and The Netherlands are relatively high-performing countries (in the top 10% of national mean mathematics literacy achievement), in Iceland (and Finland, the top-performing country in PISA 2003) school differences account for almost no variation in student mathematics achievement. This is not the case in The Netherlands where the nature of the schools—by design, structurally distinct with academic and vocational tracks—is more strongly related to student achievement, accounting for 60% of the variance in mathematics scores. However, Canadian schools, although they have relatively high levels of achievement, have a below-average proportion of variance in student achievement that can be attributed to schools, that is, less than 20%. This suggests that, although our schools perform well in relation to those of many other countries, they also tend to be more homogeneous in terms of levels of outcomes.

These examples demonstrate how the PISA measurement and modelling of school traits can lead to better understanding of educational performance as indexed by reading, mathematics, and science literacy achievement. A stark conclusion from our many resulting models of PISA data sets is that there is not a common model relating student, home, and school traits to achievement; as well, the models vary from one country to another (Goh, 2006; Gu, 2006; Hsu, 2007; Milford, 2009; Milford, Ross, & Anderson, 2010; Ross, 2008).

EXPLORATION OF PISA FINDINGS

The findings of our Pacific CRYSTAL research have gone well beyond the simple rankings of participating nations in terms of average performance scores—although we certainly noted that Canadian students perform at high levels in reading, mathematics, and science literacy in comparison to other nations that participated in PISA. The relationship between the measures of science, mathematics, and reading literacy at the student level is strong and positive—much higher than found for most interdisciplinary associations with high-stakes tests as detailed in Table 2.

The assessment measures in PISA focus on capabilities of 15-year-olds in reading literacy, mathematics literacy, and science literacy. PISA chooses the term *literacy* because it characterizes the broad, multifaceted nature of the construct being measured (OECD, 2006). Essentially, this literacy perspective focuses on the extent to which students can apply the knowledge and skills they have learned and practised at school when confronted with situations and challenges for which that knowledge may be relevant (OECD, 2005). These high correlations across all three disciplines for the majority of participating nations would appear to support PISA's contention that this assessment measures a larger association among discipline-specific "tasks relating to real life, depending on a broad understanding of key concepts, rather than limiting the assessment to the understanding of subject-specific knowledge" (OECD, 2006, p. 20).

Some of the more complex results from the multilevel models explored differences in students' educational outcomes across the nations that participated in PISA. Simply stated, the most fundamental multilevel procedures for estimating school effects indicate the relationships among student and school characteristics and schooling outcomes. The value of such analyses has been explored by Pacific CRYSTAL in several case studies, using literacy measures from PISA as the educational outcomes and background data from students and principals as student and school characteristics.

HLM CASE STUDIES

The results of the six unpublished HLM analyses of the PISA data sets for science, mathematics, and reading literacy to better understand the relationships among student performance and student, home, and community characteristics are detailed in this section.

Table 2. Correlations between literacy domains for PISA 2000, 2003, and 2006

Country	Reading and mathematics			Science and reading			Science and mathematics		
	2000	2003	2006	2000	2003	2006	2000	2003	2006
Albania	0.60	*	*	0.75	*	*	0.74	*	*
Argentina	0.64	*	0.68	0.77	*	0.75	0.82	*	0.76
Australia	0.82	0.75	0.83	0.81	0.78	0.88	0.89	0.81	0.89
Austria	0.81	0.77	0.78	0.81	0.79	0.85	0.89	0.84	0.88
Azerbaijan	*	*	0.38	*	*	0.68	*	*	0.63
Belgium	0.86	0.80	0.83	0.88	0.81	0.88	0.88	0.84	0.90
Bulgaria	0.63	*	0.77	0.78	*	0.84	0.73	*	0.85
Brazil	0.73	0.60	0.71	0.80	0.58	0.74	0.81	0.64	0.80
Canada	**0.78**	**0.75**	**0.78**	**0.80**	**0.77**	**0.84**	**0.88**	**0.80**	**0.85**
Switzerland	0.62	0.75	0.82	0.81	0.76	0.88	0.80	0.81	0.90
Chile	0.82	*	0.72	0.83	*	0.75	0.87	*	0.85
Columbia	*	*	0.57	*	*	0.61	*	*	0.68
Czech Republic	0.76	0.76	0.80	0.83	0.79	0.86	0.87	0.80	0.90
Germany	0.76	0.80	0.81	0.75	0.82	0.86	0.83	0.86	0.90
Demark	0.79	0.70	0.79	0.80	0.71	0.86	0.85	0.77	0.90
Spain	0.83	0.68	0.75	0.86	0.71	0.80	0.87	0.72	0.86
Estonia	*	*	0.82	*	*	0.85	*	*	0.89
Finland	0.75	0.68	0.74	0.76	0.72	0.81	0.80	0.76	0.86
France	0.79	0.70	0.77	0.82	0.78	0.85	0.87	0.77	0.89
United Kingdom	0.76	0.80	0.82	0.82	0.82	0.87	0.85	0.85	0.89
Greece	0.69	0.58	0.69	0.78	0.62	0.82	0.82	0.63	0.81
Hong Kong–China	0.70	0.79	0.80	0.69	0.78	0.83	0.67	0.83	0.90
Croatia	*	*	0.79	*	*	0.86	*	*	0.88
Hungary	0.84	0.71	0.80	0.82	0.75	0.85	0.90	0.75	0.89
Indonesia	0.72	0.64	0.79	0.72	0.62	0.79	0.79	0.64	0.81
Ireland	0.73	0.77	0.82	0.79	0.79	0.86	0.86	0.80	0.88
Iceland	0.77	0.73	0.80	0.78	0.74	0.85	0.85	0.76	0.86
Israel	0.80	0.68	0.76	0.76	0.71	0.83	0.82	0.74	0.84
Italy	0.76	0.76	0.69	0.72	0.80	0.76	0.78	0.79	0.83
Jordan	*	*	0.73	*	*	0.80	*	*	0.83

Table 2. (Continued)

Japan	0.78	*	0.74	0.79	0.83	0.75	0.86	0.89	0.82	0.86
Kyrgyzstan	*	*	0.66	*	*	0.67	*	*	0.72
Korea	0.82	0.76	0.81	0.83	0.79	0.87	0.89	0.82	0.88
Liechtenstein	0.79	0.75	0.83	0.82	0.79	0.90	0.83	0.82	0.91
Lithuania	*	*	0.76	*	*	0.85	*	*	0.89
Luxembourg	0.82	0.68	0.82	0.87	0.71	0.89	0.90	0.72	0.89
Latvia	0.86	0.64	0.75	0.86	0.62	0.82	0.92	0.64	0.86
Macao–China	*	0.58	0.69		0.65	0.77	*	0.66	0.82
Mexico	0.79	0.68	0.73	0.80	0.63	0.76	0.87	0.66	0.82
Montenegro	*	*	0.74	*	*	0.87	*	*	0.84
Netherlands	0.83	0.84	0.85	0.84	0.83	0.88	0.85	0.86	0.91
Norway	0.79	0.72	0.77	0.85	0.74	0.84	0.88	0.78	0.87
New Zealand	0.73	0.79	0.79	0.83	0.80	0.88	0.83	0.84	0.89
Peru	0.69	*	*	0.77	*	*	0.81	*	*
Poland	0.71	0.71	0.77	0.79	0.72	0.84	0.84	0.75	0.89
Portugal	0.77	0.71	0.80	0.84	0.76	0.85	0.87	0.78	0.89
Qatar	*	*	0.75	*	*	0.86	*	*	0.80
Romania	0.79	*	0.71	0.83	*	0.86	0.88	*	0.80
Russian Federation	0.75	0.59	0.64	0.79	0.66	0.73	0.81	0.66	0.78
Serbia	*	*	0.76	*	*	0.83	*	*	0.85
Slovak Republic	*	0.74	0.78	*	0.74	0.84	*	0.78	0.88
Slovenia	*	*	0.76	*	*	0.85	*	*	0.88
Sweden	0.76	0.73	0.79	0.79	0.76	0.84	0.80	0.77	0.89
Chinese Taipei	*	*	0.82	*	*	0.87	*	*	0.89
Thailand	0.90	0.64	0.73	0.88	0.65	0.80	0.91	0.69	0.82
Tunisia	*	0.58	0.65	*	0.54	0.73	*	0.61	0.73
Turkey	*	0.73	0.70	*	0.77	0.79	*	0.80	0.85
Uruguay	*	0.54	0.62	*	0.57	0.69	*	0.57	0.74
USA	0.85	0.81	*	0.88	0.82	*	0.91	0.83	0.90
Yugoslavia	*	0.66	*	*	0.69	*	*	0.68	*

*Not reported or nonparticipation.

Study 1. Goh (2006) looked at student-level and school-level correlates for Canadian students with results from PISA 2003 and found that students' intrinsic motivation, perceptions of teacher support, and perceptions of student–teacher relations in the school were significantly positive predicators of mathematics literacy.

Study 2. Gu (2006) compared the student-level variables of mathematical self-concept, mathematical self-efficacy, teacher support, and disciplinary climate as well as the school-level variables of student and teacher behaviour, and student and teacher morale for students from Canada and Hong Kong–China. She found similarities in the final models for both countries as student-level variables of mathematical self-concept and self-efficacy were positively associated with mathematics achievement. Similarly at the school-level, student moral, student behaviours, and disciplinary climate were also positively associated with mathematics achievement. However, teacher support was negatively associated with mathematics achievement. Differences also emerged between the two countries; Canada had a stronger relationship between student self-beliefs on mathematics achievement while Hong Kong–China had a stronger association between the school learning environment and mathematics achievement.

Study 3. Hsu (2007) also compared Canada and Hong Kong–China for PISA 2003 results but with a focus on student demographic and gender variables. She used SES, gender, family structure, and immigrant background at both the student and school levels. Student SES was significantly and positively associated with mathematics achievement in both countries (a larger influence in Canada than in Hong Kong–China), and nonnative students were predicted to achieve lower than native students. At the school level, a higher proportion of girls predicted higher mathematics achievement in Canada only while a larger proportion of students from nonnuclear families predicted lower mathematics scores in both nations.

Study 4. Ram (2007) compared students in Canada and Japan on PISA 2003. She found that males outperformed females in both nations, that SES was a significant and positive predictor of mathematics achievement (SES had a larger influence in Canada than in Japan), and that a significant and negative relationship existed between student-perceived teacher support and mathematics achievement for Canada but not Japan. Essentially, more student-perceived teacher support in Canada resulted in lower mathematics achievement on PISA but this result was not observed in Japan.

Study 5. Ross (2008) modelled the relationships between motivation and academic achievement in two distinct cultures: Western (represented by Canada, the United States, and the United Kingdom) and Asian (represented by Hong Kong–China, Japan, and Korea) on student achievement in PISA 2003. Exploring patterns of motivation and self-efficacy between these cultures is of interest in determining how Western and Asian cultures compare in the relationship between motivation and academic achievement. Student motivation and self-concept were found to be positively related to literacy achievement; students with higher levels of motivation and self-concept tended to achieve higher scores than students with low levels of these attributes. However, there were national differences in levels of student motivation and self-concept.

Study 6. Milford (2009) explored the relationships between science self-beliefs and science literacy across all nations participating in PISA 2006. Those students with higher science self-efficacy and science self-concept tended to have higher achievement within all participating nations. However, at the country level, an un-covered negative and significant correlation between science self-concept and science literacy suggests that, on average, countries with higher science self-concept tend to achieve lower on scientific literacy—and vice versa.

The individual variables that make up the holistic cultural and social capital construct (ESCS; the scaled indices of SES in PISA) account for more variance in scientific literacy on their own than does the PISA composite ESCS. Overall, these regression equations demonstrated that for all the participating nations cultural capital was the most important explanatory construct for scientific literacy. It accounted for 16% of the variance in scientific literacy scores compared to 14% for social capital, 13% for the composite ESCS, and 12% for economic capital. As has been stated, the statistical analyses of covariance like those used in this study do not imply causation, and results need to be carefully interpreted. This suggests that there may be avenues for student and family support that are outside the areas of wealth yet can have positive influence on scientific literacy.

Milford also reported a series of multilevel models exploring how patterns of science self-beliefs, SES, and immigrant status compare among nations of high immigration levels (i.e., Australia, Canada, Germany, New Zealand, Spain, and the United States) in all domains. In addition to contributing to theory, recognition of what does and what does not work for those immigrant students is essential for teachers and other education stakeholders as they strive to create education systems that are equitable for all students. For students in these nations, both science self-efficacy and science self-concept predicted increased achievement scores. Immigrant status negatively influenced achievement while ESCS was a consistently positive and significant predictor at the student level across all domains in PISA 2006. This homogeneity for final models potentially lends itself to more universal recommendations. For immigrant students, it is essential for teachers and other educa-tion stakeholders to ensure that education systems are as equitable as possible for all students.

CLOSING REMARKS AND FUTURE DIRECTIONS

The purpose of this research was—and continues to be with analyses of PISA 2009 in the planning stage—to explore the relationships of student and school characteristics to mathematics and science achievement in order to better understand educational performance. More specifically, using data from the three administrations of PISA, several analyses were conducted for the participating countries: specifically, relation-ships among student personal beliefs, motivation, and background variables and mathematics achievement across two distinct cultures—Western (represented by Canada, the United States, and the United Kingdom) and Asian (represented by Hong Kong–China, Japan, and Korea)—patterns across North, Central, and South America, and the relationship of science self-beliefs, SES, and immigrant status among nations of high immigration levels (i.e., Australia, Canada, Germany, New Zealand, Spain, and the United States).

In the first area of analysis among student-level variables and mathematics achievement in two distinct cultures, differences were found between Western and Asian countries in the results of the HLM models. For example, there were similarities between cultures for the student-level variables of motivation, mathematics self-concept, and self-efficacy with each predicting increased mathematics achievement. Similarly, SES and immigrant status were consistent across cultures with SES positively influencing mathematics achievement and immigrant status predicting lower achievement scores. However, some differences were identified in a stronger association between achievement in mathematics and student self-beliefs in Western cultures and stronger associations between achievement in mathematics and school learning environment. Our research shows that, although the relationship to achievement is positive for students in all countries, the level of self-concept is lower in some Asian countries (e.g., Hong Kong–China, Japan, and Korea) and yet the level of achievement is higher than in North America. Additionally, at the school level, a higher proportion of girls were positively associated with mathematics achievement in only Western cultures modelled in these studies.

In the second set of analyses, students with higher science self-concept and science self-efficacy tended to achieve higher academically across all nations in PISA 2006. The variables comprising the cultural and social capital constructs accounted for more variance in scientific literacy than did the composite ESCS. This might provide avenues for student and family support that are outside the areas of wealth yet can have positive influence on scientific literacy. There was a good degree of homogeneity for final models across the selected nations, which potentially leads to more universal recommendations. For all students across all countries and in all domains (with the notable exception of science self-concept in Germany for reading literacy), both science self-efficacy and science self-concept predicted increased achievement scores. Immigrant status was generally a negative—but varied—significant predictor for all nations selected for this part of the study in scientific literacy, almost all nations for reading literacy (except New Zealand) and half of the nations (Canada, Germany, and Spain) for mathematics. Finally, ESCS was a consistently positive and significant predictor at the student level across all domains in PISA 2006. Higher reported levels of ESCS were related to higher achievement. However, at the school level, patterns across country and domain were inconsistent.

Because HLM explicitly incorporates into the analysis the hierarchical structures common to many educational data sets (e.g., PISA), it is well suited to the modelling of complex social systems. One such complex system model was the recent study (Milford et al., 2009) that, in response to the increasing number of nations from the Americas participating in PISA, presented an Americas-specific example of the ways in which the PISA data set can be used for more exploratory analysis through the lens of policy and curriculum suggestions, rather than just league table comparisons. Additional efforts to use results from measures such as PISA have identified the challenges of undertaking academic research in isolation of end users (Anderson, Chiu, & Yore, 2010).

The main message arising from these results is that the relationships of student and school characteristics to educational performance as measured by mathematics and science achievement are complex and do not lend themselves to universal generalization. Certainly, schools are important in their effect on student performance; however, the magnitude of effect varies from one country to another as does the direction of relationship. To understand educational performance, a single model describing how it works is unlikely to suffice; in fact, it is unlikely to reflect reality. These results strongly suggest that careful, prolonged investigation is needed to build understandings of specific educational situations. This will require data collection designed to garner reliable information about significant student, home, and school traits. One route to attain this end is the careful design of large-scale assessment programs to serve this purpose and to further recognize that HLM modelling techniques are well suited to address questions of critical social and educational significance (O'Connell & McCoach, 2008).

The reconceptualization of student assessment programs into long-term research initiatives could better serve the purposes of not only monitoring school performance in more informed ways but also providing evidence-based understanding and evaluation for policy development and implementation. This reformation of large-scale student assessment programs should lead to programs that would monitor student achievement in important curricular areas and provide an evidentiary basis for meaningful analysis and better understanding of educational performance.

REFERENCES

Anderson, J. O., Chiu, M.-H., & Yore, L. D. (2010). First cycle of PISA (2000-2006)—International perspectives on successes and challenges: Research and policy directions [Special issue]. *International Journal of Science and Mathematics Education, 8*(3), 373–388.

Anderson, J. O., Lin, H.-S., Treagust, D. F., Ross, S. P., & Yore, L. D. (2007). Using large-scale assessment datasets for research in science and mathematics education: Programme for International Student Assessment (PISA). *International Journal of Science and Mathematics Education, 5*(4), 591–614.

Anderson, J. O., Milford, T. M., & Ross, S. P. (2009). Multilevel modeling with HLM: Taking a second look at PISA. In M. C. Shelley II, L. D. Yore, & B. Hand (Eds.), *Quality research in literacy and science education: International perspectives and gold standards* (pp. 263–286). Dordrecht, The Netherlands: Springer.

Bryk, A. S., & Hermanson, K. L. (1993). Educational indicator systems: Observations on their structure, interpretation and use. In L. Darling-Hammond (Ed.), *Review of research in education* (Vol. 19, pp. 451–484). Washington, DC: American Educational Research Association.

Camilli, G., & Firestone, W. A. (1999). Values and state ratings: An examination of the state-by-state education indicators in quality counts. *Education Measurement: Issues and Policies, 18*(4), 17–25.

Council of Ministers of Education, Canada. (2008). *Pan-Canadian assessment program (PCAP)*. Retrieved from http://cmec.ca/Programs/assessment/pancan/Pages/default.aspx

Cowley, P., & Easton, S. (2008). *Report card on British Columbia's elementary schools: 2008 edition*. Vancouver, BC, Canada: Fraser Institute.

Goh, M.-S. (2006). *Multilevel analysis of mathematics literacy: The effects of intrinsic motivation, teacher support, and student-teacher relations*. Master's thesis, University of Victoria. Retrieved from http://hdl.handle.net/1828/2155

Greenwald, R., Hedges, L. V., & Laine, R. D. (1996a). The effect of school resources on student achievement. *Review of Educational Research, 66*(3), 361–396.

Greenwald, R., Hedges, L. V., & Laine, R. D. (1996b). Interpreting research on school resources on student achievement: A rejoinder to Hanushek. *Review of Educational Research, 66*(3), 411–415.

Gu, Z. (2006). *Comparison of Canada and Hong Kong–China through hierarchical linear models: The relations among students' self-beliefs in math, the learning environment at school, and math performance*. Master's thesis, University of Victoria. Retrieved from http://hdl.handle.net/1828/2049

Hanushek, E. A. (1996). A more complete picture of school resource policies. *Review of Educational Research, 66*(3), 397–410.

Hsu, J.-C. (2007). *Comparing the relationships between mathematics achievement and student characteristics in Canada and Hong Kong through HLM*. Master's thesis, University of Victoria. Retrieved from http://hdl.handle.net/1828/2364

Kennedy, M. M. (1999a). Approximations to indicators of student outcomes. *Educational Evaluation and Policy Analysis, 21*(4), 345–363.

Kennedy, M. M. (1999b). Infusing educational decision making with research. In G. J. Cizek (Ed.), *Handbook of educational policy* (pp. 54–80). San Diego, CA: Academic Press.

Lindblom, C. E. (1968). *The policy-making process*. Englewood Cliffs, NJ: Prentice-Hall.

Lindblom, C. E. (1992). *Inquiry and change: The troubled attempt to understand and shape society*. New Haven, CT & New York: Yale University Press & Russell Sage Foundation.

Luke, D. A. (2004). *Multilevel modeling*. Thousand Oaks, CA: Sage.

Milford, T. M. (2009). *An investigation of international science achievement using the OECD's PISA 2006 dataset*. Doctoral dissertation, University of Victoria. Retrieved from http://hdl.handle.net/1828/2131

Milford, T. M., Ross, S. P., & Anderson, J. O. (2010). An opportunity to better understand schooling: The growing presence of PISA in the Americas [Special issue]. *International Journal of Science and Mathematics Education, 8*(3), 475–496.

Nonoyama-Tarumi, Y. (2008). Cross-national estimates of the effects of family background on student achievement: A sensitivity analysis. *International Review of Education, 54*, 57–82.

O'Connell, A. A., & McCoach, D. B. (2008). *Multilevel modeling of educational data*. Charlotte, NC: Information Age.

Organisation for Economic Co-operation and Development. (2005). *PISA 2003 technical report*. Paris, France: Author.

Organisation for Economic Co-operation and Development. (2006). *Assessing scientific, reading and mathematical literacy. A framework for PISA 2006*. Paris, France: Author.

Organisation for Economic Co-operation and Development. (n.d.). *PISA homepage*. Retrieved from http://www.pisa.oecd.org

Ram, A. (2007). *Multilevel analysis of mathematics literacy in Canada and Japan: The effects of sex differences, teacher support, and the school learning environment*. Master's thesis, University of Victoria. Retrieved from http://hdl.handle.net/1828/986

Raudenbush, S. W., & Bryk, A. S. (2002). *Hierarchical linear models: Applications and data analysis methods* (2nd ed.). Thousand Oaks, CA: Sage.

Rogers, W. T., Anderson, J. O., Klinger, D. A., & Dawber, T. (2006). Pitfalls and potential pitfalls of secondary data analysis of the Council of Ministers of Education, Canada, national assessment. *Canadian Journal of Education, 29*(3), 757–770.

Ross, S. P. (2008). *Motivation correlates of academic achievement: Exploring how motivation influences academic achievement in the PISA 2003 dataset*. Unpublished doctoral dissertation, University of Victoria, Victoria, British Columbia, Canada.

Shelley, M. C., II. (2009). Speaking truth to power with powerful results: Impacting public awareness and public policy. In M. C. Shelley II, L. D. Yore, & B. Hand (Eds.), *Quality research in literacy* and science education: International perspectives and gold standards (pp. 443–466). Dordrecht, The Netherlands: Springer.

Statistics Canada. (2010). International adult literacy survey. Retrieved from http://www.statcan.gc.ca/dli-ild/data-donnees/ftp/ials-eiaa-eng.htm

United States National Center for Educational Statistics. (n.d.). Trends in mathematics and science study. Retrieved from http://nces.ed.gov/timss/

Wilms, J. D. (2004). Reading achievement in Canada and the United States: Findings from the OECD programme for international student assessment: Final report. Ottawa, ON, Canada: Human Resources and Skills Development Canada. Retrieved from www.hrsdc.gc.ca/en/cs/sp/lp/publications/2004-002611/page01.shtml

Yore, L. D., Anderson, J. O., & Chiu, M.-H. (2010). Moving PISA results into the policy arena: Perspectives on knowledge transfer for future considerations and preparations [Special issue]. International Journal of Science and Mathematics Education, 8(3), 593–609.

Todd M. Milford, John O. Anderson and Jiesu Luo
Department of Educational Psychology and Leadership Studies
University of Victoria
Victoria, British Columbia, Canada

DAVID W. BLADES

12. TIME AND TEACHER CONTROL IN CURRICULUM ADOPTION

Lessons from the Lighthouse Schools Project

Canadian provinces continue to be world leaders in developing science education curricula that emphasize science literacy for all students, constructivist inquiry science teaching approaches, and authentic assessment in science education (Council of Ministers of Education, Canada, 1997). In Canada, education is the responsibility of the provinces although the national trend is toward increasing cooperation and uniformity of curriculum requirements. Curriculum change is directed by provincial ministries of education through new curriculum documents, which in British Columbia (BC) are called Integrated Resource Programs (IRPs). Such 'top-down' attempts at change invariably lead to incomplete implementation of the new curricula due to the complexity of a change process that necessarily involves teachers (Blades, 1997). Research over the past 40 years reveals that there are many factors to consider when involving science teachers in curriculum change such as the teachers' lack of science content knowledge, time constraints, limited experience to teach science beyond a textbook-dependent approach, and lack of available examples of exemplary programs (Yore, Anderson, & Shymansky, 2005). Of these factors, teachers' lack of time is considered to be a key obstacle in the adoption of a new curriculum (Campbell, 1991; Darling-Hammond & Bransford, 2005; Fullan, 1991; Futemick, 2010; Lumpkin, 2010; Sarason, 1990; Ungerleider, 2003).

This chapter reports on the case study of an elementary school where all the teachers were provided with sufficient release time to plan for the school-wide adoption of a new BC Ministry of Education (MoE) science IRP (BC MoE, 2005). The study sought to examine (a) the extent to which teachers would implement the new science curriculum in their classrooms if opportunities for planning were pro-vided and (b) whether these teachers would be subsequently willing and able to share their plans and adoption success with teaching colleagues in other elementary schools.

THE LIGHTHOUSE SCHOOLS PROJECT

This case study examined a method of curriculum adoption that focused on providing financial resources to teachers in one school to enable the school-wide adoption of a new science education curriculum and then providing the opportunity for those teachers to share their curriculum adoption with their peers. Since the focus school operated metaphorically as a *lighthouse* to help light the way for curriculum change in a school district, the project was called the Lighthouse School Project (LSP).

L. D. Yore et al (Eds.), Pacific CRYSTAL Centre for Science, Mathematics, and Technology Literacy: Lessons Learned, 203–215.

This 4-year project began with a partnership between the Centre for Excellence in Teaching and Understanding of Science (CETUS) at the University of Victoria and a K–5 school in Victoria, BC. CETUS is a university-based centre that supported K–12 school science education through teacher professional development; it played a key role in the LSP by providing $18,000 annually for teacher release time and resource acquisition. The elementary school (hereafter called Watershed Elementary School [WES], a pseudonym to protect anonymity) was selected because of its proven record of leadership in school-based initiatives, especially environmental education, and for its focus on science as part of their school planning for 2005. Teachers at this school were used to working with university researchers; thus, WES seemed the ideal location for testing an approach to curriculum change that emphasized teacher control of the curriculum implementation.

The model of curriculum adoption was a substantial investment in the school during Year 1 of the project; part of the Y2 funding enabled WES teachers to give workshops on the new science education curriculum to their peers in other elementary schools in the district. Through a case study approach, the LSP explored peer-to-peer development as a horizontal model of school change that begins with investment in a Lighthouse School, instead of the more common and typically less successful ministry-led, top-down approach to curriculum change (Blades, 1997; Fullan, 1991; Sarason, 1990). The author helped to initiate the LSP with a partnership with WES but offered only a supportive role, leaving the use of LSP funds up to the teachers. As we shall see, allocating control of the curriculum change to teachers led to significant changes to the direction of the LSP.

At inception, the LSP gained research assistance by becoming part of the Pacific CRYSTAL Project based at the University of Victoria. Pacific CRYSTAL support enabled the LSP to employ a researcher to collect field notes, engage in classroom observations, and conduct interviews as part of the case study data. This research was approved by the University's Human Research Ethics Board as well as the School District. The case study examined the extent curriculum intentions were reflected in the unit and lesson plans produced by teachers in the LSP. This method of data collection and analysis followed the recommendations of case study researchers to employ a combination of data collection methods (McNamara, 2005) to help bring understanding of a complex situation, case, or event (Soy, 1997; Stake, 1995). The data collected were analyzed chronologically to examine the research question, and those results are presented in similar chronologic fashion to address the research question (Yin, 1984).

Prior to starting the project, the author met with the WES teaching staff after school to share the general idea of a Lighthouse School and the prospect of 2 years of funding. In general, teachers supported becoming involved. Most believed that the project would promote collegial resource development and planning, create more potential for actually implementing the new science curriculum, develop school-wide responsibility for excellence in science education, and result in better science education units and resources for the school as teachers shared ideas and expertise. A key benefit recognized by all groups was a sense that involvement in the LSP would foster the more general school-wide goal of teamwork.

At this meeting, teachers were given the opportunity to express concerns anonymously through written comments. Some expressed reservations about the project, observing that the project involved a lot of time and commitment that resulted in *a loss of time from the classroom*. Some individuals worried that some teachers might not wish to be interviewed or watched as part of the case study; in the discussion afterwards, teachers were assured that involvement in such data collection was strictly voluntary in accordance with the code of ethical research. This raised concerns, however, as teachers wondered if there would be pressure on those who do not want to participate to be *team players* and join in. This important dynamic of school-wide projects suggests the possibility that some teachers might feel coerced to engage in approaches to teaching they did not wish to try. To resolve this issue, the school administration held a second meeting a week later without the presence of the researcher to discuss concerns and to assure teachers that not every teacher in the school had to participate in the project. As a result, the school teaching staff voted unanimously to participate in the LSP.

In May of Y1, the LSP officially began with a full-day workshop for the entire WES teaching staff. This workshop featured an inquiry-based approach to planning for science education and an opportunity for teachers to examine the new K–7 science IRP (MoE, 2005). At this workshop, the WES staff decided to focus on implementing topics in physical sciences for Y1, reasoning that their long-standing experience in community-based environmental education had provided the school with successful units of instruction in the biological sciences. Teachers believed that the physical sciences needed more planning; they imagined that this was an issue in other schools as well, justifying the idea of a lighthouse model.

Planning was slow due to end-of-year activities; therefore, a second workshop was scheduled for late August following the summer break. This workshop reinforced the inquiry model promoted earlier and assisted teachers to plan for science education in the year ahead. At this workshop, teachers decided to use the CETUS funding to completely plan units in physical science for each grade level as well as gather resources for teaching these units. The school set aside special storage for these supplies, creating its first science resource area. That year, the staff used 17% of available funds for resources. The remainder, almost $15,000, was allocated to the school district to hire substitute teachers so that the WES staff would have time to meet, discuss, reflect, and plan exemplary science units based on the new curriculum.

Shifts in the Concept of a Lighthouse School

The author's intention was to invite a second school to become a Lighthouse School in Y2 of the project and then expand to other elementary schools in ever-widening circles in Y3 and Y4 as a form of horizontal model of curriculum adoption. As stated in the original Pacific CRYSTAL proposal, this spiral of involvement was:

> Based on teachers working with their peers toward the development of a set of schools that can provide leadership through their exemplary science education programs. These schools are truly beacons; in each case, becoming a *Lighthouse School* involves dedication to the ongoing professional development of teachers

in other schools, ideally until *all* the schools in BC are effectively lighthouse schools. (Blades, 2004; emphasis in original text)

At the end of the first full year as a Lighthouse School, teachers were invited to reflect in groups on their involvement in the LSP. In particular, they were asked what it meant to be a Lighthouse School and to record their comments on prepared handouts. Comments were examined for pattern codes (Miles & Huberman, 1984) and organized according to frequency. Responses indicated that teachers valued most the development of what they called *teachable units* for science education, which included lesson plans and support resources and materials. Most teachers were looking forward to being a part of a Lighthouse School, believing that this designation would provide the opportunity to mentor colleagues in other schools in what they called *teachers teaching each other*. Several teachers noted that the inquiry approach provided a common language for speaking about science education planning, which they considered an advantage for peer group planning. Two teachers, however, found the LSP to be stressful because they felt pressure to perform to the expectations of the university researcher. The WES vice-principal, who was responsible for coordinating the LSP at the school level, believed that one of the most valuable consequences of involvement in the LSP was reduction in teacher isolation as teachers worked with other teachers in lesson planning. In an interview at the end of Y1, he observed that, *I think we have a lot of fun with it* [the LSP] *and the time that the teachers and the staff spend together is invaluable.*

By the end of Y1, teachers had begun work on several units and this work continued in Y2. Teachers initially did not appreciate taking time from their classrooms to plan lessons, and this sentiment became stronger in the second year. Of the nine units produced by the end of Y2, only five dealt with topics in physical science, one was on life science (botany), and three were on environmental topics, which were the particular strength of this school. As well, planning partnerships dissolved over the year as teachers completed units on their own. Essentially, in Y2 teachers fell into familiar patterns of planning and somewhat familiar topics in science despite the availability of funds for teaching release time and their initial intention to focus on physical sciences.

During Y2, teachers began to display what the vice-principal described in an interview at the end of Y2 as *institutional resistance* to the idea of leading any sort of interschool pedagogy of their peers, whether sharing models used in planning or even sharing the units developed at WES. In a report on Pacific CRYSTAL, Blades and Parsons (2007) noted that, "teachers have not, for the most part, embraced the role of 'Lighthouse School,' preferring instead to work within the boundaries of their school" (p. 1).

That report does note one exception to being a Lighthouse School, however. Two Grade 5 teachers were concerned that their students, now used to more interactive, inquiry-based science, would expect the same pedagogy when moving to the receiving middle school for Grade 6. These teachers contacted their colleagues at Creekside Middle School (CMS; a pseudonym) to inform them of the LSP at WES, which led to the author being contacted by a CMS teacher about the possibility of Creekside becoming a Lighthouse School. There was considerable support from the CMS teachers and the School District for continuing the LSP at Creekside, including a request by the school's administration for a workshop on the inquiry-based model similar to the one provided to the WES teachers. This workshop, conducted at the end of Y2 of the LSP, was led by a WES teacher and the author. In this way, the concept of Lighthouse School was reconceptualised by teachers at CMS from a system-wide *horizontal* peer-to-peer pedagogy to a *vertical* pedagogy. While the author did hope that WES teachers would be willing to share their units with other elementary school teachers during Y3 and Y4 of the LSP, this was flatly rejected by them; they preferred to remain in their schools and teach the units they had prepared. Funding support, thus, moved entirely to CMS for Y3 and Y4.

Creekside Middle School: Years 3 and 4 of the Lighthouse Schools Project

Approximately 40% of WES students move on to CMS. The other receiving middle school was not interested in becoming part of the LSP despite the availability of funds for planning. CMS was considerably more enthusiastic, partially because this school had been recently converted into a middle school and had, at that time, very limited resources for teaching science; its school plan recognized the need to improve science education pedagogy. In a preliminary meeting with CMS teachers about the possibility of being a Lighthouse School, they immediately encouraged the idea of vertical teacher development, enthusiastically suggesting that perhaps the secondary school that receives their students could be involved in Y4 of the LSP. To continue the agenda of letting the teachers decide what it means to be a Lighthouse School, funds were available ($18,000 a year for 2 years) for science education development at CMS and, again, the use of these funds was entirely left up to the teachers.

After the workshop on inquiry-based approaches to teaching science, CMS teachers met in late June at the end of Y2 to plan for the upcoming year. As a result of this meeting, which took place after school hours, attending teachers developed the following *dream* for CETUS-based funding for Y3 of the LSP:

> We would like to work toward a whole school science fair in the spring that celebrates simple life-based themes and run through the three grade curriculums. Student exploration of these themes would primarily elucidate their understanding of the processes and skills of science at each grade level.

Their plan was to meet as a staff the following September and begin by mapping out the science curriculum to articulate topics that need more attention and planning at CMS. The teachers wanted another workshop on inquiry-based pedagogies and some work on unit planning as well as the development of a school-wide science theme week.

Three weeks into the school year, the author met with the staff for "CETUS Initiation Day." An inquiry-based approach was presented; after the lunch break, teachers formed into teams to make sense of this approach for the science units they would be teaching during the school year. The author noted some difficulty by the teachers in applying an inquiry-based approach to their unit planning; in general, these teachers were used to a form of science education pedagogy that began with teacher or textbook explanations, followed by examples, which *might* include hands-on *verificational experiments* of the science concept being taught. In other words, science education pedagogy at CMS followed for the most part a traditional abstract-to-concrete pattern of conceptual development characteristic of the majority of instruction in K–12 schools (Blades, 2001).

By March of Y3, teachers had developed unit plans on the curriculum topics of body systems, forensic science, and electricity. They used approximately 40% of available funding to purchase science education resource materials (e.g., wires, batteries, resource books, etc.). Of note is that teachers at this level were reluctant to hire substitute teachers to enable more time during school hours for planning. The chief reason for this was a belief that the school curriculum is *packed* and that substitute teachers would not have the experience to move students successfully through lessons while they, the regular classroom teachers, were released to plan for science education. The result was that any planning generally occurred after school hours or during lunch breaks. Initially, planning was conducted by teams but, as the year progressed, these groups found it difficult to coordinate schedules, mainly due to after-school clubs and coaching commitments. By the end of Y3, CMS teachers were individually completing their unit plans.

With additional funds available in Y4, the lead contact teacher at CMS faced a dilemma. In their first year as a Lighthouse School, CMS teachers enthusiastically embraced the notion of a focus on science education. With the units in place they believed were most needed, teacher enthusiasm vanished. Teachers also lost interest in being a Lighthouse School for the secondary school receiving their students; at this point, the LSP was essentially over with another year of funding available. Reports from the school suggest that teachers had accomplished their objective of gathering supplies and revising key unit plans for science education; they wanted to move on to the next educational initiative.

The lead teacher contact at CMS for science education worked with the CMS vice-principal to develop a bold idea: Use the Y4 funds for a single, intensive, school-wide theme week on a topic that brings science education and ecological responsibility together. Assured that they could use the funding any way they wanted, these two individuals developed a proposal for a spring theme week on water stewardship, which they called "Flow Week."

At this point in the LSP, the CMS teachers abandoned any notion of being a Lighthouse School that engaged in district-wide, peer-to-peer teaching (i.e., collaborative professional development). However, a sort of community lighthouse effect emerged through the Flow Week. Held in late spring of Y4, the entire school spent a week in groups organized by particular topics such as creek water profiles, watershed studies, water pollution studies, oceanography, and visits to sewage treatment plants. The author was involved as a participant–observer during this week. There was tremendous energy and excitement at this interruption to regular studies. Students engaged in a host of activities, from rowing to water sampling to a run to raise funds for areas of the world suffering from drought. Students selected the general area they wished to study and then prepared reports, which were shared with their peers in a format reminiscent of science fairs.

There was a somewhat evangelistic tone to the final 2 days of presentations. Other middle schools and a few beyond district boundaries were invited to attend the research presentations by CMS students; the clear message, which seemed to be well appreciated by those attending, is that youth can do much to *save the planet*. In general, presentations were fair in their reporting on, for example, pollution in water-ways, banning plastic water bottles, careful stewardship of city reservoirs, and global warming. The audience of their peers responded by clapping hands and even cheering as the CMS students made their points. Students wrote letters to the editors of local newspapers calling for change in some municipal practices. These letters were surprisingly well informed and clearly the result of the research and studies conducted by students during Flow Week. These activities point to different types of pedagogy—a community-based pedagogy resulting from student study—that could be considered a reconceptualization of the notion of *lighthouse* in the LSP toward a larger circle of teaching.

From the observations and notes made by the author, Flow Week seemed to be an overwhelming success. There were poems in the hallways about water, and every classroom declared their *love of water* in various forms, from posters to individual projects. In a written statement to the school, one teacher confirmed the author's impressions of Flow Week:

> This week has gone by at a breakneck pace … my group had an awesome experience, with 100% participation. It has taken a strong team effort from ALL the staff to pull this week off with the level of success and positive stories I've heard from other staff … it's events like this that make [CMS] the place that it is, one of energy, enriched learning and culture.

In a special school assembly a month later, the entire school reviewed the theme of water stewardship and the students, teachers, and parents of CMS also formally thanked CETUS for funding support:

> Thank you for your important contribution. … Learning about our place here in the city is perhaps, one of the most important gifts we educators can give our students. Thank you for taking a chance on us and making our study of water possible.

And with this thanks, the Lighthouse Schools Project formally came to an end.

RESULTS OF THE LIGHTHOUSE SCHOOLS PROJECT

The Lighthouse Schools Project examined two key questions:
- To what extent are teachers from a Lighthouse School able to successfully plan and implement a new science curriculum if opportunities for planning are provided?
- To what extent would these teachers encourage through peer mentorship curriculum change in other schools?

It is clear that the teachers participating in this case study were reluctant to leave their classrooms to spend time in other schools—even with available funding and administrative support. Instead, teachers in both schools reconceptualised the idea of *lighthouse* to fit their particular, local concepts of pedagogy. In the elementary school, teachers looked to the school receiving their students while the middle school teachers looked to the greater community and students in other schools to engage in conversations about water conservation. In both cases, the research and development agenda of the LSP shifted from the university researcher to the teachers once the staff fully realized and understood that they were entirely responsible for decisions on how funding would be used and the direction of their pedagogical involvement in improving science education. What resulted, from the researcher's perspective, was unexpected—suggesting that researchers need to pay close attention to the desires and needs of teachers when forming research relationships with teaching colleagues. Such shifts are a fundamental part of community-based projects in which all participants share equally the authority and responsibility for the agenda, procedures, and decisions.

Data collected in this case study included field notes, journal entries, documents produced by teachers (unit plans), feedback sheets from teachers, interviews with key agents, and participant observation in events. Artefacts and documents were arranged chronologically and examined for emergent themes, which produced three major themes related to the two key research questions: time, unit planning, and theme week.

Time

When the author asked classroom teachers what they could use to help teach children science, these teachers invariably responded, *More time*. This usually means more time to plan effective units but also time to gather useful resources for teaching. While the lack of time in teachers' lives has been cited as a key factor in the poor implementation of new curriculum requirements (Fullan, 1991; Futemick, 2010; Lumpkin, 2010; Ungerleider, 2003), this case study indicates that the need for more time is more of a cliché than reality. The provision of funds to allow for elementary and middle school teachers to have release time to plan lessons during the school year and school day did not appear to be a key factor in curriculum adoption as evidenced by teacher unit planning.

Unit Planning

Unit plans developed in Y1 and Y2 by WES teachers and in Y3 by CMS teachers reveal the extent that an inquiry-based approach to science education was understood and incorporated into teacher planning. A total of 14 units was prepared, 5 by CMS teachers and 9 by WES teachers. In every case, the teachers prepared double sets of their plans; one set remained at the school while the other became part of the collection of resources for preservice teachers at the University of Victoria.

Without exception, unit plans were presented in large plastic bins that contained all materials necessary for the unit. For example, the electricity unit contains wires, batteries, materials for investigating static electricity, etc. Twelve units contained written unit plans composed of overviews, links to the BC science education curriculum, and detailed, individual lesson plans for each topic in the unit. Every written collection included additional print resource materials such as optional activity ideas, explanations of science phenomenon, and student worksheets.

Of the nine plans prepared by WES teachers, only three incorporated fully a constructivist approach to science education, despite two workshops on this model for teachers during the LSP. Three units begin such an approach but, as the lessons proceed, slip into a traditional pattern of teacher presentation of key ideas or teacher-led demonstrations that may be followed by some activity or, more likely, student worksheets on the topic presented by the teacher. The remaining three units are entirely traditional in approach, focusing on teacher demonstrations and discussions, which are actually teachers informing students of the concepts to be learned. One unit plan is composed of third-party worksheets, and science education in this unit comprises students completing worksheets in a sequential order.

The five units prepared by the CMS teachers display a similar pattern. Two units have no plans whatsoever, choosing to only supply equipment! Of the remaining three, all begin with an inquiry-based approach but slip into traditional, teacher-led presentations as lessons progress in the unit. What is striking about these units is the sheer amount of resource materials supplied for teachers, especially back-ground information, suggesting a strong desire by teachers at this level to present science concepts accurately. In general, the units with plans provided extensive support, strong evaluation considerations, and a tendency toward teacher-led demonstrations—although some inquiry-based pedagogy was evident, especially at the start of the unit. In every case of written plans, teachers also developed lessons that first ascertained the prior concepts of students; however, it was unclear from the plans how teachers would deal with any science-related misconceptions that might emerge during these first lessons.

Educational research results are clear that workshops for teachers are generally an ineffective method for change (Little, 1993); this was certainly indicated in the unit plans presented by teachers. Left to plan on their own or in partnerships after a workshop (or two in the case of WES), teachers in the LSP generally slipped back to planning that reflected their school and university experience of science education: A teacher-led approach emphasizing teacher (or textbook) knowledge reinforced by demonstrations and sometimes verificational experiments. The results from this LSP suggest that time for planning alone does not easily translate into teaching innovations that reflect understanding on how children learn science. In fact, pro-viding teachers with the time to reflect and plan science education lessons seems to primarily encourage resource collection over creative planning. Trusting the experiential knowledge of teachers to somehow incorporate inquiry-based learning was also ineffective; the LSP results indicate that change toward a more con-structivist approach to science education may require teachers to work with university researchers or a recognized lead teacher (science advocate) in a dynamic planning partnership that focuses on classroom practice.

The importance of a university partnership in effecting change was evident when the author visited classrooms to observe science lessons; in every case, lessons witnessed reflected an inquiry approach, even though these lessons were not reflected in the more traditional lesson plans developed as part of the unit planning.

When asked about this difference, one teacher informed the researcher that the lesson he witnessed was developed using the inquiry-based model presented in the workshops because the researcher was coming to watch a lesson! In every visit, teachers were surprised at the effectiveness of an inquiry-based approach, which reveals limited experience with this sort of pedagogy and the importance of mentorship with a university partner.

Theme Week

At the end of the LSP, the author met with a staff representative to review staff impressions of the effectiveness of using an entire year of funding in the LSP for an intensive week-long study of water stewardship. Some of the success of this experience, according to the CMS teachers, was the emphasis on inquiry-based learning and how the week helped unite the school community. Teachers especially appreciated that student work during this week was ungraded, noting that during this time *the kids no longer focused on marks, instead* [they] *focused on a desire to learn.* The week also included inviting members of the local community to the school, much like a science fair; this proved to be successful in helping the school communicate themes of water stewardship to the parents and homeowners in their local area and students in nearby middle schools.

The reporting teacher told the author that the week was *a lot of work* and that this was the key to the success of this experience. She pointed out that students continue to wear the T-shirts from the week and that sustainability issues seem to pervade conversations in and outside classrooms. The staff reportedly enjoyed the week enough to consider doing it again the following year but focused on a different environmental issue. The week did seem effective in generating a school-wide focus on sustainability and was particularly effective in linking the school with the local community. As well, this approach enabled the school to share ideas with students and staff in other middle schools; in a sense, CMS was for a week a *lighthouse* event.

IMPLICATIONS OF THE LIGHTHOUSE SCHOOLS PROJECT

Curriculum researchers observe that educational systems are remarkably resilient to efforts at curriculum change (Cuban, 1990), including innovations in science education (Blades, 1997). The LSP sought to remove one of the most cited obstacles to change: teacher time. This project found, however, that despite teacher enthusiasm about the availability of time to plan and involvement in the implementation process, the unit plans that resulted did not significantly advance a constructivist approach to science education. This suggests that curriculum change is complex and difficult; it is not easily addressed by providing time for planning or by locating teachers as the sole agents of the change process. Furthermore, time is not simply a quantity; it carries priority for these teachers. Teachers valued the mutual planning with colleagues, but this freedom came at the expense of their classroom contact with students—their highest priority. Therefore, implementation and professional development efforts, like LSP, need to explore noninstructional times that might allow these efforts to be assigned higher priority.

There are several key policy implications from the LSP for ministries of education and school districts involved in curriculum change. First, it is clear from these research results that financial resources are not sufficient to guarantee curriculum change. Even with sufficient funding to provide teacher release time, planning in the LSP remained, for the most part, very traditional in orientation. Second, given the choice between using funds for release time or to purchase resources, these teachers elected to use at least half of the funds to purchase resources, which suggests that some public schools may be underresourced to teach the topics presented in the science curriculum.

Third, it is clear that school-based resources should include teachers in schools with the pedagogical expertise to support school-wide planning in science education. Materials are insufficient for quality science education if the teachers do not know how to use them effectively. This was particularly striking at CMS where teachers elected to order useful materials but did not develop, for the most part, inquiry-based lesson plans on how to use these materials. Developing pedagogical expertise in science education might be encouraged through university-led certificate programs in science education leadership offered in school locations. In both schools, particular teachers were enthusiastic leaders for curriculum reform. The sustained effect of university-led instruction with such key teachers in schools could generate enough enthusiasm via such leaders to produce a 'tipping effect' of curriculum reform, especially if instructional materials were available.

The fourth implication is that a model of curriculum change that focuses on one school as a lighthouse for other schools depends largely on teachers' willingness to actually become involved in peer-to-peer pedagogy. Even if the teachers involved initially support such intentions, in this LSP these same teachers opted out entirely of this model of change. In general, teachers were not interested in teaching other teachers regarding their understanding of effective science education. This means that a model for change initially supported by teachers may not be realized in practice. This raises concerns about allocating resources to one school in order to position that school as a model for other schools; the LSP suggests that a more diffuse allocation, especially for resource purchases, might be more effective in enabling the adoption of at least the topics in a new science curriculum.

The BC K–7 IRP (MoE, 2005) is not only a set of topics to be taught but also a teaching orientation for instruction that emphasizes a constructivist, inquiry-based approach to learning science. Yet the majority of teachers have experienced science education as content delivery with experiments, which are not experiments in a scientific sense but typically cookbook-like proofs of teacher and textbook assertions (Blades, 2001). Given this pedagogy, it is understandably difficult to change a teacher's frame of reference concerning science education. The LSP tried to do this by providing time for planning and by trusting that workshops to explain and demonstrate the spirit and intention of inquiry-based learning would be sufficient for teachers to reorient their planning. Abdicating control of the LSP to teachers had only a superficial effect on teacher lesson planning, however.

The LSP does reveal avenues to consider when engaging in curriculum change. The theme week at CMS seemed to be an effective way to infuse a school with an orientation toward some aspects of science, particularly environmental literacy applications. Having such themes transcend grade barriers is useful in promoting science school wide and may be especially helpful at the beginning of the school year.

A more potent effect on the actual practice of teachers was the presence of the university researcher in the school and during science lessons. This effect aligns with the work of Shymansky, Yore, and Anderson (2004) on the importance of sustained engagement between universities and classroom teachers for successful curriculum implementation in science education. The LSP reveals that simply trusting the experiential knowledge of teachers is not enough to secure change. We know that theory without practical application does not effect change; the LSP reveals that practice or practical knowledge without theory is equally ineffective at enabling mandated innovation. Science education curriculum reform, then, likely requires a dynamic and sustained partnership of classroom teachers and university researchers who approach change as a shared responsibility.

There are several potential avenues that could foster partnerships in educational reform. All beginning teachers in BC are required to complete at least one university-level science course as part of their science content education. If these courses, traditionally taught in the Faculty of Science, could be more aligned to the goals of science education and in particular the reform efforts, beginning teachers would be able to link their education in science content to their education on teaching methodology. A promising example of such an initiative is the EOS 120 project reported in this book (Van der Flier-Keller, Blades, & Milford, Chapter 10 this book). In that course, one laboratory section was designed for students intending to become teachers; thus, it deliberately linked pedagogical content knowledge to constructivist instruction in earth science. Similar reinforcement of science education reform directions could be developed for university science courses that are popular choices of preservice teachers.

As mentioned earlier, change could be encouraged through more opportunities for experienced teachers to be identified as curriculum leaders in their schools, perhaps through university-sponsored certificate programs. This development could be greatly encouraged by ministerial directives that would recognize leadership status with an advancement in pay category.

Finally, it is clear that offering a single course to preservice teachers on science education pedagogy is not sufficient to ensure these new teachers can operate as agents of change once they are teaching. Teacher education needs to be a continual, seamless process of professional development that begins with content knowledge, matures through teacher education programs, and continues to support teachers as they negotiate their professional careers. In every step of the way, professors of science education and university researchers can play a decisive role. Projects described in this book reveal the importance of the researchers' presence and the positive effects of this presence in securing effective curriculum change that must be conceptualised as a series of evolving partnerships.

REFERENCES

Blades, D. W. (1997). *Procedures of power and curriculum change*. New York: Peter Lang.

Blades, D. W. (2001). The simulacra of science education. In J. A. Weaver, M. Morris, & P. Applebaum (Eds.), *(Post) modern science (education): Propositions and alternate paths* (pp. 57–94). New York: Peter Lang.

Blades, D. W. (2004). *CRYSTAL lighthouse schools: Implementing excellence through peer professional development*. Victoria, BC, Canada: University of Victoria Faculty of Education Pacific Centre for Scientific and Technological Literacy.

Blades, D. W., & Parsons, C. (2007). *Report on node #3: Lighthouse schools project*. Victoria, BC, Canada: University of Victoria Faculty of Education Pacific Centre for Scientific and Technological Literacy.

British Columbia Ministry of Education. (2005). *Science K to 7: Sciences integrated resource package 2005*. Victoria, BC, Canada: Author.

Campbell, R. J. (1991). *Workloads, achievement and stress: Two follow-up studies of teacher time in Key Stage 1*. Coventry, England: University of Warwick Policy Analysis Unit.

Council of Ministers of Education, Canada. (1997). *Common framework of science learning outcomes, K to 12. Pan-Canadian protocol for collaboration on school curriculum*. Retrieved from http://publications.cmec.ca/science/framework/

Cuban, L. (1990). Reforming again, again, and again. *Educational Researcher, 19*(1), 3–13.

Darling-Hammond, L., & Bransford, J. (2005). *Preparing teachers for a changing world*. San Francisco: Jossey-Bass.

Fullan, M. (1991). *The new meaning of educational change*. New York: Teachers College Press.

Futemick, K. (2010). Incompetent teachers or dysfunctional systems? *Phi Delta Kappan, 91*(10), 59–64.

Little, J. (1993). Teachers' professional development in a climate of educational reform. *Educational Evaluation and Policy Analysis, 15*(2), 129–151.

Lumpkin, A. (2010). 10 school-based strategies for student success. *Kappa Delta Pi Record, 46*(2), 71–75.

McNamara, C. (2005). *Basics of developing case studies*. Minneapolis, MN: Authenticity Consulting. Retrieved from http://managementhelp.org/evaluatn/casestdy.htm

Miles, M. B., & Huberman, A. M. (1984). *Qualitative data analysis*. Thousand Oaks, CA: Sage.

Sarason, S. (1990). *The predictable failure of educational reform*. San Francisco: Jossey-Bass.

Shymansky, J. A., Yore, L. D., & Anderson, J. O. (2004). Impact of a school district's science reform effort on the achievement and attitudes of third- and fourth-grade students. *Journal of Research in Science Teaching, 41*(8), 771–790.

Soy, S. K. (1997). *The case study as a research method*. Unpublished manuscript, University of Texas, Austin. Retrieved from http://www.ischool.utexas.edu/~ssoy/usesusers/l391d1b.htm

Stake, R. E. (1995). *The art of case study research*. Thousand Oaks, CA: Sage.

Ungerleider, C. (2003). *Failing our kids*. Toronto, ON, Canada: McClelland & Stewart.

Yin, R. K. (1984). *Case study research: Design and methods*. Thousand Oaks, CA: Sage.

Yore, L. D., Anderson, J. O., & Shymansky, J. A. (2005). Sensing the impact of elementary school science reform: A study of stakeholder perceptions of implementation, constructivist strategies, and school–home collaboration. *Journal of Science Teacher Education, 16*(1), 65–88.

David W. Blades
Department of Curriculum and Instruction
University of Victoria
Victoria, British Columbia, Canada

CARLOS GUSTAVO A. ORMOND, SUSAN M. TEED,
LAURA PIERSOL AND DAVID B. ZANDVLIET

13. THE DEVELOPMENT OF A PLACE-BASED LEARNING ENVIRONMENT AT THE BOWEN ISLAND COMMUNITY SCHOOL

I think, in a nutshell, that a community school has what I consider to be the best of programming and interconnectedness with the community ... I mean I have always found ways to include members of the community into the students' learning. ... When we were looking at the geology of Bowen Island, it seemed a rip-roaring idea to have a local geologist from the community in to explain exactly the rocks and the makeup of this island ... I find that a community school has the doors already open so that you can go out and find those people in the community who really are ever so knowledgeable, more than I am ... I can just form that link between the community and to the environment. It's a great way to do science, great way to use that science [in a] meaningful way with the kids, and I think that's the essence of it. (Participating teacher)

In September 2005, the Pacific CRYSTAL Project began at a Canadian elementary school, the Bowen Island Community School (BICS), to support and encourage place-based curriculum development in addition to helping the school realize its broad environmental learning goals. Besides being a part of the Lighthouse Schools (Node 3: Influencing educational policy, practice, and leadership), BICS was involved with the Ecological Education Project (EEP) within Node 2 that focused on classroom-based studies of teaching, assessment, and technology applications (see Yore & Van der Flier-Keller, Chapter 1 this book). The approach that was taken to achieve the goal of the Pacific CRYSTAL Project to promote scientific, mathematical, and technological literacy for responsible citizenship was an eco-logical one (Yore, Chapter 2 this book).

This chapter documents and describes one elementary school's attempt to investigate how ecological literacy can become a core educational standard in its school in order to promote responsible citizenship. We begin with a brief description of place-based education, learning environment research, and ecological literacy. Following that, we discuss the Pacific CRYSTAL research program at BICS in addition to providing information on Bowen Island's history and community as it relates to the school. After providing details of the methods used in this research, we review the place-based programs, events, and activities. We conclude with

L. D. Yore et al (Eds.), Pacific CRYSTAL Centre for Science, Mathematics, and Technology
Literacy: Lessons Learned, 217–234.

a summary of this study and acknowledge the important insights this research has for the development of ecological literacy programming in other places and schools.

BACKGROUND

Place-based Education

The concept of place-based education is an evolving curricular and instructional approach that over the years has also been referred to as community-oriented schooling, ecological education, and bioregional education (Woodhouse & Knapp, 2000). Due to this multidisciplinary aspect of place-based education, it is difficult to find a clear and concise definition. For the most part, this approach is "designed to help students learn about the immediate surroundings by capitalizing on their lived experiences" (Knapp, 2005, p. 278). One of its greatest appeals is its ability "to adapt to unique characteristics in particular places" (Smith, 2002, p. 584); this trait makes it a strong tool to "overcome the disjuncture between school and children's lives that is found in many classrooms" (p. 585).

Gruenewald (2003) claimed that place-based education does not have its own theoretical tradition; rather, it is an assimilation of theories belonging to experiential learning, contextual learning, problem-based learning, constructivism, outdoor education, indigenous education, environmental education, and others that emphasize the value of learning from one's own community. There is considerable literature in education research indicating the positive effects of a place-based education (Basile, 2000; Corral-Verdugo & Frais-Armenta, 1996; Cummins & Snively, 2000; Kenney, Price-Militana, & Horrocks-Donohue, 2003; Lieberman & Hoody, 1998; Lord, 1999). Numerous case studies indicate many positive effects when schools and communities work together to establish curriculum goals and design strategies; for example, student achievement improves, students' interest in their community increases, teachers are more satisfied with their profession, and community members are more connected to the schools and students (Powers, 2004). Place-based education programs are designed to motivate children at all levels of ability to interact with local content (Basile, 2000; Cummins & Snively, 2000; Kenney et al., 2003; Lord, 1999), which supports Dewey's belief that children are not interested in ideas about abstract phenomena but rather are drawn to the actual phenomena (Smith, 2002).

Learning Environment Research

Unfortunately, nontraditional fields of education such as place-based education have had difficulty being integrated into mainstream education. One reason for this is that academic institutions tend to place an emphasis on students' disciplinary content achievement. Focusing solely on content knowledge for evaluations and disregarding affective, process, and skill development risks destroying "the human qualities that make education a worthwhile experience for students" (Fraser, 2001,

p. 2). Student achievement is assessed by test-taking; therefore, there is more focus on developing pedagogical tools aimed to improve content knowledge through better methods of memorization, oftentimes with little or no regard for the learning environment. Learning environment research has provided compelling evidence to suggest that (a) the classroom environment has a strong effect on student outcomes (Fisher & Khine, 2006; Fraser, 2007; Wang, Haertel, & Walberg, 1993) and (b) actual and preferred student learning environments have a much closer fit in interdisciplinary, outdoor-based learning environments than single-discipline, classroom-based, learning environments (Ormond & Zandvliet, 2009; Zandvliet, 2007).

Ecological Literacy

Early work by Sobel (1993, 1996) described place-based education; since then, it has been expanding and developed by others in community contexts (Hutchinson, 2004), experiential learning (Woodhouse & Knapp, 2000), critical pedagogy (Gruenewald, 2003), and ecological literacy (Orr, 1992, 1994). Environmental literacy is a component of environmental education, and some may even claim it is the primary goal (Cole, 2007; Disinger & Roth, 1992; Gaylord, 2002; North American Association for Environmental Education, 2010; Roth, 1992; Volk & Cheak, 2003; Wilke, 1995). Similar to place-based education, there is no concrete definition of ecological literacy. A framework for ecological literacy contains four elements that are commonly shared among the definitions that do exist (Cole, 2007): knowledge, skills, affect, and behaviour. The idea here is that ecological literacy should aim to develop knowledge of the environment, which gives rise to the skills society needs to value both the quality of life and the environment, and to act in an environmentally responsible manner. Cole (2007) suggested that environmental literacy most often tends to focus on scientific environment knowledge solely and does not acknowledge the importance of other elements:

> Using science to construct a body of knowledge without critical explorations of its connections to culture, power, and inequity is ... dangerous. It becomes too easy to defer decision making and critical thinking to science and scientists without honouring other viewpoints, experiences, and perspectives. The question then becomes, how does environmental education move forward in ways that foster and support local and critical community environmental literacies? (p. 41)

Having this in mind, we decided to use the term *ecological literacy* rather than environmental literacy because our definition embraces both a scientific understanding of living systems and a humanistic understanding of the interdependent relationship between human beings and the greater biotic and elemental (nonliving) world around us (Orr, 1992, 1994). This chapter describes one elementary school's experiences in achieving their ecological literacy goals through the development of a place-based learning environment.

DESCRIPTION OF THE PROJECT

The reporting style of this project follows an ethnographic (Hammersley & Atkinson, 2007) format since the data were gathered from participatory observations and interviews with teachers, students, and community members. We selected this format because we believe it is the most efficient manner of documenting and communicating our experiences; we also want to acknowledge and recognize alternative research reporting styles in progressive fields of education. We recount a case study showing how ecological literacy and place-based education are being done in one part of Canada, with the goal of sharing this knowledge with others who see a need for the development of such education programming.

The story of the Bowen Island Community School began before the start of Pacific CRYSTAL. When the principal investigator (PI, David Zandvliet) moved to Bowen Island in 2004, he registered his children in the school. He soon learned that the school had several environmental educators and a rich history in environmental stewardship. As a relationship developed between the PI and BICS, there was interest from BICS teachers to support more environmental education programming. That opportunity came a year later when BICS was invited to be a part of the Pacific CRYSTAL Project and later designated a *Lighthouse School*. The Pacific CRYSTAL Lighthouse Schools Project (LSP) investigated the development of excellence in classroom instruction and exemplary practices school-wide through professional development programming. With a focus on leadership and knowledge transfer, the LSP approached curriculum implementation as an opportunity for teachers to be the primary agents of change, both in their schools and the school district. The approach taken at BICS with its LSP was an ecological one.

In addition to being a part of the LSP, BICS was involved in the EEP, which studied the complex ecology of the intersection between scientific knowledge, pedagogy, student learning, and curriculum. It identified and developed innovative approaches for teaching scientific and interdisciplinary topics around ecological education framed within the context of ecological literacy. The EEP's focus question was: How can ecological literacy become a core educational standard in our schools? To address that question, the project attempted to facilitate and support the development of place-based curriculum resources that were unique to the geographical location of BICS.

Both the LSP and the EEP complemented one another. Therefore, the BICS project (a) emphasized leadership and knowledge transfer to inform and influence educational policy and practice and (b) supported teachers to be the primary agents of change focused on understanding how ecological literacy could become a core educational standard. Thus, we, like other Lighthouse Schools (Blades, Chapter 12 this book), were not the leaders of the activities and programs that took place at BICS—the teachers were. We were there to support and facilitate their interests and objectives. This research model could be described as a participatory action research (PAR) approach, which is just one of many action research types (Hendricks, 2006). In its purest form, PAR denotes research that involves both the researcher and subject collaborating with "the aims of solving a problem and generating new knowledge" (Coghlan & Brannick, 2001, p. 3).

The participants in this research project were the teachers and administration of BICS, the surrounding community, the volunteer support of preservice teachers and undergraduate students, and the research team. The preservice teachers were students in the Global Communities Module in the Professional Development Program, and the undergraduate students were in the Summer Institute in Environmental Education, both at Simon Fraser University. They aided in the support and facilitation to BICS teachers throughout the 5 years. In addition, several preservice teachers did their teacher education practicum at BICS. The preservice teachers and the undergraduates were in programs that specifically emphasized the inclusion of ecological elements in classroom activities and required the students to think critically about how science and nonscience materials could be integrated in classrooms.

Location of Research: The Place

Bowen Island is the first island at the mouth of Howe Sound in the Metro Vancouver region of British Columbia (BC) and in the Skwxwú7mesh (also known as Squamish) territory (Figure 1). The Skwxwú7mesh are a Coast Salish cultural and linguistic group that inhabits the Howe Sound area (Squamish Nation Network, 2010; Suttles, 1990). The island derived its current English name from Rear Admiral James Bowen, an English naval officer in the 18th century, in recognition of his efforts in defeating a French fleet in 1794. Ironically, he never once set foot on the island (Bowen Island Municipality, 2010) and, thus, never experienced the sense of place.

Bowen Island's geographic location in a body of water separating it from the mainland has given rise to a unique community. The island (an area of roughly 50 km^2) is approximately 2 km from mainland West Vancouver. Daily commuters on Bowen Island connect with mainland Metro Vancouver through a 30-min ferry service to Horseshoe Bay; from there, it is a 30-min drive to downtown Vancouver.

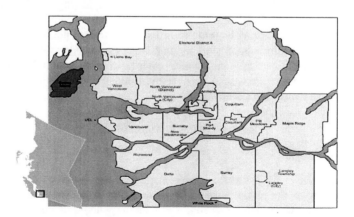

Figure 1. Metro Vancouver map with Bowen Island
(Metro Vancouver, 2010).

Having the school on an island created a unique experience for the researchers. Islands are fascinating geological formations for the sense of community that is felt when being on one and that is lost when going off the island (Zandvliet & Brown, 2006).

Quite a diverse community inhabits Bowen Island. In the early 1900s, Bowen Island became a popular destination for Vancouverites because of its natural beauty and the sense of isolation, which led to a resort being built during this period (Twigg, 1997). During the 1940s and 1950s, Bowen Island developed into a hotspot for intellectuals, artists, and writers (Lieben Artists' Colony, 2010). In the 1960s, migration to the island began to slow and led to the resort's closure. With the global push for development during the 1980s and the rise of Vancouver real estate prices, Bowen Island experienced a large migration of people seeking affordable housing. This, of course, changed the dynamics of the island; but it has kept its retreat character and strong community feel, especially with regard to music and art.

The strong sense of community extends to the only public elementary and middle (Grades K–6) school on the island. Being on an island, BICS students could see where their community began and ended. BICS is located "in an idyllic setting, just a short walk from picturesque Snug Cove" (West Vancouver School District [WVSD], 2010, para. 2), which is the main commercial area and the cove where the ferry arrives. While Bowen Island is its own municipality in the Metro Vancouver Regional District, BICS is one of 17 schools in the WVSD. For the most part, students attending this school are from Bowen Island but there are a number of students who come from West Vancouver. As one teacher explained, *Over the years, BICS teachers have gained a reputation for being able to deal well with eccentric children, and because of that some parents in the West Vancouver school district have chosen to send their children here for Kindergarten to Grade 7.* This should be no surprise as the school prides itself on focusing on the "Educational needs of individual students … through a variety of programs. In addition to active, meaningful classroom learning experiences, [they] offer support through [a] Learning Assistance Centre, and Challenge Program." (WVSD, 2010, para. 3). In addition, its supportive and stimulating learning environment is created not only by teachers at the school but also by support staff and numerous community volunteers. Unlike other schools, BICS acts as a community centre—offering continuing education courses and active programs, such as yoga and running clubs with the help of the local Parks and Recreation Commission.

REFLECTIONS AND RESULTS

Early Developments

The first initiative at BICS was the establishment of a collaborative planning group. The Eco-Team, as the group came to be known, was organized by the teachers. Prior to this research beginning, we had met with the school principal and teachers who were interested in having support for environmental learning at BICS. At those early meetings, the teachers recommended that if this research program was to take place at the school then a group from BICS should meet with the researchers once a month. Once the Pacific CRYSTAL Project began at BICS, these meetings were used to reflect on the project and discuss ideas for future environmental education programming. The creation of this group was the first teacher-led activity associated with this research and modelled perfectly the framework of teachers as the primary change agents and, in turn, this research. The following content is a result of the Eco-Team meetings.

One of the first products from this PAR partnership resulted from the participation of BICS teachers in focus groups that contributed to the development of an environmental education curriculum guide that was later published by the BC Ministry of Education. The BICS teachers took part in focus and working groups that were conducted in communities around the province and included broad representation from various stakeholder groups (e.g., the Ministry, informal education organizations, preservice and inservice teachers, and academics). This type of inquiry enabled a study that placed research capabilities into the hands of the educator–subjects and provided these educators research tools with which they could generate knowledge. Focus groups and teacher interviews conducted over a 16-month period informed a collaborative writing process that involved the BICS teachers. The resulting framework, *Environmental Learning and Experience* (ELE; MoE, 2007) aimed to assist BC teachers of all subjects and grades to integrate environmental concepts into their classrooms. The creation of the ELE, involving BICS teachers in the process, was perceived as an empowering activity. In our experience, teachers after years of working in the educational system become disempowered as top-down learning objectives and outcomes are mandated to them. The ELE document was created from the bottom-up with teachers as the primary agents and later adopted by the MoE.

Another early BICS teacher-led initiative was the revitalization of the annual dive and field trip to Bowen Bay. The event had been dependent on volunteers who would take the interpreter role and lead a marine intertidal activity. The teachers reactivated the activity as two of the researchers were certified SCUBA divers. This activity appeared to be popular with the students, likely because the activity took place at Bowen Bay, a popular place to visit; therefore, students may have been enjoying the internal contradiction of being in an area of play while being in school. This was a perfect example of the effects an environment has on learning. These early experiences for children to be exposed to alternative learning environments can prove to be beneficial as they do not become accustomed to the assumption that learning only occurs in an indoor classroom. It also acknowledges the importance of exposing children early on to outdoor learning.

The BICS teachers also developed an accompanying lesson plan book to this beach activity entitled *Beach Studies in a Bucket* (BICS, 2006). The title, a play on words, was appropriately named because not only did the activity involve a bucket as part of the lesson but the same bucket was also the housing for all the lesson plans, equipment, and handouts used on the beach. Having lessons specifically tailored for this trip to Bowen Bay allowed even the teachers to enjoy themselves. This was an important observation to us—because we had planned to focus on observing the students and their environmental learning, we had forgotten that the teachers were also becoming more knowledgeable of their community through such activities.

With all the activity occurring at BICS around environmental learning, the principal proposed the idea of establishing environmental goals, along with literacy and numeracy goals. The school board accepted the proposal and supported BICS's plan to place environmental learning as a focus of the school, which allowed school funding to be used for environmental programs. Including ecological literacy as a school goal was another example of the teachers being the primary change agents and how they informed and influenced policy and practice. The principal, who was also an Eco-Team member, saw firsthand at these meetings how passionate the teachers were about implementing more environmental education programming in the curriculum. One of the first programs resulting from this was a professional development (Pro-D) day for teachers prior to the start of classes. This Pro-D day exposed the teachers to numerous activities and connected them with environmental education organizations and networks. Representatives from Metro Vancouver, the Environmental Educators Professional Specialist Association of the BC Teachers' Federation, and Green Learning (http://www.greenlearning.ca/) presented place-based environmental education resources. This Pro-D workshop presented an opportunity for the teachers that, in turn, created serious interest in trying new activities in their classrooms. The early success of the EEP led the Pacific CRYSTAL Project to appoint BICS a Lighthouse School.

Seaquaria in Schools Program

Through collaborations within the Pacific CRYSTAL Project, BICS had the opportunity to run and host a *Seaquaria in Schools* program. This program brings local marine ecosystems into schools through permanent saltwater aquaria and curriculum-linked programming (see Zandvliet, Holmes, & Starzner, Chapter 5 this book). One of the main barriers for involving environmental education programs in the BICS curriculum is simply the lack of funding for field trip travel. Having a seaquarium at BICS increased the likelihood for place-based education to develop. Also, while Seaquaria in Schools has obvious "tools for teaching about the environment, science, nature, and environmental stewardship, ... [it also has] exceptionally flexible tools for multi-disciplinary teaching, bridging school-based and field programs, potentiating the effectiveness of other resources and programs, and enhancing learning and responsible behaviour of all kinds—particularly for people with learning disabilities" (WestWind SeaLab Supplies & World Fisheries Trust, 2008, p. 9).

The teachers and the researchers decided that in order to authentically represent the local marine community we would do a local dive at Bowen Bay to collect marine organisms for the school's new seaquarium. This activity's value to the project was that it involved teachers, students, and researchers in its development, with no hierarchy of responsibility or roles. It was a school-wide effort. The students took great care in transporting their new marine friends to the seaquarium. Having had a role in bringing these marine organisms to their school, the students had an instant attachment to and responsibility for them (Figure 2).

Figure 2. The Seaquarium at BICS.

Over the 2 years that the seaquarium was at BICS, it played numerous roles for Grades K–7. The first one, most obviously, was its intended role to be a hands-on, supplemental resource for the K–7 teachers to use alongside classroom texts. Thus, Seaquaria in Schools was integrated into the classroom curriculum through links to the life science curriculum for each grade. Teachers would send groups of 8 students to the seaquarium where one of the researchers would lead them in an activity. While these students were at the seaquarium, we gave teachers an activity they could lead in their classrooms, such as a storybook or a *Science Times* (see Teed, Zandvliet, & Ormond, Chapter 9 this book) topic focused on the marine world. These introductory activities focused on identifying the organisms in the seaquarium and engaging the students about their current knowledge of the marine animals around Bowen Island. A large majority of the students had had personal experiences with the marine world and were eager to tell their stories. Since the teachers were not able to take part in this activity, we oriented them prior to the activity in addition to engaging them during their breaks in the staff room. We felt this was a critical strategy, as it helped the teachers feel more comfortable with this new resource and acknowledge our support in helping them integrate the program into their classrooms. We posted a schedule in the staff room for teachers to choose when they wanted our assistance. While most teachers used Seaquaria in Schools to complement their life science texts, some early grade (K–4) teachers used it along with fine arts and English language arts activities.

The most observable effect of the seaquarium was the increased knowledge of marine ecology. Its location near the school's front entrance served as a conversation piece for students, teachers, and parents. Students began to anthropomorphise their marine friends in the seaquarium, creating deep connections with them. In particular, a crab had been collected with no left claw; it was known as *Lefty* and became the mascot of the school. Why this is so important is that students created such a strong

225

connection to their marine friends that they began to question having them in the seaquarium and taking them away from their *family* and habitat. This sentiment became visible to the school when a problem arose with the water pump of the seaquarium, changing its climate and in turn risking the lives of the marine organisms. While the seaquarium was fixed eventually, this event became a teachable moment as now the students began to think critically. We were amazed and happy to see this debate arise naturally from the students. These critical actions embodied the four elements of ecological literacy: knowledge, skills, affect, and behaviour. The students had to have developed knowledge and skills to become aware of the ethical issues of having marine organisms out of their habitat. Those students that were critical, one could argue, were acting, as they would believe, in an environmentally responsible manner.

The seaquarium also played other surprising roles. For one Grade 2 student, it helped him develop social skills with the rest of his classmates. This student was autistic and very knowledgeable of the local marine ecosystem. Seeing this interest, we asked him to help us with teaching classmates about the marine world. Another such moment was with a Kindergarten student who had anxiety separation issues. Having seen the student come by a number of times to the seaquarium and knowing the student's interest in it, we began to use the seaquarium as a way to connect and relax the young student.

Teaching Trails

One immediate request from the BICS teachers at an Eco-Team meeting was for help in their classrooms. One of the expressed goals was to revitalize a place-based environmental education resource that had become outdated. The *Bowen Island Teaching Trails* was an earlier collaboration between EcoLeaders (Husby & Fast, 2002) and BICS teachers to develop lesson plans focused on local park trails. The resource contained an outdoor activity designed for each grade, with links to the (then current) BC K–12 curriculum. When the MoE changed several K–8 prescribed learning outcomes (PLOs), it became important to revise this resource. While this may seem like a simple request, the importance of this revision should not be undervalued. Teachers are bombarded constantly with new curriculum aids from various interest groups. Unfortunately, unless they are linked and mapped to the PLOs, teachers have little time to make those connections themselves so these resources gather dust on the bookshelf. The revised *Teaching Trails: Bowen Island Community School* (Husby & Fast, n.d.) will be useful for a number of years, allowing it to become part of the BICS culture. This became evident as this trail guide inspired and paved the way to the creation of two more outdoor environmental education activities, called Quests.

Questing

With all the focus on updating the Teaching Trails, one teacher voiced her interest in questing—an outdoor activity she had read about and believed could be adopted locally. Questing is a community-based treasure hunt with the goal of sharing the unique natural and cultural heritage of an area (see *Questing: A Guide to Creating Community Treasure Hunts* by Clark & Glazer, 2004). Questing adds local, organic, authentic, interdisciplinary, and intergenerational components to learning. Clark and Glazer (2004) explained their reasoning behind creating some of the original quests: "Questing emerged from our suspicion that a great way to build people's sense of place would be to invite them out into the landscape to play." (p. 2). After the group learned more about questing, the majority believed this would be an excellent way to excite and involve students in place-based education. Two quests were developed: *Bowen Island Salmon Forest Quest* (BICS, 2009) and *The Grafton Lake Watershed Quest* (Nicolson & Blair Whitehead, 2009).

One teacher shared how the experience and questions from students during the quests had sparked new wonders for her: *Where do slugs go in the winter? What is the difference between an epiphyte and a bryophyte? Are mosses epiphytes?* She also encouraged students to record some of their wonders in their journals: *How do leaves make that shape? How come one type of moss is lighter than another?* Besides fostering curiosity of ecological phenomena, this activity appeared to be a valuable socializing tool for some students. One student in particular, who most often was nonsocial and shy to start a conversation, acted to the contrary during the quests. Teachers were amazed by the amount of new information they learned about Bowen Island, even though they lived and walked these trails often. In some manner, this activity seemed to have benefited the teachers more than the students because it had the teachers investigate and research their local community's history and its natural landscape. By doing so, they became exposed to using the forest around the school as a lesson context and were comfortable in doing so. Such moments have helped us to learn to discard the assumption that our questions as educators have to be simple and that we have to know the answers to them ourselves. We have also found that 'It depends ...' is a great way to draw out possibilities for linking the wonder at hand to its nest of contingent relationships. In this way, we realize that one wonder is contingent on many other relations—one story linked to many others.

Great Canadian Shoreline Clean-up

One of the longest lasting programs that has become part of BICS culture over the years is the nation-wide *Great Canadian Shoreline Clean-up* that is organized by the Vancouver Aquarium and the World Wildlife Fund. It "is a grassroots direct action conservation program that aims to promote understanding and education about shoreline litter issues by engaging Canadians to rehabilitate shoreline areas through cleanups." (Great Canadian Shoreline Clean-up, 2010, para. 1). On Bowen Island, this clean-up occurs annually at the beginning of the school year when students visit every beach around the island to pick up garbage. The students find out how much and what kind of garbage washes on to the shores, which they inventory and send the results to the Great Canadian Shoreline Clean-up database. Not only did we witness the development of responsible environmental stewards but also an aesthetic appreciation for the ocean. We got the sense that after this activity the students became much more protective of their beautiful beaches. Here, we believe, was the success of this activity. As stated in ELE (MoE, 2007), "an aesthetic appreciation, along with other understandings of nature, encourage students to learn and act to protect and sustain the environment, [in addition to contributing] to self-awareness and personal fulfillment." (p. 13).

Stream to Sea

Successful collaborations inspired and encouraged teachers to revisit and rejuvenate other programs. A former BICS teacher had run the *Stream to Sea* aquatic steward program developed by Fisheries and Oceans Canada (2010). This program, which has been running for over 20 years in BC and the Yukon, focuses on the lifecycle of salmon, connecting their lives and the importance of both the marine and freshwater environments (e.g., salmon streams and rivers). In the *Salmonid in the Classroom* activity, students watch and record the development of salmon from eggs to release as smolts in nearby salmon streams. Unfortunately, the program ended when the teacher who led this activity transferred to another school. A current BICS teacher, seeing the connections to the Salmon Forest Quest and Teaching Trails, took on the restart of the Stream to Sea program and asked us for help in preparing the freshwater aquarium found in the school storage area because of our experience working with Seaquaria in Schools.

With a team effort, the freshwater aquarium got underway a few months before the January intake of salmon eggs. When it was time to release the smolts, a day was planned for the K–2 classes to take the trails around the school that had been used in the Salmon Forest Quest and Teaching Trails to the Bowen Island Hatchery. This was a great opportunity for teachers to adapt the quest to their younger students who had not yet developed the literacy skills to read the complicated riddles. Therefore, they linked the Salmonid program to the K–2 life science and processes of science PLOs to local places: salmon streams and rivers. In addition, this program provided another valuable participatory activity involving students, teachers, and researchers that exudes ecological literacy. With the teachers' experience of having the Salmonid program for one school year and having the opportunity to see the connections to their learning goals, it looks promising that knowledge of this program will remain at BICS.

Community Garden and Journaling

With the support of the Bowen Island Community School Association, a community food garden was built at the back of school in an area overlooked by four classrooms (Figure 3). This activity had an immediate effect because students' interest was on the garden once it was created. Several hands-on lessons on food knowledge and safety were adopted into the curriculum.

We encouraged the teachers to use journaling in their classroom as a reflective activity because it has the potential to positively influence student relationships with the environment (Hammond, 2002). We assisted teachers by leading journal activities

Figure 3. BICS community garden (Photo: David Keoplin).

outdoors to the community garden and the trails behind the school. Students became deeply connected to what they were observing, drawing, or writing about this activity. In doing so, they were strengthening their connection to the more-than-human world. Some student comments support this observation: *I like how I am always able to come up with my own creations instead of being told exactly what to do. Drawing makes me look at things differently, like the way the branches move in the wind; I usually run around but this* [journaling] *makes me stop and notice. I like drawing outside because it makes me feel calmer. Journaling outside just feels different ... there are all sorts of smells and sounds. It makes me feel good inside. Instead of hearing or reading about it we get to actually see, smell, and feel nature.*

The development of this deep connection led to students wanting to find out more about the natural object they were observing or drawing, thereby creating a natural interest in ecological knowledge; for example: *You notice that everything is more detailed than you thought, like this leaf that I drew has all these holes and cracked edges. Being able to journal in the garden is cool. I learned that there are all different kinds of plants. My friend and I even found a leaf that looks like a cup!* The teachers also journaled with their students throughout the year, and some kept a personal journal. In doing so, they reaffirmed the process of journaling as a worth-while experience. The students often asked the teachers and researchers: *Can I see your journal? How did you draw it? What kind of pencil do you use?* Teachers were also learners in the discovery of their connection to place.

Missions Possible and Green Games

The last activity of the Pacific CRYSTAL EEP in some way represents this 5-year program at BICS. Each year Science World, in collaboration with the MoE and with the financial support of BC Hydro and Terasen Gas, holds a competition called *The BC Green Games* (Science World BC, 2010). The competition allows K–12 schools to submit a video presentation that shows their school's environmental stewardship. After a meeting, it was decided that BICS would enter the competition. With the support of a parent who was a documentary filmmaker, BICS decided to submit a video entitled *Missions Possible*. This presentation would focus on each grade's environmental goals. At the beginning of the year, each class had to select an environmental action; some classes chose to go around and turn off lights during recess and lunch breaks in order for the school to use less energy; others chose to gather all the compost from the school to place in the school's community garden; others chose to help encourage recycling in and around the school. Although there was no official reason provided, we believe that this activity was chosen instead of the others that have been mentioned in this chapter because it was the easiest to organize the involvement of the entire school. BICS won the Viewers' Choice Award voted on by the general public. What made this award so special is at an earlier meeting the BICS teachers had asked us to lead this submission; however, this was not the case: BICS did it all on its own. For us, the community-wide interest in this activity was indicative that ecological literacy had genuinely become integrated into the school's core curriculum and culture.

This award went alongside another external symbol of recognition for the school's place-based environmental learning programs. In 2007, the BC Ministry of the Environment presented BICS with a BC Provincial Award of Excellence for Leadership in environmental education and stewardship. The teachers were presented the award by the Premier at a ceremony held at the school with the entire Bowen Island community attending.

DISCUSSION

During Pacific CRYSTAL's LSP and the EEP at BICS, the local environment was used as an organizing theme for interdisciplinary teaching with an infusionist approach. This educational approach was taken in order to find numerous ways for how ecological literacy could become a core educational standard in the school and embedded into specific subject area units. Over the 5 years, we believe the BICS case study has provided several ideas for the infusion of ecological literacy.

One of the most important conclusions from this study was the role of the teacher. The BICS teachers played critical leadership roles from the inception of the Eco-Team to the organizing of Missions Possible. We can confidently state that these activities would not have occurred if the teachers had not been the primary change agents. It was the support and enthusiasm of a few teachers who acted as environmental education advocates at the beginning of this research project that led to the school-wide support for ecological literacy.

As important as having teachers as leaders was the incorporation of activities and programs that were collaborative efforts in which all participants (i.e., students, teachers, administrators, community members, and researchers) were equal. Participatory research methods, such as the one practiced during this project, acknowledge the value of involving both the researcher and subject collaborating with "the aims of solving a problem and generating new knowledge" (Coghlan & Brannick, 2001, p. 3).

Another observation is the valuable role that the community plays in the development and successful implementation of place-based activities. Every activity described in this chapter was contextualized to Bowen Island with the help of the community. Resources such as the Teaching Trails, Beach Studies in a Bucket, and Quests could not have come about without the expertise and support of community members. BICS was fortunate for its strong links to the community and environmental organizations. Other programs that were not developed particularly for Bowen Island, such as Seaquaria in Schools, appear to have become much more valuable when they were adapted for the school's local environment. It is believed that because the marine organisms in the seaquarium were from the students' backyards, they became closely attached to them, developing empathy for them.

A final point to make with regard to this Pacific CRYSTAL Project at BICS was a development after the project had ended. The teachers and principal believed that the place-based environmental education activities and associated resources could be beneficial to urban schools that do not have current access to such experiences. The BICS teachers now became ambassadors for ecological literacy in their own school district and others. So confident were they that the WVSD is now considering BICS as a destination school—a true Lighthouse School.

CLOSING REMARKS

Both the LSP and the EEP complemented one another with their focus on leadership, knowledge transfer, and supporting teachers as the primary change agents in their schools and the school district. The LSP supported the EEP's focus on understanding how ecological literacy became a core educational standard in schools by providing professional development for teachers. After 5 years of the Pacific CRYSTAL Project at BICS, there was visible and documented evidence for the development of a supportive and positive place-based learning environment, which fostered the infusion of ecological literacy into the school's curriculum.

At its core, this research study's greatest contribution to understanding how to introduce ecological literacy into the core educational standard of a school is by acknowledging the importance of involving teachers as primary agents for change. Ecological literacy became part of the school's core curriculum by the BICS teachers taking an infusionist and place-based approach to adopting it into the school's culture. At BICS, ecological literacy was more than simply a learning goal—it was adopted to help students contextualize their learning in their local community and environment. Therefore, ecological literacy was not presented to students using abstractions but rather as actual phenomena in their own community. By doing so, BICS teachers acknowledged the importance of both knowledge of science and knowledge of community and exemplified that ecological literacy is both a scientific understanding of living systems and a humanistic understanding of the interdependent relationship between human beings and the greater biotic and elemental (nonliving) world around us.

ACKNOWLEDGEMENT

We would like to thank the staff and administration of Bowen Island Community School in School District 45 (West Vancouver) for allowing us the opportunity to work with them over the course of this project.

REFERENCES

Basile, C. (2000). Environmental education as a catalyst for transfer of learning in young children. *Journal of Environmental Education, 32*(1), 21–27.

Bowen Island Community School. (2006). *Beach studies in a bucket.* Bowen Island, BC, Canada: Author.

Bowen Island Community School. (2009). *Bowen Island salmon forest quest.* Bowen Island, BC, Canada: Author.

Bowen Island Municipality. (2010). *About Bowen Island website.* Retrieved from http://www.bimbc.ca/about_bowen

British Columbia Ministry of Education. (2007). *Environmental learning and experience: An interdisciplinary guide for teachers.* Victoria, BC, Canada: Author.

Clark, D., & Glazer, S. (2004). *Questing: A guide to creating community treasure hunts.* Lebanon, NH: University Press of New England.

Coghlan, D., & Brannick, T. (2001). *Doing research in your own organization.* London, England: Sage.

Cole, A. G. (2007). Expanding the field: Revisiting environmental education principles through multidisciplinary frameworks. *Journal of Environmental Education, 38*(2), 35–44.

Corral-Verdugo, V., & Frais-Armenta, M. (1996). Predictors of environmental critical thinking: A study of Mexican children. *Journal of Environmental Education, 27*(4), 23–28.

Cummins, S., & Snively, G. J. (2000). The effect of instruction on children's knowledge of marine ecology, attitudes toward the ocean, and stances toward marine resource issues. *Canadian Journal of Environmental Education, 5,* 305–326.

Disinger, J. F., & Roth, C. E. (1992). *Environmental literacy.* Retrieved from ERIC database. (ED351201)

Fisher, D. L., & Khine, M. S. (2006). *Contemporary approaches to research on learning environments: World views.* Singapore: World Scientific.

Fisheries and Oceans Canada. (2010). *Stream to Sea website.* Retrieved from http://www.pac.dfo-mpo.gc.ca/education/index-eng.htm

Fraser, B. J. (2001). Twenty thousand hours: Editor's introduction. *Learning Environment Research, 4,* 1–5.

Fraser, B. J. (2007). Classroom learning environments. In S. K. Abell & N. G. Lederman (Eds.), *Handbook on research in science education* (pp. 103–124). Mahwah, NJ: Lawrence Erlbaum.

Gaylord, C. G. (2002). Environmental literacy: Towards a shared understanding for science teachers. *Research in Science & Technological Education, 20*(1), 99–110.

Great Canadian Shoreline Clean-up. (2010). *Homepage.* Retrieved from http://shorelinecleanup.ca/en/about/our-mission

Gruenewald, D. (2003). The best of both worlds: A critical pedagogy of place. *Educational Researcher, 32*(4), 3–12.

Hammersley, M., & Atkinson, P. (2007). *Ethnography: Principles in practice.* London, England: Routledge.

Hammond, W. (2002). The creative journal: A powerful tool for learning. *Green Teacher, 69,* 34–39.

Hendricks, C. (2006). *Improving schools through action research: A comprehensive guide for educators.* New York: Allyn & Bacon.

Hutchinson, D. (2004). *A natural history of place in education.* New York: Routledge.

Husby, W., & Fast, S. E. (2002). *Bowen Island teaching trails.* Retrieved from http://ecoleaders.ca/

Husby, W., & Fast, S. E. (n.d.). *Teaching trails: Bowen Island community school.* Retrieved from http://ecoleaders.ca/Introduction/mainpage.html

Kenney, J., Price-Militana, H., & Horrocks-Donohue, M. (2003). Helping teachers to use their school's backyard as an outdoor classroom: A report on the watershed learning center program. *Journal of Environmental Education, 35*(1), 15–21.

Knapp, C. E. (2005). The "I – thou" relationship, place-based education, and Aldo Leopold. *Journal of Experiential Education, 27*(3), 277–285.

Lieben Artists' Colony. (2010). *Homepage.* Retrieved from www.lieben.ca

Lieberman, G. A., & Hoody, L. L. (1998). *Closing the achievement gap: Using the environment as an integrating context for learning. Results of a nationwide study.* Retrieved from ERIC database. (ED428943)

Lord, T. (1999). A comparison between traditional and constructivist teaching in environmental science. *Journal of Environmental Education, 30*(3), 22–28.

Metro Vancouver. (2010). *Map of Bowen Island.* Retrieved from http://en.wikipedia.org/wiki/File: GVRD_Bowen_Island.svg

Nicolson, C., & Blair Whitehead, D. G. (2009). *The Grafton Lake watershed quest.* Bowen Island, BC, Canada: Author.

North American Association for Environmental Education. (2010). *Excellence in environmental education: Guidelines for learning (K–12).* Washington, DC: Author.

Ormond, C. G. A., & Zandvliet, D. B. (2009, April). *Place-based learning environments and teacher education.* Paper presented at the annual meeting of the National Association for Research in Science Teaching, Garden Grove, CA, USA.

Orr, D. W. (1992). *Ecological literacy: Education and the transition to a postmodern world.* Albany, NY: State University of New York Press.

Orr. D. W. (1994). *Earth in mind.* Washington, DC: Island Press.

Powers, A. L. (2004). An evaluation of four place-based education programs. *Journal of Environmental Education, 35*(4), 17–32.

Roth, C. E. (1992). *Environmental literacy: Its roots, evolution, and directions in the 1990s.* Retrieved from ERIC database. (ED348235)

Science World British Columbia. (2010). *The BC green games home page.* Retrieved from http://www.bcgreengames.ca/about/for-parents.html

Smith, G. (2002, April). Learning to be where we are. *Kappan, 83*, 548–594.

Sobel, D. (1993). *Children's special places.* Tucson, AZ: Zephyr Press.

Sobel, D. (1996). *Beyond ecophobia: Reclaiming the heart in nature education.* Great Barrington, MA: Orion Society.

Squamish Nation Network. (2010). *Homepage.* Retrieved from http://www.squamish.net/

Suttles, W. (1990). Central Coast Salish. In W. Suttles (Ed.), *Handbook of North American Indians* (Vol. 7, pp. 453–594). Washington, DC: Smithsonian.

Twigg, A. M. (1997). *Union steamships remembered.* Campbell River, BC, Canada: Author.

Volk, T. L., & Cheak, M. (2003). The effects of an environmental education program on students, parents, and community. *Journal of Environmental Education, 34*(4), 12–25.

Wang, M. C., Haertel, G., & Walberg, H. J. (1993). Toward a knowledge base of school learning. *Review of Educational Research, 73*, 249–294.

West Vancouver School District. (2010). *About Bowen Island Community School (BICS).* Retrieved from http://www2.sd45.bc.ca/schools/bowenisland/About/Pages/default.aspx

WestWind SeaLab Supplies & World Fisheries Trust. (2008). *Seaquaria in schools: An educator's guidebook and manual.* Retrieved from http://www.worldfish.org/images-pdfs/Projects/Seaquaria/Seaq%20Manual%20%2011%20Feb.pdf

Wilke, R. (1995). Environmental literacy and the college curriculum. *EPA Journal, 21*(2), 28–30.

Woodhouse, J. L., & Knapp, C. E. (2000). *Place-based curriculum and instruction: Outdoor and environmental education approaches.* Retrieved from ERIC database. (ED448012)

Zandvliet, D. B. (2007, April). *Learning environments that support environmental learning*. Paper presented at the annual meeting of the National Association for Research in Science Teaching, New Orleans, LA, USA.

Zandvliet, D. B., & Brown, D. (2006). Framing experience on Haida Gwaii: An ecological model for environmental education. *Canadian Journal of Environmental Education, 11*, 207–219.

Carlos Gustavo A. Ormond, Susan M. Teed, Laura Piersol
and David B. Zandvliet
Faculty of Education
Simon Fraser University
Burnaby, British Columbia, Canada

V. CLOSING REMARKS AND IMPLICATIONS FOR THE FUTURE

LARRY D. YORE AND EILEEN VAN DER FLIER-KELLER

14. EPILOGUE OF PACIFIC CRYSTAL—LESSONS LEARNED ABOUT SCIENCE, MATHEMATICS, AND TECHNOLOGY LITERACY, TEACHING AND LEARNING

Pacific CRYSTAL involved a diverse collection of investigators and projects within the first-ever Centres for Research into Youth, Science Teaching and Learning (CRYSTAL) funded by the Natural Sciences and Engineering Research Council of Canada (NSERC). Being a new endeavour for the funding agency and many of the researchers—in terms of the scope and size of the project as well as the breadth of disciplines and cultures involved with the CRYSTAL program—meant that refinements and revisions to the goals, policy interpretations, procedures, organization, and operations were inerrable. Within this implementation phase, it took 18 months to build a degree of consensus and mutual trust, shared understandings, and internal procedures to produce a mission statement, an evolutionary process for idea development and application, and cooperative management structures and procedures that utilized the diversity of talents and opportunities, emphasized collaboration and shared authority, and blended cultures and reward systems of various universities, academic departments, and nongovernmental agencies. These deliberations advanced methods for conducting community-based research and development (R&D) projects while leveraging NSERC funds with other government, university, and private sources; in addition, they set the R&D agenda using cooperative decision-making mechanisms that recognized multiple perspectives and priorities.

From the outset, Pacific CRYSTAL was proposed to be a research-oriented effort to generate and publish academic research reports in the traditional sense involving a diverse collection of science, mathematics, and technology (SMT, where the T includes engineering, computer science, and other techno-scientific disciplines) academics, university educators, school personnel, and nongovernmental awareness-of-SMT advocates and practitioners. During early project-wide and Advisory Board meetings and the first meeting of the five CRYSTAL projects across Canada, it became apparent that performance benchmarks solely focused on peer-reviewed publications were not fully embraced by all participants—nor was it reasonable to expect of emergent R&D activities focused on youth and the teaching and learning of SMT literacies if program goals including influencing policy and the teaching and learning landscapes were to be attained. These issues were addressed by developing (a) a mutually agreeable mission statement and deliverables that more completely captured the visions and desires of all participants, (b) a strategic

L. D. Yore et al (Eds.), Pacific CRYSTAL Centre for Science, Mathematics, and Technology Literacy: Lessons Learned, 237–252.

understanding of how ideas could evolve over the duration of the project, and (c) an organization and management plan that reflected community-based principles of shared authority and responsibility, which aligned with the funding agency's refined intentions.

The Pacific CRYSTAL mission statement says that it intends to *promote scientific, mathematical, and technological literacies (including underserved and underrepresented groups) for responsible citizenship through research partnerships with university and educational communities.* To this end, Pacific CRYSTAL's functional structure consisted of three R&D nodes designed to facilitate an evolution of connected ideas and an administrative node charged with facilitating the R&D activities (~18–25 projects and ~42 principal investigators, partners, and research associates). The projects evolved in focus, function, and number over the duration of the project as people entered and left Pacific CRYSTAL and as tested ideas were implemented more widely. Node 1, an incubation centre (*Build*), involved extracurricular authentic science, mathematics, and technology experiences; Node 2, a classroom testing environment (*Expand*), field-tested instructional ideas and strategies to develop evidence-based resources and practices; and Node 3, lighthouse schools (*Lead*), involved systemic change, knowledge transfer, and leadership opportunities that adapted, demonstrated, and disseminated tested ideas, resources, and strategies to a much broader education community to influence public policy and educational decisions about SMT learning and teaching. The early years of Pacific CRYSTAL emphasized the *Build* intentions, while the middle years emphasized the *Expand* intentions, and later years emphasized the *Lead* intentions. Budget and resources were assigned accordingly, in a transparent manner, to achieve the current emphasis while maintaining prior efforts and supporting future endeavours. This chapter provides an epilogue of Pacific CRYSTAL, reflections on the lessons learned, and insights into future R&D related to SMT literacies.

REFLECTIONS ON LESSONS LEARNED

Multiple readings of the chapters and discussions amongst the co-directors, section editors, project leaders, and authors revealed themes flowing from one or more chapters and projects. Most of these themes were anticipated in the original NSERC proposal, others morphed in character with the evolution of the project, and unanticipated opportunities allowed other themes to be developed. Themes identified included community commitment and action planning, expanded and shared understanding of SMT literacies, evidence-based instruction and resources, professional learning (teacher education and professional development), student performance (identities, career awareness, and SMT literacies), and leadership and advocacy.

Community Commitment and Action Planning

Pacific CRYSTAL was built on a long history at the University of Victoria in which the Faculty of Engineering, Faculty of Science, and Faculty of Education collaborated to provide graduate (i.e., Master of Science Education, Master of Mathematics Education) and outreach programs for professional development (e.g., Continuing Studies in Education, UVic Speakers Bureau, etc.). Furthermore, the Faculty of Engineering, the Engineering Students Association, and the Faculty of Science have supported and facilitated numerous science awareness and understanding outreach efforts over the last 20 years; for example, Science Venture, Women in Science, Science Fairs, EdGEO teacher workshops, Scientists in the Schools, Let's Talk Science, Year of Science, a variety of programs for aboriginal students, and after-school programs in computer science such as Solving Problems with Algorithms, Robots, and Computer Science (SPARCS).

Pacific CRYSTAL revitalized these cooperative networks amongst members of the Faculties of Engineering, Science, and Education, other universities (i.e., Simon Fraser, Vancouver Island, Royal Roads), nongovernmental agencies (i.e., SeaChange Marine Conservation Society, World Fisheries Trust, WestWind SeaLab Supplies), and British Columbia and First Nations school districts and schools on Vancouver Island and the lower mainland. The Pacific CRYSTAL proposal recruited participants from these diverse groups without fully recognizing the desires, needs, and differences of the individuals and groups. More open and face-to-face deliberations, which were not possible because of the short development timeline for the NSERC proposal, would have revealed the need to clarify involvement, recruitment of research assistants/graduate students, budget allocations, and management procedures that were later developed during Years 1 and 2. This lack of initial clarity caused some tensions and led to some project leaders leaving the Pacific CRYSTAL Project. The original proposal accurately identified some authentic SMT learning opportunities and experiences that were anchored in the involvement of academic scientists, engineers, technologists, and mathematicians in collaboration with SMT educators. However, funding allocations, project implementation processes, and interpersonal interactions amongst the diverse group of co-investigators were not fully anticipated or clarified. While some obstacles to involvement in such an interdisciplinary project were identified in the science and engineering community, especially in terms of research focus and university reward systems, the interdisciplinary networking facilitated by Pacific CRYSTAL overall proved to be highly effective in improving SMT outreach and education approaches.

The systemic change action plans assumed that (1) high-quality professional learning combined with (2) high-quality evidence-based resources would lead to (3) enhanced classroom teaching and assessment that reflect *best practices*, which in turn would promote (4) enhanced student SMT literacies outcomes (Banilower, Boyd, Pasley, & Weiss, 2006). The relationships among factors 1, 2, and 3 in this action plan are reasonably well established, but their influence on student achievement remains tentative (Shymansky, Yore, & Anderson, 2004). Several researchers (Czerniak, Beltyukova, Struble, Haney, & Lumpe, 2005; Geier et al., 2008; Johnson, Fargo, & Kahle, 2010; Revak & Kuerbis, 2008; Romance & Vitale, 1992) have—and continue to—successfully documented the relationships among professional development, instructional resources, classroom practices, and disciplinary literacy (e.g., fundamental literacy, disciplinary understanding, and fuller participation in the public debate about science, technology, society, and environment [STSE] issues).

The design, development, and evaluation of most Pacific CRYSTAL projects were implicitly guided by these assumptions while the implementation of the systemic change action plan varied across projects, depending on their initial intentions and development. These challenges could not be addressed effectively without systems thinking that recognized the nested structures of elementary, secondary, and postsecondary education and networks of scientists, engineers, educators, educational researchers, teachers, administrators, students, and parents. This collaboration between diverse constituencies represents a new approach to advancing SMT literacy, and NSERC is to be congratulated for its vision and foresight in facilitating such interdisciplinary networks.

Engaging scientists and engineers in the Pacific CRYSTAL program has yielded many benefits:
- facilitating opportunities and authentic internships for students in working laboratories with researchers
- providing up-to-date SMT research expertise and understanding to direct the development of high-quality resources and experiences as part of Node 1
- mentoring for Pacific CRYSTAL teachers
- promoting an improved understanding of the cultures and nature of SMT enterprises and their relevance to society.

The last item is an essential component of SMT literacy: informed participation in the public debate of STSE issues using the knowledge, epistemic and ontological assumptions, habits of mind, plausible reasoning, and language of SMT.

For the SMT academics involved, the value of the collaboration with science, mathematics, and environmental educators and their communities cannot be overstated. Interactions over the course of the project have provided these benefits:
- access to new insights into constructivist pedagogy and classroom realities
- increasing the effectiveness of existing outreach programs
- informing new professional development and teacher education projects being developed
- sharing of insights and tools for program evaluation and student assessment has provided critical guidance for future R&D activities into professional learning, instructional resources, classroom practice, and student SMT literacy achievement.

A further advantage of the collaboration is that science, engineering, and education HQP (highly qualified personnel) are interacting together and sharing their diverse cultures and expertise. However, SMT academics involvement is not without risk, as some engineering and science environments within universities/colleges undervalue their faculty members' education and awareness outreach efforts in terms of promotion, tenure, and salary considerations.

For SMT students, this project has far-reaching implications both in terms of any future teaching they may do as part of their careers and for improving their effectiveness in informal environments focused on the public awareness of SMT (e.g., classroom visits, community events, etc.).

Expanded and Shared Understanding of SMT Literacies

Pacific CRYSTAL has focused on various aspects of SMT literacies; it has attempted to address the critical nature of disciplinary literacies and the need to develop both the fundamental and derived senses of SMT literacies such that people can participate more fully in the public debate about STSE issues and socioscientific issues (SSI). The goal is an informed public who can produce informed decisions and arrive at sustainable solutions to or actions for pressing societal issues, many of which require an understanding of SMT. Teed, Zandvliet, and Ormond (Chapter 9) differentiate the newer SSI and the historical STSE issues by identifying common and unique attributes of each—multidisciplinary issues based in science, society, and politics; forming opinions; cost benefits; and trade-offs—but SSI are more ill-defined and stress values and ethical reasoning. Frequently, STSE is considered a flexible and optional context for curriculum development while SSI is an instructional approach that engages science–technology–society interdependency and promotes moral and ethical development.

Pacific CRYSTAL has made concerted efforts to move the STSE and SSI away from the exclusive socio-emotional perspective of earlier efforts in environmental education (EE) and to address pressing issues with a more balanced approach that considers (a) underlying SMT and social science understandings, (b) ways of doing science (including observing, thinking, experimenting, and validation, utilizing both logic and imagination grounded in social activity skills such as discussion, negotiation, and dissemination), and (c) evolving SMT knowledge based on evidence, inherent values, ethical perspectives, and other contemporary local issues relevant to the learners. Pacific CRYSTAL focused its efforts on specific societal-relevant topics including water quality, climate change and weather, processes in the Earth's crust such as plate tectonics, natural hazards (e.g., earthquakes, volcanoes, etc.), environmental processes, marine ecosystems, Earth history, as well as the mathematical and technological tools and approaches needed to engage in these SMT topics.

Throughout the duration of Pacific CRYSTAL, members have struggled to develop and share working definitions or frameworks of SMT literacies that would (a) capture the synergy of fundamental literacy in SMT, understanding of SMT, and engagement of SMT-related issues, careers, and studies; (b) guide the implementation of these discipline-specific literacies into the established school curricula; (c) revitalize and refresh the current science and mathematics education reforms; and (d) direct second-generation reforms in SMT education. The conceptual frameworks for SMT literacies (Yore, Chapter 2) advocated in Pacific CRYSTAL stress a new Vision III that incorporates Vision I—knowledge about the big ideas and unifying themes of a discipline, and Vision II—application of these ideas in relevant contexts (Roberts, 2007). Vision III provides a mediating structure to enhance understanding and application to STSE issues using the underemphasized importance and utility of fundamental literacy (i.e., cognitive and metacognitive abilities, habits of mind, reasoning, information communication technologies [ICT], mathematical and natural languages) in the specific discipline. Heretofore, few SMT educators have recognized the essential nature of fundamental literacy: language, especially print-based language, plays critical roles in constructing SMT knowledge claims (understandings), communicating these claims or understandings to others, and persuading others of their validity and usefulness.

Milford, Jagger, Yore, and Anderson (2010) demonstrated that after 12 years the Pan-Canadian Framework for Science (Council of Ministers of Education, 1997), which promotes science literacy for all Canadians, has influenced current curricula in every province and territory. Similar, delayed effects are also visible in mathematics curricula and the revised version of the NCTM (United States National Council of Teachers of Mathematics, 2000) and the WCNPM (Western and Northern Canadian Protocol for Collaboration in Education, 2006), which have refreshed reform efforts in the USA and western and northern Canada. Clearly, science education reforms require similar renewal (United States National Research Council [NRC], 2010) and the efforts to infuse technology, engineering, and computer science into the extant curricula needs increased effort. The SMT literacies frameworks that integrate the cognitive, linguistic, pedagogical, and philosophical aspects of disciplinary literacy might well serve as a foundation for second-generation SMT reforms and renewal efforts. The design of the common framework for SMT literacies can be used to justify and develop stand-alone curricula in these content areas, infused or integrated curricular modules, or map common goals onto existing curricula in language arts, mathematics, social studies, and science. Whichever strategy is used will be partially determined by the current crowding of school programs and the availability of professional learning experiences for teachers that retain the essential nature of the fundamental and derived components of discipline-specific literacy, leading to fuller participation in the public debate about STSE issues.

Evidence-based Instruction and Resources

School reforms and improvement efforts have called for implementation of best practices and evidence-based instructional strategies and resources (Shelley, 2009). Analyses of instructional recommendations involving literacy, language, and science learning and teaching in science teacher journals from Australia, the United Kingdom, and the United States indicated the lack of evidentiary basis for most of the recommended practices (Hand, Yore, Jagger, & Prain, 2010). A more in-depth analysis of literacy, language, and science instructional recommendations in National Science Teachers Association publications for K–12 teachers indicated that 61% of the recommendations lacked a sufficiently strong evidence base (Jagger & Yore, 2010). Pacific CRYSTAL has tried to address this problem by developing and testing innovative approaches to SMT education, as provided in the following.

Some authentic SMT activities, which might be better called extracurricular approaches since they were extensions beyond the normal classroom, include:
- laboratory internships (Hsu, 2008)
- field trips (de Oliveira Jayme, 2008)
- Seaquaria in Schools (Zandvliet, Holmes, & Starzner, Chapter 5)
- EcoRowing (www.seachangelife.net).

Other Pacific CRYSTAL activities grounded in the prescribed curricula include:
– Possible Selves (Marshall et al., Chapter 3)
– problem solving with computer science (Carruthers, 2010; Carruthers et al., Chapter 6; Gunion, 2010)
– community mapping (Jagger, 2009)
– weather unit, lesson plans, resources, and maps (Weaver, http://www.victoria weather.ca/)
– Science Times (Teed et al., Chapter 9)
– Lighthouse Schools (Blades, Chapter 12; Ormond, Teed, Piersol, & Zandvliet, Chapter 13)
while others were integrated with the normal K–12 school organization:
– First Nations internships (Wright, Claxton, Williams, & Paul, Chapter 4).
Other innovative applications pursued by Pacific CRYSTAL are represented by:
– Earth Science activities (Van der Flier-Keller, Blades, & Milford, Chapter 10)
– middle school science literacy (Tippett, in progress; Tippett & Anthony, Chapter 8)
– ICT (Francis Pelton & Pelton, Chapter 7)
– enriched mathematics (Francis Pelton & Pelton, Chapter 7; Willers, 2005).

Collectively, these projects and participants illustrate that *Schools and schooling are constructs, NOT constructions* and that *Curricula define a journey's endpoints (outcomes) and do not prescribe the road map (instruction)*. Innovative teachers can move freely between the formal and informal environments to capture the importance of EE, aboriginal education, and place-based learning and to engage learners in relevant local issues and phenomena. Formal and informal environments for learning about SMT must be considered and integrated in the development of SMT literacies and in building the public awareness of and engagement in SMT as well as the public debates about STSE issues. Schools, museums, parks, summer programs, weekend activities, and after-school experiences (e.g., Science Ventures, EcoRowing, Seaquaria in Schools) internships, lighthouse schools, and others often provide the SMT foundation as well the opportunity for engagement and enrichment for all learners, but in particular for underserved students. Additionally, these informal learning environments and innovative experiences provide opportunities for the general public to expand and deepen their understanding and improve their SMT identities and self-efficacies (NRC, 2009; Yore, Kottová, & Jagger, 2010).

Technology in Pacific CRYSTAL has been considered to be a discipline (design), a component of fundamental literacy (ICT), and an instructional delivery system (instructional technologies, IT). Carruthers et al. (Chapter 6) explored key concepts and engineering design of technology, specifically computer science, as derived understandings of technology literacy. Francis Pelton and Pelton (Chapter 7) illustrated applications of ICT (computer quests, conceptual comics), IT (personal response systems), and technological design (LEGO MINDSTORMS®). The middle school literacy project (Tippett & Anthony, Chapter 8) attempted to engage teachers with ICT in science, but there was little uptake of readily available software, hardware, and related strategies (e.g., Inspiration/Kidspiration, electronic weather stations, graphing software, earthquake modelling software, etc.) other than the Internet. Unfortunately, none of the projects were able to fully develop ICT as cognitive tools that modelled how scientists, engineers, and mathematicians used these technologies in doing SMT and that could become integral parts of the SMT literacies.

Professional Learning—Teacher Education and Professional Development

Professional education of SMT teachers must be based on a seamless program that illustrates best practices justified by empirical evidence of how people learn SMT leading to SMT literacies; it should provide teachers with knowledge about the disciplinary content, pedagogy and, most importantly, pedagogy related to specific SMT ideas appropriate for the target learners. Clearly, we need to produce beginning SMT teachers who are critical thinkers and reflective practitioners, which involves more than mimicry, mechanical use, and classroom management of inquiry, design, and problem-solving oriented approaches. When such teachers are challenged by pedagogical issues that require deliberation about alternatives, they will reflect on the situation and determine the best solution and will justify their instructional decisions. These principles should be a fundamental part of professional learning—teacher education and professional development programs. SMT teacher educators and professional development providers are frequently disappointed when preservice and inservice teachers quickly adopt, or revert to, the traditional practices of their colleagues, abandoning the constructivist inquiry, design, and problem-solving teaching strategies promoted in their on-campus courses and professional development experiences. It is essential that components of teacher education and professional development programs present an internally consistent rationale for—and expectations of—SMT teaching.

The principal investigators in Pacific CRYSTAL implicitly or explicitly emphasized content (CK), pedagogical (PK), and pedagogical content (PCK) knowledge related to SMT literacies. Scholars and teacher educators have stressed the importance of PCK in science (van Driel, Verloop, & de Vos, 1998; Veal & MaKinster, 1998), mathematics (Ma, 2010; Marks, 1990), instructional technology (Hughes, 2005; Mishra & Koehler, 2006), and disciplinary literacy (Love, 2009). PCK—the craft knowledge master teachers develop from their reflection on actions and the implicit study of their teaching practice in service of learners—has been demonstrated by many effective teachers. These teachers have well-developed, deep, flexible, and accessible CK, PK, and PCK of their disciplines and "ways of representing and formulating [their] subject[s] that ... [make them] comprehensible ... [to] others. ... [They develop] the most powerful analogies, illustrations, examples, explanations, and demonstrations" (Shulman, 1986, p. 9) that make abstract ideas accessible, comprehensible, and learnable! These insights include the nature—more correctly termed the ontological and epistemological assumptions and contemporary views—of SMT.

Many teacher professional learning programs, especially in the early years, are fragmented, misaligned, disconnected, and distributed among academic faculties and degrees, teacher education programs, and professional development components. Teaching in SMT content courses frequently is based on large-group lectures that stress knowledge transmission, coupled with weekly laboratories to verify and apply the knowledge provided earlier. This traditional deductive approach focuses on CK that is not aligned with contemporary models of how people learn SMT and interactive-constructivist teaching (e.g., modified learning cycles, project-based programs, cooperative strategies, etc.) and other inductive and hypothetico-deductive approaches promoting conceptual change and growth, high-order thinking, problem solving, inquiry, and design. Likewise, teaching methods courses in teacher education programs stress PK about generalized models and theories of learning and teaching. Some methods courses and clinical experiences focus on PCK that addresses specific conceptual demands of SMT topics and learners' prior knowledge, personal beliefs, and assumptions about SMT. Such a disconnect in the professional learning progression leads to SMT ideas being presented in abstract forms or as mathematical equations and totally disregards the learners' potential misconceptions and prior understanding about the nature of SMT and SMT topics. Furthermore, university/ college SMT experiences appear to have a lasting influence on how students teach since little has changed in elementary and middle schools over the last 50 years.

The EOS 120 project (Van der Flier-Keller et al., Chapter 10) illustrates (a) how the fragmentation of a program can be addressed within the constraints of multiple faculties and traditional university organization and (b) how contemporary constructivist approaches can be used in both the content and pedagogical components of teacher education and professional development programs to form a seamless model for SMT professional learning. The EOS Education Laboratory (EdLab) serves as an interface between the traditional science lecture that emphasizes knowledge transmission and a modified learning cycle approach (EDU) that emphasizes a constructivist inquiry approach, which allows students to construct new understanding based on prior knowledge and concurrent experiences in a sociocultural context. The EdLab not only enhances students' achievement in laboratory and lecture, it also provides the preservice teachers experiences that serve as foundations for their pedagogical beliefs and PCK about how to teach specific Earth Science topics to specific learners.

The Departments of Curriculum and Instruction and of Mathematics and Statistics have jointly developed and instructed first- and third-year courses (MATH 161, 162, 360) designed to fulfil the mathematics entry requirements and to provide advanced CK for the elementary teacher education program. The successes and challenges of these courses have been reported to be similar to EOS 120, but they have not been formally documented. Similar interface arrangements or bridge courses could be developed for other science, mathematics, and engineering domains.

Professional learning is a continuous process encompassing the preservice programs, entry into the teaching profession, and continued renewal. The transition from university programs to early teaching and career successes is challenging. Professional development to ensure continued effectiveness as well as to meet changing curricular and instructional demands of SMT education has been the focus of several Pacific CRYSTAL projects (Francis Pelton & Pelton, Chapter 7; Tippett & Anthony, Chapter 8; Teed et al., Chapter 9; Van der Flier-Keller et al., Chapter 10; Blades, Chapter 12; Ormond et al., Chapter 13). These efforts placed importance on rational, evidence-based decisions about what to teach, how to teach, and what data justify learning and teaching effectiveness. These professional development projects have in common the delivery of PCK; involvement of expert teachers as partners in development and delivery; in-context, situated experience with the recommended innovation as participant observers; provision and exploration of necessary classroom resources (robot kits, trade books, rock and mineral samples, observation and data collection tools, etc.); and, in several cases, ongoing mentoring and coaching. Effective PD must provide complete innovation and implementation resources and support that address real and perceived barriers to change, not just a description of an abstract idea.

Student Performance (Identities, Career Awareness, SMT Literacies)

Some Pacific CRYSTAL projects attempted to document the connections among PD, instructional resources, classroom practices, and student achievement regarding some or all components of SMT literacies. The researchers focused on understanding of SMT concepts and critical attributes of inquiry, problem solving, and design (Carruthers et al., Chapter 6; Van der Flier-Keller et al., Chapter 10); development of fundamental literacy in these disciplines involving affective dispositions, processes, plausible reasoning, ICT strategies, and language competence (Marshall et al., Chapter 3; Wright et al., Chapter 4; Zandvliet et al., Chapter 5; Tippett & Anthony, Chapter 8); and the participation in the public debate about STSE issues (Teed et al., Chapter 9). Other researchers explored the relationships within the fundamental understanding and public engagement of SMT literacies (Milford, Anderson, & Luo, Chapter 11; Ormond et al., Chapter 13). Each of these projects contributed confirmatory evidence to the claim that student achievement was connected to other factors in the action plan (e.g., PD, resources, classroom practice), but none of them made a compelling argument with strong evidence to claim best-practice status. This was due to the small-scale case studies and comparison–treatment group designs. Much more robust, random controlled trials or random field trials are needed to fully establish the final link in the action plan model. However, Tippett (in progress) has conducted a metasynthesis of four case studies and a verification study to document the links among visual competence in science, student-constructed representations, constructivist teaching, and PD in middle schools.

A critical issue facing many people involved in SMT education is being aware of the current career and study opportunities available in the 21st century. *Why So Few?* (Hill, Corbett, & St. Rose, 2010) documents the demographics and barriers for women in science, technology, engineering, and mathematics in the USA. Women, First Nations, and other underserved populations in some SMT areas in Canada have made progress, but these advances are not evenly distributed across all SMT areas. Elementary, middle, and secondary school teachers and counsellors need to be aware of the barriers for these populations and ensure that students engage SMT opportunities in their K–12 education. Possible Selves (Marshall et al., Chapter 3) illustrates the critical importance for underserved and under-represented people to engage and become aware of SMT-related careers and further studies and to develop SMT identities that will fully realize their personal attributes and interests. Traditional school SMT courses do not fully reflect the changing opportunities for and needs of students, especially for new Canadians, women, First Nations, and other underserved students. Marshall and her team continue to promote career awareness, mentorships, and other real-world experiences to more fully alert students to opportunities and to keep doors to future decisions and solutions open.

Various secondary analyses of large-scale assessments of student performance uncovered relationships and correlates of mathematics, reading, and science literacies, of school features, and of family/home characteristics (Milford et al., Chapter 11). They focused on the Programme for International Student Assessment (PISA)—one large-scale assessment that is often used to report school and country rankings in reading, mathematics, and science literacies based on an extracurricular definition of literacy involving adult survival in an information economy, which decouples the tests from existing curricula in language arts, mathematics, and science to indicate what might be possible. These researchers and others found surprisingly high correlations amongst these literacies and between these literacy performances and school and family/home characteristics using hierarchical linear modelling (HLM). These correlations tended to support the relationships amongst fundamental literacy, disciplinary understandings, and public engagement of SMT (Yore, Chapter 2). Furthermore, other HLM results provide insights into the relationships amongst family/home, school, and student performance in reading, mathematics, and science literacies. The 2009 PISA, which emphasizes reading literacy and provides associated mathematics and science literacies results, is another rich data set that deserves further considerations (search 2009 PISA on http://www.oecd.org).

Leadership and Advocacy

Increasing leadership capacity was a critical feature of most Pacific CRYSTAL activities. There is a drastic need for leaders, advocates, and agents for change from within the formal and informal SMT learning communities—elementary, middle, secondary, and postsecondary education levels—regarding extracurricular public awareness, engagement, and understanding environments. The lists of project leaders, authors, and the HQP Appendix formally document many new and established researchers, leaders, and advocates in these arenas. The Pacific CRYSTAL projects incorporated a cascading leadership approach that systematically decentralized responsibilities and shared authority as much as was possible under the terms of the NSERC grant and operational procedures. These lists illustrate how cascading responsibility, academic civility, and distributed expertise were achieved by many new researchers through research fellowships and internships, and the collaborations amongst principal investigators and team members that are characteristic of effective research groups (Florence & Yore, 2004). However, these people are only part of the leadership legacy.

The transfer of responsibility and cascading leadership for teacher participants varied in success across various projects. The Watershed Elementary and Creekside

Middle Schools (pseudonyms) resulted in substantive transfer of decision making but did not result in district-wide leadership (Blades, Chapter 12). Participating teachers in these Lighthouse Schools were fully willing to accept responsibility for identifying educational goals and developing resources within their grade levels and classrooms, but many teachers were reluctant to serve as advocates for SMT education within their schools or school district and beyond. The Middle Schools Explicit Literacy in Science project illustrated similar results regarding enacting responsibility for curriculum design decisions but resulted in somewhat more leadership and advocacy for scientific literacy (Tippett & Anthony, Chapter 8). The lead teachers (advocates) developed embedded literacy tasks in science and associated PD activities and materials. They were willing to deliver the PD within their school and to participate in district-wide committees, but these highly qualified teachers were reluctant to get involved in professional development and conference activities at the district, regional, or provincial levels.

The most successful examples of leadership and advocacy were in the EE and First Nations internship projects. The participants in the Bowen Island Community School (Ormond et al., Chapter 13), Seaquaria in Schools (Zandvliet et al., Chapter 5), and EcoRowing (www.seachangelife.net) projects were passionate about the EE causes at both the professional and personal levels. These teachers and volunteers willingly accepted the responsibilities for curriculum development, implementation, and dissemination of the instructional resources and pedagogical strategies. They frequently presented at regional and provincial science and EE conferences and workshops, supported new participants within the projects as mentors, and contributed to provincial curriculum revisions. The SNIT☐E☐ First Nations Internship project illustrated the innovative development of leadership capacity and the transfer of responsibility in which the principal investigator facilitated knowledge and responsibility transfer, developed leadership skills, and revitalized connections between traditional ecological knowledge and wisdom (TEKW) and western scientific knowledge sources (Wright et al., Chapter 4).

Transfer of knowledge and influence of educational policies, decisions, and practices were central considerations of Pacific CRYSTAL. Many education R&D funding agencies require consideration of public advocacy to enhance SMT education policies and decisions. Grant writers are quick to accept this charge without fully understanding the implications (Yore, Shelley, & Hand, 2009). Informing and influencing public policy involves a unique skill set and communications not common amongst most SMT researchers and educators (Shelley, 2009). Promotion of SMT best practices requires an evidence base and thoughtful implications that are not found in most science teacher magazines in North America (Jagger & Yore, 2010), the UK and Australia (Hand et al., 2010), and most research journals (Brickhouse, 2006).

Presentation styles and rhetorical procedures need to recognize the end users, windows of opportunity, and the political process. Most busy politicians, bureaucrats, policy consultants, and decision makers do not have the time or backgrounds to read, interpret, and translate isolated academic and research reports. They require systematic reviews, metasyntheses, meta-analyses, and other secondary analyses of empirical research written in user-friendly forms to initiate and inform their actions. Journals (e.g., *Educational Leadership, Phi Delta Kappan,* etc.) along with advocacy websites—such as the Society for Research in Child Development (http://www.srcd.org/), Best Evidence Encyclopedia (http://www.bestevidence.org/), Campbell Collaboration (http://www.campbellcollaboration.org/), Comprehensive School Reform Quality Center (http://www.csrq.org/), and What Works Clearing-house (http://ies.ed.gov/ncee/wwc/ —provide examples of useful, written reports to meet the communication and persuasion functions necessary to inform and influence policies and decisions.

Advocates for SMT literacies need to recognize the windows of opportunity and the education policy and curriculum cycles so as to be ready for action when such opportunities surface and to be persistent (Milford et al., 2010). The most important consideration for passionate and idealistic advocates is to realize that politicians may use parts of their brief to initiate incomplete policy or use the brief to support their own perspective. This is illustrated by the influence of the Bowen Island Community School participants on the EE learning and experience guide (http://www.bced. gov.bc.ca/environment_ed/); they provide an excellent example of successful advocacy for change. Their actions led to a strong framework of principles (com-plexity, aesthetics, responsibility, ethics) and increased visibility of EE, resulting in an interdisciplinary document outlining how approaches and topics could be mapped onto existing curricula in mathematics, science, and social studies. These outcomes likely do not fully reflect their desired goals; however, they represent a significant and positive step forward and an effort to overcome less rational EE actions.

CLOSING REMARKS

Funding agencies that are concerned about changing the quality of SMT learning, teaching, curriculum, and instructional resources need to realize that substantive, robust, and lasting changes represent a process, not an event, and that it is a long-term commitment to efforts that challenge existing policies, programs, procedures, and practices. Many curriculum and instruction reforms have evaluated proposed innovations without applying similar scrutiny to existing programs and approaches. We need to focus our efforts on learning rather than teaching—teaching has to be in service of learning; if there is no meaningful learning, there is no meaningful teaching. Traditional approaches frequently focus on teaching as a performance indicated on observational checklists and learning as improved test scores, with little attention to process skills, problem solving, critical thinking, self-concept, and self-efficacy toward SMT. Pacific CRYSTAL made significant contributions to high-quality resources and practices, high-quality professional learning experiences, and enhanced classroom practices—but it did not provide substantive evidence on student performance. However, several projects did attempt to elaborate learning in terms of both fundamental and derived components of SMT literacies and in terms of fuller participation in the public debate about STSE issues leading to informed decisions and sustainable actions.

Future R&D efforts dealing with SMT literacies need to establish a program of study that moves beyond isolated case and small-scale, quasi-experimental studies toward cross-study metasyntheses or meta-analyses and random control trials to establish cause-effect mechanisms and convincing arguments. The studies in this book have initiated development and documentation of promising SMT experiences and instructional practices, but none yet provide a strong evidence basis for claiming best-practice status. Likewise, several studies have explored and described promising professional learning experiences and approaches for SMT teacher education and professional development that addressed CK, PK, and PCK as well as border-crossing between traditional and scientific knowledge about nature and naturally occurring events. As with most R&D efforts, more questions arise that require further investigation.

The 5-year CRYSTAL pilot project was a valiant attempt by NSERC to establish collaborations focused on SMT literacies, but the luxury of hindsight affords some insights for future efforts. First, the initial competition should have tried to identify 8–12 promising proposals or potential centres rather than to immediately identify the five centres to be funded. The initial competition could have been based on a letter of intent and brief proposal (including documentation of the actors) and authorization of the involved agencies. These 8–12 proposals could have been awarded $50,000–80,000 planning grants to pilot their proposed ideas using small-scale efforts, to develop productive collaborations and management procedures, and to generate a comprehensive proposal. During this year, the NSERC program director and staff could have searched for natural synergies amongst these pilot centres in a geographic region or research focus. Second, the 4–6 successful final proposals could have been awarded a 4-year grant of $700,000–800,000 to conduct the R&D projects outlined in the second-level competition. This would have involved the same amount of money as the 2005–2010 CRYSTAL pilot ($5,000,000) but it would have resulted in a more productive competition, more effective collaborations, and involvement of science, technology, and engineering faculties, and likely better-quality R&D results.

REFERENCES

Banilower, E. R., Boyd, S. E., Pasley, J. D., & Weiss, I. R. (2006). *Lessons from a decade of mathematics and science reform: A capstone report for the local systemic change through teacher enhancement initiative*. Chapel Hill, NC: Horizon Research Inc.

Brickhouse, N. W. (2006). Celebrating 90 years of science education: Reflections on the gold standard and ways of promoting good research [Editorial]. *Science Education, 90*(1), 1–7.

Carruthers, S. (2010). *Grasping graphs*. Master's thesis, University of Victoria. Retrieved from http://hdl.handle.net/1828/3193

Council of Ministers of Education, Canada. (1997). *Common framework of science learning outcomes, K to 12 Pan-Canadian protocol for collaboration on school curriculum*. Retrieved from http://publications.cmec.ca/science/framework/

Czerniak, C. M., Beltyukova, S., Struble, J., Haney, J. J., & Lumpe, A. T. (2005). Do you see what I see? The relationship between a professional development model and student achievement. In R. E. Yager (Ed.), *Exemplary science in grades 5–8: Standards-based success stories* (pp. 13–44). Arlington, VA: NSTA Press.

de Oliveira Jayme, B. (2008). *Elementary students' and teachers' interactions during out-of-classroom activities*. Master's thesis, University of Victoria. Retrieved from http://hdl.handle.net/1828/1027

Florence, M. K., & Yore, L. D. (2004). Learning to write like a scientist: Coauthoring as an enculturation task. *Journal of Research in Science Teaching, 41*(6), 637–668.

Geier, R., Blumenfeld, P. C., Marx, R. W., Krajcik, J. S., Fishman, B., Soloway, E., et al. (2008). Standardized test outcomes for students engaged in inquiry-based science curricula in the context of urban reform. *Journal of Research in Science Teaching, 45*(8), 922–939.

Gunion, K. (2010). *FUNdamentals of CS: Designing and evaluating computer science activities for kids*. Master's thesis, University of Victoria. Retrieved from http://hdl.handle.net/1828/2750

Hand, B., Yore, L. D., Jagger, S., & Prain, V. (2010). Connecting research in science literacy and classroom practice: A review of science teaching journals in Australia, the UK, and the United States, 1998–2008. *Studies in Science Education, 46*(1), 45–68.

Hill, C., Corbett, C., & St. Rose, A. (2010). *Why so few? Women in science, technology, engineering, and mathematics*. Washington, DC: AAUW.

Hsu, P.-L. (2008). *Understanding high school students' science internship: At the intersection of secondary school science and university science*. Doctoral dissertation, University of Victoria. Retrieved from http://hdl.handle.net/1828/1096

Hughes, J. (2005). The role of teacher knowledge and learning experiences in forming technology-integrated pedagogy. *Journal of Technology and Teacher Education, 13*(2), 277–302.

Jagger, S. (2009). *The influence of participation in a community mapping project on grade four students' environmental worldviews*. Master's thesis, University of Victoria. Retrieved from http://hdl.handle.net/1828/2816

Jagger, S., & Yore, L. D. (2010). *Evidence-based practice in science literacy for all: A case study of 1998–2009 NSTA articles as self-directed professional development* [Manuscript submitted for publication].

Johnson, C. C., Fargo, J., & Kahle, J. B. (2010). The cumulative and residual impact of a systemic reform program on teacher change and student learning of science. *School Science and Mathematics, 110*(3), 144–159.

Love, K. (2009). Literacy pedagogical content knowledge in secondary teacher education: Reflecting on oral language and learning across the disciplines. *Language and Education, 23*(6), 541–560.

Ma, L. (2010). *Knowing and teaching elementary mathematics: Teachers' understanding of fundamental mathematics in China and the United States* (2nd ed.). New York: Routledge.

Marks, R. (1990). Pedagogical content knowledge: From a mathematical case to a modified conception. *Journal of Teacher Education, 41*(3), 3–11.

Milford, T. M., Jagger, S., Yore, L. D., & Anderson, J. O. (2010). National Influences on science education reform in Canada. *Canadian Journal of Science, Mathematics and Technology Education, 10*(4), 370–381.

Mishra, P., & Koehler, M. J. (2006). Technological pedagogical content knowledge: A framework for teacher knowledge. *Teachers College Record, 108*(6), 1017–1054.

Revak, M., & Kuerbis, P. J. (2008, January). *The link from professional development to K-6 student achievement in science, math, and literacy*. Paper presented at the annual international meeting of the Association for Science Teacher Education, St. Louis, MO, USA.

Roberts, D. A. (2007). Scientific literacy/science literacy. In S. K. Abell, & N. G. Lederman (Eds.), *Handbook of research on science education* (pp. 729–780). Mahwah, NJ: Lawrence Erlbaum.

Romance, N. R., & Vitale, M. R. (1992). A curriculum strategy that expands time for in-depth elementary science instruction by using science-based reading strategies: Effects of a year-long study in grade four. *Journal of Research in Science Teaching, 29*(6), 545–554.

Shelley, M. C., II. (2009). Speaking truth to power with powerful results: Impacting public awareness and public policy. In M. C. Shelley II, L. D. Yore, & B. Hand (Eds.), *Quality research in literacy and science education: International perspectives and gold standards* (pp. 443–466). Dordrecht, The Netherlands: Springer.

Shulman, L. S. (1986). Those who understand: Knowledge growth in teaching. *Educational Researcher*, *15*(2), 4–14.

Shymansky, J. A., Yore, L. D., & Anderson, J. O. (2004). Impact of a school district's science reform effort on the achievement and attitudes of third- and fourth-grade students. *Journal of Research in Science Teaching, 41*(8), 771–790.

Tippett, C. D. (in progress). *Exploring middle school students' representational competence in science: Development and verification of a framework for learning with visual representations.* Doctoral dissertation, University of Victoria, Victoria, British Columbia, Canada.

United States National Council of Teachers of Mathematics. (2000). *Principles and standards for school mathematics.* Reston, VA: Author.

United States National Research Council. (2009). *Learning science in informal environments: People, places, and pursuits* (P. Bell, B. Lewenstein, A. W. Shouse, & M. A. Feder, Eds.). Board on Science Education, Center for Education, Division of Behavioral and Social Sciences and Education. Washington, DC: The National Academies Press.

United States National Research Council. (2010). *A framework for science education* (H. Quinn & H. A. Schweingruber, Eds.). [Preliminary public draft]. Board on Science Education, Center for Education, Division of Behavioral and Social Sciences and Education. Washington, DC: The National Academies Press.

van Driel, J. H., Verloop, N., & de Vos, W. (1998). Developing science teachers' pedagogical content knowledge. *Journal of Research in Science Teaching, 35*(6), 673–695.

Veal, W. R., & MaKinster, J. G. (1998). Pedagogical content knowledge taxonomies. *Electronic Journal of Science Education, 3*(4).

Western and Northern Canadian Protocol for Collaboration in Education. (2006). *The common curriculum framework for K–9 mathematics.* Retrieved from http://www.wncp.ca/english/subjectarea/mathematics/ccf.aspx

Willers, M. (2005). *Enriched mathematics 10/11: Focus on the NCTM process standards.* Unpublished master's thesis, University of Victoria, Victoria, British Columbia, Canada.

Yore, L. D., Kottová, A., & Jagger, S. (2010). Review of the book *Learning science in informal environments: People, places, and pursuits* by P. Bell, B. Lewenstein, A. W. Shouse, & M. A. Feder (Eds.). *International Journal of Environmental and Science Education, 5*(3), 377–382.

Yore, L. D., Shelley, M. C., II, & Hand, B. (2009). Reflections on beyond the Gold Standards era and ways of promoting compelling arguments about science literacy for all. In M. C. Shelley II, L. D. Yore, & B. Hand (Eds.), *Quality research in literacy and science education: International perspectives and gold standards* (pp. 623–649). Dordrecht, The Netherlands: Springer.

Larry D. Yore
Department of Curriculum and Instruction

Eileen Van der Flier-Keller
School of Earth and Ocean Sciences
University of Victoria
Victoria, British Columbia, Canada

APPENDIX

Pacific CRYSTAL Project: Highly Qualified Personnel

Numerous postdoctoral, graduate, and undergraduate research fellows and research assistants, interns, and community researchers were integral parts of the Pacific CRYSTAL projects. The following people and their graduate projects, theses and dissertations, universities, completion dates, and other academic and instructional products are listed by their research node. The entries for each of these highly productive persons' scholarship are limited to five; however, several have many more works.

NODE 1 — BUILD: AUTHENTIC SCIENCE, MATHEMATICS, AND TECHNOLOGY EXPERIENCES

Carruthers, Sarah

Grasping graphs. (2010). Master of Science thesis, University of Victoria, Victoria, BC. Retrieved from http://hdl.handle.net/1828/3193

Articles
Carruthers, S., Milford, T. M., Pelton, T. W., & Stege, U. (2010). Moving K-7 education into the information age. In *Proceedings of the ACM SIGCSE 15th Western Canadian Conference on Computing Education (WCCCE'10)* (pp. 1–5).

Carruthers, S., Gunion, K., & Stege, U. (2009). Computational biology unplugged! (Invited workshop). In *Proceedings of the ACM SIGCSE 14th Western Canadian Conference on Computing Education (WCCCE'09)* (p. 126).

Murdoch, J., Agah St. Pierre, A., Coady, Y., Carruthers, S., et al. (2007). SPARCS from the University of Victoria: Supporting sustainable and integrated outreach activities for educators and young minds. In *IEEE meeting the growing demand for engineers and their educators 2010–2020* (pp. 1–15). Retrieved from http://hdl.handle.net/1828/2750

Conference Presentations
Carruthers, S. (2010, March). *Computer science education: Thoughts and directions.* Poster presented at the 41st ACM Technical Symposium on Computer Science Education (SIGCSE'10), Milwaukee, WI, USA.

Carruthers, S. (2010, March). *Relational graphs: What are they?* [DVD]. Presented at the 41st ACM Technical Symposium on Computer Science Education (SIGCSE'10), Milwaukee, WI, USA.

Claxton, Earl, Jr.

Conference Presentations
Williams, L., & Claxton, E., Jr. (2007, October). *Ecological restoration and education.* Presented at the CANEUEL (Working Together) Series to the Community-based Research Conference, University of Victoria, Victoria, BC.

Williams, L., Paul, T., & Claxton, E., Jr. (2007, September). *SNIT□E□: Connecting to place.* Presented at the National CRYSTAL Meeting, University of Alberta, Edmonton, AB.

APPENDIX

de Oliveira Jayme, Bruno

Elementary students' and teachers' interactions during out-of-classroom activities. (2008). Master of Arts thesis, University of Victoria, Victoria, BC. Retrieved from http://hdl.handle.net/1828/1027

Articles

de Oliveira Jayme, B., Reis, G., & Roth, W.-M. (2010). Egomorphism: Discursive pedagogical artefact for science education. Submitted to *Canadian Journal of Environmental Education*.

de Oliveira Jayme, B., Roth, W.-M., Reis, G., & van Eijck, M. (2007). Group monopolization and collaborative work: The making of a science video project. In T. W. Pelton, G. Reis, & K. Moore (Eds.), *Proceedings of the University of Victoria Faculty of Education Research Conference–Connections* (pp. 111–116).

de Oliveira Jayme, B., Reis, G., & Roth, W.-M. (2006, May). Step back! The use of student-produced digital movies as a metacognitive tool to assess non-formal activities. In T. W. Pelton, G. Reis, & S. Stewart (Eds.), *Proceedings of the University of Victoria Faculty of Education Research Conference–Connections* (pp. 51–56).

Conference Presentations

de Oliveira Jayme, B., Reis, G., & Roth, W.-M. (2008, March). *Computer collaborative work in science lessons: The flow of students' mutual understanding within working groups.* Poster presented at the annual meeting of the American Educational Research Association, New York, NY, USA.

de Oliveira Jayme, B., Roth, W.-M., & Pozzer-Ardenghi, L. (2008, March). *The role of interjections in students' engagement during science field trips.* Poster presented at the annual meeting of the American Educational Research Association, New York, NY, USA.

Demchuk, Tania Ellen

Surficial geology of the Komie Creek map area and an investigation of an ice-contact glaciofluvial delta, northeast British Columbia. (2010). Master of Science thesis, University of Victoria, Victoria, BC.

Article

Van der Flier-Keller, E., Blades, D. W., & Demchuk, T. E. (2006). Empowering student teachers to teach Earth science: A collaboration between science and education at the University of Victoria, Canada. In *Proceedings of the GeoSciEd V International Geoscience Education Organisation "Geoscience Education: Understanding System Earth"* (p. 98). Bayreuth, Germany.

Conference Presentations

Demchuk, T. E., Vander Flier-Keller, E., & Blades, D. W. (2007, October). *First year Earth Science labs for pre-Education students at the University of Victoria, British Columbia, Canada.* Presented at annual meeting of the Geological Society of America, Denver, CO, USA.

Blades, D. W., Van der Flier-Keller, E., Demchuk, T. E., & Pryhitka, A. (2007, April). *Grounding Earth Science in classrooms: The effects of a "pre-ed" lab section for prospective education students on achievement, science literacy and attitude in an introductory college Earth Systems course.* Presented at the annual meeting of the National Association for Research in Science Teaching, New Orleans, LA, USA.

Blades, D. W., Van der Flier-Keller, E., & Demchuk, T. E. (2007, May). *The pedagogy of Earth Science: Does instructional approach make a difference for pre-Education students?* Presented at the Connections 2007 Research Conference, Faculty of Education, Dunsmuir Lodge, Victoria, BC.

Fisher, Kate

Aboriginal students' high school mathematics experiences: Stories of opportunities and obstacles. (2010). Master of Arts thesis, University of Victoria, Victoria, BC. Retrieved from http://hdl.handle.net/1828/3103

Conference Presentation

Marshall, E. A., Guenette, F. L., Ward, T., & Fisher, K. (2009, October). *Utilizing task-based methods to enhance data quality in narrative interviews.* Symposium presented at the 8th Annual Advances in Qualitative Methods Conference, Vancouver, BC.

Giasson, Julie

Conference Presentation

Van der Flier-Keller, E., & Giasson, J. (2008, September). *Science in the media: What is covered in our newspapers?* Presented at the Third National CRYSTAL Conference, Sherbrooke, PQ.

Guenette, Francis L.

Work and career supports and barriers for youth and families in a rural community affected by social and economic restructuring. (in progress). Doctoral dissertation, University of Victoria, Victoria, BC.

Articles

Hsu, P.-L., Roth, W.-M., Marshall, E. A., & Guenette, F. L. (2009). To be or not be? Discursive resources of (dis)identifying with science related careers. *Journal of Research in Science Teaching, 46,* 1114–1136.

Guenette, F. L., Marshall, E. A., & Morley, T. (2007). Career experiences and choice processes for secondary science students. In *Proceedings of the University of Victoria Faculty of Education Connections Conference* (pp. 77–84).

Conference Presentation

Marshall, E. A., Begoray, D., Rawdah, N., Lawrence, B. C., & Guenette, F. L. (2009, October). *The possible selves mapping process: Research and practice to facilitate transitions for emerging adults* (innovative session). Presented at the 4th Conference on Emerging Adulthood, Atlanta, GA, USA.

Instructional Resources

Marshall, E. A., Guenette, F. L., & Ward, T. (in progress). *Possible selves mapping process: A manual to facilitate the career development exploration process.* University of Victoria, Victoria, BC.

Marshall, E. A., & Guenette, F. L. (2008). *Possible selves mapping process: A career development exploration process for teachers and students* [DVD]. University of Victoria, Victoria, BC.

Gunion, Katherine

FUNdamentals of CS: Designing and evaluating computer science activities for kids. (2010). Master of Science thesis, University of Victoria, Victoria, BC. Retrieved from http://hdl.handle.net/1828/2750

Articles

Gunion, K., Milford, T. M., & Stege, U. (2009). The paradigm recursion: Is it more accessible when introduced in middle school? *Journal of Problem Solving, 2*(2), 142–172.

Gunion, K., Milford, T. M., & Stege, U. (2009). Curing recursion aversion. In *Proceedings of the 14th Annual ACM SIGCSE Conference on Innovation and Technology in Computer Science Education (ITiCSE 2009)* (pp. 124–128).

Carruthers, S., Gunion, K., & Stege, U. (2009). Computational biology unplugged! (Invited workshop). In *Proceedings of the ACM SIGCSE 14th Western Canadian Conference on Computing Education (WCCCE '09)* (p. 126).

Hammond-Todd, Michael

Scientific literacy and the mobile curriculum: Emerging possibilities and challenges for diverse learning populations. (in progress). Doctoral dissertation, University of Victoria, Victoria, BC.

APPENDIX

Resources

Hammond-Todd, M. A., & Van der Flier-Keller, E. (2010). *Science to understand our forests: What conifers live near you?* Year of Science, Faculty of Science, University of Victoria, Victoria, BC.

Hammond-Todd, M. A., Van der Flier-Keller, E. (2010). *Mathematics and society: Using statistics to understand how people vote.* Year of Science, Faculty of Science, University of Victoria, Victoria, BC.

Holmes, Mary

Gently down the stream: Reflections on a Seaquarium journey. (2010). Master of Education project, University of British Columbia, Vancouver, BC.

Hsu, Pei-Ling

Understanding high school students' science internship: At the intersection of secondary school science and university science. (2008). Doctor of Philosophy dissertation, University of Victoria, Victoria, BC. Retrieved from http://hdl.handle.net/1828/1096

Articles

Hsu, P.-L., & Roth, W.-M. (2010). Interpretative repertoires for talking (about) science-related careers. In W.-M. Roth & P.-L. Hsu (Eds.), *Talk about careers in science* (pp. 19–41). Rotterdam, The Netherlands: Sense.

Hsu, P.-L., van Eijck, M., & Roth, W.-M. (2010). Students' representations of scientific practice during a science internship: Reflections from an activity-theoretic perspective. *International Journal of Science Education, 32,* 1243–1266.

Hsu, P.-L., & Roth, W.-M. (2009). An analysis of teacher discourse that introduces real science activities to high school students. *Research in Science Education, 39,* 553–574.

Hsu, P.-L., Roth, W.-M., & Mazumder, A. (2009). Natural pedagogical conversations in high school students' internship. *Journal of Research in Science Teaching, 46,* 481–505.

Hsu, P.-L., Roth, W.-M., Marshall, E. A., & Guenette, F. L. (2009). To be or not be? Discursive resources of (dis)identifying with science related careers. *Journal of Research in Science Teaching, 46,* 1114–1136.

McCarter, Patsy

Enhancing ocean literacy: Professional development in a networked community of practice. (2010). Master of Arts action research report, University of Phoenix, Arizona, USA.

Moore, Karen

Changing the way we teach mathematics: An examination of the numeracy support program in Newfoundland and Labrador. (in progress). Doctoral dissertation, University of Victoria, Victoria, BC.

Articles

Pelton, T. W., Francis Pelton, L., & Moore, K. (2007). Geotrekking: Connecting education to the real world. In C. Crawford, et al. (Eds.), *Proceedings of Society for Information Technology and Teacher Education International Conference 2007* (pp. 2082–2088).

Francis Pelton, L., Pelton, T. W., & Moore, K. (2007). Learning by communicating concepts through comics. In C. Crawford, et al. (Eds.), *Proceedings of Society for Information Technology and Teacher Education International Conference 2007* (pp. 1974–1981).

Conference Presentations

Pelton, T. W., Francis Pelton, L., & Moore, K. (2010, April). *Creating comics: Connecting mathematics, art, and writing to explain concepts.* Paper presented at the annual meeting of the National Council of Teachers of Mathematics, San Diego, CA, USA.

Moore, K., & Barron, N. (2009, April). *Numeracy games: I have... who has... and more.* Paper presented at the annual meeting of the National Council of Teachers of Mathematics, Washington, DC, USA.

Pelton, T. W., Francis Pelton, L., & Moore, K. (2008, May). *Teaching teachers technology by teaching their students* (technology outreach workshops). Paper presented at the annual meeting of the Canadian Society for the Study of Education, Vancouver, BC.

Morley, Tara

Article

Guenette, F. L., Marshall, E. A., & Morley, T. (2007). Career experiences and choice processes for secondary science students. In *Proceedings of the University of Victoria Faculty of Education 2007 Connections Conference* (pp. 77–84).

Neill, Brian W.

New 'ways of knowing' at the confluence of Indigenous knowledge and Euro-western science. (in progress). Doctoral dissertation, University of Victoria, Victoria, BC.

Article

Neill, B. W., & Francis Pelton, L. (2010). *Performance of Aboriginal students in British Columbia's science and mathematics curricula articulates a need to 'indigenize' science at the secondary level* (book chapter in review).

Conference Presentation

Neill, B. W. (2010, May–June). *Analysis of the British Columbia grade 12 science and mathematics curricula articulates a need for 'indigenizing' science at the secondary level.* Paper presented at the XXXVIIIth Annual Conference of the Canadian Society for the Study of Education (CSSE), Montreal, PQ.

Paul, Tammy

Conference Presentation

Williams, L., Paul, T., & Claxton, E., Jr. (2007, September). *S̲N̲IT□E□: Connecting to place.* Presented at the National CRYSTAL Meeting, University of Alberta, Edmonton, AB.

St. Cyr, Bob

Mobile and online applications to improve parental support when helping their children with mathematics homework. (in progress). Doctoral dissertation, University of Victoria, Victoria, BC.

Articles

Francis Pelton, L., Pelton, T. W., & St. Cyr, B. (2009). Enhanced instructional presentations and field-webs. In P. Rogers, G. A. Berg, J. Boettcher, C. Howard, L. Justice, & K. Schenk (Eds.), *Encyclopedia of distance learning* (2nd ed., pp. 907–914). Hersey, PA: IGI Global.

St. Cyr, B., & Pelton, T. W. (2008). Parents as co-learners, tutors & teachers. In K. McFerrin, R. Weber, R. Carlsen, & D. A. Willis (Eds.), *Proceedings of the Society for Information Technology and Teacher Education International Conference 2008* (pp. 4542–4547).

Conference Presentations

St. Cyr, B., & Pelton, T. W. (2008, March). *Parents as co-learners, tutors & teachers.* Paper presented at the 19th International Conference of the Society for Information Technology and Teacher Education, Las Vegas, NV, USA.

St. Cyr, B., & Pelton, T. W. (2006, February). *ePortfolios.* Paper presented at the Illinois Online Conference 2006.

Starzner, Matthias

Listening to kids: Developing and inclusive evaluation process for environmental education. (2010). Master of Arts thesis, Royal Roads University, Victoria, BC.

Conference Presentation

Starzner, M. (2009, May). *Exploring success in place-based environmental education.* Poster presented at the 5th World Environmental Education Congress, Montreal, PQ.

van Eijck, Michiel

Articles

van Eijck, M., & Roth, W.-M. (2010). Towards a chronotopic theory of "place" in place-based education. *Cultural Studies of Science Education, 5*(4), 869–898.

van Eijck, M., & Roth, W.-M. (2009). Authentic science experiences as a vehicle to change students' orientation toward science and scientific career choices: Learning from the path followed by Brad. *Cultural Studies of Science Education, 4*(3), 611–638.

van Eijck, M., Hsu, P.-L., & Roth, W.-M. (2009). Translations of scientific practice to "students' images of science. *Science Education, 93*(4), 611–634.

van Eijck M., & Roth W.-M. (2007). Improving science education for sustainable development. *PLoS Biology, 5,* 2763–2769.

van Eijck, M., & Roth, W.-M. (2007). Keeping the local local: Recalibrating the status of science and traditional ecological knowledge (TEK) in education. *Science Education, 91*(6), 926–947.

Ward, Tanya

The work and educational aspirations of young single mothers in rural communities. (2009). Master of Arts thesis, University of Victoria, Victoria, BC. Retrieved from http://hdl.handle.net/1828/1973

Conference Presentations

Marshall, E. A., Guenette, F. L., Ward, T., & Fisher, K. (2009, October). *Utilizing task-based methods to enhance data quality in narrative interviews.* Symposium presented at the 8th Annual Advances in Qualitative Methods Conference, Vancouver, BC.

Ward, T., Guenette, F. L., & Marshall, E. A. (2009, May). *Career aspirations with high school students: A longitudinal study using possible selves mapping.* Poster presented at the 2009 University of Victoria Faculty of Education Connections Conference, Victoria, BC.

Marshall, E. A., Guenette, F. L., Ward, T., et al. (2008, May). *Community-university partnerships: Building relationships with Aboriginal and non-Aboriginal communities.* Symposium presented at the Community-University Expo Conference, Victoria, BC.

Instructional Resource

Marshall, E. A., Guenette, F. L., & Ward, T. (in preparation). *Possible selves mapping process: A manual to facilitate the career development exploration process.* University of Victoria, Victoria, BC.

Williams, Lewis

Conference Presentations

Williams, L., & Claxton, E., Jr. (2007, October). *Ecological restoration and education.* Presented at the CANEUEL (Working Together) Series to the Community-based Research Conference, University of Victoria, Victoria, BC.

Williams, L., Paul, T., & Claxton, E., Jr. (2007, September). *S̲N̲IT□E□: Connecting to place.* Presented at the National CRYSTAL Meeting, University of Alberta, Edmonton, AB.

NODE 2 — EXPAND: CLASSROOM APPLICATION OF EVIDENCE-BASED PRACTICES

Cui, Yanping

Beliefs about Chinese teaching and learning: A study of Chinese teachers and non-native learners of Chinese language. (in progress). Doctoral dissertation, University of Victoria, Victoria, BC.

Conference Presentation

Cui, Y., Anthony, R. J., & Pelton T. W. (2009, May). *Using item response theory to validate an interactive-constructive science reading awareness model.* Paper presented at the 2009 University of Victoria Faculty of Education Connections Conference, Victoria, BC.

Jagger, Susan

The influence of participation in a community mapping project on grade four students' environmental worldviews. (2009). Master of Arts thesis, University of Victoria, Victoria, BC. Retrieved from http://hdl.handle.net/1828/2816

Articles

Jagger, S., & Yore, L. D. (submitted). Evidence-based practice in science literacy for all: A case study of 1998–2009 NSTA articles as self-directed professional development. *School Science and Mathematics.*

Milford, T. M., Jagger, S., Anderson, J. O., & Yore, L. D. (2010). National influences on science education reform in Canada. *Canadian Journal of Science, Mathematics and Technology Education, 10*(4), 370–381.

Hand, B., Yore, L. D., Jagger, S., & Prain, V. (2010). Connecting research in science literacy and classroom practice: A review of science teaching journals in Australia, the United Kingdom, and the United States, 1998–2008. *Studies in Science Education, 46*(1), 45–68.

Yore, L. D., Kottová, A., & Jagger, S. (2010). Learning science in informal environments: People, places, and pursuits by P. Bell, B. Lewenstein, A. W. Shouse, & M. A. Feder (Eds.) [Book Review]. *International Journal of Environmental and Science Education, 5*(3), 377–382.

Conference Presentation

Yore, L. D., & Jagger, S. (2010, March). *Connecting research in science literacy and classroom practice: A review of popular science teaching journals in North America, 1998–2009.* Paper presented at the annual meeting of the National Association of Research in Science Teaching, Philadelphia, PA, USA.

Teed, Susan

Coming to terms with the education system: Words from a departing teacher. (in progress). Doctoral dissertation, Simon Fraser University, Burnaby, BC.

Article

Teed, S. (2010). Incorporating controversial, socio-scientific issues into science education through role-play. *Northwest Passage: Journal of Educational Practices, 8*, 31–46.

Conference Presentations

Teed, S., Zandvliet, D. B., & Ormond, C. G. A. (2011, March). *Science Times: Current, socio-scientific news stories written for students.* Presented at the annual meeting of the National Science Teachers Association, San Francisco, CA, USA.

Ormond, C. G. A., Piersol, L., Teed, S., & Zandvliet, D. B. (2010, April). *Case-studies in the development of place-based learning environments.* Paper presented at the 2010 International Conference on Inter-personal Relationships in Education, Boulder, CO, USA.

Ormond, C. G. A., Zandvliet, D. B., Teed, S., & Piersol, L., (2010, March). *The development of a place-based learning environment.* Paper presented at the annual meeting of the National Association for Research in Science Teaching, Philadelphia, PA, USA.

Resources

Zandvliet, D. B., & Teed, S. (2008–2010). *Science Times* magazine. News and resources. Retrieved from http://sciencetimes.ca/

Tippett, Christine D.

Exploring middle school students' representational competence in science: Development and verification of a framework for learning with visual representations. (in progress). Doctoral dissertation, University of Victoria, Victoria, BC.

Articles

Tippett, C. D. (2010). Refutation text in science education: A review of two decades of research. *International Journal of Science and Mathematics Education, 8*(6), 951–970.

Anthony, R. J., Tippett, C. D., & Yore, L. D. (2010). Pacific CRYSTAL project: Explicit literacy instruction embedded in middle school science classrooms. *Research in Science Education, 40*(1), 45–64.

Norton-Meir, L. A., Tippett, C. D., Hand, B., & Yore, L. D. (2010). Professional development in teaching disciplinary writing in the context of international science reform efforts. In G. A. Troia, R. K. Shankland, & A. Heintz (Eds.), *Putting writing research into practice: Applications for teacher professional development* (pp. 115–153). New York: Guilford.

Tippett, C. D. (2009). Argumentation: The language of science. *Journal of Elementary Science Education, 21*(1), 17–25.

Conference Presentation

Tippett, C. D. (2010, August). *Middle school students' construction of visual representations from science text.* Poster presented at the biennial conference of the European Association for Research on Learning and Instruction Special Interest Group (Text and Graphics), Tübingen, Germany.

NODE 3 — LEAD: INFLUENCING EDUCATIONAL POLICY AND PRACTICE AND LEADERSHIP

Goh, Ming-Sze

Multilevel analysis of mathematics literacy: The effects of intrinsic motivation, teacher support, and student-teacher relations. (2006). Master of Arts thesis, University of Victoria, Victoria, BC. Retrieved from http://hdl.handle.net/1828/2155

Conference Presentation

Anderson, J. O., Ross, S., Goh, M.-S., et al. (2007, January). *Hierarchical linear models of student and school indices of writing, numeracy, and reading in Grades 4 and 7*. Paper presented at the Hawaii International Education Conference, Honolulu, HI, USA.

Gu, Ziemei

Comparison of Canada and Hong Kong-China through hierarchical linear models: The relations among students' self-beliefs in math, the learning environment at school, and math performance. (2006). Master of Arts thesis, University of Victoria, Victoria, BC. Retrieved from http://hdl.handle.net/1828/2049

Conference Presentation

Anderson, J. O., Ross, S., Goh, M.-S., Gu, Z., et al. (2007, January). *Hierarchical linear models of student and school indices of writing, numeracy, and reading in Grades 4 and 7*. Paper presented at the Hawaii International Education Conference, Honolulu, HI, USA.

Hsu, Jui-Chen

Comparing the relationships between mathematics achievement and student characteristics in Canada and Hong Kong through HLM. (2007). Master of Arts thesis, University of Victoria, Victoria, BC. Retrieved from http://hdl.handle.net/1828/2364

Conference Presentation

Anderson, J. O., Ross, S., Goh, M., Gu, Z., Hsu, J.-C., et al. (2007, January). *Hierarchical linear models of student and school indices of writing, numeracy, and reading in Grades 4 and 7*. Paper presented at the Hawaii International Education Conference, Honolulu, HI, USA.

Luo, Jiesu

School characteristics and family environment on student's academic achievement: Results from PISA. (in progress). Doctoral dissertation, University of Victoria, Victoria, BC.

Article

Macdonald, S., Stockwell, T., & Luo, J. (2010). The relationship between alcohol problems, perceived risks, and attitudes toward alcohol policy in Canada. *Drug and Alcohol Review*, doi: 10.1111/j.1465-3362.2010.00259.x.

Conference Presentations

Luo, J. (2010, August). *Rethinking ethnic disparities in education: In a global perspective*. Paper presented at the 36th annual conference of the International Association for Educational Assessment, Bangkok, Thailand.

Macdonald, S., De Wit, D. J., Maguin, E., Nochajski, T. H., Safyer, A., & Luo, J. (2010, June). *Strengthening families program and children's conduct disorder: Example from children of alcoholic parents*. Paper presented at the international conference on Applied Psychology, Paris, France.

Macdonald, S., Stockwell, & Luo, J. (2009, June). *The relationship between alcohol problems, perceived risks and attitudes toward alcohol policy in Canada*. Paper presented at the 35th annual meeting of the Kettil Bruun Society, Copenhagen, Denmark.

Milford, Todd M.

An investigation of international science achievement using the OECD's PISA 2006 data set. (2009). Doctor of Philosophy dissertation, University of Victoria, Victoria, BC. Retrieved from http://hdl.handle. net/1828/2131

Articles

Milford, T. M., Jagger, S., Anderson, J. O., & Yore, L. D. (2010). National influences on science education reform in Canada. *Canadian Journal of Science, Mathematics and Technology Education, 10*(4), 370–381.

Milford, T. M., Ross, S. P., & Anderson, J. O. (2010). An opportunity to better understand schooling: The growing presence of PISA in the Americas. *International Journal of Mathematics and Science Education, 8*(3), 453–476.

Anderson, J. O., Milford, T. M., & Ross, S. P. (2008). Multilevel modeling with HLM: Taking a second look at PISA. In M. C. Shelley II, L. D. Yore, & B. Hand (Eds.), *Quality research in literacy and science education: International perspectives and gold standards* (pp. 263–286). Dordrecht, The Netherlands: Springer.

Conference Presentations

Anderson, J. O., Ross, S., Goh, M.-S., Gu, Z., Hsu, J.-C., Huang, J., et al. (2007, January). *Hierarchical linear models of student and school indices of writing, numeracy, and reading in Grades 4 and 7.* Paper presented at the Hawaii International Education Conference, Honolulu, HI, USA.

Milford, T. M., et al. (2007, May). *Modeling student performance using large-scale assessment data.* Paper presented at the University of Victoria Faculty of Education Connections Conference, Victoria, BC.

Ormond, Carlos Gustavo A.

Investigating learning environments in place-based education settings: A participatory action research approach. (in progress). Doctoral dissertation, Simon Fraser University, Burnaby, BC.

Conference Presentations

Teed, S., Zandvliet, D. B., & Ormond, C. G. A. (2011, March). *Science Times: Current, socio-scientific news stories written for students.* Paper presented at the National Science Teachers Association National Conference, San Francisco, CA, USA.

Zandvliet, D. B., & Ormond, C. G. A. (2010, May). *Validating the place-based learning and constructivist environment survey (PLACES) in diverse settings.* Paper presented at the annual meeting of the American Educational Research Association, Denver, CO, USA.

Zandvliet, D. B., & Ormond, C. G. A. (2010, April). *Developing and describing place-based and constructivist learning environments.* Paper presented at the 2010 International Conference on Interpersonal Relationships in Education, Boulder, CO, USA.

Ormond, C., Zandvliet, D. B., Teed, S., & Piersol, L. (2010, March). *The development of a place-based learning environment.* Paper presented at the annual meeting of the National Association for Research in Science Teaching, Philadelphia, PA, USA.

Zandvliet, D. B., & Ormond, C. G. A. (2009, May). *'Learning' environments.* Paper presented at the 5th World Environmental Education Congress (5WEEC), Montreal, PQ.

Ram, Anita

Multilevel analysis of mathematics literacy in Canada and Japan: The effects of sex differences, teacher support, and the school learning environment. (2007). Master of Arts thesis, University of Victoria, Victoria, BC. Retrieved from http://hdl.handle.net/1828/986

Conference Presentation

Anderson, J. O., Ross, S., Goh, M.-S., Gu, Z., Hsu, J.-C., Huang, J., et al. (2007, January). *Hierarchical linear models of student and school indices of writing, numeracy, and reading in Grades 4 and 7.* Paper presented at the Hawaii International Education Conference, Honolulu, HI, USA.

Ross, Shelley P.

Motivation correlates of academic achievement: Exploring how motivation influences academic achievement in the PISA 2003 dataset. (2008). Doctor of Philosophy dissertation, University of Victoria, Victoria, BC.

Articles

Milford, T. M., Ross, S. P., & Anderson, J. O. (2010). An opportunity to better understand schooling: The growing presence of PISA in the Americas. *International Journal of Mathematics and Science Education, 8*(3), 453–286.

Anderson, J. O., Milford, T. M., & Ross, S. P. (2008). Multilevel modeling with HLM: Taking a second look at PISA. In M. C. Shelley II, L. D. Yore, & B. Hand (Eds.), *Quality research in literacy and science education: International perspectives and gold standards* (pp. 263–286). Dordrecht, The Netherlands: Springer.

Anderson, J. O., Lin, H.-S., Treagust, D. F., Ross, S. P., & Yore, L. D. (2007). Using large-scale assessment for datasets for research in science and mathematics education: Programme for International Student Assessment (PISA). *International Journal of Science and Mathematics Education, 5*(4), 591–614.

Conference Presentation

Ross, S. P. (2007, January). *Secondary data analysis: How alternative approaches to methodology and analysis can improve educational research.* Paper presented at the Hawaii International Conference on Education, Honolulu, HI, USA.

Stith, Ian

Cogenerative dialogue praxis in a lighthouse school: Contradictions, ethical concerns, expansive learning, and "kids being kids". (2007). Doctor of Philosophy dissertation, University of Victoria, Victoria, BC. Retrieved from http://hdl.handle.net/1828/242

Articles

Stith, I., & Roth, M-W. (2010). Teaching as mediation: The cogenerative dialogue and ethical understandings. *Teaching and Teacher Education, 26*(3), 363–370.

Stith, I. (2006). Responsibility and coteaching: A review of "warts and all". *Forum: Qualitative Social Research, 7*(4), article 22 & #8211.

Stith, I., et al. (2006). The ethics of cogenerative dialogue: A cogenerative dialogue. *Forum: Qualitative Social Research, 7*(2), article 44 & #8211.

Taveira, Marcilia

English as a foreign language curriculum adaptation: A constructivist model for enriching teacher class planning at a language institute in Brazil. (2007). Master of Education project, University of Victoria, Victoria, BC.

ADMINISTRATIVE NODE

Kottová, Alena

Discovering the social side of science: Using film production to capture the "story of science" and find the impact on student's emotional attachment to science. (in progress). Doctoral dissertation. University of Victoria, Victoria, BC.

Articles

Kottová, A. (2010). Childhood memories in career plans: How past memories shape our identities. In W.-M. Roth & P.-L. Hsu (Eds.), *Talk about careers in science* (pp. 83–95). Rotterdam, The Netherlands: Sense.

Yore, L. D., Kottová, A., & Jagger, S. (2010). Learning science in informal environments: People, places, and pursuits by P. Bell, B. Lewenstein, A. W. Shouse, & M. A. Feder (Eds.) [Book Review]. *International Journal of Environmental and Science Education, 5*(3), 377–382.

Instructional Resources

Informal environments literature review in comparison to conclusions and findings of United States National Research Council of the National Academies project. (2009). Retrieved from http://education2.uvic.ca/pacificcrystal/literature/index.html

Pacific CRYSTAL Archive: Website restructuring, completion, and consolidation to allow accessibility after the project's closure. Retrieved from http://education2.uvic.ca/pacificcrystal/

Waldron, S. Winona

The possible implications of approaching food issues from a critical literacy perspective in education. (in progress). Master of Arts thesis, University of Victoria, Victoria, BC.

Instructional Resources

Informal environments literature review in comparison to conclusions and findings of United States National Research Council of the National Academies project. (2009). Retrieved from http://education2.uvic.ca/pacificcrystal/literature/index.html

Pacific CRYSTAL Archive: Website restructuring, completion, and consolidation to allow accessibility after the project's closure. Retrieved from http://education2.uvic.ca/pacificcrystal/

INDEX